D1715183

For a Dollar and a Dream

For a Dollar and a Dream

a Dream

State Lotteries in Modern America

JONATHAN D. COHEN

OXFORD
UNIVERSITY PRESS

Oxford University Press is a department of the University of Oxford. It furthers
the University's objective of excellence in research, scholarship, and education
by publishing worldwide. Oxford is a registered trade mark of Oxford University
Press in the UK and certain other countries.

Published in the United States of America by Oxford University Press
198 Madison Avenue, New York, NY 10016, United States of America.

Library of Congress Control Number: 2022940623

ISBN 978–0–19–760488–5

DOI: 10.1093/oso/9780197604885.001.0001

1 3 5 7 9 8 6 4 2
Printed by Sheridan Books, Inc., United States of America

Contents

.

To my parents

Acknowledgments

WRITING A BOOK about lotteries has taught me a lot about luck.

I have been lucky to learn from generous scholars and mentors. My thanks begin with Grace Hale. As a graduate adviser and a friend, she has been a mentor in scholarship and in life. Thanks to the many other faculty members at the University of Virginia, particularly Brian Balogh, Matthew Hedstrom, and Sarah Milov, for helping train me as a historian and for their feedback on this project at various stages of its development. Also at UVA, thanks to Kathleen Miller and Jennifer Via for their invaluable assistance throughout my graduate studies. I am appreciative, too, of all the other scholars I have had the pleasure to learn from and work with over the years: Bryant Simon for prompting me to think bigger about gambling and American history; Thomas Jundt, Len Moore, Jason Opal, and Gil Troy at McGill University; as well as Roxanne Harde, Roger Launius, June Skinner Sawyers, and Irwin Streight. My thanks to Peter Mickulas for his advice throughout the publication process and to Jim Cullen for his help tracking down a key quotation.

I have been lucky to work with a fantastic team at Oxford University Press. Thank you to Susan Ferber for inviting me to submit my manuscript and for her careful edits, her guidance, and her advocacy on behalf of this project. My gratitude, too, to two anonymous reviewers for their thoughtful comments, to Jeremy Toynbee for his expert oversight of the production process, and to Patterson Lamb for her careful copyediting.

I was lucky to enlist—a better word might be coerce—numerous friends to read portions of the manuscript: Kirk Benson, Danielle Deluty, Daniel Gastfriend, Raffi and Charlotte Grinberg, Ben Lang, Victoria Pilger, Noemi Schor, Julie Shain, Sarah Trager, and many others. Monica Blair, Cecilia Marquez, and Joey Thompson read the entire manuscript in its dissertation phase. Even if it took me a few years to come around on their advice, they always made the project better. My sister-in-law Rafaella Schor read every chapter (some multiple times) and was a thought partner on images, chapter titles, and everything in between. Her feedback was invaluable.

I am lucky to have friends from all walks of life who helped keep me going through the research, writing, and editing processes. Specials thanks to Clayton Butler, Benji Cohen, Mary Draper, Erik Erlandson, Jack Furniss, Shira Lurie, Cecilia Marquez, and Joey Thompson for making Charlottesville feel like home during graduate school. My friends from Gann have been with me for over a decade and a half. It would take another book to list their names and the names of all of their partners and children, but I look forward to having them in my life for many decades to come.

For the last two years, I have been lucky to serve as a program officer at the American Academy of Arts & Sciences, where I have the opportunity to work on some of the nation's most pressing problems while participating in conversations that helped inform this personal, side project. My gratitude to Katherine Gagen, Darshan Goux, Victor Lopez, and Liza Youngling—among many others—for being fantastic, supportive colleagues, and to Academy leadership, particularly President David Oxtoby and Tania Munz.

I was lucky to receive financial support from numerous organizations over the course of my research: the Andrew W. Mellon Foundation and the American Council of Learned Societies; the Tobin Project; the Office of the Vice President for Research at the University of Virginia; the New York State Archives; the Rockefeller Archive Center; the Raven Society at the University of Virginia; the Center for Gaming Research at the University of Nevada, Las Vegas; the Jewish Studies Program at the University of Virginia; the Walter P. Reuther Library at Wayne State University; the Kentucky Historical Society; and the Jefferson Scholars Foundation. Additionally, this project would not have been possible without the archivists and librarians at 27 different facilities who helped me track down hundreds of thousands of documents, many of which had been lying unexamined for years. A special thank you to Su Kim Chung and the staff at the Special Collections and Archives at the University of Nevada, Las Vegas, where I spent extended time in their unparalleled gambling collection. My gratitude to Caitlin Flangan for her work processing and analyzing documents from the Arizona State Archives and to Abbie Cohen for her help with the Denver Public Library records. Thanks also to Sven Beckert for his comments on Chapter 3 and for sponsoring my stay in the History Department at Harvard University for the last two years of my graduate work. Some material from Chapter 1 is adapted from a chapter in the edited collection *All In: The Spread of Gambling in Twentieth-Century United States* published by the University of Nevada

Press as well as as an article in the the *Journal of Policy History,* published by Cambridge University Press.

Where I have been luckiest of all is my family. Thanks to my siblings Ava and Josh, Ezra, and Hannah, and Noemi and Mike—and Matan—and Rafaella for their patience and their encouragement. A special thank you to my in-laws, Lori and Josh, who have always been incredibly supportive of my endeavors, professional and otherwise. This book is dedicated to my parents, Miriam May and Shaye Cohen, who understand the sacrifices required to produce a book like this, who taught me to be resilient in the face of unexpected challenges, and who supported me in more ways than I could know.

Some of my best luck occurred just after I finished this book: my son Caleb was born two days after I sent the completed manuscript to Oxford. I cannot wait to see him grow and to grow along with him. My greatest thanks are for my wife Shayna for her humor, her fortitude, and for always lifting my spirits. The Powerball tickets we bought on our first date didn't win anything, but it has been clear since that night that I absolutely hit the jackpot.

For a Dollar and a Dream

Introduction

LEO MCCORD HAS played the Illinois Lottery every day for almost 50 years. A lifelong resident of Chicago, McCord is 70 years old, black, and rents a home on the West Side, not far from where he grew up. Since 2013, he has worked for the Chicago public school system as a security officer and an aide for students with disabilities, a position he took after two decades holding various jobs for the city government. When the lottery started in 1974, he was working as a taxi driver and would spend about $5 a day on tickets: "I saw it as an investment I could afford," he remembered. But as the national and local economy soured, he lost his job and fell on hard times. In the 1980s, he did odds jobs, shoveled walks, and collected cans—whatever he could to make a legal buck. As his desperation increased and his future prospects dwindled, his relationship to the lottery changed. Tickets became more than a side investment. He began to see a jackpot as his last, best, and only chance to change his situation. The size of his investment shifted accordingly. McCord would spend however much money he could put together on tickets, as much as $15 a day. Even after years of losses, he kept dreaming. "Not a day went by I didn't think of what it would be like living the life of a rich man, planning what I would do if my six numbers came up in the Lotto and I became one of the instant millionaires," he told the *Chicago Tribune* in 1986. Between the daily fantasies and the advertisements promising a quick jackpot that were ubiquitous in his poor, predominantly African American neighborhood, a lottery win seemed like a sure thing. "The worst part is," he noted, "you start believing a poor man is smart to take a chance."

McCord still believes he has a chance. These days, he mostly plays daily numbers and rollover jackpot games, with an occasional scratch ticket. He prays every day for a windfall, and he plays some special numbers: 245, which came to him in a dream one night, and 1007, part of his payroll code with the city, which "hasn't done anything yet" but he thinks is due to hit eventually. Around 2007, he won $100,000, most of which he used to fix up his mother's house and buy himself a new car. However, even with this payout and a few smaller hits over the years, he knows that he has lost more than he has won. By his own admission, he spends more than he should on tickets, though he is always sure to take care of necessities first. He plays because he still dreams of what he calls "the big one," not any specific amount, just enough to leave him set for life, and then some. The bigger the better. The way he sees it, some people spend money on movie tickets or alcohol. He buys lottery tickets to try to fulfill his dream of instant riches. So he plays. And he prays. And he waits for the jackpot he has been chasing for almost 50 years, which he is sure will arrive someday soon.[1]

Every week, 33 million Americans like Leo McCord spend a few dollars on the dream of a life-changing lottery jackpot. At convenience stores, gas stations, and supermarkets in nearly every corner of the country, gamblers buy their favorite scratch tickets, fill out slips for the daily numbers, or take a chance on a rollover jackpot game. Roughly half of American adults play the lottery at least once a year, and one in four do so at least once a month, holding out hope that they will overcome the odds standing between them and a massive windfall. Americans spend more on lottery tickets every year than on cigarettes, coffee, or smartphones, and they spend more on lottery tickets annually than on video streaming services, concert tickets, books, and movie tickets *combined*. The state lottery era began in 1964 with one state and $5.7 million in sales. In 2020, sales from 45 states totaled $91.4 billion. The United States has become a jackpot nation.[2]

Lottery tickets are popular because many Americans judge the long odds of a jackpot to be their best chance at a new life. Gambling has been a prevalent pastime in the United States for centuries, and luck has always held deep cultural resonance in a society that prided itself on its work ethic.[3] For people like Leo McCord, the lottery is more than just a game. It represents the likeliest path to financial stability, not to mention wealth. In 2006, almost 40 percent of households with incomes under $25,000 believed their best means of accumulating several hundred thousand dollars in their lifetime was through the lottery. A 2010 poll asked respondents to name the most likely way for them to get rich; 20 percent said by starting their own business and 19 percent said by securing a high-paying job. However, almost as many respondents (15 percent) chose chance: winning the lottery or receiving an inheritance.[4] During periods of economic decline, casino and horserace gambling revenues typically drop. Meanwhile, lottery sales increase as incomes fall, unemployment grows, and poverty rates rise.[5] More than any other form of gambling, players see the lottery as an alternative means of upward mobility.

Economic circumstances of the late twentieth century played a crucial role in encouraging Americans to turn to the long odds of lottery tickets. Over the last half-century, rates of relative intergenerational mobility have stagnated. The demise of high-paying manufacturing jobs, the rise of a low-wage service sector, and the concentration of high-growth industries in certain parts of the country have shut many Americans out of paths to greater prosperity. As a larger share of gains flew into the hands of the already rich, children born later in the century were less likely to earn more than their parents. Meanwhile, many Americans face acute financial insecurity: as of 2020, 36 percent of adults—including over half of black and Latino adults—reported being unable to cover an unexpected $400 expense.[6] Educational achievement and hard work provide no guarantee of success as the promise of economic opportunity proves increasingly elusive. As more financial risk was heaped onto American families in the name of personal responsibility, many of those same families embraced the risk inherent in the lottery to try to get ahead. "We sell hope in this depressed economy," an Ohio Lottery executive explained in 1975. "We don't sell lottery tickets. We sell dreams."[7]

For five decades, scholars have studied who exactly plays the lottery. Their research has proven that lotteries are regressive—meaning they take relatively more from those with lower incomes. Because Americans from almost every walk of life at least occasionally buy tickets, participation rates generally vary little along lines of income, race, and education. In fact, some studies find that, due to a lack of disposable income, the very poor may have the lowest rates of lottery play. Crucially, however, the frequency of play and the amount bet by those who do gamble is particularly high among lower-income, nonwhite, and less-educated Americans. Studies find that the top 10 percent of players account for half of total lottery sales and that the top 20 percent account for as much as 70 to 80 percent. Relative to the overall population, this group is disproportionately black or Latino, male, lacking a high school diploma, and below the twentieth income percentile. The amount spent on tickets—both in raw dollars and as a percentage of household income—declines as incomes rise. Furthermore, every single lottery game is regressive, especially daily numbers games and scratch tickets.[8] When pressed about these statistics, lottery officials and gaming industry executives utilize numerous statistical sleights of hand to obscure their industry's reliance on poor bettors. The evidence, however, is overwhelming. Lotteries represent a source of state revenue that draw heavily from those who can least afford to gamble.

At first glance, the demographic breakdown of lottery players seems to validate the age-old critiques that lotteries are a "stupid tax" or a "tax on people who are bad at math." By this reasoning, bettors buy tickets because they are irrational people driven by a wishful fantasy, or they simply do not understand how unlikely it is that they will win. Certainly, many lottery players overestimate their odds and have ideas about lucky numbers or divine control over jackpots that defy basic principles of probability. However, even if they cannot recall the precise likelihood of winning, players are generally aware of their small chance at a windfall. That they choose to play anyway is the result of the conclusion that, no matter how long the odds, an improbable jackpot offers their best shot at wealth. The lottery "is for dreamers and fools," one Virginia gambler acknowledged in 1991, but "any way you slice it, [the] lottery still gives a working stiff a better chance than the big bosses."[9] The popularity of lottery tickets is an unmistakable sign that tens of millions of people feel they lack other opportunities to get ahead. In a society increasingly bereft of economic opportunity, where it can feel impossible to build wealth no matter how hard one works, Americans have turned to gambling for a chance to make their dreams come true.

Players' dreams changed over the course of the lottery era, and shifting definitions of success helped drive the popularity of lottery tickets. The aspiration for more—whether money, land, power, or something else—is a long-standing theme in American culture. Dreams, though, are a reflection of their time, of a period's values and economic circumstances. In the immediate post–World War II era, the dominant aspiration—what might be called the

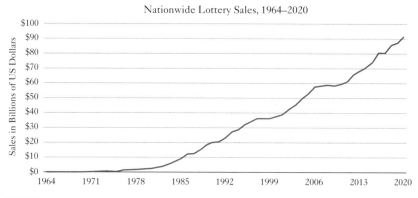

Nationwide Lottery Sales, 1964–2020

FIG I.1

American Dream—centered around the suburban home, a refuge of financial and familial security in a nation that had overcome depression and war.[10] Over the course of the late twentieth century, though, as inequality grew and economic opportunity dwindled, standards of financial success moved into greater heights. Starting in the 1980s, definitions of the good life became tethered to the beachfront mansion instead of the white picket fence. Success meant wealth and luxury, not stability and comfort.

Lottery prizes paralleled and helped facilitate this new enthusiasm for wealth. In the 1960s and 1970s, lottery players were primarily white working- and middle-class Americans who gambled for prizes that were considered large at the time but that pale in comparison to today's top jackpots. Lotteries opened with raffle-type drawing games that were infrequent and boring, and that offered an occasional top prize of $1 million (around $5 million in 2021 dollars) generally paid out in taxable installments over 20 years. Jackpots represented a chance at a comfortable life—a shot at climbing a rung or two up the economic ladder, not obscene opulence. In the 1970s, states introduced instant scratch tickets and daily numbers games. These attracted new players but did not fundamentally alter the scale of lottery prizes or the scope of lottery dreams.

Lotto did. In the 1980s, rollover jackpot games produced multimillion-dollar prizes. Though they bore the worst odds of any lottery game, these jackpots grew larger over time, setting off periods of lottery fever, days or weeks when those who played frequently and those who rarely played all rushed for tickets, pursuing the dream of life as a lottery multimillionaire. The lottery came to represent one of the only means of entering the highest reaches of economic inequality. As the rich got richer and got more ostentatious with their wealth, large jackpots meant everyone had a chance— however small—of joining them. Any American could live out the ultimate rags to riches story. All it would take would be their lucky numbers finally coming through.

Over time, gamblers' appetite for jackpots grew, and the size of the prize needed to set off a lottery frenzy became bigger. This prompted states to join together to form multi-state lotto games, which today offer gargantuan prizes. In 1964, New Hampshire awarded the nation's first lottery prize: $100,000 to each of six different winners (equivalent to $854,000 each in 2021). In 2016, John and Lisa Robinson of Munford, Tennessee; Maureen Smith and David Kaltschmidt of Melbourne Beach, Florida; and Marvin and Mae Acosta of Chino Hills, California, split a $1.58 billion Powerball jackpot. In a nation of growing disparities between rich and poor, winning the lottery has come to represent not just incremental mobility and financial security but mind-boggling wealth, the possibility of fulfilling seemingly any fantasy.

For many lottery players, the fantasy is the point. Gamblers buy tickets for the chance to dream, the opportunity, for a few days or a few moments, to imagine what it would be like to hit the jackpot and spend their newfound riches. Tucked inside this fantasy, though, is an understanding that it might just come true, that every ticket provides a small though very real chance of winning. Because hitting the jackpot is so unlikely, and because money has for so long been rhetorically tied to merit, winning the lottery seems to represent more than simply defying probability. Lotteries give Americans the chance to be chosen by luck, by God, or by whatever other force they see behind the game. If they could overcome the odds, they could be marked as blessed, worthy of money they may not have been born with but which they certainly felt they deserved. The word "lottery," after all, derives in part from a Germanic word meaning someone's lot in life, their share, their portion, their due. For many players, getting their due is what the lottery is all about. "People will tell you that they gamble to win, but I don't believe them," a Las Vegas casino shift manager once noted. "It's those brief seconds before you know the outcome that really turn you on. Those are the moments when you learn if you are a . . . winner or a loser."[11] In a nation where being poor is still often equated with personal failure, lottery tickets offer a singular opportunity to dream, to throw oneself at the hands of fate and maybe, just maybe, come out a winner.

For their part, states have been happy to inculcate the dream of a lottery ticket as a sure-fire route to a life of ease. Lottery commissions behave like no other government agency as they entice the public to purchase a consumer product. These enticements—which, through their content and their placement at times target lower-income and nonwhite Americans—center around the fun of playing and the lure of winning. "In America, we do not have kings or queens," one early 1990s California Lottery commercial explained. "What we have is something far more democratic. It's called Super Lotto and it gives each individual a chance for untold wealth. So, play Super Lotto, because even though you can't be born a king, no one ever said you can't live like one."[12] Many players retain a wishful, mistaken belief in an inevitable jackpot, a belief fostered by advertising that for decades has suggested that anyone can win, that winning is the ultimate fantasy, and that the American Dream is just one more ticket away.

Like few other activities, the nation's lottery habit sheds light on how Americans responded to the economic trends of the late twentieth and early twenty-first centuries. By offering a lifeline to those who feel they do not have other opportunities, lotteries helped acclimate Americans to a new economic order. Most players understand that winning is a long shot. Despite the odds, it is a bet they feel they have to make.

———————

Gamblers are not the only ones who have been captivated by lottery dreams. Like bettors wagering on a windfall, states legalized lotteries hoping to hit a jackpot of their own. Between 1963 and 2018, voters and policymakers in 45 states enacted lotteries because they believed legalized gambling was a panacea. All government policy entails a measure of risk, its enactment driven by an uncertain promise of how exactly it will improve people's lives. The politics of state lotteries made clear just how much of a gamble policymaking can be. Lotteries were seen as budgetary miracles, the chance for states to make revenue appear seemingly out of thin air, much the same way a lottery ticket might be worthless one moment and worth millions the next.

Lotteries appeared to present voters and policymakers with a painless solution to pressing budgetary problems. Specifically, lotteries offered states a seemingly simple way to fund public services without new taxes to pay for them. "Lotteries have proven to be catnip for elected officials who fear taxation," wrote Richard Leone, a member of a 1990s federal gambling commission. "Like gamblers themselves," states "hope to get lucky and put off tough choices about taxes and spending by chasing increased gambling revenues." Eager for a tax-free bonanza, supporters thought states could avoid traditional, established solutions to budget issues by taking a chance on gambling. Even as evidence emerged that lotteries could provide only a small percentage of state revenue, and even as data mounted about their regressivity, states kept passing them, kept advertising, and kept adding new games, desperate for their long-shot gamble to pay off. "For them and for us," Leone concluded, "it's a sucker's bet."[13]

Voters and legislators across the country bet on betting because of the economic and political circumstances facing state governments in the late twentieth century. Many of the same factors that have bred public fervor for lottery tickets also increased states' need for new revenue. In particular, lottery legalization was the result of states' attempts to preserve the mid-century social compact as the foundations of postwar prosperity crumbled.

The period from the 1930s through the mid-1970s was, in historian Jefferson Cowie's words, a "great exception," an era of government commitment to collective economic rights sandwiched between periods of inequality, polarization, and political deference to business.[14] In this unique historical moment, American government sought to provide economic opportunity and security to white working- and middle-class men—and, to a significantly lesser extent, African American men—through major public investments, especially in universities, housing, infrastructure, and social services. Crucially, government provided these services while generally keeping taxes low.[15] This arrangement was possible thanks to a unique convergence of American overseas influence and, relative to today, the even distribution of the economic gains.

Fractures in this era of economic exceptionalism began to emerge in the 1960s, leading to the first wave of lottery legalization. Due to a variety of factors, including population growth, shifting economic conditions overseas, and voters' ever-expanding appetite for new services, it was becoming increasingly difficult for state governments to keep their budgets balanced. By the late 1960s, states, especially northeastern states that had larger social safety nets and that put more into the federal pot than they received in return, needed to increase taxes to prevent massive cutbacks.

Voters, however, rebuffed the possibility of either reduced state spending or new taxes. Faced at long last with the prospect of having to shell out more for the services they demanded, legislators and taxpayers turned to government-run gambling. The first lottery was enacted in tax-averse New Hampshire in 1964, and lotteries swept across the Northeast and parts of the Rust Belt between the late 1960s and the mid-1970s. For gambling proponents, these were not merely extra sources of revenue. Lotteries were seen as silver bullets. Supporters believed a lottery would singlehandedly prevent a tax increase and allow for the continued expansion of state services. Though New Hampshire's sweepstakes benefited education, most states channeled profits directly into the general fund on the assumption that a lottery could subsidize a wide array of services. A "lottery operated by the state could raise enough revenue to permit reducing taxes," a West Belmar, New Jersey, resident wrote to his local newspaper in 1964. "New Jersey could have larger and better schools, better hospitals, and provide senior housing and medical care for the senior citizens."[16] As states struggled to fund existing services through old funding models, lotteries seemed to offer a chance to shore up the mid-century status quo. With a government-run sweepstakes, states could have it all.

In this period, dubious projections of revenue relied primarily on the prevalence of illegal gambling, especially daily lotteries knows as numbers games. At the time, numbers games were hugely prominent, particularly in urban black communities in the Northeast and Rust Belt. Voters and lawmakers in these states reasoned that gambling was already big business. A government-run game would allow bettors—especially Africans Americans—to keep gambling and would transmit the profits to the state instead of racketeers or organized crime.

It quickly became clear that lotteries could not come close to meeting northeastern voters' outsized expectations. Lotteries did generate revenue but not nearly enough to prevent cutbacks or a tax increase. And perceptions of a panacea made it harder for policymakers to raise taxes, as voters assumed states were already flush with lottery revenue. It was difficult to accept that the time of seemingly unfettered growth was nearing an end, that taxpayers would need to pay higher taxes both for new services and for those they already enjoyed. "There's no way to know just how New Hampshire's experiment will finally turn out," the *Wall Street Journal* concluded at the dawn of the lottery era. Though "it is plain to see that a state's hopes of getting schoolbooks for kids by playing the sweepstakes aren't much brighter than are the average gambler's dreams."[17]

Gamblers, however, are not known for giving up after a few losing bets. While they tempered their expectations somewhat, legislators and voters in other parts of the country retained the faith that a lottery could underwrite the costs of government. These hopes led to a second wave of lottery expansion. In the late 1970s, as voters in California and elsewhere began slashing their own taxes, many refused to accept the prospect of reduced government services. Particularly in western states, lotteries were a key component of the

State Lotteries by First Date of Ticket Sales

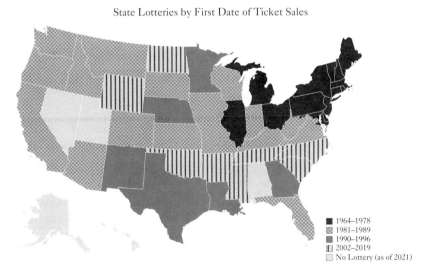

1964–1978
1981–1989
1990–1996
2002–2019
No Lottery (as of 2021)

FIG I.2

tax revolt and the growth of anti-tax sentiment more generally. Despite their failure in the Northeast, lotteries appeared to resolve the contradiction at the heart of the tax-cutting project. In the 1980s, in the face of potential service reductions, lotteries promised that states could have both low taxes and big government. A lottery offered pre-tax revolt spending without pre-tax re-volt taxes. Gambling proponents were encouraged in these beliefs by lottery ticket manufacturer Scientific Games Inc. Eager to create new markets for its products, the company brought lotteries to California and other states through ballot initiatives. The previous decade had proven that lotteries could not subsidize full state budgets, so Scientific Games tied its ballot proposals to individual budget areas, such as education, emergency services, or public parks. Expectations for revenue changed. The jackpot mentality endured.

By the 1990s, states had embraced what historian Bryant Simon calls "cheap government."[18] The anti-taxation chorus only grew louder, and, in much of the country, spending for dramatic new programs to bolster eco-nomic security was off the table—unless states could procure funding without taxes. Lotteries offered a unique opportunity, particularly for southern states, to implement new education programs in an era of bipartisan aus-terity. Gambling revenue had not come close to covering western states' des-ignated programs. Despite another lesson in the limits of the lottery, states held out hope for a windfall. In the third wave of lottery expansion, which occurred primarily in the Southeast, states tied lotteries to new education initiatives, specifically a college scholarship targeted at white suburbanites and a pre-kindergarten program meant to attract African American voters. If the panacea of the lottery could not be visible at the state level, it could be realized by individual households who lawmakers promised would benefit directly from lottery-funded education initiatives. For southern Democrats clinging to their last years in power in the region, lotteries represented a way to fund a popular expansion of government without a politically destructive tax increase.

Despite their Democratic affiliation in the South in the 1990s, lotteries, like other types of gambling, have been a thoroughly cross-partisan enter-prise. While lottery politics were different in every state, the promise of tax-free revenue enticed red and blue voters alike. Opposition also came from across the political spectrum. Critiques of lotteries have been remarkably consistent over the last 60 years, and many of the same arguments invoked against New Hampshire's lottery proposal in 1963 resurfaced in debates over a lottery in Mississippi in 2018. For decades, opponents' primary concern has revolved around effects on the poor. Lotteries appeal to lower-income people, opponents charge, tempting families to spend more than they could afford. Additionally, lotteries undermine the work ethic, encouraging Americans to try to get ahead through luck rather than pluck, education, and hard work. They could also foster problem gambling. It was one thing for states to legalize gambling, opponents often noted, but another entirely for state governments to encourage citizens to bet. States should not put their own bottom line ahead of the common good.

The loudest lottery opponents have consistently been conservative evangelical Protestants. Despite the lack of biblical prohibitions against gambling, evangelicals lambasted lotteries for their social impact and for what they saw as an ungodly veneration of chance. Lotteries, then, represent a forgotten terrain in the culture wars of late twentieth-century politics, a period in which evangelicals emerged as a powerful voting bloc within the Republican Party and in American politics more generally.[19] However, the vast majority of lottery proposals that went before voters were approved, almost always over evangelicals' strenuous objections. Lotteries present an issue on which evangelicals proved woefully out of step with the political mainstream, including many of the fiscally and culturally conservative voters they often counted on for support. When faced with gambling proposals, Americans have consistently put social, moral, and religious concerns aside in favor of nontax revenue.

Voters and legislators of nearly every political persuasion were taken with the prospect of a gambling windfall for government. Over time, hopes for lottery revenue gradually shrank. Lotteries represented an attempt to subsidize entire state budgets in the 1960s, then just a single budget line item (such as education or public parks) in the 1980s, and then specific education programs in the 1990s. Nonetheless, dreams of a tax-free jackpot persisted, and not just from a lottery. Over the course of the twentieth century, lotteries helped cleanse deep-rooted cultural and political skepticism of legalized gambling. Though lotteries were often not the first form of betting to receive government sanction—in most states bingo or horserace betting preceded lotteries—they were sufficiently broad based to change public and lawmaker attitudes in ways other games could not. Lotteries paved the way for casinos in Atlantic City, on tribal lands, and in cities across the country; riverboat gambling in the Midwest; and, since a 2018 Supreme Court decision, sports betting. Hopes for a nontax windfall persist to this day, even as gambling remains a marginal source of government income. Over the last 60 years, states have gone all in on gambling. In most cases, though, they are still waiting for their long-shot wager to pay off.

Lotteries were by no means an invention of twentieth-century American state governments. They have a long history as methods of public finance, a longer history as forms of entertainment, and an even longer history as decision-making devices. The first lotteries date back over four millennia. In the Old and New Testaments, the casting of lots is used to select land allocations (Numbers 26:55), kings (1 Samuel 10: 17–22), invasion targets (Ezekiel 21: 21–22), apostles (Acts 1: 24–26), and even the recipient of Jesus's garments following the crucifixion (Matthew 27:35). For societies without mathematical understandings of probability, lotteries were divinatory tools, and the drawing of lots served as a way to discern divine will. The reading of thrown animal bones was used in China as early as 1000 BCE, and lottery-type games became widespread pastimes in many parts of Asia. In ancient Rome, nobles and emperors distributed gifts to dinner party guests via drawings, with prizes ranging from terracotta vases to human slaves. The emperor Nero, too, offered massive, life-changing prizes through raffle tickets.[20]

The first lotteries used to fund government programs date at least to the fifteenth century. Lotteries were held for numerous purposes in Flanders in the 1440s, particularly raising money for city fortifications. The games quickly spread to Italy, where they were organized privately by business owners and then by the Venetian government to subsidize a variety of civic needs. Lotteries also made their way to England, where Queen Elizabeth I commissioned the sale of tickets for a lottery to raise money on behalf of "publique good works" in 1567.[21]

Lotteries became a popular pastime in Britain and were crucial to financing the colonization of North America. In the early 1600s, the Virginia Company of London held a series of lotteries to fund its outpost at Jamestown, with one Company member observing that lotteries were the "real and substantial food, by which Virginia hath been nourished."[22] Lotteries were common in the colonies, too. Due to a scarcity of liquid capital, they were important means of raising funds for infrastructure and construction projects, including churches and some of the nation's oldest and most prestigious universities. Additionally, if someone wanted to sell their estate but could not find a buyer with sufficient cash on hand, it was common to hold a lottery instead. In 1769, the British Crown enacted a prohibition on colonial lotteries, partly to exercise its authority over the increasingly disobedient colonists but also to squash competition for the sale of tickets for the English State Lottery. In November 1776, to fund the war against England and prevent the further depreciation of its recently issued paper dollars, the Continental Congress authorized a lottery with $10 million in prizes. Thomas Jefferson wrote approvingly of lotteries as a tax "laid on the willing only," one that to his mind did not entail significantly more chance than farming, shipping, or other commercial ventures.[23]

Lotteries remained a widespread practice in the early years of the United States. In a society defined politically by its aversion to taxation, state governments authorized lotteries to fund a wide variety of municipal works. As they had for much of the eighteenth century, state governments doled out authorizations for lotteries to raise money for specific purposes, especially infrastructure projects. "Every part of the United States abounds in lotteries," one Boston newspaper noted in 1791.[24] The games appealed to eighteenth- and nineteenth-century Americans for many of the same reasons they are popular today: they offered gamblers a chance to dream of instant affluence and provided a rare opportunity for the poor to hit it big. An early example of lotteries' dramatic social leveling was the case of Denmark Vesey, an enslaved man in South Carolina who purchased his freedom in 1799 after winning $1,500 in a local lottery. He later became known for allegedly plotting a rebellion against slave owners.

The tide against lotteries began to turn in the 1820s. Due to concerns over fraud, mismanagement, and the games' effect on the poor, states began banning lotteries. By the Civil War, every state other than Delaware, Kentucky, and Missouri had prohibited the practice. Though lotteries made a brief return after the war, the emergence of commercial banking and a full-throated capitalist economy reduced their importance. They quickly fell out of favor again, and by the 1880s the last remaining sweepstakes was the infamous Louisiana State Lottery Company. Known as the "The Serpent" or "The Golden Octopus" for its tentacular reach into states that had banned gambling, the company also earned its nicknames from notoriously corrupt dealings in Louisiana politics. Lottery officials bribed state lawmakers into granting its initial charter in 1868, a document that provided the company exclusive rights to sell lottery tickets in the state, with the company promising to contribute $40,000 a year to a charity hospital in exchange. These were the only taxes paid on an enterprise that in 1890 made $28 million in sales, amounting to $8 million in gross profit. From 1868 to 1892, the Louisiana State Lottery bribed its way through every Louisiana legislature to preserve its monopoly, avoid additional taxation, and prevent the loss of its charter. Finally, in the early 1890s, Congress enacted a series of bills designed to slay the Octopus, by, for instance, blocking the transportation of lottery tickets and advertisements over state lines.[25] These acts brought an end to the second period of legal lotteries in the United States.

Lotteries did not disappear, though. Gambling remained widespread around the country, including illegal lotteries, private card games, sports bets with bookies, underground casinos, or lotteries based overseas. Beginning in the 1920s, by far the most prominent form of illegal gambling was the numbers, daily three-digit lotteries that could be played for as little as a few pennies. These games were a pervasive part of urban African American life in New York, Chicago, and many other cities. Until the rise of state-run sweepstakes, numbers games informed most Americans' beliefs about how lotteries worked and who played them.

Despite the popularity of the daily numbers and other types of illegal gambling, from the mid-1800s through the 1920s, legal gambling was on the run in the United States. This nadir proved short-lived. Due to the potential for revenue, as the nation shook off its Victorian and Progressive prudishness, states began a gradual process of legalization. The return of state-sanction started with horserace betting during the Great Depression, and four states went so far as to legalize slot machines to meet budgetary needs and satiate residents' desire for action. Even though many of these laws did not last, a nation that had long wanted to bet was slowly creating ways for people to do so legally.

Because of their association with the Octopus and illegal numbers games, and because they are designed to reach as many people as possible, lotteries were not a part of the initial return of legalized betting. Puerto Rico, at the time an unincorporated American territory, formed a lottery in 1932 and the US Virgin Islands did so in 1937. But when legislators began pushing for state-run sweepstakes in the 1930s, their bills did not attract a great deal of attention. Neither did attempts in the 1940s to create a national lottery to help offset the costs of World War II despite polling that indicated general public support for government-run lotteries. For decades, lottery bills were floated in Congress and in state legislatures across the country. Again and again, lawmakers brushed these proposals aside. Lotteries were seen as unbefitting of American government and a rightly discarded relic of an earlier era.

Then, in 1963, legislators in New Hampshire approved a bill creating a state lottery to benefit education. Tickets went on sale the following year. The 70-year wall of lottery restrictions had been broken. A new era of legal lotteries had begun.

For a Dollar and a Dream picks up the story in the 1960s, drawing on sources from nearly 30 archives in 18 states to chart the spread of lotteries and the surge in lottery sales over the course of the late twentieth and early twenty-first centuries. This book opens in New Jersey in the 1960s, where white suburban voters hoping to preserve an inequitable state financing system and capitalize on illegal black gambling were convinced that a lottery represented a veritable budgetary panacea. Chapter 1 shows that although New Jersey was the third state to pass a lottery, it struck gold with a new game design that sparked the spread of lotteries across the region. Chapter 2 looks at northeastern lottery players in the 1970s, a cohort that consisted primarily of white working-class bettors. Amid a period of economic tumult and religious revival, many lottery winners claimed that divine forces were responsible for their jackpots, in the process expanding traditional conceptions of the American meritocracy.

After being confined to the Northeast for over a decade, lotteries arrived west in the early 1980s. Chapter 3 recounts how Scientific Games Inc. swamped the ballot initiative process in California, Arizona, Oregon, and other states, convincing voters already angry about taxes that a lottery would allow them to receive state services without having to pay for them. Thanks to Scientific Games' efforts, by the mid-1980s, lotteries were becoming a national phenomenon, and over the course of the decade a new rollover jackpot game—lotto—took lottery states by storm. Lotto, Chapter 4 illustrates, drew much of its popularity from the cultural and economic climate of the 1980s, a decade defined by the valorization of wealth on the one hand and rising inequality and growing financial insecurity on the other. Chapter 5 explores lottery advertising to highlight the contradiction inherent in the fact that lotteries are arms of the state charged with raising money by convincing people to gamble, thereby defying the nominal goal of government to pursue the public good. Chapter 6 shows how the lotteries spread to the South in the 1990s. In the midst of political realignment, Georgia governor Zell Miller tied the lottery to merit scholarships and pre-kindergarten programs, cementing lotteries' connections to education and crafting a model that was replicated across the region. The conclusion follows developments in state lotteries through the COVID-19 pandemic and asks whether lotteries remain a befitting activity of American government in the twenty-first century.

The state lottery story can only be told through the lives of both hopeful gamblers like Leo McCord and the policymakers and taxpayers (many of whom were also gamblers) who ushered in lotteries in the first place. This story is one that also includes mobsters and basketball star Michael Jordan, *Star Wars* and Donald Trump, the rise of the convenience store and a court case to decide, once and for all, whether God picked lottery winners. All were responsible, one way or another, for the nation's lottery habit. Together, these stories explain the reemergence of the state lottery system and the rebirth of an often-overlooked national pastime.

—•—

At first glance, the long history of gambling may imply that the nation's current lottery obsession is inescapable. Gambling represents a seemingly inexorable human enterprise, an activity that has always existed in some form. Lotteries, in particular, have been part of the social and political life of the nation since before its founding. The state-lottery era, then, appears to be just the latest manifestation of Americans' never-ending dance with the forces of chance. As a federal gambling commission concluded in 1976, "Gambling is inevitable."[26]

However, the legal status of gambling, the types of games people play, and the dreams that inspire players to bet are far from inevitable. It was not preordained that states enact lotteries, not predetermined that they introduce games that appeal to lower-income and nonwhite Americans, and certainly not unavoidable that southern states use revenue in ways that exacerbate lotteries' regressivity. The notion that gambling is an inescapable impulse bolsters the idea that lottery players are too irrational to understand the odds against them. According to this logic, they are not playing due to any specific economic circumstances but due to human instinct and an intrinsic misunderstanding of probability.

Gambling is a reflection of its time. The history of state lotteries reveals that the same conditions that compelled bettors to pursue long-shot prizes also compelled states to pursue gambling as a budgetary silver bullet. For all involved, lotteries appeared to present an easy answer to difficult economic problems. The lottery era has been defined by Americans' embrace of risk and the persistence of hope in the face of seemingly impossible odds. For states and for players, jackpots have proven illusory. But the fantasy endures, a fantasy captured in a 1980s New York Lottery advertising campaign: "All you need is a dollar and a dream."

An Astronomical Source of Income

THE RETURN OF STATE LOTTERIES

IN THE SWELTERING summer of 1967, the city of Newark, New Jersey, erupted. On July 12, two police officers arrested John W. Smith, a black taxi driver working despite having a suspended license, and beat him before bringing him into the station. Rumors spread in the black community that he had been killed by police, and the city was quickly embroiled in a five-day-long uprising in which 26 people were killed—nearly all of them by the city's police department, the New Jersey State Police, or the National Guard. Hundreds of stores were looted, mostly by black Newark residents, and millions of dollars in property was destroyed. Though host to one of the largest, longest, and most prominent incidents, Newark was hardly the only site of black protest and resistance in this period. Historian Elizabeth Hinton dubs these uprisings "rebellions," and she documents nearly 100 such episodes in 46 different communities in New Jersey alone—many in small cities and towns—between 1966 and 1972.[1]

After the fires were put out and the National Guard was sent home, local, state, and federal officials sought to understand what caused the uprisings in Newark, in other parts of New Jersey, and across the country. Governor Richard Hughes formed the Governor's Select Commission for the Study of Civil Disorder in New Jersey, known as the "Lilley Commission" for its chairman, New Jersey Bell Telephone CEO Robert Lilley.

The commission surveyed people across the Newark area. White residents generally blamed the uprising on bored youth, outside troublemakers, or "criminals and hoodlums." They denied that the riot—as it was labeled by newspapers and the commission—held any deeper political meaning. Black respondents told a different story. The problems at the heart of the rebellion, they insisted, were systemic: poor housing, lack of economic opportunity, and broken promises from city leaders, among other issues. Newark's history reveals that the events of July 1967 were, in fact, a culmination of processes that had built up over decades. As white families moved to the suburbs in the post–World War II period, the city's tax base crumbled. With few state-level taxes, property tax rates on remaining residents skyrocketed, which prompted even more white families to move away, while black families were explicitly or implicitly barred from buying homes in the suburbs. The decline in tax revenue had a harmful, trickle-down effect on city services, particularly education. Meanwhile, Newark was the second major city in the country with a majority of African American residents—it also boasted a significant Latino population—but it remained governed by Italian American politicians who were felt by local leaders to be unresponsive to the needs of the black community. Many of these needs were economic. Good-paying jobs had fled the city along with its white residents, exacerbating high unemployment rates, particularly among young people of color. In an era of ostensibly national prosperity, residents of Newark's black neighborhoods saw little opportunity for material comfort or the American Dream.[2]

Another major problem reported to the Lilley Commission was the behavior of the Newark Police Department. Even if the rumors about the cab driver's death were not true, black residents experienced constant police harassment and frequent brutality. They also witnessed pervasive corruption, especially in the area of anti-gambling enforcement. Numbers games—illegal daily lotteries—were ubiquitous in black and Latino neighborhoods in Newark and cities across the country. Because seemingly everyone participated as either a bettor or an employee of a gambling operation, numbers gave police the chance to hassle or arbitrarily arrest nonwhite citizens. The games also provided a network of bribes and payoffs to ensure that officers looked the other way and did not make any high-level arrests. One Newark assemblyman told the commission that graft was so extensive and so lucrative that "despite all the dangers of being involved in this all-black community, you couldn't run some of the white officers away from there." It was well known at the time that many of these games fed into the pockets of organized crime. Even the federal government's own commission to study the uprisings—the National Advisory Commission on Civil Disorders, known as the Kerner Commission—specifically noted the prevalence of the Mafia in Newark.[3] Police abuse was not solely centered around numbers games, but officers' capricious application of anti-gambling laws provided more proof to Newark's black residents that the system was rigged against them.

The two issues that helped spark the rebellion in Newark—New Jersey's local tax structure and the failed efforts to restrict illegal gambling—were also crucial in generating support for a surprising policy proposal: a state-run lottery. White suburbanites turned to the lottery hoping to protect the very same property tax system that had turned Newark and numerous other American cities into powder kegs. In the 1960s, these voters wanted their state government to increase its array of services but opposed using a sales or income tax to pay for such an increase. Especially after July 1967, many believed that any state-level tax would funnel money out of the suburbs into predominantly nonwhite urban centers like Newark. Recognizing that their state needed more money but opposed to any broad-based tax, the white middle-class turned to a lottery.

For voters and policymakers in the Garden State and across the Northeast and Rust Belt, a lottery was not just another source of government revenue. They saw it as a panacea, a fiscal savior, a painless, nontax way for states to expand their services. Proponents chose to ignore the temperate revenue projections put forth by their governors' offices and the lackluster results from the nation's first two lotteries, clinging instead to exaggerated projections of their own making. Despite mounting evidence to the contrary, lottery supporters held out hope for a windfall. In 1969, a referendum for a New Jersey state lottery won by what was at the time the largest margin of votes of any referendum in state history.

In New Jersey, as well as other early adopting states like Maryland, Michigan, and Illinois, white suburban voters had a specific idea about where profits would come from: urban African Americans. Given the prevalence of numbers games, they reasoned that states should legalize lotteries to capture this revenue for themselves rather than allow money to continue to flow to organized crime. Black numbers gamblers, many assumed, would become legal lottery players, and state-run gambling would allow African Americans to fund the public services that white voters expected would disproportionately benefit them anyway. For their part, black and Latino voters in Newark and elsewhere also overwhelmingly favored legalization. A state-run lottery, they believed, could offer legitimacy and government sanction to the numbers games that sat at the center of the underground urban economy and at the center of many of their issues with the police. Even if voters were skeptical of the grandiose promises of revenue, a legal lottery represented a major change to decades of failed gambling enforcement.

The passage of a lottery in New Jersey reverberated across the region. After disappointing results from the nation's first two state lotteries, the Garden

State introduced a number of innovations in game structures that increased sales and quickly set a new standard for lottery revenue. Even though sales fell short of voters' wild expectations, New Jersey's relative success led to the adoption of lotteries in 11 states between 1971 and 1977. The state served as a model for other states as they implemented their own sweepstakes and hoped for their own nontax windfall. While these hopes, like those of so many lottery players, ultimately failed to come to fruition, voters in New Jersey ushered in the lottery age.

The modern state lottery system began in New Hampshire. In the early 1960s, the state's financial situation created an acute need for revenue, and in 1963 legislators approved a bill creating a state sweepstakes to benefit education. Despite skepticism and occasional outright hostility from the federal government, the state captured headlines nationwide when tickets went on sale in March 1964.[4] Facing a similar budgetary situation, neighboring New York began a lottery of its own in 1967. Sales were slow in both states, and the drawings were complicated, mostly based on a convoluted system involving previously run horse races. While sales fell short of advocates' initial expectations, New Hampshire and New York legitimized a new revenue-generating tool for any state desperate for cash.

New Jersey was desperate indeed. The biggest problem facing the Garden State was its woefully underfunded public services. In the 1960s, one-third of the state's highways were deficient, 50,000 students attended school in ill-equipped classrooms, and state colleges and universities could accommodate only half of the state's college applicants.[5] The state government, however, was in no position to make the necessary improvements as it faced a budget shortfall that grew larger every year and threatened to eliminate an already dwindling surplus. New Jersey needed to make dramatic upgrades to its public services without further imperiling an already shaky financial situation.

The Garden State was not alone in facing a moment of budgetary reckoning. In many states, particularly in the Northeast and the Rust Belt, the economic foundations of the post–World War II status quo were starting to unravel. Beginning with Harry Truman's Fair Deal, the primary aim of American government had been to promote upward mobility, protect economic security, and, to a somewhat lesser extent, help the economically vulnerable. From subsidizing housing loans to exerting power overseas to create sources for cheap raw materials and markets for American products, the federal government helped build the white middle class and shore up widespread—though far from universal—prosperity. With the Great Society, Lyndon Johnson brought elements of this promise to African Americans. Thanks to an expanding economic pie and the relatively even distribution of the benefits of growth, aid to specific vulnerable populations did not entail reducing the benefits or high costs for others. As historian Molly Michelmore observes, a crucial dimension of the postwar social contract was that even as government expanded, taxes were kept low. Johnson's initial refusal to raise taxes as he expanded military action in Vietnam and launched a domestic anti-poverty agenda spoke to the priority of low taxes as a matter of both politics and public policy.[6]

Even before the economic crisis of the mid-1970s, the era of unencumbered growth was grinding to a halt. Rising inflation, population growth, increasing competition from rebuilt European and Japanese economies, and the costs of the Vietnam War brought on a new era of austerity and threatened the low tax/big government arrangement. Johnson promised in 1967 that his foreign policy agenda would not impede progress on domestic issues, that the nation could have both "guns and butter." However, one reporter observed that his proposed 1969 budget "melt[ed] down much of the butter," decelerating elements of the Great Society.[7] Rising war costs forced lawmakers of both parties to pick and choose. In 1968, Congress slashed billions from the federal budget while raising some of the personal and corporate income taxes Johnson had cut earlier in his administration. After years of low taxes and increased foreign and domestic spending, the nation was entering an age of limits.

This new epoch spelled trouble for state governments, which, like the federal government, had undergone a period of massive expansion. State government spending nationwide increased 50 percent per capita in the 1950s and 80 percent in the 1960s. New Jersey was typical of this trend. Total state expenditure doubled between 1950 and 1960 and then quintupled over the course of the next decade.[8]

However, between population growth, citizens' appetite for more spending, and a slowdown of economic growth, it was becoming increasingly difficult for states to uphold their end of the postwar bargain without raising taxes. Across the Northeast and Rust Belt and even in the booming Sun Belt, state budgets were in turmoil. Rising education, welfare, and Medicaid costs and growing demands from city governments pushed expenditures to new heights. In a 1970 survey of budget officers from all 50 states, 19 said spending was higher than expected, 8 had already cut expenditures, and only 3 reported spending below initial estimates (20 said it was as expected). States did not receive a corresponding increase in revenue so, in 1971, for the first time in more than a decade, total spending by state governments exceeded total state government income.[9] States pleaded with the federal government for more money, and overall Washington aid to state and local governments did increase fourfold between 1962 and 1972. But legislators facing a rising tide of austerity needed more. One Massachusetts state lawmaker warned in 1972 that his commonwealth was "on the brink of financial disaster."[10]

New Jersey faced a similarly dire situation, one made even more complicated by a unique—and uniquely regressive—tax structure. In the United States, localism has long been a powerful force in paying for government services, especially education. In New Jersey, public services were funded primarily by property taxes, which were collected and spent almost entirely at the local level by the state's 567 municipalities and townships and 578 school districts. This tax system became particularly important after World War II when New Jersey became the most suburban state in the nation. The local tax approach, historian Lizabeth Cohen notes, insulated white homeowners from paying for government services for anyone outside of their leafy green suburbs. After fleeing the state's urban centers in the 1950s and 1960s, suburbanites did not want to pay any state-level taxes. Especially in the context of the Great Society and in the aftermath of the urban rebellions, homeowners assumed state taxes would be funneled into welfare programs for the African American poor. By keeping their tax dollars local, suburbanites ensured that they paid for only the services that benefited them. Much of this was typical of suburban politics in other states.

However, the Garden State took the localist tradition to new extremes. More so than elsewhere, white suburbanites in New Jersey kept their state government starved for revenue. Until 1966, New Jersey was one of only three states without either a sales or income tax (the other two were Nebraska and New Hampshire). The largest taxes that supported the state government were generally out of sight, such as cigarette, gasoline, corporate income, and excise taxes. In 1967, the New Jersey state government received the lowest percentage of combined state and local taxes in the country.[11] Even if they had wanted to, lawmakers in Trenton simply did not have enough money to help urban governments match the spending of suburban areas. In 1969, New Jersey's state government spent less per resident than any other state.[12]

New Jersey's tax system was possible only because the state subsidized local governments, providing roughly 14 percent of their budgets. Most of the subsidies were for education and, to a lesser degree, highways and public welfare. Despite relying on handouts from the state, local governments left it to fend for itself financially, as legislators were expected to run the state and provide aid to local governments on limited sources of income. The Lilley Commission dubbed this arrangement "the most regressive tax system in the country." Little help was forthcoming from Washington. In 1968, New Jersey state and local governments received less federal aid per capita than any other state.[13]

"New Jersey has long been proud of the taxes it does not have," the state's tax commission wrote in 1963, but it has "paid a price" for this source of pride. Though designed to keep taxes low, locally financed services were inefficient, leading to redundancies and high costs. As a result, New Jersey residents paid some of the highest property taxes in the nation: a middle-income New Jersey homeowner paid more in property taxes than a New Yorker with the same income paid in property, income, and sales taxes combined.[14]

This left legislators with a dilemma. Homeowners wanted more government services but were overburdened by property taxes and refused to support a broad-based sales or income tax. New Jersey voters' hostility to state-level taxes was well established. In 1935, to help offset rising relief costs caused by the Great Depression, the state had passed a 2 percent sales tax. Public outcry, however, led to its repeal after just four months as well as the electoral defeat of nearly every politician who had supported it. For years, Republicans and Democrats alike shied away from tax proposals, and a common phrase in Trenton maintained that "taxers [are] losers" who would not last long in elected office.[15] Even as the state's financial problems mounted, even as voters demanded more state subsidies for local government, and even as a new age of limits threatened the old economic order, suburbanites remained steadfast in their opposition to a state-level tax. Voters rejected bond issues for school and highway financing in 1963. The following year the state legislature turned away five different tax proposals.

By the mid-1960s, the New Jersey state government could no longer survive on the crumbs left for it by local governments. Lawmakers in other northeastern states may not have had to reckon with the same degree of hyper-localism, but they did encounter similar issues. If they wanted to improve state services and balance their budgets, legislators could not depend on unpopular tax increases or even less popular cuts to government services. They would have to find the funding elsewhere.

—•—

Across the Northeast, voters and politicians turned to lotteries. New Jersey had legalized horserace betting in 1939, bingo for charitable purposes in 1953, and games of chance at amusement parks in 1959. These were relatively small sources of state revenue. Yet the gradual expansion of gambling helped set the stage for the lottery debates. It also increased the fervor of supporters. "New Jersey is having financial problems which are likely to get worse before they get better," the *Trenton Times* explained in 1964, "so it is in the cards that someone suggest legalized betting to raise the extra cash needed to maintain the state government in the style to which it has become accustomed."[16]

More often than not, that someone was William Musto. A Democratic state legislator from Hudson County, Musto had for years beseeched his fellow lawmakers to consider a lottery as a new, creative source of state revenue. He sponsored eight gambling bills between 1954 and 1969, most of which were met with skepticism and generally did not receive genuine consideration. By the mid-1960s, however, the state's budget crisis caused his fellow lawmakers to start taking his proposal more seriously. "Almost all of us will acknowledge that New Jersey must soon find substantial additional revenues to meet the cost of vital building programs and other services," Musto told the State Assembly Judiciary Committee. "A State lottery . . . would provide a most simple, effective and painless way out of our pressing fiscal problems."[17]

Initially, support for Musto's lottery extended all the way to the governor's mansion. After New Hampshire took the sweepstakes plunge in 1964, New Jersey's Democratic governor, Richard Hughes, claimed he would investigate the viability of a lottery, and the state treasury department projected possible net profits of $25 or $35 million per year.[18] By 1968, flagging sales in New Hampshire and disappointing results in the newly formed New York Lottery tempered these estimates. Hughes's office anticipated profits of $20 million per year while the state's Economic Policy Council predicted closer to $13 million.[19] New Jersey needed additional annual income of at least $50 to $100 million to balance its budget and would need even more to keep pace with standard annual spending increases. "It would be the worst of poor judgment," Hughes explained in his 1968 budget address, "to believe that a lottery could do anything more than scratch the surface of our genuine requirements for funds."[20]

Lottery proponents both in and outside Trenton were hardly so modest when it came to estimates of gambling revenue. Though they did not coalesce into an organized movement, politicians and voters across the state championed a lottery as the savior of New Jersey. Their support was built on hyperbolic expectations of the amount of money it would raise. Devised through a wide variety of methods, supporters' estimates invariably showed that a massive windfall awaited the state. In 1966, for example, the president of the state's Junior Chamber of Commerce projected $156 million in annual sales. He claimed his calculation was based on returns from New Hampshire's newly enacted lottery, notwithstanding that lottery sales in the Granite State were just $5.7 million in 1964 and had fallen in both 1965 and 1966.[21] As the decade went on and sales in New Hampshire and New York fell millions or tens of millions of dollars below initial expectations, Hughes's projection of lottery revenue declined accordingly. Yet, as New Jersey's budget crisis worsened, lottery supporters' forecasts grew larger, regardless of how poorly other lotteries were performing. By 1969, one Republican state legislator projected $200 million in annual sales, while a northern New Jersey Democratic congressman claimed the state could take in the monstrous sum of $500 million (equivalent to $3.5 billion in 2020 dollars). Musto promised that a lottery would "without any question supply hundreds of millions of dollars toward solving . . . the urgent needs of the state."[22] While it remains unclear how much they were influenced by lawmakers' projections, voters developed lofty expectations of their own. "The 'take'" from a lottery, one Turnersville resident predicted, "would be more than enough to fill the coffers of the state treasury to the brimful."[23] No matter how bad the financial crisis got, proponents claimed a lottery could provide what the state needed.

Exaggerated revenue estimates rested in part on the premise that New Jerseyans were already buying lottery tickets in New York. In this period, the passage of a lottery in one state spurred momentum for a sweepstakes in neighboring states. In 1970, a member of the New York Lottery Commission estimated that as many as 25 percent of tickets were bought by Garden State residents.[24] Statistics like these and newspaper stories about New Jersey residents winning the New York Lottery led many voters to reason that if its people were playing anyway, New Jersey might as well enact a lottery of its own. A Plainfield resident explained: "[It's] a shame . . . when I pick up a New York newspaper and see the thousands who are throwing away (yes, I mean throwing away) a buck for lottery tickets." He was not happy that his neighbors were squandering money on lottery tickets. Nonetheless, he implored the governor to "think of the thousands of bucks we should see coming into the coffers of New Jersey. . . . We need it a lot."[25] Even as lawmakers in Albany agonized over upsettingly low sales in New York, taxpayers on the other side of the Hudson River were enraptured by the idea that a large windfall was already made from gambling, a windfall that the Garden State should be keeping for itself.

Projections of huge sums of revenue led to the view that a lottery was not just another new source of state income but one that would permanently ward off a sales or income tax. A lottery offered to reconcile the contradiction between voters' desire for local services, state subsidies to municipalities, and school and infrastructure improvements, all without a broad-based tax. At a public hearing for one of Musto's lottery bills, Joseph Diaz, the president of a New Jersey anti-tax organization, excoriated the state for its lack of spending, especially its low rankings in per capita expenditure on education, health, and welfare. The state needed to improve in all these areas, he declared, though it should not do so through taxes, which Diaz called a "sickness" that would lead to the "death of our state." Diaz instead backed a lottery "to prevent and avoid the imposition of any new taxes," articulating the popular view that a lottery and taxes were equivalent means of raising revenue. Diaz's organization held four demonstrations in favor of the lottery in 1964 because gambling was essentially the only means of raising what he called "painless" revenue—in contrast with implicitly painful taxes.[26] Neither Republicans nor Democrats seriously considered reducing state spending to solve the state's financial problems. It was taken as a given that Trenton needed additional funding to preserve the arrangement that had carried the day in the 1950s and early 1960s. The only question was where the necessary funds should come from—taxes or a lottery?

Governor Hughes had a definitive answer: taxes. He refused to rely on a lottery to fund New Jersey's rapidly expanding budget and he disputed prognostications that gambling would be a quick fix for the state's problems. Though he had initially supported a lottery, Hughes spent much of his second term attempting to raise revenue through more traditional means. He proposed a massive spending increase for education in 1967 because he presumed the passage of a broad-based tax. Both parties, in fact, recognized that the condition of public schools and highways in New Jersey necessitated a new source of state revenue. Around this time, lawmakers across the country were making the same realization. Nationwide, state governments passed 410 new taxes or tax increases between 1959 and 1970, including the introduction of a sales or income tax in 20 states.[27] States wanted to preserve the postwar system of robust social services but needed more from taxpayers in order to do so.

After a landslide reelection in 1967, Hughes pushed an income tax through the state legislature, where it drew bipartisan support. However, the bill was rejected by the Democratic-controlled state senate. According to a Hughes biographer, senators saw it as a means of taking money from the suburbs to help the urban poor. Taxpayers, who were overburdened with property taxes, were reluctant to support an income tax that would draw more from richer areas to benefit less prosperous ones. Progressive taxes were considered so loathsome that in 1969, lawmakers organized hearings to consider adding a ban on state income taxes to the New Jersey constitution.[28]

With his budget in limbo, Hughes made a threat that no state legislator wanted to hear: if a broad-based tax did not pass, he would have to cut the budget. Crucially, the first item on his list would be $115 million the state was slated to contribute to local education, highway, and health budgets.[29] Suburbanites may not have liked the prospect of a broad-based tax, but they liked budget cuts even less. Unsurprisingly, the legislature overwhelmingly passed a 3 percent sales tax in April 1966. Lawmakers' preference for a sales tax over an income tax proves highly telling. Because everyone pays the same tax rate on the goods they purchase, sales taxes are highly regressive, as they force the poor to contribute much higher proportions of their income. If the state was going to institute its first broad-based tax, suburbanites ensured that their contributions would be kept relatively low.

Despite his disappointment at the failure of the income tax, Hughes claimed the new sales tax would "turn New Jersey's face to the future, and let us not fall back into inaction and mediocrity." The *New York Times* was much less optimistic: "Slowly and painfully, New Jersey is moving to provide the revenues it so urgently needs to meet the problems of its increasingly urbanized, industrialized economy."[30] The state, it seemed, was finally taking concrete steps to pay for the services that voters had come to expect.

The passage of the sales tax only increased the fervor for legalized gambling. Voters hoped that the sales tax would finally offer relief from burdensome property taxes. They failed to realize, though, that New Jersey needed a new tax just to keep its head above water, not to reduce the taxes already in place. Calls for a lottery became even louder in 1968 as legislators began debating the possibility of increasing the sales tax. As the *Times* had predicted, the 3 percent tax merely scratched the surface of the state's financial needs. Additionally, Hughes hoped to use the revenue from a tax increase to support the state's Medicaid program, set to begin in 1970. He also hoped to bolster urban aid in the aftermath of the Newark uprising. While the governor had previously voiced his support for a lottery, he understood the wild expectations that had captured the imaginations of lottery supporters. Hughes did not want a lottery referendum in 1968 because "it would be fatal for the interests of the state" if voters thought a lottery could prevent the need for a bond issue or new taxes.[31] In his view, a lottery referendum would shut down any possibility of tax reform, as voters would insist on a lottery instead of new taxes, even though gambling would not raise nearly enough money. The lottery had evolved from a curious political proposal into a way for taxpayers to avoid addressing the fundamental flaws in the state's revenue structure.

—•—

The other major question hovering over state-run lottery proposals related to illegal gambling and organized crime. The fight against the mob was a major political and social issue in the 1950s and 1960s, one that shaped the political conversation around almost every proposal for every form of legalized gambling. In the Northeast and parts of the Rust Belt, where underground black numbers games were especially prevalent and where the mob problem was especially acute, promises of revenue alone might not have been sufficient to secure the passage of state lotteries. Enactment hinged on voters' beliefs about what would happen to organized crime and illegal lotteries.

From its earliest days in the United States, organized crime was involved in illegal gambling. For many Americans, the connection between the two was solidified in the early 1950s by the Senate Special Committee to Investigate Crime in Interstate Commerce, also known as the Kefauver Committee. In the late 1940s, a number of newspaper exposés and state-level investigations brought mob corruption to light, particularly the widespread practice of bribing police officers to prevent scrutiny of illicit betting operations. These local inquiries set the stage for a groundbreaking Senate investigation into organized crime in 1950–1951. Committee chairman Estes Kefauver (D-TN) focused the committee's efforts on the mob's dealings in legal gambling in Nevada as well as illegal betting around the country. "Gambling profits," the senator alleged, "provide the financial resources whereby ordinary criminals are converted into big-time racketeers, political bosses, pseudo businessmen, and alleged philanthropists."[32] Advancing a theory that would define political discourse around the mob for decades, Kefauver argued that gambling revenue was not the product of organized crime's power. It was the source of that power.

The Kefauver Committee revealed the scale of the mob menace for the American public. Many of the hearings were televised and, in the days of limited viewing options, they attracted more viewers than the World Series. "Never before," *Life* magazine explained in 1951, "had the attention of the nation been so completely riveted on a single matter. The Senate investigation into interstate crime was almost the sole subject of national conversation."[33] For many, that conversation entailed the first discussions of a sinister, mysterious crime organization called the "Mafia." Until the 1950s, most Americans—including FBI director J. Edgar Hoover—were skeptical that such a syndicate existed. Kefauver's committee cemented the connection between gambling and organized crime. He introduced the public to the possibility that the nation was home not just to rogue, individual gangsters but to a centralized criminal network that coordinated a range of illicit activities all over the country.

The Kefauver investigation proved to be the opening salvo in a decades-long federal war against the mob. Thanks to Kefauver, stopping illegal gambling was considered synonymous with stopping organized crime. As a result, when lawmakers turned up the heat on the Mafia, special attention was placed on the fight against betting. In the late 1950s, Senator John McClellan (D-AR) launched his own inquiry into organized crime and illegal betting, culminating in the passage of five bills to aid the fight against organized crime, including three focused on gambling.

In the 1960s and 1970s, Lyndon Johnson and Richard Nixon launched a war on crime, one that heavily targeted urban African Americans. The campaign against the mob represented a central, but often overlooked, component of this effort. Both presidents affirmed Kefauver's belief, as Nixon stated in 1969, that "gambling income is the lifeline of organized crime." Johnson placed the fight against the mob first on a list of the federal government's "special" law enforcement responsibilities, and his Commission on Law Enforcement and Administration offered more recommendations pertaining to organized crime than to drugs, alcohol abuse, and gun control combined.[34] In 1970, Nixon created a National Council on Organized Crime to help coordinate national strategy. That year, Congress passed the Organized Crime Control Act, which introduced a range of new measures to aid law enforcement, most prominently the Racketeer Influenced and Corrupt Organizations (RICO) Act, and also stiffened penalties for operating an illegal gambling ring. The Organized Crime Control Act also launched a new commission to investigate national gambling policy. Released in 1976, the commission's final report revealed just how connected gambling and the mob had become in the public imagination over two and a half decades: 87 percent of Americans surveyed by the commission believed illegal gambling profits were used for narcotics and loan-sharking operations.[35]

States escalated their efforts against the mob, too. The 1968 Omnibus Crime Control and Safe Streets Act authorized states to use wiretaps, and numerous states, New Jersey among them, approved their use in court-approved circumstances, including gambling enforcement. New Jersey also passed funding for special grand juries as well as for 50 state troopers dedicated to investigating organized crime. In 1970, voters elected Republican

William Cahill, former FBI agent and congressman, to the governorship. While in Congress, Cahill authored a crucial amendment to the 1968 crime bill and dedicated his administration, as he declared in his inaugural address, to "destroy[ing] the corrupt and the corrupted wherever they exist" in New Jersey.[36] Other states were similarly concerned with the mob question. In Connecticut, a gubernatorial committee to investigate illegal gambling recommended a range of new police powers. In New York, Governor Nelson Rockefeller increased penalties for illegal gambling, including mandatory minimum sentences and making it a felony to operate a gambling syndicate. By 1973, 35 states had formed either an organized crime prevention council or an anti-mob investigative or prosecutorial unit.[37]

Given the prominence of the war on organized crime and the association of gambling with the mob, many voters were hesitant about government-run lotteries. Kefauver's argument held that even legalized betting might invite crime. To lottery skeptics, enterprising mobsters would follow the money to infiltrate state lotteries. No legal restrictions could ever keep them at bay. A concerned East Orange resident wrote that a lottery "would stimulate unlawful gambling. . . . There would be greatly increased crime, drug abuse, and immorality of all kinds, including much graft."[38] For critics, government-sanctioned betting would offer organized crime a beachhead to infiltrate civil society and from which low-level street crime and high-level corruption would proliferate. Gambling was associated with crime beyond the particular circumstances of illegal betting in the United States. To opponents, gambling was an inherently corrupting enterprise, and its inherent corruption is what attracted gangsters in the first place. Legalization would not cut off gambling as a source of revenue for the mob nor would it cleanse gambling of its criminal associations. Nothing ever could.

Lottery supporters had an answer for crime-concerned cynics. Proponents promised that legalized gambling would not embolden criminals but would take money from illegal gambling and funnel it into state coffers. As historian David G. Schwartz notes, postwar investigations into organized crime had an ironic consequence: they produced a steady stream of headlines and hearings that detailed exactly how lucrative betting was for the mob. In the process, they bolstered projections of how much a state lottery could rake in. The Johnson administration's crime commission estimated that the total amount wagered illegally nationwide in horserace, lottery, and sports betting was around $20 billion per year. After prizes and expenses, this amounted to approximately $6 or $7 billion in annual profits for organized crime. In New Jersey, state law enforcement officials estimated that illegal gambling was a $1.5 billion per-year business, with profits of $100 million from Newark alone.[39] These reports were particularly useful for lottery advocates given the slow sales in New Hampshire and New York. Illegal gambling seemed to offer proof that there was a market for gambling and that the nation's first two sweepstakes had simply failed in their execution. New Jersey congressman Cornelius Gallagher projected that "if [illegal gambling] revenue could be channeled to the state through a legal lottery, we could abandon all taxation in New Jersey and increase every service in our state four times over."[40]

When lottery proponents like Gallagher talked about redirecting revenue from illegal gambling operations, they often had one specific kind of betting in mind: numbers games. These games had deep roots in American history. In the nineteenth century, anyone who could not afford the often-hefty price of a lottery ticket could place a side bet on the drawing, a practice known as "insuring the lottery" or, more commonly, "policy." Policy gradually became popular in its own right, and it remained particularly prevalent among black gamblers. In policy, between 11 and 15 numbers ranging from 1 to 78 were drawn from a box or wheel. Players could bet that a specific number would be drawn or that a certain number would be drawn at a certain position.[41]

Policy remained the lottery game of choice for black gamblers until the 1920s when a resident of Harlem—generally believed to be Casper Holstein, a black immigrant from the West Indies—devised the plan for numbers games. Players selected a three-digit number, which could be bet in a variety of ways for as little as a few cents. The winning number was generally decided through a highly public source that was printed in the newspaper, if someone knew where to look. Initially the number was derived from the last two digits of the bank clearings of the New York Clearing House and the third digit of the Federal Reserve Bank balance. If the Clearing House had a printed value of $1<u>23</u>,000,000 and the bank balance was $4<u>5</u>6,000,000, the number would be 236. While the source of the number changed—in many cities to a more complicated formula based on the total amount bet each day at a certain horserace track—what was important was that the number was accessible and could not be rigged in the house's favor. Players could bet their chosen numbers in a variety of ways, including a straight bet, a bet on any combination of three specific digits (a "boxed" bet), or bolita, a wager on only the final two digits. Numbers quickly spread across the country, especially to cities with large black populations in the Northeast and Rust Belt (though policy remained the game of choice in Chicago). In 1927, a black New York newspaper reported that Asbury Park, New Jersey, was "'number' mad." "Harlem, in the days of its wildest orgies . . . could not approach the passion of the Jerseyites to get two cents down on 726 and a nickel on the bolita."[42]

Numbers games were huge institutions in urban black communities. The games enticed Latino and white working-class players as well, but especially by the middle of the twentieth century, African Americans constituted the primary clientele. "Practically everyone played every day in the poverty-ridden black ghetto of Harlem," Malcolm X writes in his autobiography.[43] The game appealed to bettors for a variety of reasons: it was easy to understand, was widely available in certain neighborhoods, and could be played for as little as a few pennies. Numbers also provided marginalized bettors their best chance at a large amount of cash. Given the social and legal barriers facing African Americans in the traditional economy, stringing together a few wins or hitting on a major bet offered a rare chance at a quick windfall. Across the country, dream books, which translated names, world events, or dreams into three-digit numbers, were bestsellers. For those willing to bet on their dreams, numbers games could, in fact, provide a stepping stone to the black middle class. One such gambler was a South Bronx shipping clerk and Jamaican immigrant named Luther Theophilus Powell. Sometime in the late 1950s, a three-digit number appeared to Luther in a dream. He and his family scraped together all the money they could to place a $25 bet. Miraculously, the number came through. The $10,000 jackpot let the Powells move to Queens and purchase their first home. The family's only son, Colin Powell, would go on to serve as US secretary of state and chairman of the Joint Chiefs of Staff.[44]

Numbers games were originally run by black entrepreneurs. Though their wealth was built off the nickels, dimes, and dollars of their neighbors, operators made a point of reinvesting portions of their wealth back into their communities. The games were also crucial sources of employment for young African Americans—including both Malcolm X and musician Ella Fitzgerald—who collected numbers bets, as well as some black women who defied gender and racial stereotypes to run their own numbers operations.[45] But many games did not remain community outfits for long. Especially after the repeal of Prohibition, white mobsters forcibly took over the larger numbers rings in big cities, though on a day-to-day basis many games were still run primarily by African Americans.

White suburbanites knew all about the prevalence of daily lotteries in black neighborhoods. Prior to the start of the war on drugs in the mid-1960s, "gambling was the principal site of racially targeted policing" in urban America, according to historian Matthew Vaz. Given police priorities, the war against organized crime often manifested as police harassment of black numbers workers. Meanwhile, white gamblers—including the mobsters who actually owned many of the black lotteries—were spared from law enforcement scrutiny.[46] This heavy-handed policing did not escape the public eye. Articles detailing the arrest of numbers operators or charges against police officers caught taking bribes from game organizers were fixtures in state and local newspapers. African Americans were hardly the only illegal gamblers in this period, but the predominance of numbers games in black communities and the disproportionate focus of police enforcement on this subset of gamblers made urban black lotteries seemingly synonymous with illegal betting writ large.

The notoriety of numbers games had important implications for white suburbanites' beliefs about the viability of a state-run sweepstakes. Lottery tickets, these voters presumed, would be purchased by black gamblers who already wasted their money on numbers games. "How can you stop them?" Gladys Mason of Trenton asked. "The poor play the numbers, so why not have a lottery?"[47] Using "the poor" as code for "African Americans," Mason reasoned that black communities already bet millions every year. In her mind, gambling was an innate activity in African American communities. Like the voters who pointed to their neighbors buying tickets in New York, for Mason a lottery would capture money already spent on gambling. A state-run sweepstakes would not increase the total amount bet but would put extant betting revenue into taxpayers' pockets.

Mason's comment reflected emergent ideas about the inevitability of gambling. In criminological circles, gambling—as well as public intoxication, sex work, drugs, and vagrancy—was increasingly seen as a "victimless crime," a new phrase that came into public use in the early 1970s. For these activities, experts pointed to the ineffectiveness of harsh police enforcement and called for decriminalization instead of continued crackdowns. While 12 states did experiment with marijuana decriminalization between 1973 and 1978, legalization efforts in this period were generally rejected. Gambling, however, was an exception.[48] Given its presence in so many Americans' everyday lives and the fact that many states had already legalized bingo or horserace betting, gambling represented a unique issue where the victimless crime rhetoric found widespread purchase. In 1978, for example, just 16 percent of northeastern urban residents said they would be willing to report an illegal bookie. Two and a half decades after the Kefauver hearings, gambling was still associated with organized crime, and law enforcement officials insisted that it remained their economic lifeblood. Nonetheless, public appetite for continued gambling enforcement was on the wane.[49]

The widespread willingness to change approaches to gambling was tied to the abject failure of the war on illegal betting. Oblivious to the fact that they were in the process of repeating the same mistakes with the budding war on drugs, law enforcement, state policymakers, and the general public questioned the effectiveness of difficult-to-enforce gambling penalties. These laws, many came to realize, were onerous for police departments, costly to states, and unsuccessful at actually stopping illegal gambling. In a 1978 poll, 90 percent of northeasterners who knew about an illegal numbers games in their city believed the police also knew about it, and 75 percent believed the games persisted because of police corruption.[50] If numbers games continued despite police pressure and if bookmakers or numbers operators could simply pay off police officers, then no amount of enforcement would ever adequately put a stop to illicit operations.

A state lottery, then, promised to accomplish what federal and state crackdowns never could: run the mob out of business. Instead of continued futile attempts at enforcement, the state would end criminals' monopoly over the lottery market, cutting off gambling as a source of funds for organized crime and raising tax revenue in the process. Proponents drew parallels between the campaign against gambling and the unsuccessful attempt 40 years earlier to ban alcohol. According to the common understanding of Prohibition, the government had tried to outlaw a popular, unavoidable activity. A legal ban only fed into the hands of the underworld that profited from rum-running in ways they could not have if alcohol was legal. "The situation with gambling today is the same as existed during [P]rohibition," a doctor from Brick Township wrote in 1963. A government-run lottery would "derive an astronomical source of income for the state," the doctor wrote, and "eliminate the crime syndicate."[51] Voters envisioned that the repeal of anti-gambling statutes would end the reign of organized crime. They ignored the reality that the repeal of Prohibition had catalyzed many mobsters' embrace of gambling in the first place, and therefore the implication that the legalization of gambling would simply lead organized crime to a new source of income.

By connecting illegal gambling to the prohibition of alcohol, proponents did not deny the aura of crime and corruption that surrounded gambling. On the contrary, they embraced gambling's illicit reputation. Motivated by the lottery play they believed to be irrepressible in black communities, they saw a way to make black gamblers pay for the state services suburbanites assumed would benefit them anyway. White voters wanted government to tap into this new source of income, to strike a blow against organized crime, and create a new wellspring of revenue.

Not all New Jersey residents were convinced that a lottery would raise a windfall for the state. As momentum for gambling grew across the Northeast in the 1960s, a small but vocal cadre spoke out against the lottery. The primary opposition to lotteries came from the Protestant clergy, which has served as the center of anti-lottery campaigns since the nineteenth century. While opponents—like supporters—generally did not form dedicated anti-gambling organizations, individual church leaders took to the airwaves and attended public hearings to voice their hostility to legalized betting.

Opponents' main argument against the lottery was that the games would prey on the poor. This represented a long-standing critique. Since roughly the advent of lotteries as means of public finance, critics had raised concerns that the public who would finance these projects would consist of individuals staking their limited funds on a life-changing windfall. As early as 1621, King James I's crackdown on lotteries in England was motivated in part by growing opposition to the levels of participation by poor laborers. Similar fears informed states' bans on lotteries in the United States in the nineteenth century.[52] In the post–World War II period, the popularity of numbers games in urban black communities seemed to provide further confirmation that lotteries were naturally appealing to the less fortunate.

As a result, even before any data on the demographics of lottery players were available, lawmakers and religious leaders assumed that tickets would attract poorer and less-educated people. A lottery would not create income out of thin air, as proponents imagined, but would further entice people to bet once they had the chance to do so legally. Those most tempted would be lower-income Americans. A Republican Bergen County assemblyman noted, "How many lottery tickets do you think Governor Rockefeller of New York has bought? I don't know. But I do know they'll be buying them in droves in ghetto neighborhoods in New Jersey by people who can least afford them." Poor African Americans, he suggested, should not be tricked into subsidizing state services. Concerns of regressivity represented the most popular critique of legalized lotteries. A 1972 survey in New York found that twice as many people opposed state-run gambling because of its effects on the poor compared to those who thought it was "morally wrong."[53] While a subset of lottery opponents saw gambling as inherently immoral and some worried that it would invite organized crime, many more feared that a legal lottery would expand access to gambling and induce poor people to spend money on desperate, long-shot wagers.

Opponents also pointed to the folly of a lottery as a source of state revenue. They rejected the idea that a state-run sweepstakes would present a bountiful fountain of revenue for New Jersey. Instead, they offered sober reflections on the state's financial situation, warning that only a broad-based tax would lead the Garden State out of its budgetary morass. "We are not surprised that proposals like this are made because too many people are looking for financial miracles to happen to pay the cost of government," Reverend Samuel Jeanes stated in 1964. The pastor of a Baptist church in Merchantville, Jeanes was the anti-lottery movement's answer to William Musto. In addition to launching campaigns against abortion, drug legalization, and alcohol, Jeanes spent decades fighting the expansion of gambling in New Jersey. While he acknowledged the state's troubled situation, Jeanes argued that a lottery is "not realistic. [Lotteries] represent a very shallow approach" to financial problems.[54] As a search for "financial miracles," Jeanes framed the lottery as a foolhardy, speculative, and naïve venture, what many opponents deemed a quest for "something for nothing." This phrase implied that lottery proponents exaggerated calculations of revenue and underestimated the true depth of the state's financial situation. Support for the lottery, opponents charged, rested not on sound economics but on wishful thinking.

Caution about estimates of state revenue melded with concerns about legalized gambling's impact on the poor. A lottery would be harmful to lower-income people by modeling irresponsible financial behavior. Taxpayers, opponents charged, were trying to use a lottery to receive state services without paying for them. So too, gamblers would buy tickets hoping to be miraculously catapulted into a new life without having to work for it. "I don't feel this state should encourage a something-for-nothing, pie-in-the-sky or get-rich-quick attitude," one Republican assemblyman explained, warning that a lottery would lead bettors to put their faith in chance as a mechanism of social mobility. Jeanes worried specifically about the message that would be relayed to the state's children. Young people, he wrote in 1963, would first see that their parents "have tried to bypass an old-fashioned American tradition of paying for education with old fashioned American tax dollars."[55] Like gamblers betting on a fortune and like voters trying to make a quick buck for the state, children would learn to seek out shortcuts and to take a chance on a windfall. A lottery was unbecoming of the state. The jackpot mentality associated with gambling should not be allowed to proliferate.

But proliferate it did. Between projections of hundreds of millions of dollars in annual revenue and the prospect of stamping out the mob, by the late 1960s the vast majority of voters in New Jersey and growing majorities across the Northeast and Rust Belt believed that a lottery was a good idea. In 1969, legislation for a lottery referendum passed both houses of the state legislature with bipartisan support. The bill designated revenue for education and the state general fund. On November 4, nearly 2 million voters cast ballots on the lottery question: almost 1.6 million voted in favor with only 363,000 opposed, the first referendum in state history to win by over 1 million votes.[56] Support came from across the state. At least 58 percent of voters in every county voted for it. In William Musto's Hudson County, over 90 percent of voters approved the measure. The county lay on the New York border, so voters were especially aware of the popularity of New York Lottery tickets in the Garden State. Significantly, the county was also a longtime epicenter for New Jersey's organized crime operations.[57] Fighting the mob remained a chief concern for voters statewide. On the same 1969 ballot, New Jerseyans also elected organized crime fighter William Cahill to the governorship, the first Republican to win the office since 1949.

While the lottery won widespread support statewide, suburban taxpayers felt they had been the driving force behind the bill's passage. Two weeks after the referendum, a Ship Bottom resident wrote to Cahill, "I hope you will bear in mind the fact that the lottery was most definitely approved by the so-called middle class, senior citizens, also persons who are at the breaking point of high property taxes."[58] The lottery was supposedly a suburban endorsement of localism. Legalized gambling would mean the state government could continue subsidizing local services without new tax revenue.

Suburban support for the lottery was supplemented by even stronger approval among minority voters in metropolitan areas. In Newark, which was 52 percent black and roughly 10 percent Latino, the lottery was approved by a 10–1 margin, compared to an almost 3–1 margin statewide. In urban areas, lottery voters looked a lot like the people who were expected to be lottery players. As Matthew Vaz shows, in the 1960s, black lawmakers and civic leaders saw legalization as an opportunity for legitimacy for the numbers games that were so central to their community. Rather than displace illegal games, they hoped a state lottery would offer a path to legal employment for numbers workers and bring an end to decades of police harassment.[59]

With a mandate from the populace, the newly formed New Jersey Lottery Commission set about creating the nation's third state-run lottery. After careful study of New York's operation, the commission introduced a series of innovations in American legalized gambling. As lottery pioneers, New York and New Hampshire had striven for respectability. In New Hampshire, players were required to write their names on their tickets, which bore pre-printed numbers and cost $3. In the Empire State, tickets cost $1 and were sold in hotels, government offices, and—until 1968 congressional legislation outlawed the practice—banks. Drawings were infrequent, and winners were selected through a complicated process involving multiple raffles tied to horse races. The expensive tickets and affiliation with the sport of kings were meant to mark the lottery as a highbrow form of gambling, avoid a federal excise tax on non-horserace gaming, and assure the public that the lotteries could not be rigged. But the games were boring and the drawings too sporadic to generate consistent interest. "The Lottery takes too long," an African American barber in Harlem complained in 1967. "Who wants to wait three or four weeks to get some action? . . . Most people want some action . . . every weekday like with numbers."[60]

New Jersey did not initially hold daily drawings but did adopt a harder-sell tactic, putting profit over propriety to meet the exaggerated projections that had facilitated the passage of the 1969 referendum. The state started with a weekly $50,000 drawing, tickets for which cost just 50¢, and shortly thereafter added a biannual $1 million drawing, with tickets for $2.50. Tickets could be purchased at supermarkets, taverns, newsstands, and corner stores. Though players could not pick their own numbers, they did not have to write their address and contact information on every ticket stub. Winners were determined through randomized drawings involving ping-pong balls and the results of an already run horse race, as the state did not immediately embrace the live drama of horseracing.

On December 16, 1970, the first New Jersey Lottery tickets went on sale. The innovative game design quickly set a new standard for the nascent lottery industry. Consumers bought 1.5 million tickets on the first day—three times the officially anticipated figure—and many of the state's nearly 2,000 vendors ran out of tickets by noon. This initial wave of enthusiasm remained high, and in its first year, the lottery raised, on average, $2.75 million for the state every month. By contrast, the New York Lottery raised an average of only $2.9 million for the state in its first year, even though New York boasted more than twice New Jersey's population.[61] The New Jersey Lottery sold $72 million in tickets in its first full year. The following year, sales nearly doubled. By 1972, 80 percent of New Jerseyans had bought at least one ticket, and over 90 percent said they approved of the lottery.[62]

After the disappointments in New Hampshire and New York, the relative success of the New Jersey Lottery catalyzed the spread of lotteries across the Northeast and Rust Belt. While it remained to be determined whether the lottery had solved New Jersey's budget crisis, reports of Garden State sales figures led voters across the region to believe that a lottery might be the answer to their financial issues. Other states faced the same fiscal crunch as New Jersey, circumstances that whetted appetites for tax-free lottery revenue. In states like Connecticut, where legislators were mired in debates over enacting a new income tax, the apparent success in New Jersey further bolstered gambling proponents' case. "I hope you will sign the bill to put a lottery system in the state of Connecticut," one West Hartford woman wrote Governor Timothy Meskill in 1971. She noted that New Jersey is "doing well with a lottery system" and hoped Connecticut would enact its own to prevent an income tax.[63] In Michigan, the size of Detroit's numbers games led voters to reason, as one Hillsdale housewife noted, "Gambling is done anyway. We might as well legalize it." Additionally, in the early 1970s Michigan was mired in political fights over busing to integrate Detroit's school system. Historian Kelly Goodman notes that the lottery became a favored tool of white suburban anti-busers seeking to protect localized education financing. On the same day they voted overwhelmingly for George Wallace and his anti-busing campaign in the 1972 Democratic presidential primary, Michigan voters approved a lottery. A few months later, they rejected ballot measures to distribute property tax revenue statewide and to create a state income tax. In Michigan, as in New Jersey, the lottery attracted white voters who wanted public services but did not want to pay for them with taxes that flowed out of the suburbs and into the coffers of the state government.[64]

Once they saw the initial sales figures from New Jersey, previously skeptical lawmakers became enamored with the possibility of tax-free revenue. In 1971, officials from Pennsylvania, California, and over 20 other states sent inquiries to New Jersey about its lottery, and officials from Connecticut and Massachusetts visited New Jersey to examine its games firsthand. Both states—as well as Michigan and Pennsylvania—began selling lottery tickets in 1972. All four modeled their lotteries on the Garden State, and Massachusetts went so far as to pay the New Jersey Lottery $25,000 for the guidelines behind its weekly lottery game.[65] Previously established lotteries sought to imitate New Jersey as well. In the early 1970s, New Hampshire and New York restructured their games to match the cheaper tickets, more frequent drawings, and—they hoped—higher sales that made New Jersey the nation's first successful state lottery.[66] By 1977, 14 states, all in the Northeast and Rust Belt, had enacted lotteries.

While states across the country were in need of revenue, three factors help explain why residents of northeastern and upper midwestern states were especially receptive to lotteries. First, states were influenced by the passage of a lottery in a neighboring state. One study concludes that it was only during the first wave of lottery legalization—1963 to 1977—that the enactment of a lottery in one state significantly increased the likelihood that an adjacent state would enact one as well.[67] Once New Hampshire and then New York took the lottery plunge, they set off a domino effect across the region. Second was support for legalized gambling among Catholics, as economists have found a direct relationship between the proportion of a state's Catholic population and the likelihood that it enacted one of the nation's first lotteries.[68] The third was organized crime. The mob had long posed a problem in New Jersey, and the presence of organized crime was an important predictor of states' early lottery adoption. The 1967 Johnson administration crime report, *The Challenge of Crime in a Free Society*, identified 17 states where organized crime members lived and operated. With the exception of Florida (which enacted a lottery in 1986) and Wisconsin (1988), every state east of the Mississippi River tabbed as a home for organized crime enacted a lottery in the first wave of legalization. Forty-seven percent of mob states were early lottery adopters compared to just 15 percent of non-mob states, meaning states identified as hubs of organized crime were over three times more likely than other states to adopt a lottery in this period.[69] Other than New Hampshire, every state that adopted a lottery in the first wave was either a mob hotbed or bordered a state with a lottery.

Lotteries remained confined to the Northeast and Rust Belt until the 1980s. But after the failures in New Hampshire and New York, New Jersey provided a model that set the standard across the region and across the country. The Garden State legitimized a creative way to raise revenue for any state in need.

———•———

Voters in New Jersey and across the region ushered in lotteries as fiscal saviors. However, legalized gambling simply did not raise enough revenue to uphold the postwar status quo. Initial sales in the Garden State were high relative to New Hampshire and New York but extremely low compared to supporters' estimates of $300 or $500 million in annual income. Most important, revenue was also small in relation to the state's budgetary needs. Few proponents had

Table 1.1 The First Wave of Lottery Legalization,
1963–1977

State	Year lottery enacted
New Hampshire	1963
New York	1966*^
New Jersey	1969*^
Connecticut	1971^
Pennsylvania	1971*^
Massachusetts	1971*^
Michigan	1972*
Maryland	1972^
Ohio	1973*^
Rhode Island	1973*^
Maine	1973^
Illinois	1973*
Delaware	1974^
Vermont	1977^

* Indicates a state identified by *The Challenge of Crime in a Free
Society* as one where members of organized crime lived or operated.

^ Indicates a state that shared a border with at least one lottery
state at the time of lottery enactment.

accounted for the fact that actual net profits represent only a fraction of gross
sales. In its early years, the New Jersey Lottery returned roughly 43 percent of
gross sales to the state, with 45 percent to prizes, 6 percent to the retailers that
sold each ticket, and 5 percent to operating expenses. In 1971, $72 million in
sales netted $33 million for the state, amounting to approximately 2 percent
of the state's $1.5 billion total revenue. This was a notable source of income,
to be sure, but hardly enough to forestall a tax increase, bankroll a massive
array of new government services, or balance the budget, not to mention all
three. In 1969, voters had enacted a lottery hoping it would singlehandedly
end the budget crisis. In February 1970, less than four months after the lottery
vote, Governor Cahill signed legislation increasing the sales tax in the face of
a projected $300 million deficit.[70]

Lawmakers and lottery officials had to face the fact that gambling revenue
could not come close to meeting the state's needs. Even the lottery's most avid
advocates acknowledged that it might not have the impact they predicted.

After the referendum, William Musto explained, "Revenue is my last consideration. Whether it makes $1 million or $100 million is not important," implausibly claiming that he simply wanted New Jersey residents to have access to the excitement of lottery tickets. As early as 1964, Musto had accounted for the possibility that a lottery would not solve the state's problems. In a State Assembly hearing, he declared, "One thing is certain: The State cannot lose money on a lottery. If it does not bring in enough to meet needs, we can then turn elsewhere, and the 'illusion' of lottery riches will not impede the proponents of new taxes."[71]

Except that is exactly what happened. In the early 1970s, as spending continued to increase, some state officials began calling for New Jersey to pass its first income tax. As expected, they faced resistance from a public long wary of state-level taxes and armed with a new weapon in their rhetorical arsenal. Voters argued that because of the millions of dollars pouring in from the lottery, New Jersey could continue to provide the same level of state services without new taxes. "There is no need for a state income tax," a Point Pleasant Beach resident wrote emphatically in 1976. Thanks to the lottery, "there is a surplus of cash in the state's treasury."[72] Years after the lottery's passage, hope for a gambling windfall persisted, hope that stood in the way of the taxes that most lawmakers understood were the actual answer to the state's budget problems.

Many lottery supporters refused to acknowledge that gambling revenue would not be enough to prevent a new tax. They understood that the lottery was providing millions for the state, though they neglected to consider those millions relative to the overall state budget. Instead, voters charged that the only reason New Jersey needed an income tax was because the state had mishandled the lottery money. In a climate in which many Americans were becoming increasingly distrustful of government in the aftermath of Vietnam and Watergate, the inability of the lottery to solve the state's problems offered further proof of bureaucratic corruption and incompetence. "Why should the people trust the governor or the Legislature?" a Moorestown man argued in 1975. "The excuse for the sales tax was it would reduce property taxes. This was a laugh. The excuse of the lottery was it would aid the schools. This was another disaster."[73] Voters expected immediate, visible results after the lottery passed. When none were forthcoming, instead of remembering the governor's caution to lower their expectations, they blamed the state. By doing so, they could cling to the belief that gambling represented a panacea. Some voters pushed state officials to expand the lottery's operations, hoping that a wider variety of games—especially a daily three-digit game to compete directly with numbers operations—would finally meet the impossible revenue benchmarks. New Jersey did in fact introduce the nation's first daily lottery drawing in 1972 and then a numbers game in 1975. Overall sales grew gradually but still could not come close to offsetting a tax increase.

By the mid-1970s, it appeared that New Jersey residents had learned that gambling could not solve their state's financial problems. Shortly after the passage of the lottery, state officials began discussing the possibility of legalized casino gambling, particularly in Atlantic City. However, in 1974, by a 3–2 margin, voters defeated a referendum that, after a five-year test period in Atlantic City, would have allowed any New Jersey municipality to authorize casino betting, thereby creating the only legal casinos in the country outside of Nevada. The bill was presented as another revenue windfall. For Atlantic City residents in particular, historian Bryant Simon explains, casinos were a "magic bullet": "No matter the problem" facing the city, "unemployment, urban decay, or race relations," proponents promised that casinos "would fix it." Other advocates claimed that casinos represented a means of staving off a state income tax, echoing the lottery campaign by dubbing casinos a "painless" source of revenue.[74]

Casino proponents hoped the lottery referendum signified that the public had changed its mind about all forms of legalized gambling. Their hopes were dashed, at least initially. Voters had been duped by revenue promises before, and some New Jerseyans attributed their opposition to the casino measure to the disappointment of the lottery. A Middletown Township voter opposed the referendum because "in 1969 promoters of the lottery said it would yield approximately $200 million annually to the state." With sales of just $89 million in 1974, "the voting public, led to believe that the lottery would solve our problems in funding education, has been sadly disillusioned."[75] Voters were newly skeptical about promises of overflowing state coffers. If casino supporters wanted to drum up public support, it appeared they would have to do more than frame their measure as a windfall for the state.

Yet the desire for government services subsidized by gambling revenue endured. In 1972, Cahill proposed a state income tax, which he promised would lower property taxes. After months of debate, a bipartisan group of lawmakers defeated the bill in the state legislature. Some were explicit that they opposed it because they saw the bill as a way to funnel money from the suburbs into urban areas. One West Bergen Republican said his constituents told him that they did not care about the problems of the cities. He voted no.[76] Nonetheless, the suburbs quickly found themselves facing a fiscal crunch, too. In the mid-1970s, amid growing unemployment and surging inflation in the national and state economies, New Jersey's deficit continued to rise, reaching a point where lawmakers began seriously considering severe service cuts. In this context, a 1976 referendum legalizing privately owned casinos in Atlantic City passed easily. Following their defeat in 1974, casino supporters, including William Musto, shifted the debate more squarely onto the economic benefits casinos could provide, highlighting the revitalization of Atlantic City as well as a portion of gambling revenue that would benefit the state's elderly population—borrowing from the Pennsylvania Lottery, which channeled all of its profits into elder-care programs. As one assemblyman noted, "At a time when the Governor is cutting [Medicaid benefits] . . . we should look seriously to casino gambling as a way of financing these worthwhile services."[77] Voters had finally been forced to reckon with the possibility of reductions in government programs. Advocates presented casinos as a way to prevent these cuts. Despite the failure of the lottery, voters hoped a bet on legalized gambling would finally pay off.

Even as it became clear that a lottery could not replace new taxes, the something-for-nothing ethos that drove lottery legalization remained. In its first six years, the New Jersey Lottery raised, on average, 2.5 percent of total annual state revenue. For a brief period, the panacea promoted by lawmakers and voters boasted the highest per capita lottery sales in the nation. Yet even such record-breaking sales fell far short of the expectations that had grabbed the public imagination in the 1960s. Lottery revenue remained around 3 percent of annual state government income. The same was true in other states. In Massachusetts, which by 1974 had taken the crown as the state with the highest per capita ticket sales, lottery profits amounted to roughly 2 percent of state revenue.[78]

The lottery was slightly more effective in its mission of thwarting illegal gambling, albeit not the mob. There are indications that organized crime may have already moved out of the numbers racket by the time the lottery measure passed, and the mob continued to thrive after the enactment of lotteries. The gambling-focused anti-crime measures were largely a bust. As one former chief of a state organized crime strike force admitted, "We would investigate a couple of low-grade bookmakers, call them organized crime figures and go after them."[79]

State lotteries did, however, mark the beginning of the end for large-scale illegal lotteries. Initially, black gamblers stayed loyal to numbers games, as weekly state-run raffle games appealed to a different player base. However, once states introduced their own numbers games—and once those games began offering higher payouts and better odds than illegal games—numbers

games did not stand a chance. Ultimately, the end of the numbers led to unemployment for thousands of young black men who had worked as numbers
runners and operators, many of whom had long arrest records that barred
them from legal employment. As with the legalization of marijuana in recent
years, the advent of state-approved gambling did not expunge the criminal
records of the thousands of black people previously arrested for this newly
legal activity. The numbers games that had been a source of both pride and
apprehension in black communities were swallowed up by the state.

While state lotteries did turn illegal gambling money into tax revenue,
they had another impact many proponents had not considered. Instead of
simply siphoning revenue already being spent on gambling, lotteries led to a
massive increase in the total amount spent on gambling. Lotteries provided
the first real gambling opportunity for any non-horserace bettor or bingo
player who had been wary of playing illegally. Though voters had envisioned
a lottery as a crime-fighting measure, once enacted it grew to a scale larger
than any illegal game could ever hope to achieve. Ultimately, lotteries helped
further shift the burden of paying for government away from the wealthy,
increasing the share of revenue drawn from those with less means.

Nonetheless, after the lottery failed to prop up New Jersey's unique tax
structure, white suburban homeowners were finally forced to reckon with the
inequities of a system built around property taxes. In 1970, a northern New
Jersey lawyer brought suit against Governor Cahill on behalf of Kenneth
Robinson, an African American sixth-grader from Jersey City. The suit alleged that the state's property-tax based system was unconstitutional because
it abandoned students like Kenneth to poorly funded school districts. Due to
the fact that the tax structure failed to provide sufficient funding to Jersey City
schools, the state allegedly violated Kenneth's right under the New Jersey constitution to a "thorough and efficient" public education, thereby also violating
his rights under the equal protection clause of the Fourteenth Amendment.
In *Robinson v. Cahill* (1973), the State Supreme Court agreed with the plain-
tiff, deeming New Jersey's localist system unconstitutional. After three years
of follow-up court rulings, failed tax proposals, and negotiations, the court—
led by chief justice and former governor Richard Hughes—ruled that New
Jersey could provide funding for urban education or not provide any education at all. In a dramatic measure (that would have been more dramatic had it
not occurred during the summer), the court closed public schools statewide
until the legislature settled on an acceptable formula for equitable education
funding. Reluctantly, a bipartisan group of lawmakers passed the state's first
income tax in 1976. The state government gradually assumed a greater role in

education funding, though the new tax distribution formula continued to favor wealthier areas.[80]

The debates over a state-run lottery in New Jersey and across the Northeast and Rust Belt in the 1960s and early 1970s signal voters' attempts to bet on painless answers to complicated budgetary problems. Taxpayers ignored mounting evidence of the ineffectiveness of gambling as a means of public finance. Instead, as the economic foundations of postwar prosperity began to collapse and states faced growing budgetary problems, voters clung to the belief that a lottery would preserve government services while allowing states to maintain relatively low taxes. In addition to subsidizing government, a lottery would have the added benefit of singlehandedly putting an end to a decades-long crusade against the mob's illegal gambling operations. In a 1969 editorial, the *Trenton Times* pointed to the parallels between gamblers and state officials, "The lure of getting something for nothing, which draws millions of Americans to . . . illegal numbers and policy rackets, obviously has some appeal to New Jersey legislators."[81] Voters and lawmakers across the northeast held out hope that supposedly painless government income could underwrite the cost of state services. Inspired by New Jersey, risk-taking legislators and voters resurrected state lotteries as methods of public finance and brought the nation into a new era of sweepstakes gambling.

2

Not Luck, but the Work of God

MERIT AND MIRACLES IN THE 1970S

DAYSI FERNANDEZ WAS desperate to change her luck. An immigrant from the Dominican Republic, Fernandez lived in Washington Heights with her husband Delio and their three children. Delio drew a steady salary from his job at a nearby factory, but like many blue-collar households in the 1970s, it never seemed to be enough. Fernandez frequently fretted over her family's finances. "I dream all the time of money," she explained. "Not big, you know, but little money [*sic*]. Every time I'm thinking of my children . . . [and] their education." Beginning in 1978, she sought extra funds for her children's education through the New York Lottery, playing four different games weekly.[1] Despite praying for a jackpot, she never successfully picked the winning numbers.

Even after three years, Fernandez did not waver in her belief that heavenly forces could attract a life-changing windfall. On June 27, 1981, with the grand prize for the New York Lottery's rollover game at a then-state-record $2.87 million (roughly $9 million in 2022 dollars), Fernandez took action to improve her odds. She asked Christopher Pando, a deeply devout friend of her eldest son, to purchase four tickets on her behalf, hoping his piety would help her win. As Pando later testified, "Mrs. Fernandez, knowing that I am religious and a strong believer in [the Santeria deity of] St. Eleggua asked me . . . whether or not I could get my Saint to win the Lottery. I told her that I did not know, but I would try." Pando went to a local liquor store where he purchased the tickets. To fulfill his promise to Fernandez, he prayed to St. Eleggua while he selected his numbers.[2] Two days later, the duo discovered that, at approximately 4-million-to-one odds, Fernandez's ticket bearing the numbers 17-22-23-26-31-37 was worth nearly $3 million. Her financial troubles were over. The jackpot, however, brought on new problems of its own.

At a lottery commission press conference to celebrate her prize, Fernandez attributed her windfall to God. "All the time I prayed to my Lord," she stated, painting the jackpot as a testament to the power of faith.[3] In her mind, the prize had been God's answer to her years of prayers, a way of rewarding her and providing for her children's education. She did not mention Pando, though, nor did she discuss any plans to share her winnings. Once it became clear that she had no intention of splitting the money, Pando felt cheated. He thought his prayers had led to the miraculous win and that he deserved a share of the prize. Pando was so sure he had a right to her winnings that he filed suit in court, claiming that he was owed a portion of Fernandez's new-found millions.

Pando's suit was initially rejected on the grounds that he could not prove that his prayers had made them win the lottery. New York Supreme Court Justice Edward Greenfield reasoned that Pando and Fernandez's agreement rested on divine intervention. "The condition was not that the numbers chosen would win," Greenfield wrote, "but that the saint was to make the numbers win." In order to recover a share of the winnings, Pando would have to "demonstrate that his prayers caused the miracle to occur." This, Greenfield held, was impossible. "In the modern courtroom, there is no way to prove that his faith in prayer brought about the winning ticket. . . . He can testify that he prayed, but who is going to provide the proof that his prayers were efficacious and that the saint caused the numbers to win?"[4] Unless Pando could prove St. Eleggua had caused the jackpot, he had no claim over the prize.

Two years later, the New York Court of Appeals reversed Greenfield's decision. Pando's fulfillment of the agreement was not contingent on proving that he had persuaded St. Eleggua to intervene. Rather, the court maintained, Pando's "prayers in this scenario had value to [Fernandez] because she believed in their power to help effectuate the desired end."[5] By asking Pando to pray over the tickets, Fernandez made it clear that she thought prayer could improve her chances of winning. Legally, it did not matter if Pando's actions had actually affected the drawing. Because she believed they would help, the two of them had formed a legally binding verbal contract to split the winnings. Consequently, the court opened the doors for a jury trial to decide Pando's share of the prize. In 1988, seven years after the drawing that made Daysi Fernandez a multimillionaire, Christopher Pando was awarded half of her jackpot. "It took the patience of a saint," one headline read, but his prayers were finally answered.[6]

While theirs was a uniquely dramatic case, Daysi Fernandez and Christopher Pando exemplify the contested claims about merit, luck, and divine intervention that became prevalent among American lottery players in the 1970s. Lotteries are built around uncertainty, around the distribution of money through games built on pure randomness. However, many bettors do not approach lotteries as vehicles of chance. American lottery players have long employed a variety of tactics to try to help them win, from prayer to lucky numbers to precognition. This behavior is rooted in the belief that an individual can affect the result of an event outside of their observable influence. These types of practices—often characterized as "superstition" or "magical thinking"—have been intrinsic to gambling for centuries and are ubiquitous across the globe.[7]

One aspect of gambling, though, is unique to the United States. In a practice that began in the early 1970s, many American lottery winners attributed their jackpots to God, claiming that supernatural forces intervened on their behalf to grant them a windfall. Due to the overwhelming unlikelihood of winning, winners like Daysi Fernandez reasoned that mathematical probability could not sufficiently explain their good fortune. Instead of acknowledging that they had gotten extremely lucky, these winners constructed retrospective theological narratives that erased luck, framing their windfall instead as the product of a supernatural miracle and divine interposition. These types of statements remain relatively uncommon outside the United States. Studies from South Africa, Finland, and Taiwan find gamblers who utilized religious practices but almost no winners who expressed gratitude to divine forces for their prizes.[8]

By asserting that God had provided them with a windfall, religious American lottery winners expanded conceptions of the meritocracy. For centuries, merit has been at the center of most tellings of the American story: those who were virtuous and smart were destined to rise. Those who were not would not. Traditional meritocratic principles celebrated hard work as the only proper way to get ahead. Even as states began to legalize lotteries in the 1960s and 1970s, gambling was looked down on, as forces of chance disrupted the sacrosanct connection between virtue and success. Lottery winners had other ideas. Through claims that their windfall had been an act of God, winners made the case that they deserved their prize. If God had intervened to reward them with a jackpot, then surely God had reason to reward them. By explaining to newspapers and at press conferences that divine forces had provided their windfall, winners made the case that the lottery was not a mechanism of chance but a tool to reward the deserving, a meritocratic

means of distributing wealth. Not every lottery winner made such a statement, and it is impossible to determine what percentage of winners made re-
ligiously inflected declarations of gratitude. But any winner who sought to
claim that they deserved their prize almost invariably attributed it in some
fashion to the divine. These statements were particularly significant amid the
economic and religious context of the 1970s. In these years, lotteries appealed
primarily to a white, working-class, and Catholic player base, a group ad-
versely affected by deindustrialization and other economic trends. These
developments heightened the importance of lotteries as mechanisms of social
mobility, made players more willing to take a chance on a jackpot, and made
a lottery win seem that much more miraculous.

Of course, most people who bought tickets in this period did not win the lottery. Those who did win, though, constitute a significant proportion of the available record. The practice of interviewing hopeful lottery players as they bought
tickets did not become common until the rise of rollover jackpot games in the
1980s, so, beyond demographic data, sources on lottery players from the 1960s
and 1970s consist primarily of the stories of lottery winners mediated through
newspapers, interviews, and press conferences. As Daysi Fernandez's court case
indicates, the stories of these winners—particularly those who claimed divine
intervention—warrant close examination. Christopher Pando's prayers to St.
Eleggua only entered the historical record, for instance, because he filed suit.
Otherwise, Fernandez would have simply declared that her supplications had
caused a jackpot and there would be no evidence of Pando's efforts. Regardless
of the veracity of winners' statements, narratives of God and gambling were
many Americans' first exposure to lottery winners. These narratives reveal the
betting practices of early lottery players and the connection between merit,
money, and miracles that has become a pervasive part of American life.

Do people get what they deserve? Do they deserve what they get? For many
Americans for many years, the answer was yes. Success represented a question of individual achievement—behaving the right way, making the right
decisions, and having the right work ethic. Anyone who worked hard would
surely become rich and successful, so anyone who was rich and successful was
surely deserving of a fortune. By extension, anyone who had not succeeded
lacked the ambition, fortitude, or ingenuity to make it. These ideas provided
the basis of a meritocracy, a society where the most virtuous and worthy
people rose to the top. Under the principles of the meritocracy, both rich and
poor deserve their lot.[9]

The American meritocracy has religious origins, specifically in the idea of grace. In *The Protestant Ethic and the Spirit of Capitalism* (1905), German social theorist Max Weber explains that Puritans were obsessed with questions about their standing in the eyes of the divine. Calvinist doctrine, though, maintained a strict theology of predestination. This meant the living could never know their divine status, nor could they do anything to help facilitate their salvation. Puritans, Weber argued, did see their vocation as part of their heavenly calling, so they poured themselves into work, not for the sake of earning money but for the glorification of God. However, this devotion to labor laid the groundwork for a recognition of human agency in facilitating grace. Philosopher Michael Sandel explains, summarizing Weber, "as the Calvinist notion of work in a calling evolved into the Puritan work ethic, it was hard to resist its meritocratic implication—that salvation is earned, and that work is a source, not merely a sign, of salvation."[10] Gradually, it became more difficult to avoid the connotation that working hard improved someone's chances at grace.

The relationship between work and grace helped pave the way for merit. Calvinist predestination was replaced by an acknowledgment that everyone had control over their lives and could determine their own outcomes. What emerged was a meritocratic ideal, which held that the successful earned their status through their own good work, though many continued to endow their achievements with a tinge of divine providentialism. These ideas form a pillar of what historian Jackson Lears calls a "culture of control," a strain in American thought and life of "a coherent universe where earthly rewards match ethical merits."[11] The culture of control left no room for chance, attributing outcomes to each individual's virtue. Since the mid-nineteenth century, the culture of control has been used to rationalize inequality and create a moral and religious justification for the more distasteful corners of the free market. If everyone made their own luck, then everyone had it within themself to grab their own bootstraps and change their fate. The culture of control remains alive and well in American culture. "Do you want to believe that it's just the luck of the draw and bad things can happen to you at any time? . . . That you have no control over your circumstances?" Australian author Rhonda Byrne writes in the bestselling self-help book *The Secret* (2007), "Or do you want to believe and *know* that your life experience is in your hands?"[12] For much of the nation's history, rhetoric surrounding success has centered on the belief that everyone's life experience does indeed lie in their own hands.

Forces of luck present a powerful countercurrent to an ostensibly monolithic meritocracy. Lears explains that the culture of control has always been in conflict with another formulation, the "culture of chance." This culture acknowledges life's unpredictability, that not everything happens for a reason. Anyone who was successful—or unsuccessful—could not be entirely to blame, as there could be no straight line between work, merit, and life's outcomes without room for luck in between. Whereas the culture of control was embodied by the quintessentially American self-made man (and depictions were invariably of men), the culture of chance was personified by an oft-reviled but no-less quintessential figure: the confidence man— someone willing to gamble, to embrace a future of uncertain possibilities.[13]

The culture of chance had a variety of origins and champions. Divinatory rituals played important roles in Native American and West African culture and, through the early years of the United States, the practice of Protestantism left room for magical elements seemingly outside of God's control. By the mid-nineteenth century, a nascent industrial capitalist economy made the influence of luck undeniable. American commerce, French aristocrat Alexis de Tocqueville wrote in 1840, resembled "a vast lottery." The rise of insurance, the growth of land, stock, and commodity speculation—a practice at times indistinguishable from gambling—and the simple reality that many hard-working and virtuous farmers and entrepreneurs failed while others succeeded all reinforced the power of randomness. In the twentieth century, the capriciousness of death in war overseas as well as the popularization of credit, financial commodities, and investment bolstered the belief that someone's fate was not entirely in their own hands, especially when it came to their finances.[14]

Gambling was the ultimate embodiment of the culture of chance. Historian Jim Cullen explains that gambling has long offered a "competing notion of the American Dream," one that ran up against the much more celebrated ethos of hard work and rugged individualism. Since the earliest days of the republic, games of chance offered alternative means of upward mobility for those unable or unwilling to navigate the traditional meritocracy. From sweepstakes players of the colonial period to black numbers bettors in the twentieth century, lotteries, more so than other games, offered gamblers the chance to get ahead. Historian Ann Fabian notes that the campaign against lotteries in the 1820s was driven largely by concerns that the poor were not just spending their scant resources on the games but were also counting on lottery tickets as a way of climbing the class ladder. Cullen writes that while the wealthy insisted that "the universe was a fair and orderly place," gambling spat in the face of a meritocratic system. Even if they are not always conscious of the fact, gamblers tend "to believe that the world's arrangements are, if not arbitrary, then not finally knowable in any rational way."[15] The world of gambling was one where luck reigned supreme, where social class was not a matter of birthright, natural ability, virtue, or even providence. It was just a roll of the dice.

The rise of state lotteries in the 1960s and 1970s tapped into a key dimension of the American allegiance to luck. Closely tied to the culture of chance was a belief in the possibility of instant, transformative wealth, that someone's good fortune could arrive in the form of an unexpected and life-changing payday. From European colonists seeking cities of gold to Anglo settlers headed to California on their own quest for gold in the 1840s, Americans have long sought out, read about, and imagined miraculous windfalls. The nineteenth-century novels of Horatio Alger, for instance, feature stories of virtuous and hard-working paupers benefiting from acts of financial grace by members of the bourgeoisie who come across them by happenstance. Inspired in part by the popularity of Alger's books, actual rags-to-riches stories became a cultural obsession around the turn of the century. Journalists were constantly on the lookout for tales of fast fortunes, from unknown entrepreneurs striking it big to Cinderella stories of poor women who caught the eye of an aristocrat and married into luxury.[16] Another well-trod narrative was a surprise inheritance from a long-lost relative, a tale frequently featured in turn-of-the-century newspapers and in the 1902 novel *Brewster's Millions*, subsequently adapted into a 1906 play, a 1937 radio show, and seven film versions between 1914 and 1985. In a similar vein, one of the most popular programs in the Golden Age of Television was *The Millionaire*. Running from 1955 to 1960, in each episode a fictitious benefactor would grant a fictional individual $1 million and then watch from afar as they spent their new fortune. Even if actual opportunities for rags to riches remained as rare as ever, American popular culture was obsessed with windfalls.

As northeastern and Rust Belt states began enacting state-run sweepstakes, the possibility of instant riches became as simple as purchasing a lottery ticket. No longer did someone have to dream of a letter bearing news of a surprise inheritance or hope to woo a member of the aristocracy to strike it rich. Notably, lotteries in this era offered a very specific degree of wealth. Until the introduction of rollover jackpot games in the late 1970s, the size of every lottery prize was decided in advance by state lottery commissions. Given how new the games were, seemingly any prize was attractive to players, and lottery administrators did not feel pressured to ramp up the jackpots. New Jersey introduced the first $1 million drawing in 1971. Other states followed, and New York introduced a game with a grand prize of $50,000 a year for life (minimum total payout of $1 million). In general, lotteries opted for a larger number of smaller prizes, with a grand prize or two and multiple five- or six-figure prizes. Almost every prize was paid out in taxable annual installments rather than a lump sum. Most winners won guaranteed income for the next few decades, not an immediate payout that would appear in their bank account the next day.

In this period, then, the lottery represented incremental class mobility. Between 1974 and 1978, sociologist Roy Kaplan surveyed lottery winners in New Jersey, western New York, and other states, including one-third of the nation's lottery millionaires. Players fantasized about a jackpot, imagining that any prize from $25,000 to the coveted $1 million would end their financial woes. But the actual purchases of lottery winners reflected the relatively limited size of jackpots, especially compared to those that would emerge in the years to come. In fact, in 1978, a prize with an annual payout of $50,000 was not enough to place lottery winners in the top one percentile of individual income.[17] Winners were able to buy a home and quit their jobs, and most became comfortable, if not outright wealthy. The biggest significance of the lottery, though, was in creating a reliable opportunity for anyone to change their station. Kaplan writes that "for the man struggling to make his mortgage payments and keep his car from the finance company, or the widow eking out an existence on Social Security payments, the lottery is the grist of which fantasies are made."[18]

Of course, the chance at a windfall of any size remained appealing, though lottery tickets enticed some Americans more than others. In their early years, lotteries attracted a primarily white, blue-collar clientele. Until the 1980s, most African American and Latino gamblers remained wedded to illegal numbers games. White working-class players did play the numbers, but also became avid lottery players. In Illinois in 1975, gamblers who spent more than the state average on lottery tickets were disproportionately white, aged between 45 and 64, and blue collar, with incomes around the state median. One six-state study estimated that industrial workers, craftsmen, and foremen accounted for 40 percent of scratch ticket sales from the mid-1970s through 1980. Of the first 37 winners of New Jersey Lottery jackpots, almost all worked blue-collar jobs, all were white, and not a single one had a college degree.[19] The lottery was a white working man's game.

Economic conditions in the 1970s cultivated the popularity of lottery tickets among the northeastern white working class. As inflation and unemployment wracked the economy, millions found themselves financially pressed by the sudden collapse of what was already a tenuous postwar economic order. Even before the mid-decade financial crisis, many American workers had been frustrated with their growing powerlessness in an increasingly corporatized economy, a feeling exacerbated in the 1970s by long lines at gas stations, rising unemployment, a rebellious youth counterculture, the apparent impotence of American power overseas, and the federal government's inability to solve any of these problems. In 1972, blue-collar wages failed to rise for the first time since 1947 and rates of social mobility began to stagnate. Well-paying factory jobs, too, were becoming harder to find in the Northeast and Rust Belt, as manufacturing relocated out of the region. Politically, this period marked the emergence of what political scientist Jacob Hacker calls the "great risk shift," a process by which more and more economic risk was taken off the plate of government and business and heaped onto American families. The middle class that had long been attainable for blue-collar Americans was growing out of reach. Northeastern workers had entered the decade hoping for a greater sense of professional dignity and self-worth. By the end, many were hoping just to hang on.[20] Lotteries had served as mechanisms of upward mobility over the course of the nation's history, and state-run games reemerged right at the moment when the working class came under siege.

The return of lotteries also coincided with a growing individualism, the fracturing of an economic egalitarianism that had held sway in the postwar period. In a 1976 essay, Tom Wolfe famously dubbed the 1970s "the 'Me' Decade." As postwar prosperity came undone and as nonwhite Americans gained full rights of citizenship in the aftermath of the civil rights movement, many people turned inward and away from some of the collective, government-oriented solutions of the previous two decades. Wolfe's fellow cultural observers also noted a shifting cultural ethos. *Boston Globe* journalist Ellen Goodman wrote about a "subtle, changing consciousness, a new sense of individualism in mid-1970s America." Sociologist Robert Nisbet detected "enlarging aggregates of atom-like individuals." For *Harper's*, Peter Marin described a "world view emerging among us centered solely on the self. . . . An unembarrassed denial of human reciprocity and community."[21] This culture of me had a wide variety of implications and manifestations, among them the further solidification of the culture of control. If individuals were charged with their own self-improvement and had no accountability to their community, then they were all responsible for their own financial outcomes, no matter the circumstances of their birth or the vagaries of their life. Historian Christopher Lasch wrote in his aptly titled *The Culture of Narcissism* (1979), "People perceive their social position as a reflection of their own abilities and blame themselves for the injustices inflicted upon them." No matter inflation, unemployment, or the oil crisis. The 1970s saw the solidification of an ethic of personal responsibility.[22]

The financial pressures on the white working class and the rising tide of individualism also explain why lottery tickets were consistently more popular among men than women in this period. Surveys from New York, Michigan, Pennsylvania, and New Hampshire found that the percentage of men who played the lottery was roughly 5 to 10 points higher than the percentage of women. In much of the country in the postwar period, expectations of a single-income household reigned supreme, a model based around a working father and a stay-at-home mother.[23] While many working-class women already held jobs outside the home, the economic contractions of the 1970s led to a large increase in working women as families added a second income to try to maintain their economic status. As blue-collar jobs provided a less-reliable path to the good life, and as single-income families were becoming harder to sustain, the lottery offered northeastern men an alternative way to try to fulfill their widely understood obligation as breadwinners. Millions of women were also attracted to the lottery for its promise of an instant fortune. In the 1970s, though, and even since, lottery tickets were especially appealing to men facing familial responsibilities and uncertain financial futures.

The other crucial demographic trend among early lottery players was religion. While Americans of all faiths gambled, Catholics were the most avid bettors and the most enthusiastic proponents for legalized gambling. In 1963, 66 percent of American Catholics supported the creation of state-run lotteries, compared to 43 percent of Protestants. In 1974, 80 percent of Catholics said they engaged in some form of betting, and the percentage of Catholics who had bought a lottery ticket in the last year was 20 points higher than the percentage of Protestants. The results of a New York State Lottery promotion epitomized the popularity of gambling in Catholic communities. In 1980, the lottery commission offered cash rewards to the individual or organization that collected the most losing stubs from a specific scratch-off lottery game. A group of Buffalo nuns undertook a ticket drive to raise money for their convent, amassing over 70,000 losing tickets from local parishioners. However, this sum qualified them for only third place and a $25,000 check. The grand prize was won by an organization that had conducted a ticket drive of its own: the New York State Federation of Catholic School Parents.[24]

The enthusiasm for lotteries among northeastern Catholics can be explained in part by the Catholic Church's doctrinal position toward gambling. Though there is no specific injunction against gambling in the Bible, conservative Protestants condemned the practice as anti-biblical, immoral, and unethical and associated it with a range of evils, particularly the dereliction of familial responsibilities. On the other hand, the *Catholic Encyclopedia*—a turn-of-century sourcebook of church doctrine—maintains that "apart from excess or scandal, it is not sinful to stake money on the issue of a game of chance."[25] While the church did not encourage gambling, the *Encyclopedia* assured readers that betting in moderation was permissible. As a result, gambling was a fixture in twentieth-century Catholic communities. Catholic churches across the nation and especially in the Northeast and Midwest used bingo and raffles to raise revenue, a practice that states began to legalize in the mid-twentieth century. By 1978, 34 states had authorized nonprofit organizations to raise money from bingo. In New York, Illinois, and many other states, political battles over bingo laws often boiled down to clerical squabbles between supportive Catholics and oppositional Protestants. Catholics had a good reason to put up a fight, as bingo was a huge moneymaker. In 1978, for example, bingo games hosted by Ohio Catholic high schools took in more money than the state's lottery.[26]

Amid the financial uncertainty of the 1970s, lotteries offered northeastern Americans—especially white working-class Catholic men—a reliable way to take a chance on transformative wealth. For many, it became the locus of dreams for a sudden change in financial standing, even if it meant pursuing a fortune through luck instead of pluck and hard work. Whether or not it fit into conceptions of the meritocracy, gambling retained its important place in American social and economic life.

Questions about merit and chance loomed especially large for those few gamblers fortunate enough to win the lottery. In the economic climate of the 1970s, winners had to come to terms with the fact that they had become instantaneously well-off through highly improbable means. Many had been struggling, but their ship had finally come in. Some accepted their good fortune. The culture of chance, after all, meant that luck could make anyone rich at any time. "I'm both shocked and thrilled," a Rochester teacher declared upon finding out she had won a spot in a 1967 grand prize drawing. "It's the first time I ever got lucky."[27]

Others, however, sought to understand and rationalize their windfall. For them, sheer probability failed to explain such a life-changing occurrence. Instead, their jackpot appeared to be nothing less than a miracle, something attributable to divine forces. A New York Lottery winner declared that the odds of his windfall were "only fifty-fifty, because either God is going to give it to you or He's not." Another early winner claimed his prize "was not luck, but the work of God."[28] Probability was immaterial. If someone won the lottery, it could only have been through an act of God.

These winners fell prey to a common cognitive bias around unlikely events. When the improbable occurs—whether negative (such as a rare disease diagnosis) or positive (like a lottery jackpot)—many have an instinct to try to understand why. In these moments, explanations rooted in probability and randomness often do not suffice. Lottery winners focused only on the distant odds that the jackpot would happen to them rather than the near certainty that it would happen to someone, somewhere, sometime.[29] This led to the unfounded belief that their win was mathematically impossible and that other forces had must have been at work.

The idea that God would bother to intervene in something so cosmically inconsequential as a jackpot drawing is reflective of changes in American religion in the early lottery years. In the same essay in which he dubbed the 1970s the "'Me' Decade," Tom Wolfe also declared it the "Third Great Awakening," a moment of religious revivalism akin to the mid-eighteenth and early nineteenth centuries. Typical accounts of this awakening focus on two trends. On the one hand was the Christian Right, which mobilized politically and gained adherents through an emphasis on the individual experience of being born again. On the other hand was New Age spiritualism, a hodgepodge of beliefs and practices oriented around self-awareness, self-improvement, and achieving higher levels of consciousness. As dissimilar as these trends appeared on the surface, historian Bruce Schulman writes, both actually reflected a similar trend: the rise of individualized faith practices based on personal feelings and detached from old ways and old institutions.[30] Religion offered a clear embodiment of the rising tide of individualism, and it was increasingly common for Americans to explain how the divine worked through them or worked to shape their lives. In this context, why wouldn't God get involved in the lottery to help someone's pocketbook?

By these winners' calculus, luck and God were opposites. Whereas luck was unpredictable and haphazard, God was purposeful and precise. If God was responsible for the jackpot, that meant the winner had been specifically chosen, not just randomly rewarded. Police officer William Inman, the fifth winner of the Illinois Lottery's million-dollar drawing, noted, "I personally believe in God, and I personally believe He did it. I just wonder why out of all these people God had to pick me. . . . He probably had His reasons."[31] As the person who had actually won the lottery, Inman claimed the authority to declare the forces responsible for his jackpot. He understood that some might see his win as chance. He insisted it was anything but.

For winners like Inman, God and luck served as oppositional forces not because of their theological differences but because of their inherent similarities. Theologian Kathryn Tanner argues that faith, like gambling, is built around the promise of an uncertain reward from an unknowable system. Hence, Pascal's Wager, the philosophical argument that humans should believe in God because the temporary inconveniences of religiosity on Earth are outweighed by the infinite potential rewards that await in the afterlife if God does, in fact, exist. As seventeenth-century French mathematician and Catholic theologian Blaise Pascal acknowledged, religion was a gamble. For their part, some Protestants resisted gambling precisely because they saw it as competing with the religious ordering of the universe. Many modern-day Christians of all denominations believe their life hinges at least in part on a divine system outside of human control. "Religious life and games of chance," Tanner writes, "are both ways of dealing . . . with life's precarious prospects."[32] Luck and God each impose an order on the universe, an order that could account for the cause of a lottery windfall. When winners hit the jackpot, they faced a choice. If they could not or would not admit that their win was due to pure chance, there was only one other possible explanation.

Crucially, lottery winners discussed the role of supernatural forces only after they had already won. By definition, gamblers could not declare they had received a gift from God before they actually obtained their prize. Afterward, though, they took great pains to construct stories that centered on divine intervention. The case of Curtis Sharp illustrates the importance of the retrospective nature of these narratives. Sharp was working as a mail porter for Bell Laboratories in New Jersey in 1982 when a coworker offered to buy New York Lottery tickets on his behalf. With his coworker's departure for New York imminent, Sharp quickly jotted down number combinations for three tickets. His final set of numbers matched those drawn in the lottery, and he won $5 million, at the time one of the largest jackpots ever awarded in the United States. In a press conference shortly after he won, Sharp explained that he had picked his numbers randomly, that they had "popped into [his] head."[33]

In the weeks and months that followed, Sharp's newfound wealth brought major changes to his life. He became a spokesman for the New York Lottery, appeared on late-night talk shows, held a lavish wedding, bought a 14-room house, and was flooded with requests for money from prospective business partners and passersby in Manhattan. "I could walk down the street," he later remembered, "and [strangers] would come up to me and ask for autographs and talk to me like they've been knowing me for years." In addition to accosting him for money, they would try to touch his hands or his clothes, treating him like a religious talisman in an attempt to rub off some luck. As Sharp's circumstances changed, so did his story of how he had won the lottery. In an interview with *Ebony* magazine a few months after his jackpot, Sharp claimed that as he began writing his third, ultimately winning, set of numbers, "God started guiding my hand."[34]

Sharp's revision of his lottery narrative was not a simple change in his media talking points. It was an indication of the forces that he came to believe were responsible for his jackpot. In the aftermath of his win, Sharp's life changed rapidly. Faced with appeals for money from family members, acquaintances, and strangers, many winners chose—or were forced—to quit their jobs or move into new homes. As a result, Roy Kaplan explains, winners felt "powerless" and "turned to the supernatural in an attempt to explain and direct their lives, which were becoming increasingly confused and meaningless."[35] Though God had not played a role in Sharp's initial account of how he had won, as his circumstances shifted, he sought to explain the disruptions as more than the product of randomness. By attributing his prize to God, Sharp absolved himself of responsibility for the changes the lottery brought to his life, denying his own agency to such a degree that he claimed God had physically taken control of his hand to ensure that he selected the proper numbers.

More important, Sharp's narrative made the case that he deserved his jackpot. If God had ensured that he won the money, then certainly Sharp had been dubbed worthy of the prize. By asserting that divine intervention had occurred, Sharp made the case that his win demonstrated something about him as a person. "The fortunate is seldom satisfied with the fact of being fortunate," Max Weber writes. "Beyond this, he needs to know that he has a *right* to his good fortune. He wants to be convinced that he 'deserves' it, and above all, that he deserves it in comparison with others. He wishes to be allowed the belief that the less fortunate also merely experience his due."[36] Lottery winners had to reason around the fact that they had won and every other hopeful gambler had lost. Any story rooted in chance would imply that Sharp had gotten lucky and would not draw any meaning from the fact that, of all the lottery players in New York, his had been the numbers that came through. Amid the rise of me-centric religious practices in the 1970s, a divinely caused lottery win was yet another way of revealing something about the self. Because God had chosen the numbers for Sharp, his windfall marked him as blessed.

So, while many lottery players were believers in luck when they bought tickets, after winning, they maintained that the game's seemingly arbitrary outcome in fact obeyed a meritocratic logic. Despite their affinity for gambling, winners' narratives marked an adherence not to the culture of chance but to its counterpart, the culture of control. Like the supposedly self-made men of the past, lottery winners claimed that their success had been divinely approved and, as a result, that they had earned their jackpot. "God gave me my money," oil tycoon John D. Rockefeller once remarked, a sentiment shared by Curtis Sharp and other lottery winners who felt their fortunes had been nothing less than acts of providence.[37]

However, the culture of control was historically not welcoming to gamblers, and this remained the case in the state lottery era. The work ethic, in particular, represented an important cultural touchstone. "Everything valuable in life requires some striving and some sacrifice," President Richard Nixon declared in his 1972 Labor Day address. "The work ethic holds that it is wrong to expect instant gratification of all our desires, and it is right to expect hard work to earn a just reward." In the 1960s and 1970s, the very idea of hard work became a part of the culture wars. The work ethic—which Nixon contrasted in his address with a "welfare ethic"—served as a coded way to elevate white middle- and working-class families above supposedly lazy and government-dependent African Americans and countercultural youth.

The work ethic defined itself by what it was not: it was not a handout and it was not luck. Lottery tickets were popular among Nixon's beloved Silent Majority, his imagined constituency of white working- and middle-class families who opposed the counterculture and racial liberalism. Nixon chose to overlook this fact. "The work ethic tells us that there is really no such thing as 'something for nothing,'" using the same phrase employed by lottery critics to disparage the wishful thinking of pro-gambling voters. Instead, merit was about work and vice versa. American society, in Nixon's mind, was a meritocracy where chance held little sway. "Above all," he concluded, "the work ethic puts responsibility in the hands of the individual, in the belief that self-reliance and willingness to work make a person a better human being."[38] It was impossible, the president implied in a clear articulation of the culture of control, for someone to work hard and not reap rewards for their labor. Any failure was the result of personal shortcoming. If someone did not succeed, it was because they lacked the necessary effort, skill, or virtue, not because they were unlucky.

By the mid-1970s, though, the economic foundations that had helped build the postwar blue-collar work ethic were being shaken to their core. Companies were increasingly moving industrial jobs away from the Northeast and the Rust Belt, where unions were relatively strong and manufacturing costs were high. Ten out of the 14 early-adopting lottery states had private-sector job loss above the national average between 1969 and 1976. Later in the decade, these states, especially Michigan and Ohio, were hit again as a wave of shutdowns and slowdowns struck the auto manufacturing industry. Deindustrialization was a gradual process, and it had a deleterious impact on both the affected workers themselves and on entire communities where factory jobs had been an economic lifeblood.[39]

For the lottery's working-class player base, these conditions fostered a change in thinking about the relationship between merit and money. After all, it was difficult to equate virtue with hard work if factory jobs were moving south and there was no work to be found. In her study of workers at an Elizabeth, New Jersey, sewing machine factory in this period, anthropologist Katherine Newman explains that blue-collar men of the 1970s believed in the value of hard work. Yet, despite the rising ethic of personal responsibility, many were reluctant to accept that they were fully in control of the fate of their jobs. As long as they worked hard when the opportunity presented itself, it was not their fault if they were out of work because their job disappeared. "They see themselves at the mercy of remote decision makers," Newman explains. "These inaccessible authorities control their fortunes."[40] Rather than understand factory closures as a matter of luck, workers saw them as the product of human decision-making—just not the decision of the workers themselves. Working-class northeasterners believed that some elements of their economic fate lay out of their hands. The lottery offered them a way to turn this to their advantage. For once, the enigmatic forces that determined their financial fortunes might bestow not another pink slip, but a windfall.

Furthermore, the lottery could recognize virtue in a way a work could not. Many industrial jobs entailed repetitive and occasionally dehumanizing work, and, as Kaplan notes, most lottery winners in this period held jobs that provided few opportunities to demonstrate merit through their work. Nixon insisted that "no job is menial in America if it leads to self-reliance, self-respect, and individual dignity," that the value of work lay in the act of working, regardless of how unpleasant the job might be. But even if they worked hard and even if they were able to support their families, many Americans—blue and white collar alike—lacked ways to distinguish themselves through their professions. By tying their jackpots to their merit, lottery winners found a way to make their prize signify their character. The jackpot gave them an opportunity to be marked as special and virtuous in a way their work did not.[41]

Even as the working class's allegiance to the culture of control seemed to fracture, unease with gambling wealth persisted. Though job status may not have been entirely in their own hands, there was still a hierarchy of wealth. Unfortunately for lottery winners, they were at the bottom. Many Americans continued to look down on those who gambled or who had gotten rich through gambling. Much of this antagonism was due to the fact that lottery playing had for so long been an activity associated with urban African Americans. One midwesterner stated in 1978 that he would not sell his home to "any buck who just happened to hit it big playing the numbers."[42] A derogatory term, "buck" was often used to refer to African American or Native American men, and the reference to "the numbers," even after states had legalized lotteries, indicated how large illegal games loomed in popular understandings of gambling. His comment made clear that gambling marked someone as undeserving of affluence because they had chased luck instead of trying to make money the old-fashioned way. Wealth was not simply about money. It was about someone's character. Those who got rich from gambling were wealthy because they were lucky, not because they deserved it. Under the terms of the era's cultural norms, lottery winners had come by their wealth dishonestly and did not have the moral fortitude to match their financial standing.

Societal discomfort with so-called unearned wealth helped create the myth of the miserable lottery winner. In the first decade of the state lottery era, newspapers avidly covered winners—both in the United States and overseas—whose gambling luck was followed in short order by misfortune: bankruptcy, divorce, or even death. Stories of this sort have long followed lotteries. They were fixtures in American newspapers as early as the eighteenth century and would become even more prominent beginning in the late-1980s and 1990s.[43] The return of the tale of the miserable winner in the postwar period highlights enduring uncertainty about gambling as a means of class mobility. Overall, the actual incidence of dramatic calamity befalling lottery winners was—and remains—rare. Nonetheless, a few outstanding cases seemed to prove the rule: it was not healthy to win a windfall. The implication of these stories was that if individuals won money through gambling, they had somehow violated the natural order of the universe and would inevitably suffer a comeuppance to restore things to their proper place. A further implication held that had they worked for their fortune, they would have truly deserved it and would have known how to live with it, and such a fate would not have befallen them. The tale of the regretful winner seemed to confirm that a society built on luck was dangerous, even for the very lucky.

Winners, then, had good reason to claim that their prizes reflected a moral order. By asserting that God had provided their jackpots, winners like

Curtis Sharp sought to expand the boundaries of the American meritocracy. For decades, if not centuries, ideas about meritocratic wealth had explicitly excluded those who relied on luck, especially gamblers. By denying
that his prize was random, Sharp instilled it instead with divine authority,
arguing that it had been no less than God's will for him to bypass socially accepted methods of wealth accumulation. Lottery winners, then, rhetorically
reinforced the meritocracy. In the process, though, they sought to detach it
from the work ethic. Sharp did not assert that he had worked for his prize,
though this did not mean he did not deserve it. Lottery winners agreed with
proponents of the work ethic that wealth depended on merit. Money did go
only to the deserving. However, it may arrive to them in curious ways. The lottery was a part of the culture of control and represented a perfectly reasonable
way for people to receive their due.

Lottery winners were not the only Americans in the 1970s who thought God
was looking out for their finances. The first state lotteries emerged contem-
poraneously with the flowering of the prosperity gospel, a Christian theology
that held that material abundance and physical health were given by the grace
of God. With roots in New Thought, Pentecostalism, and positive thinking,
the prosperity gospel built on ideas about the connection between earthly
well-being and divine favor that been a strain in American religion since
Max Weber's Puritans. As documented by religious historian Kate Bowler,
the prosperity gospel crossed into mainstream American Christianity in the
post–World War II period and then took off in the 1960s and 1970s. In this
period, preachers held revivals, created Christian television stations soaked in
prosperity rhetoric, and broadened the reach of the movement to accommodate a multidenominational cohort of Catholic and Protestant believers. The
first years of the state lottery system also represented the period in which the
prosperity gospel became what Bowler calls "the foremost Christian theology
of modern living."[44]

   The same economic forces that propelled the appeal of lottery tickets also
facilitated the popularity of the prosperity gospel. In the 1970s, the nation
faced both rising unemployment and inflation, which economic orthodoxies
dictated should not occur simultaneously. For many Americans, inflation
represented the most pressing issue of the decade. "It affects every American
in a very palpable way," wrote one adviser to President Jimmy Carter. "It causes
insecurity and anxiety. It affects the American Dream." To help cope with
inflation and rising instability, many households turned to consumer credit,

and total credit card spending increased from almost $14 billion in 1973 to $66 billion by 1982. Unsurprisingly, debt increased too, and total consumer borrowing nearly doubled between 1975 and 1979. In the early lottery years, then, Americans were becoming accustomed to seemingly mystical financial mechanisms whereby money seemed to appear, disappear, and even change in value of its own volition. "I don't know what's going to happen next week, let alone next year," a Boston carpenter complained. "It doesn't seem to matter how hard you work anymore; you can't keep up with these prices."[45] Caught in the vicissitudes of a tumultuous economic climate, many Americans were searching for order.

Prosperity theology promised to restore that order. The gospel rested on the idea that everyone received what they deserved. Because God looked out for believers' well-being, the gospel affirmed the providential nature of financial success. In a market system that seemed to give and take at random (and which in the 1970s did a lot more taking than giving) and amid the rise of a religious outlook increasingly focused on the self, the gospel maintained that outcomes were the product of each individual's divine virtue. The economy had nothing to do with it. Neither did luck. Instead, believers were drawn to what sociologist Tony Tian-Ren Lin calls a "miraculous meritocracy," a system that promised miracles on behalf of the devout. Adherents waited for God to supply them with a financial bounty or with physical healing, though they needed to take action to attract the promised rewards. In this period, the dominant strain of prosperity theology held that, if believers followed specific steps—usually some combination of prayer, fasting, tithing, attending church, and maintaining a positive attitude—God would not deny their request. If they did not receive a reward, it was not because God was not listening. It was because they had failed to properly attract what they wanted. Just as the work ethic guaranteed rewards for hard work, so too did the prosperity gospel guarantee rewards for proper observance. Per Bowler, the gospel of health and wealth made "financial miracles an everyday prospect."[46]

The lottery represented an ideal avenue for everyday financial miracles. Winning the lottery was the very definition of an unlikely event, so defying the odds of a jackpot represented the ultimate example of the miraculous. However, religious lottery winners' claims about their jackpots differed in a key way from the principles of prosperity theology. The prosperity model that predominated in the 1970s placed agency almost entirely in human hands, implying that God could not and would not refuse a properly executed request from a worthy adherent. By contrast, early religious lottery winners endorsed a milder theological formula. Some, including Curtis Sharp, suggested that their windfall was a complete surprise, that they had bought tickets with little expectation of winning, and certainly not expecting God to provide them with a life-changing fortune. Most winners who attributed their prize to God, though, explained that they had taken action to solicit a jackpot. But winners did not see a prize as guaranteed. They had intentionally solicited divine intervention and this action, they argued, was crucial in attracting a jackpot. The prize had not been promised. God had chosen to answer their request. It was left to them to try and figure out why they had been deemed worthy of a windfall.

Prayer represented the most common way for gamblers to seek divine aid. Of course, other than buying more tickets, players do not have any means at their disposal to improve their odds. Some were content with this arrangement. They would win or lose, and the outcome was simply a matter of luck. Religious gamblers, though, thought they might be able to shape the odds in their favor or render probability immaterial. The impulse to turn heavenward to assert control over randomized outcomes is intrinsic to gambling. Archaeologists have uncovered an ancient Roman game board with an inscription requesting Jesus's help winning dice games. Numerous passages in ancient and biblical literature make clear that supplications to divine forces were fixtures of lottery drawings hundreds of years before the games became mechanisms of public finance.[47] Yet, just as the lotteries of the 1970s looked very different from those of 197 BCE, so too did gamblers' supplications look different. Prayer is historically grounded, a product of its time, place, and context.[48] So, while turns to the heavens have been a part of gambling for centuries, the financial and religious atmosphere of the 1970s shaped how, why, and when lottery players prayed for help with their bets.

Lottery players offered numerous types of prayers at various stages of their betting. Crucially, the act of praying predetermined how gamblers interpreted the results of the drawing. If they won, their win was a confirmation of the power of prayer, proof that supernatural forces had answered their request. If they did not win, then God simply had not chosen them. More specifically, God had not chosen them *yet*. Most were confident a jackpot was coming; they just needed to keep the faith. At the press conference to celebrate his jackpot, railroad worker Ronald Carlson explained that as he was a born-again Christian, his jackpot was the second most important event in his life following his acceptance of Christ. He asserted that "gambling is wrong" even as he declared that God had rewarded him through the lottery: "I prayed for the Lord's will in my life. I didn't pray to win, but to have the Lord's testimony in my life." Carlson bought tickets for three months in the search of that "testimony," specifically a jackpot of at least $10,000 with which to buy a new home. "It wasn't real gambling which takes money from the family," Carlson insisted, engaging in a discursive dance to deny that his lottery playing constituted gambling. For him, buying a few lottery tickets was merely a search for divine validation.

For Carlson, as for other lottery winners, prayer was important because it worked. After he prayed for money and subsequently won the lottery, he felt he knew exactly why the jackpot had come to him. "I viewed it as a testimony," Carlson noted. "*He* willed it. The Lord wouldn't give it to you if you couldn't take care of it. God is in your life if you are with Him. If you're in the faith, God is in you and your life, and He'll answer your prayers."[49] God would only answer the prayers of those who deserved to have their prayers answered. Like the meritocracy, Carlson's reasoning rested on circular logic. His prayers had been answered, so clearly God had determined that he deserved the winnings. Yet, he deserved the winnings because his prayer had been answered.

However, the results were not entirely up to God. Though God "willed" his prize, Carlson's prayers—his statement of what he wanted—had convinced God to reward him with a jackpot. He suggested that had he not prayed, he would not have won. Here was the culture of control: because God had chosen to answer his prayer, his win was not simply about his prayers but his merit. Though God did not approve of gambling, God did support believers. The lottery was one of many ways God could confer blessings onto the faithful, the virtuous, and the deserving.

While Carlson's prayers had some elements in common with the prosperity gospel, his theological formula worked in retrospect. Prosperity theology promised imminent wealth or health. Believers announced what they wanted, performed the required rituals, and kept performing them until their reward came through. Similarly, lottery players like Carlson bought tickets expecting to win, expecting God to work a miracle on their behalf. After days, weeks, or months of fruitless play, many still held out hope that God would reward them. However, prosperity gospel adherents acknowledged from the outset that God answered prayers and that wealth and health were signs of divine merit. Lottery winners made no such acknowledgment. Once he hit the jackpot, Carlson ignored his three months of prayer that had received no response, interpreting the win as confirmation that the heavens shone down on him. In retrospect, that period represented a time in which God was considering his prayers, not three months of lottery losses. Unlike prosperity adherents waiting for an answer to their prayers, lottery players waiting for a jackpot were unlikely to endorse the sweepstakes as a godly meritocracy.

Conveniently, they waited until after they won to declare that the results of the lottery represented a referendum on divine merit.

Prayer was a particularly common part of lottery play in the 1970s because of the structure of the games. In the early years of state lotteries, most grand prizes were awarded through a process involving multiple drawings. Lottery commissions first selected a small number of tickets through a raffle or instant game. Winners of these games were guaranteed a minor prize as well as entry to a grand prize drawing where each player's odds of taking home the jackpot could be as low as 1-in-10. With as long as a few weeks between receiving notice that they were finalists and the actual drawing, gamblers turned the time before the final drawing into periods of intense prayer. When asked what he had done leading up to the drawing that won him $300,000 in 1974, elevator mechanic Joseph Mariano of Morton Grove, Illinois, replied that he and his wife Louise were both Catholic and "prayed all the way here. . . . Really, this whole week we've been praying." Mariano suggested a correlation between the amount of time the couple had prayed and the chance that God would award them with the jackpot. Louise went to church one final time before the drawing to offer an appeal to the Virgin Mary: "If this is what you want us to have, we'll go along with it. If it's not best for us, we don't want it."[50] Thus, she would interpret any result, win or lose, as determined by heavenly forces. Stuck with a long wait before a drawing where they had a relatively good chance of winning, players sought to exert control over an event that was completely out of their hands. This liminal period served as a metaphorical purgatory, one in which prayer represented the only way to attract a windfall.

The Marianos' story also exemplified the power of newspaper reports about lottery winners. As remains common practice today, media outlets featured human interest stories on nearly every local lottery winner, including quotes with their reactions to their win and the strategies that had supposedly led to their windfall. Many of these profiles contained some form of statement expressing gratitude to a higher power for the jackpot. Reporters did little editorializing around these claims, instead simply reproducing winners' narratives about divine intervention or about sheer luck to highlight the human drama surrounding the lottery. These stories helped instill the belief among hopeful gamblers that prayer could work for them too. A *Chicago Tribune* cartoon a few days after the Marianos' jackpot depicted a long procession of people headed into a church past someone selling newspapers with a headline declaring " 'Prayers Pay Off'—Couple Wins $300,000." Standing on the steps and admiring the rush of congregants, a priest remarks to a smiling colleague "Funny about attendance. . . .[L]ast week we were down to a handful." As the cartoon acknowledged, news of someone attributing a jackpot to prayer could spur imitators hoping to strike it rich, to believe that God might also work for them. The Marianos proved that prayer did indeed pay off, and if church attendance surged, it was not out of increased piety but the possibility that religious devotion could increase the probability of a jackpot. Chicago Catholics saw religion as a means to a monetary end.

Stories about religious lottery winners became self-reinforcing. When the media published winners' statements that their prize was a gift from God, other gamblers could be primed to see their own jackpot as a divine act or could become more likely to openly discuss their prayers when they won the lottery. In response to the story about the Marianos, one Pana, Illinois, resident poked fun at this cyclical process—and, by extension, the fact that newspapers regurgitated lottery winners' narratives without comment. "It seems that God is going to be in trouble," he wrote. Joseph Mariano "says that he and his wife really prayed to win, and they did win. Now what if every holder of a lottery ticket prays to win, what is God going to do?"[51]

What was God going to do, particularly for those many Americans who turned to the lottery in moments of desperation? Gamblers prayed to win the lottery in a variety of circumstances. Ronald Carlson prayed regularly for three months with the hopes of winning enough money to buy a house. Joseph and Louise Mariano prayed in the days and hours ahead of the final drawing. For others, though, prayers for a jackpot were a vehicle of last resort, a place to turn in moments of despair in the hope that God would end their acute financial troubles with a lottery win. Before the 1960s and 1970s, if someone did not want to play the numbers, there were few places to turn for a quick payout, other than a loan shark.[52] Now, there was the lottery, which had the added benefit of state sanction. After being laid off from a steel mill, Peter Pulaski found work as a taxi driver in New York. At one point, he was in "such bad shape" that he had no choice other than to go to church to pray for money. "I was there in the chapel and I told God that I realized it wasn't right to pray for money, but I really needed it." He lit three candles and, as part of the Catholic practice of writing prayer intentions, he wrote "To win the lottery." Upon leaving the church, Pulaski found a pencil and a dollar in the street. He paid for a lottery ticket with the dollar, picked his numbers with the pencil, and won $100,000.[53] Pulaski saw no other way to quickly acquire money other than the lottery and no other way to win the lottery other than to ask for God's help. Both the pencil and the dollar, he implied, were critical to his lottery win. His story bore a familiar religious structure: Pulaski found himself in desperate straits, so he turned to the heavens for help. He received

"Funny about attendance ... last week we were down to a handful."

FIG 2.1 On August 22, 1974, Joseph and Louise Mariano of Morton Grove, Illinois, won $300,000 in the Illinois Lottery and dubbed the prize an answer to their prayers. Three days later, *Chicago Tribune* cartoonist Wayne Stayskal poked fun at Illinoisans seeking to replicate the Mariano's miracle and at his own paper for the way it reported on the couple's lottery win. Wayne Stayskal, *Chicago Tribune*, August 25, 1974, A6. Stayskal/ TCA.

a strange sign that ultimately led to salvation, in this case in the form of a miraculous lottery win.

His narrative also sought to justify the doctrinally prohibited portion of his prayer. According to the *Catholic Encyclopedia*, Catholics may ask for "our daily bread, and all that it implies[:] health, strength, and other worldly or temporal goods... [W]e should ask for nothing unless it be strictly in accordance with Divine Providence."[54] Catholics were not supposed to ask God for money directly. Instead, they could pray for the fulfillment of God's plan and could pray for God's plan to include a windfall. Prayer was not meant to be a guarantee, rather a means of opening the door to divine assistance. Yet, for Catholics, as for other Americans, the 1970s was a time of breaking old rules when it came to religion. The Second Vatican Council (1962–1965) had introduced major reforms to the church, including the elimination of the Latin Mass. Historian Joseph P. Chinnici explains that the council's verdict also affirmed increasingly personalized faith practices.[55] As such, more Catholics were willing to adapt their faith to suit their needs and adopt beliefs that resembled the prosperity gospel. For Peter Pulaski, this meant enlisting God to help him win a jackpot. Pulaski's desperation and his admitted violation of church edict inferred that he had made an exception by praying. He suggested that God, too, would make an exception by answering the prayers of those truly in need and those truly worthy of divine aid.

One way around the Catholic aversion to direct prayer was negotiation. As they awaited lottery results, gamblers tried to entreat, bargain with, or persuade God to reward them, offering prayers premised on the notion that God would respond to specific offers in real time. Some offers, apparently, were more tempting than others. In 1976, 19-year-old high school dropout Bob Netto was one of 65 million New Yorkers to buy a ticket for a $1,000 a-week-for-life prize from the New York State Lottery. Netto won a guaranteed jackpot of at least $5,000 and one of 100 spots at the drawing to compete for the grand prize. He later reported that while waiting for the results at the final drawing, "I was praying, 'Please Jesus, let me win.' ... I said 'Jesus, if you let me win, I'll give something to the Church.'" Netto believed divine aid could secure him the jackpot and also that Jesus would only grant him a windfall once he promised to contribute a share of his winnings. After he won, Netto was certain his offer had secured the jackpot. He told his archdiocese's newspaper, "We owe God. What else could it be? One out of 65 million. It has to be the Holy Spirit. We prayed and we won—what else is there to say?"[56] What else there was to say is that Netto believed God helped him overcome the odds because of the precise terms of his offer. God wanted to give him the prize because the church stood to benefit.

Given how many winners asserted that they won through prayer, the lottery presented a dilemma for clergy members. Certainly, even non–prosperity gospel clergy wanted congregants to express gratitude to the divine, to understand their newfound wealth as, in some fashion, a gift from God. However, non–prosperity clergy did not want to endorse a prosperity gospel theological model that drew a direct connection between faith and material rewards. Such an acknowledgment might lead to the unsustainable expectation that God could be cajoled through prayer to work miracles on demand. When asked in 1979 whether someone could win the lottery with prayer, Jesuit priest John J. O'Callaghan of Hyde Park, Illinois, argued that the faithful should pray for their needs but that he did not see "God as the god of the lottery. I think we drag him down when we start making him a kind of good-luck charm." This type of prayer, O'Callaghan suggested, veered from theology into superstition, treating the divine as a simplistic force concerned with trivial matters. A Lutheran theologian was even more scandalized by the apparently widespread belief in the connection between God and gambling. Prayers for winnings, he noted, are based "on the rather magical notion that God intervenes in events from outside the world."[57] The idea that the divine shaped the results of the lottery led logically to the idea that God shaped every event on earth, that everything that happened—good, bad, and in between—was actively caused by God. Some things, these clergy members implied, really were just a matter of chance.

Prayer represented just one method for gamblers to try to attract divine assistance. Players also employed seeding, the prosperity gospel practice of donating money to religious causes in the hope of receiving a reward of that sum many times over. In the mid-1970s, Lidia Dubinsky won $54,000 in the New York Lottery. Dubinsky frequently donated money to prosperity preachers, including Rex Humbard, a televangelist who appealed particularly to working-class audiences. A few days before her jackpot, Dubinsky reported "a funny feeling," telling her children that she felt she was about to win the lottery. When her daughter heard that Dubinsky had won, she exclaimed, "See, Mother? You give slowly and God gave you back in a big chunk," interpreting the jackpot as a direct reward for Dubinsky's donations. Dubinsky agreed, attributing her success in the lottery—as well as bingo and her trips to Las Vegas—to her faith. "If you help others," she stated, "God helps you."[58] Though prosperity theology promised ten- or hundred-fold returns on donations to the church, preachers were often vague on precisely how God would multiply seeders' donations. By gambling, Dubinsky felt she was providing God with the opportunity to reward her for her charity.

Whether they won through prayer or precognition, winners' retrospective narratives made them sound like prosperity gospel practitioners. For both, material blessing was a definitive sign of God's favor and, by extension, of the recipients' virtue. Blessings came to those who deserved to be blessed, and those who had their prayers for a jackpot answered must have deserved their winnings. Unlike the prosperity gospel, in the lottery, one person's win was always someone else's loss. While God had theoretically unlimited capacity to create wealth, state lottery commissions did not. Unlike prosperity gospel adherents, then, lottery players' connection of merit to their jackpot hinged on the idea that God had a choice. There was no sure-fire formula to attract a windfall. There were only prayers, perhaps aided by premonition, that would alert God to human need. It was up to heavenly forces to decide who was worthy. So when gamblers received what they asked for, they attributed it to higher powers, which, in their mind, were simply giving them what they deserved.

As they gambled, lottery players were buoyed by the belief that they could improve their odds of winning, that they could in some sense control the outcome to ensure a financial miracle. Winners' narratives make clear that many gamblers bought tickets expecting a jackpot, certain that God would reward them. Through their narratives, winners not only maintained that they deserved their lottery prize but also painted the entire lottery system as meritocratic. Rather than focus on their own win and the miracle that had befallen them, they extrapolated the theological implications of their jackpot. Because they felt they deserved their prize, they reasoned that God answered all prayers for those who were worthy of having their prayers answered. They had won, so surely all other deserving gamblers also won and all other winners were deserving. Lotteries were means of rewarding the faithful and the worthy. Through their narratives, winners rhetorically transformed the quintessential vehicle of chance into an extension of the meritocracy and the culture of control.

In the 1970s, lotteries' white working-class player base needed the meritocracy to change. In a deindustrializing economy, the work ethic that had for so long formed the basis of the connection between merit and money was slipping out of reach. It should hardly be surprising, then, that Americans sought out the chance for an instant fortune. And in the context of rising tide of individualism, it should hardly be surprising that when they won, gamblers tried to turn their jackpot into a referendum on their merit.

While lottery players associated their wins with their divine virtue, these narratives also entailed multiple erasures. As they spoke about God's role in their jackpot, winners erased most of their previous experience with the lottery. Nearly every gambler acknowledged divine control over their win while implicitly denying supernatural involvement in their months or years of lottery losses. After they won, they claimed that these losses were not reflective of their merit. Their win was.

Winners' stories validate the old idea that the archival record favors history's victors. For every gambler who understood their jackpot as the result of an answered prayer, many more prayed to win the lottery and came away empty-handed. Unsurprisingly, newspapers and state lottery commissions remained largely silent about those whose hopes, dreams, and prayers failed, whose lottery playing left them poorer, not richer. Despite winners' claims, lotteries do not present meritocratic means of wealth distribution. Only a fraction of players had their financial difficulties solved with a jackpot. Though it has largely been erased from the historical record, the most common connection between faith and gambling has been the unanswered prayer.

3

Rivers of Gold

THE LOTTERY INDUSTRY AND THE TAX REVOLT

"A COMBINATION OF wishful thinking, institutionalized greed, and very bad business": this was how Lieutenant Governor Leo McCarthy described Proposition 37, a 1984 ballot initiative slated to make California the nation's eighteenth lottery state. The revenue from the proposed lottery would benefit education, but McCarthy remained skeptical, railing against the irrational hopes for a windfall that surrounded the proposal. The wishful thinkers McCarthy had in mind were not potential lottery players chomping at the bit for a chance to buy tickets. Rather, his scorn was reserved for the voters and state legislators who supported the initiative. They were foolish to think that they could raise significant sums for the government without taxes, merely by selling tickets promising instant wealth. They were the real wishful thinkers. "The lottery," he concluded, "takes that 'something for almost nothing' appeal" of gambling "and institutionalizes it by making it an official function—almost a patriotic duty."[1] Gambling was not a proper way to fund government, and the state should not place the hopes of its education system on the luck of the draw.

Government officials like McCarthy were especially concerned about Proposition 37 because voters had been duped by the promise of something for nothing only a few years earlier. In 1978, California had sparked a nationwide tax revolt with the passage of Proposition 13, a ballot initiative that struck an apparent blow to the state's liberal establishment by drastically reducing property taxes. Though taxpayers had been promised that state services would not suffer following a tax reduction, the resulting budgetary shortfall forced the legislature to make dramatic spending cuts, especially to education. By 1984, millions of Californians who had benefited from tax cuts yearned for the reinstatement of pre-1978 levels of state spending. They were reluctant, though, to restore pre-1978 taxes. Voters turned instead to the idea of a state lottery, hoping that, notwithstanding its spotty success on the other side of the country, legalized gambling could restore the golden age of government services to the Golden State.

Into this climate rode Scientific Games, Inc., which bankrolled the lottery campaign. The creator of instant, scratch-off lottery tickets, Scientific Games was not satisfied with competing against other firms over contracts to supply states with lottery tickets. Between 1980 and 1984, the company facilitated the passage of lotteries in California, Arizona, Oregon, Colorado, Missouri, Iowa, and the District of Columbia. Scientific Games promised that lotteries represented bountiful sources of revenue. Taking advantage of an environment in which voters were cutting their own taxes but bemoaning the service cuts that followed, the company spent millions of dollars to convince tax-wary Americans that legalized gambling represented a financial panacea. "A group of outsiders is attempting to change the Constitution and to put California directly into the gambling business," an anti-lottery Sacramento minister warned in 1984. "They are dangling before us the age-old gambler's promise of easy money painlessly acquired."[2] Scientific Games presented lotteries as simple solutions to states' financial problems. Like gamblers hoping for a jackpot, voters agreed to take a bet on betting.

The politics of lottery expansion in the 1980s were different from those of the first wave of legalization. In previous decades, most lotteries supported state general funds, and voters viewed the legalization of gambling as a means of raising revenue for the entire state. When these hyperbolic promises proved unrealistic, Scientific Games shifted toward a more specific, though similarly exaggerated, financial pledge. The company tied the lottery to a single cause—education in California, for example—and convinced voters that a lottery represented a windfall for this particular program. Amid the threat to government services caused by the tax revolt, lotteries offered to restore post-World War II era programs without postwar taxes. Through advertising campaigns and the work of lobbyists, spokespeople, and lawyers, Scientific Games sought to turn the debate over its lottery initiatives from a discussion about legalized gambling into a referendum on the possibility of a new, nontax funding source for a specific area of government. Rather than weigh the social merits of a lottery, the company convinced voters that, if they supported this government program and if they wanted it to have more money, then they should support a lottery. Lotteries were not simply a result of the economic aftermath of Proposition 13 but were themselves part of the tax revolt. They were a manifestation of the seemingly incompatible desire for reduced taxes and improved services that marked many voters' relationship with government in the late twentieth century.

For decades, scholars have studied how lotteries spread. Some attribute the proliferation of gambling to intra-state dynamics—budgetary problems, voter demographics, and the prevalence of illegal numbers games—while others focus on inter-state politics, particularly the passage of a lottery in a neighboring state.[3] In the early 1980s, the enactment of state lotteries was not an organic response to states' internal or external political circumstances. Beliefs about taxes alone could not overturn voters' long-standing skepticism of legalized lotteries, especially in states with little illegal gambling. Rather, Scientific Games was the key factor in the spread of state lotteries in this period. The company facilitated the expansion of lotteries through the initiative process, exploiting states' soft legislative underbellies to circumvent hesitant legislators or oppositional governors. In a textbook case of a practice known as "astroturfing" (the artificial manufacturing of a grassroots movement), Scientific Games hired lobbyists, drafted company-friendly legislation, paid signature gatherers, sponsored pro-lottery advertising, and created citizens' groups to manufacture the illusion of popular support. The company summarily won the contracts to supply states' instant tickets. To date, only five of the nation's 45 state lotteries were formed through initiatives. All five initiatives were passed between 1980 and 1984, and Scientific Games played a major role in all of them. By utilizing a newly professionalized and technologically proficient political campaign industry, over the course of just four years Scientific Games convinced voters of gambling's economic promise and restarted the spread of state lotteries across the American commercial landscape.

———

The private sector played an important role in the operation of the nation's first state-run lotteries. In the 1960s and 1970s, a small group of software and printing companies competed over a similarly small supply of contracts, vying to provide states with ticket production services, computer software setup, market analysis, and game management. These contracts were paid out of the roughly 10 percent of gross ticket sales allocated for lottery administration. Initially, the leading firm was Systems Operations Inc. (SOI), a subsidiary of New Jersey–based Mathematica. By 1976, SOI had helped implement, design, or operate 11 of the nation's 13 state lotteries. SOI lobbied legislators in nongambling states, arguing that lotteries represented an alternative to taxes.

Ultimately, SOI focused on providing services to existing lotteries rather than facilitating the creation of new markets for its products.[4]

Eventually, other companies began competing with SOI for lottery contracts. One of these firms, Scientific Games Inc., was formed outside of Atlanta in 1973 with the goal of shaking up the lottery industry. Company cofounders Dan Bower and John Koza met while developing contests for gas stations and supermarkets. Koza, who held a PhD in computer science, believed that the promotional scratch-off games run by grocery stores and gas stations could revitalize stagnant sales for northeastern state lotteries. In 1970, SOI introduced weekly drawings in New Jersey that represented a significant improvement over the monthly or semi-annual sweepstakes in New Hampshire and New York, but sales declined over time. Koza and Bower reasoned that even weekly lottery games operated too slowly. "There wasn't enough action," one Scientific Games executive noted.[5] Initial bursts of sales would wear off, leaving a small cohort of primarily older and infrequent lottery players.

To attract a younger and more committed group of gamblers, Scientific Games introduced the first scratch-off—or instant—lottery ticket. Instant games relied on the simple premise that players should be able to discover whether they had won immediately. Every ticket contained a set of numbers or symbols covered by an opaque latex or foil coating, and bettors scratched the film to discover if they were a winner. A winning ticket featured a specific set of numbers or symbols that guaranteed a prize ranging from a free ticket to thousands of dollars, including possible qualification for a secondary jackpot drawing. These games provided players with the illusion of control. For drawing games, players received a ticket with pre-selected numbers (with the exception of numbers games, gamblers could not select their own lottery numbers until the introduction of lotto in 1978). Instant games, on the other hand, allowed players to participate in the lottery experience by scratching their tickets, even though the contents of that ticket had been determined weeks earlier during the printing process. Scientific Games knew how to capitalize on this feeling of control and designed tickets that left gamblers wanting more. If players scratched a 3 or a 13 and were looking for a match, they might uncover a 31, a 2 or a 12 (to give the feeling of being just one number away), or even an 8, which at first glance might resemble a 3. Daniel Bower dubbed these tickets "heartstoppers." The goal, he confirmed, was to give players the instantaneous feeling of winning before realizing that they had lost, a feeling that would inspire them to buy more tickets in pursuit of a winner.[6]

The nation's first instant lottery tickets went on sale in Massachusetts in 1974. Tickets cost $1 each, with Scientific Games pocketing approximately 2 cents per ticket. The heartstoppers worked to perfection. In the first 10 weeks, the state sold an average of 1.7 million tickets per week, approximately double the sales of its weekly, raffle-like lottery. Based on their popularity in Massachusetts, other lottery commissions sought to introduce their own instant games. Surveys indicated that scratch tickets attracted younger players as well as those who had never played the lottery before. In Illinois, 28 percent of all lottery players—and 42 percent of instant players—said scratch tickets were the first tickets they ever purchased, and 80 percent of players said they bought tickets spontaneously after seeing them at a retailer.[7] Instant games were popular in their own right and had the added benefit of serving as a gateway to other lottery games. By the end of 1975, Scientific Games' scratch tickets were available in six states, including New Jersey, where players bought 68 million instant tickets in less than six months. By 1976, every state lottery had added instant tickets or was in the process of doing so.[8]

As instant tickets grew in popularity, Scientific Games' revenue ballooned. In 1976, after just three years in operation, the company grossed approximately $10 million, and by 1980 it produced 85 percent of all instant tickets sold in the United States. By its own estimate, the company also cornered 96 percent of the early private market for lotto and numbers games tickets (not including states that opted to print these tickets themselves).[9] In 1981, Koza and Bower agreed to sell their firm to Bally Corporation, an entertainment concern whose portfolio included slot machines, an Atlantic City casino, the Six Flags amusement parks, and the Pac-Man franchise. The following year, Scientific Games printed its 5 billionth ticket and annual revenue reached $30 million. Thanks to its industry dominance and the fact that it printed 1 million lottery tickets every hour, one spokesperson dubbed Scientific Games the "McDonald's of lottery companies."[10] The comparison was meant to reflect Scientific Games' status as the gold standard in a crowded industry, but the lottery firm bore other resemblances to the Golden Arches. Like McDonalds, Scientific Games relied on selling large volumes of inexpensive goods, counting on the ubiquity of outlets to distribute instantly gratifying alternatives to traditional products.

However, McDonalds and Scientific Games faced significant differences in terms of their access to new customers. In the mid-1980s, McDonalds opened, on average, one store per day in the United States in addition to undertaking an aggressive expansion into foreign countries.[11] Scientific Games, meanwhile, faced major limitations in the expansion of its customer base. In

1979, only 14 states had a legal lottery, and the company had done business with all of them except for Rhode Island. Koza started pushing Scientific Games into international markets, stationing an executive in England in 1977 to compete for European lottery contracts. The company printed tickets for lotteries in Israel, Switzerland, Thailand, and other countries, but Koza believed the United States offered untapped potential for lottery sales. "We are quite frankly interested in seeing new lotteries," a company executive noted in 1980. "The only way we can build domestic business is by adding new business in new jurisdictions."[12]

To create opportunities for new contracts, Koza and Bower ramped up Scientific Games' American political operations. They started with lobbyists. In the early 1980s, the company hired Paul Silvergleid, former head of the Connecticut State Lottery, to lobby legislators in Minnesota, Alabama, Nebraska, and New Mexico. Additionally, Scientific Games became one of the first companies to advertise in *State Legislatures*, a magazine geared toward state lawmakers. In 1983 and 1984, with advertisements on the magazine's inside-front and back covers, the company enticed state officials to legalize gambling by highlighting the available windfall. Under the headline "Is Your State Losing Its Share of $2,500,000,000?" one advertisement featured a map of the United States with non-lottery states highlighted. A certain dollar amount was placed on each non-lottery state—$452 in California or $24 in Montana, for example—referring to the millions of dollars in annual revenue these states could ostensibly make from a lottery. Suitably placed in an edition on the crisis of state education funding, the ad promoted lotteries as substantial, painless sources of government income, and the company offered assistance to any state interested in pursuing a lottery. Koza also took proactive efforts to ward off concerns that lotteries were regressive, authoring industry-friendly studies that unsurprisingly concluded that lotteries did not prey on the poor.[13]

These initial promotional efforts were ineffective. None of the states lobbied by Silvergleid passed a lottery until the late 1980s, and only two states—Washington (1982) and West Virginia (1984)—enacted lotteries without help from Scientific Games in this period. While legislators considered lottery bills in almost every non-lottery state between 1983 and 1984, the vast majority of these bills petered out. Even if lawmakers had been persuaded by the company's enticements, a reluctant governor could reject the legislation. In Iowa, for example, Scientific Games lobbyists shepherded lottery proposals through the legislature in 1983 and 1984 but Governor Terry Branstad vetoed both bills.[14] Stymied in these early attempts, Koza and Bower realized that they would need to pursue a different tactic to spread the lottery gospel.

Scientific Games found its answer in the ballot initiative process. Initiatives allowed any citizen to place a law on the state ballot by collecting a certain number of signatures. If more than 50 percent of voters supported the initiative at the subsequent election, the bill became law, beyond the reach of tepid legislators or oppositional governors. Populist lawmakers in western states created the ballot initiative in the 1890s to place political power in the hands of citizens rather than corporations or the political elite. Between 1898 and 1918, 24 states—mostly in the West and Midwest—legalized the initiative process, though its use gradually declined over time. Nationwide, fewer than 90 citizen-initiated questions qualified for ballots in the 1960s.[15]

Initiatives reemerged as a political tool in the 1980s, partly as a result of the landmark passage of Proposition 13 in California. In the late twentieth century, though, this form of direct democracy looked different from what the Populists had envisioned decades earlier. The ballot initiative was increasingly a tool of corporations seeking industry-friendly legislation, another terrain for rising corporate political power in the United States. In the 1970s, some business groups expanded their involvement in partisan politics while others sought to increase profits by passing pro-business legislation at the federal and state levels. Despite the tax revolt's reputation as a grassroots movement, for example, Proposition 13 received crucial funding and organizational support from the Los Angeles Apartment Owners Association.[16] The Supreme Court's *Buckley v. Valeo* (1976) decision ruled that campaign spending limits violated the First Amendment, lifting restrictions on political donations and further enabling the flow of corporate cash into politics. Shortly thereafter, especially during the Reagan administration, corporate lobbying became an entrenched phenomenon in Washington and in state capitals around the country.

The corporatization of the ballot initiative was aided by the expansion of the political consultant industry. Since the Reagan years, consultants have formed what political scientists deem an "initiative industrial complex," a group of professionalized companies with the ability to place seemingly any initiative question on a state ballot and subsequently secure a majority of votes.[17] Consultants offered an array of services unavailable previously, including precise polling, media management, and computers to facilitate direct mailings. Navigating the initiative process was also becoming more expensive, further ensuring that only groups with deep pockets could plan for a successful campaign. In 1976, total expenditure on California ballot initiatives was $9 million. In 1984, it was $34 million (including Scientific Games' spending on the Proposition 37 campaign), and four years later spending hit $127 million. In 1987, more money was spent on initiatives in California than on lobbying in Sacramento. Initiatives became so commonplace that a state campaign finance commission dubbed them "the fourth branch of government."[18] A political measure designed to circumvent corporate power had become yet another tool for business interests.

Unlike other lottery companies, Scientific Games embraced the ballot initiative and the campaign consulting industry. While every firm stood to gain from the chance to bid on contracts when states enacted lotteries, Scientific Games' competitors confined themselves to the associational position that had defined the industry in the 1970s. These companies bid on contracts when states created lotteries but refused to wade into state politics. Harry Hutton, executive vice president of Glendinning, one of Scientific Games' chief competitors, stated that his company's "policy is that we will not encourage, promote, or assist in any other way a lottery that is going on the books. That is for the citizens to decide." In addition to concerns about interfering in the democratic process, Hutton was wary of investing capital in an initiative when there could be no guarantee that his firm would subsequently win the contract. Barry Fadem, Scientific Games' initiative lawyer for the California campaign, attended the annual meeting of the National Association for State Lotteries in 1983 and 1984 to solicit other firms to join the company in the drive for a California lottery. Every company declined. This reticence was not, however, due to a lack of excitement over the possibility of winning the California ticket contract. Because of its population size, the state represented the crown jewel of untapped lottery sales. "Everybody is waiting for California because it is so big," Hutton admitted. "California is the bonanza."[19]

But lottery legislation had a troubled history in California. In 1964, voters overwhelmingly rejected an initiative that would have created a privately run state lottery, and, between 1965 and 1983, 11 different campaigns for lotteries failed to garner the minimum number of signatures required for a spot on the ballot. One of these failed attempts played an instrumental role in inspiring Scientific Games' use of the initiative process. In 1980, San Diego toy manufacturer Roger Chapin began work on an initiative for a statewide sweepstakes to raise money for medical research. Chapin retained Republican campaign consulting firm Butcher Forde—which had also worked on Proposition 13— and political lawyer Barry Fadem, who contacted Scientific Games in the hope that the company would assist the campaign. Ultimately, Chapin did not gather the required number of signatures, but Scientific Games' brief involvement in his initiative sparked Koza and Bower's interest in using the initiative process to bring lotteries to the West Coast. The unsuccessful bid also introduced the company to Fadem, who wrote the Proposition 37 initiative for Scientific Games and was its official proponent, filing the required paperwork with the California Secretary of State's office and serving as the technical and legal proponent of the initiative.[20] However, the company opted to practice its politicking before the major effort that would be required in California. In May 1980, Koza and Bower hired a political operations firm in Phoenix to begin a drive for a lottery initiative in Arizona while also retaining Butcher Forde to help with campaigns in Arizona, Colorado, and Washington, DC.[21]

Scientific Games did not choose Arizona—or any state where it pursued a lottery initiative—at random. The company narrowed its search first by identifying states with regularly used and simple initiatives processes, where signature requirements were relatively low and voters were in the habit of approving the ballot measures placed in front of them. Then, the company hired pollsters to gauge popular support for a lottery. Bower claimed that polls invariably revealed untapped enthusiasm for lotteries. Lotteries typically polled around 60 percent, and Bower maintained that this revelation presented "a great source of amazement for legislators, because they have no idea there is that ground swell, so to speak, for legalized gambling."[22]

However, public approval could not organically translate into political action. Where polling proved favorable, the company took action. Bally vice president William Peltier noted that the lottery movement in California needed "a push here and there . . . getting it on the ballot to see what the people say."[23] Peltier and Bower's comments framed lotteries as grassroots causes that sprang up from public demand. To them, Scientific Games was not an out-of-state, self-interested corporation meddling with the ballot process but a democratic champion working on behalf of a silenced mass of pro-gambling voters.

Koza had a number of ideas regarding how Scientific Games could give lottery campaigns a "push." One key effort involved sponsoring signature gatherers to ensure that lottery bills reached state ballots. The company did not care if the signers of its petitions were avid lottery supporters. In California, the head of the signature gathering firm retained by Scientific Games stated that his petitioners first asked voters what county they were registered in and if they would sign a petition for a state lottery. "If they want more information, you have a second line. California lottery is good for schools. . . . *After*

two or three lines it doesn't become cost effective to argue with a person." Without
any evidence, the inquiring public was presented with the simple proposition
that the lottery would aid schools. Collectors had no incentive to debate the
merits of a California lottery but to present it as a windfall for education to
as many people as possible as quickly as possible. In Arizona, a professional
signature gathering firm registered every person in line to see the latest install-
ment of the *Star Wars* film franchise. "If we had not had *The Empire Strikes
Back* [1980] in town," campaign director Bill Meek confessed, "we literally
would not have made it," indicating that the petition's signers were bored
moviegoers, not enthusiastic lottery supporters.[24] In state after state, the use
of paid signature gatherers proved crucial for measures that had public approval but did not inspire grassroots activism.

In addition to gathering signatures, Scientific Games also hired lawyers
to draft lottery legislation. Every bill written by Scientific Games relied on a
standard boilerplate that generally resembled the laws passed in eastern states
in the previous decade. In the mid-1980s, Koza sent the sample lottery bill to
legislators and officials in non-lottery states with the hope of drumming up
interest. While each of the company's bills offered some legalistic differences,
the Oregon and California lottery laws, both adapted from the company's
template by Barry Fadem, offer nearly line-for-line similarities.[25] Scientific
Games, then, utilized a similar tactic to that employed by the American
Legislative Exchange Council (ALEC), the political organization founded in
1973 that provides template legislation for landmark conservative issues such
as right-to-work laws and abortion. The company conducted a comparable
operation via the initiative process, with an eye for profit rather than partisan
politics.[26]

Scientific Games was not wary of investing in initiative campaigns because a clause it inserted in the bills gave the company an inside track to the
ticket provision contracts. Specifically, Scientific Games' legislation required
extensive financial documentation from the executives of any firm submitting
a bid to supply the state with lottery tickets. Crucially, the laws also required
disclosures from the heads of that firm's parent company. This stipulation was
designed to target Scientific Games' biggest competitors. Webcraft Games,
for example, was founded through a merger of SOI with a technology firm
and was a subsidiary of Beatrice Foods, which recorded over $9 billion in rev-
enue in 1984. In order to comply with the disclosure clause, Webcraft would
have had to submit financial forms from over 150 executives to vie for a contract that represented one-half of 1 percent of Beatrice's total annual sales.
A Webcraft executive stated that his company would not bid on the lucrative

California contract under the terms of the law: "It has nothing to do with what we're trying to withhold. It's that we cannot comply." Scientific Games, on the other hand, was well suited to provide these disclosures. Though the company had been purchased by Bally in 1981, Bally provided extensive financial documentation to the New Jersey Casino Control Commission when it applied to open an Atlantic City casino in 1980.[27] It had all the necessary paperwork at the ready.

Scientific Games justified the disclosure requirements as a protective measure to prevent the infiltration of organized crime. The connection between gambling and the mob, solidified decades earlier, endured into the 1980s, and Scientific Games took advantage of gambling's questionable reputation. Company representatives claimed that the financial disclosures would protect state lottery commissions from criminal interests. In a statement issued during debates in Iowa, one company lobbyist explained, "In lotteries around America, law enforcement worries more about vendors than any other aspect. . . . Copies of tax returns prevents [*sic*] the possibility of infiltration by any element of organized crime." Without these provisions, the company implied, lotteries would be vulnerable to mob-connected gambling firms. Competitors proved skeptical as to whether disclosure documents would actually protect against organized crime. The president of Glendinning explained, "If you have a criminal element in the business, they're not going to announce they are crooks on their tax forms."[28] Other lottery firms saw through Scientific Games' efforts, arguing that the disclosure requirements were put in place solely to keep out competition.

The company had a particular incentive to require this seemingly superfluous documentation. In 1978, because of his alleged ties to organized crime figures, the New Jersey Casino Control Commission forced Bally president, founder, and chairman William O'Donnell to resign from the company. Though Bally did not purchase Scientific Games until 1981, allegations concerning Bally's underworld connections frequently followed its lottery subsidiary. Scientific Games used the accusations against Bally and the connection between crime and gambling to its advantage. Looking back, Koza dubs the disclosure requirements an "offensive and defensive" measure.[29] These stipulations absolved the company of association with organized crime while simultaneously preventing other companies from bidding on the contracts.

Another provision was similarly self-interested and similarly designed to effectively ensure states came knocking on Scientific Games' door immediately after the initiatives passed. The Arizona, Oregon, Missouri, and California bills specified that after election day, governors and the state senate had 30 days to appoint and confirm a director and members of the lottery commission, a way of preventing legislators opposed to gambling from delaying the creation of the lottery. More significantly, in California and Oregon, the commission was obligated to start lottery sales no later than 135 days after the initiative vote, including the time for confirmations. Fadem justified this measure by claiming that most lotteries had been started within this timeframe.[30] In fact, of the 18 lotteries enacted between 1963 and 1982, only three—Maryland, Michigan, and Washington State—began sales within 135 days of the passage of the final piece of legislation setting up the lottery. Startup took, on average, 265 days. In addition to forcing states to move quickly, the requirement would condense the pace of the bidding process and narrow eligible companies down to those with the capacity and the experience to work quickly. It would also effectively guarantee that states opened their lotteries with instant games, which were much faster to set up than lotto or numbers or raffle games. The timeline provisions ensured that new lotteries would begin operations with Scientific Games' signature product and that they would turn to the industry leader.

With the help of lawyers and signature gathering firms, Scientific Games placed company-friendly lottery legislation on the ballot in Oregon, California, Arizona, and other states. Once the initiatives made the ballot, however, the company faced a different question entirely: how could it convince the public to reverse its long-standing skepticism of legalized gambling?

＊

Scientific Games lured voters to its initiatives through the most important section of its lottery bills. The company designated the beneficiary of lottery revenue on a state-by-state basis. The goal was to pick the cause in each state that would be most enticing to voters in order to provide them with a clear expectation of the outcome if a lottery bill passed. Results from northeastern lotteries indicated that Scientific Games could not market its initiatives as fiscal cure-alls for entire state budgets. Duane Burke, president of the Public Gaming Research Institute, observed in 1982, "In previous years you could have gotten away with promoting the lottery as a panacea for revenue problems. I think it would be very difficult today." The question for new lotteries, Burke explained, would be whether the revenue "can do you some good for programs you are interested in."[31] Rather than a magic bullet for the entire state, Scientific Games proposed lotteries as a windfall for specific programs, retaining the promise that lotteries offered something for nothing but providing a more particular fiscal promise than the one that had carried the first wave of legalization.

The company set up focus groups and polls to determine the program that would make voters most likely to support a lottery initiative. When asked about the services they thought should receive lottery revenue, 81 percent of Arizonans approved of more spending for flood control, while just 14 percent wanted additional funding for arts and humanities programs. As company cofounder Daniel Bower noted, "You have tremendous variance. . . . [T]he cause itself can change the perception of a lottery as much as 60 or 70 percent. Certainly you wouldn't want to start a lottery for the arts and humanities in Arizona."[32] Ultimately, legal restrictions forced the company to tie its Arizona initiative to the state general fund, though this did not stop supporters from championing the proposition as a panacea for their preferred projects.

Selecting a specific state program was particularly important in the context of 1980s national politics. Large, bloated government represented a popular target for Democrats and Republicans alike in this period. A long-standing strain in American politics that had been heightened under presidents Nixon, Ford, and Carter, the campaign against bureaucratic waste found its most stalwart champion in President Ronald Reagan who declared in his first inaugural address that "government is not the solution to our problem; government is the problem."[33] The rising rhetorical animus toward government had a variety of origins, from Vietnam, Watergate, and the 1970s economic crisis to the civil rights movement and the racialization of welfare programs. Northeastern lotteries, too, had played a small part in fostering a belief in government ineptitude. In 1975, New York was forced to suspend its lottery after a slew of problems, including hundreds of duplicate tickets printed for one game, another game that failed to award prizes for half of its drawings, and a revenue surplus that was remitted to the state only after an audit. Around the same time, the Delaware, Maine, Ohio, and Rhode Island lotteries were all enveloped in controversies related to ticket errors, improper payments to lottery contractors, or bribery of state officials. Then, in 1980, in an event that captured headlines nationwide, federal investigators caught a television broadcaster rigging the Pennsylvania Lottery's daily numbers game.[34] State-run lotteries appeared to validate the long-standing critique that gambling was inexorably corrupting and gave further fuel to those skeptical of government's ability operate efficiently, honestly, and transparently.

Most voters were not deterred by these scandals. In fact, by supporting a state lottery they supported the creation of a new state agency as well as government entry into the gambling marketplace. However, rising misgivings about big government did make voters distrustful of the designation of lottery revenue for state general funds. Whereas 9 of the first 14 state lotteries initially devoted revenue to general funds, this type of unrestricted revenue proved untenable in the political climate of the early 1980s. In a poll commissioned by Scientific Games in Arizona, the use of lottery revenue for a specific purpose held a 10 percent advantage over allocation to the general fund. Barry Fadem remembers that company research indicated Californians did not want lottery revenue "to go into the black hole, i.e., the general fund, for the legislators to dole out to whatever they wanted."[35] The general fund did not present an obvious, tangible benefit for citizens, as gains would be absorbed into the broader budget. From Scientific Games' perspective, the general fund threatened to obscure the promised financial windfall. The allure of the lottery would be lost.

While taxpayers looked unfavorably on government in the abstract, particular programs remained popular. Voters differentiated between the general fund and individual state services, even those paid for out of the general fund. Richard Demmer of Newport Beach, California, wrote in 1983 that if "a lottery is adopted I feel strongly that the total proceeds should be earmarked for statewide education at all levels and not merely put into the general fund for less worthy causes."[36] Demmer's view of the general fund as "less worthy" validated the company's decision to tie the lottery to a single, identifiable aspect of state government. Revenue for the general fund implied a political pork barrel. Designation for a specific program supposedly meant that voters would know exactly how lottery money would be spent.

In California, many taxpayers agreed with Demmer that education represented the most deserving recipient of lottery revenue. Education sat at the heart of the nation's ideas of a meritocracy, the belief that if all children had access to good schooling, they would have an equal chance at economic success in the marketplace. As a result, education provided a potent political—but nonpartisan—symbol. One Crestline lottery supporter noted, "What could possibly be wrong or sinful with . . . such an important undertaking as providing our public schools with badly needed funds consummating in better education for our children?"[37] Any political measure that benefited education was worthwhile, even one that undermined the meritocracy by celebrating the role of luck. Concerns for children's welfare should outweigh political, moral, or religious concerns regarding the legalization of gambling. For voters, the ends justified the means.

Scientific Games played up the benefits a lottery would supply for education. At a Sacramento hearing, Barry Fadem declared that "for every day that goes by that . . . the lottery is not in effect," California lost out on "approximately $2 million for public education." By discussing revenue in terms of daily income and by relying on best-case scenario projections of annual sales, Fadem portrayed the revenue as slipping through the state's fingers. To emphasize this point, he explained that a local second-grader had knocked on his door with her mother, asking " 'Would you contribute a dollar?' I said 'What do you need a dollar for?' [My] school district . . . was attempting to raise money for a field trip to the zoo." Fadem put a human face on Proposition 37 and on the state's education budget. "To me, those are the type of people that when we ask about [starting a lottery quickly], we're talking about an educational system that is desperate for money."[38]

Though not as desperate as Fadem suggested, education represented a particular concern for Californians in the mid-1980s because of the impact of the tax revolt. Resistance to property taxes in the Golden State began in earnest in the 1950s and reached a fever pitch in the 1970s. Over the course of the decade, surging inflation sparked bracket creep, pushing households into higher tax brackets even as their purchasing power declined. Additionally, the California Supreme Court's *Serrano v. Priest* (1971) ruling—a precursor to *Robinson v. Cahill* in New Jersey—maintained that it was unfair for school spending to remain tied to property taxes, forcing the legislature to standardize education expenditure across California. This decision, coupled with national economic conditions, changes to the state's tax assessment system, and a series of political miscues by state and local officials, helped bring suburban voters of both political parties into a broad coalition of tax rebels.[39] Proposition 13 cut homeowner and business property taxes by an average of 57 percent, limited annual property tax rate increases, and made it more difficult for the legislature to increase taxes. With this initiative, Californians— primarily white suburbanites—rebelled against ballooning property taxes that no longer had a direct bearing on their local school systems. One Los Angeles resident dubbed Proposition 13 "the Watts riot of the white middle class," comparing the taxpayer revolt to the 1965 rebellion in the Los Angeles black community over police violence. As black Angelenos had destroyed property, so too were white voters destroying the capacity of the state government to easily provide a robust array of services. On the surface, the tax revolt appeared to be populist pushback against redistributive tax policies, a manifestation of a conservative Sun Belt homeowner ethos associated with a preference for small, locally controlled government and a resistance to liberal welfare programs perceived to benefit black and Latino urban centers.[40]

However, opposition to large government and rising taxes did not necessarily entail a desire for material reductions in state services. Political scientists David O. Sears and Jack Citrin summarize the perspective of the majority of California tax rebels as "Taxes, No! Big Government, No! Services, Yes!" Proposition 13 supporters were buoyed by the belief that tax cuts would eliminate government waste and would trim the state bureaucracy but would not affect state services. On the eve of the initiative vote, for example, 50 percent of voters believed the state government could provide the same level of services with a 25 percent budget cut.[41] As the head of the campaign, Howard Jarvis told voters that by cutting their own taxes they could force the government to offer the same programs with increased efficiency. Californians' support for the tax revolt rested on the belief that they could have something for nothing.

Jarvis's assurances could not forestall the inevitable. In the immediate aftermath of Proposition 13, the legislature began drawing from its hefty surplus. By 1984, all reserve funds had long been exhausted. Even as lawmakers slashed budgets for a range of programs, the drastic reductions in property tax revenue submerged the state's education system in crisis. One 1982 financial report concluded that with the exception of the state's libraries, "the impact of Proposition 13 has been greater upon education than upon any other expenditure category." Before the initiative passed, school districts received 43 percent of their budgets from the state government and 50 percent from local property taxes. After Proposition 13—and after *Serrano*—the state government provided 67 percent of districts' funding while property taxes accounted for just 26 percent. Proposition 13 increased Sacramento's share of education funding even as it cut annual state revenue by approximately $9 billion. California per-student spending on education dropped from 10th in the nation to 35th, and most school districts reduced the number of nurses, counselors, and custodians and lowered expenditure on books and school maintenance. "We always try to cut as far away from the classroom as possible," the budget director for the Los Angeles public school system admitted, though teachers disclosed a shortage of state-provided supplies in their classrooms as well.[42]

The state's situation was exacerbated by the threat of reductions in aid from Washington. Reagan's first budget consolidated certain federal categorical grants to states into block grants while also cutting overall grant funding. As a result, in 1982, federal aid to state and local governments declined for the first time since 1946. While the threat of a wholesale reorientation of the federal grants program proved short-lived—other than in 1987, aid to states increased every year of the Reagan administration—the possibility of reorganized or lessened federal funds hung over states. "With the federal government cutting a great number of services, the states have a revenue need,"

Lottery Players Magazine explained in a profile of Scientific Games. "And where there's a revenue need, there's a place for a lottery as a buffer against increased taxation."[43]

Facing a fiscal crunch, by the time of the Proposition 37 campaign in 1984, Californians had soured on the tax revolt. After passing a cap on state spending in 1979, voters rejected two bills put forth by Jarvis because they recognized that further tax reductions would result in more cuts to education and other state programs. This skepticism reflected the broader failure of Proposition 13 nationwide. Only two states—Idaho and Massachusetts—passed initiatives similar in scope, while copycat ballot proposals were rejected in seven states (some multiple times) between 1979 and 1984, though 24 states did pass more measured tax- or budget-restricting bills in this period.[44] Like cuts in federal funding, the threat of a tax revolt still loomed large. "We need a way of raising money that doesn't 'ring out' as a TAX," an Oregon teacher wrote his governor in 1984, pleading for a lottery to benefit education. "If Oregon waits too long, a California type Proposition 13 will surely arrive by public demand." In California, voters still had to reckon with the consequences of their 1978 vote, and a lottery quickly drew attention as an alternative way to fund a robust state government. A Republican state legislator noted the week after Proposition 13 passed that while his lottery bills had been rejected in the past, he had "a better chance now because we need the money more."[45]

Californians saw a lottery as a crucial measure to help save their state. "Let's be realistic about the predicament our state currently faces," one Los Angeles resident wrote in 1983. "We have a tremendous revenue dilemma, and legal forms of gambling that are heavily taxed offer a remedy that is a viable alternative to California's current economic plight." Voters wanted a lottery in large part because they knew the state needed revenue but also knew that a tax increase was off the table. As sociologist Isaac William Martin argues, Proposition 13 became an untouchable "third rail" of California politics shortly after its passage.[46] Californians wanted their state to provide more services. However, few supported repealing the tax cuts they had passed in 1978. In the aftermath of the fiscal crisis brought on by Proposition 13, the lottery appeared to offer a singular means of restoring education funding without restoring property taxes.

Like the tax revolt, then, support for the lottery initiative rested on voters' belief that they could continue to receive services without paying for them. The relationship of Proposition 13 and Proposition 37 was on full display at a September 1984 hearing in a conversation between Democratic state senator Bill Greene, a former civil rights activist who represented South Central

Los Angeles, and Lynn Thompson, president of the board of trustees of the Pajaro Valley Unified School District. Thompson listed some of the ways her school district might spend supplemental income provided by the lottery, including uniforms for the school band. Greene undertook a different line of questioning:

GREENE: How did your community vote on Prop. 13?

THOMPSON: For Prop. 13.

GREENE: Well, you made your decision then, didn't you?

THOMPSON: On what? Not on Prop. 37.

GREENE: . . . You voted to cut the funding you now want to replace with this proposition. . . . And you've named band uniforms. Why is it that your parents and the people in your community cannot pay for them themselves?

THOMPSON: I suppose they can. I don't know if you're familiar with Watsonville, but it is a low-income area. A lot of kids do go without things.

. . .

GREENE: Okay, but they knew that when they voted for Prop. 13; they knew that they were going to affect educational funding; they knew there were going to be some things they were going to have to do without. Right?

THOMPSON: Prop. 13 was against taxes, enforced by the Legislature. This is not.

GREENE: Those taxes supported education, not the Legislature. Those taxes effected [sic] education.

Despite Greene's exasperation, Thompson articulated the view of many Californians who supported both Proposition 13 and the lottery initiative. Though she had voted to reduce her own tax burden in 1978, she did not expect state services to suffer as a result. Greene tried to point out that Thompson should have understood that by paying less in taxes she should expect less in return from the state. However, Thompson revealed that she wanted more state funding for education, and she wanted the lottery to pay for it. She had voted to cut revenue for the state legislature—which was associated with waste, welfare, and bureaucracy—not to cut funding for education, even though almost half of the state education budget came from the general fund and from the legislature. Crucially, unlike taxes, the lottery was voluntary. Thompson noted that Proposition 37 "is not . . . the county sending me a bill for property taxes and saying: Pay this. This my free agency [sic]. If I want to go out and buy $500 worth of lottery tickets, I can do it."[47] Voters had backed Proposition 13 without acknowledging that lower taxes meant "there were going to be some things they were going to have do without." Her support for the lottery entailed the admission that Proposition 13 had curtailed programs that she wanted the state to provide. Rather than have to choose between a tax reduction and service cuts, the lottery offered a painless way to have it all.

The tax revolt bore particular influence over the lottery debates in Arizona, California, and Oregon because voters considered tax cut initiatives and Scientific Games' lottery initiatives on the same ballot. The 1980 Arizona ballot included Proposition 106—a copy of Proposition 13—alongside the lottery initiative, Proposition 200. William Adams, a supporter of both the tax revolt and the lottery, argued that the lottery would alleviate any negative side effects from the tax revolt: "Some feel if 106 passes we'll be headed for bankruptcy. We offer 200 to help." Adams implied that by supporting both initiatives, Arizonans could vote to reduce their own taxes without losing government services. He did not mention, though, that Proposition 106 would cut an estimated $300 million from the state budget while the lottery was projected to bring in just $30 million.[48] Adams created a false equivalency between the two initiatives, implying that any measure to provide state revenue could make up for any measure to cut taxes. The lottery represented an act of tax rebellion, an economic mechanism by which anti-tax forces justified their support for reduced state revenue.

State officials feared that voters would draw similar conclusions about the relationship of the lottery and tax cuts. In addition to Proposition 37, in 1984 California voters considered "Jarvis IV," Howard Jarvis's fourth tax revolt initiative, which promised to "Save 13" by closing loopholes exploited by local governments and the state courts to preserve some property taxes at pre-1978 levels. Nancy Jenkins, a volunteer for the state Parent Teacher Association, worried that voters would connect Jarvis IV with the lottery initiative. Specifically, Jenkins feared that the passage of the lottery would "delude the voters of our state into thinking that they have . . . addressed public funding of education" when in fact the tax revolt measure might create another budgetary crisis and result in no net gain for education whatsoever.[49] Jenkins's concern centered on the symbolic politics of the lottery. She recognized that voters viewed the lottery as a windfall for education. She hoped that a lottery would in fact improve California's schools. She feared, though, that voters might believe that a lottery meant that no further funding would be required for the state's education budget.

These concerns extended to the highest reaches of state government. In 1982, California Governor Jerry Brown Jr. explained that he did not approve of lotteries because they led voters to believe "that somehow—without any pain, without any change in their private behavior—funds can be generated for a great university, fine schools, honest cops, good transit and all the rest of the things that government does." This sort of thinking was unfair and untrue, and Brown cautioned against "the false image that a gambling program can solve our problems." Brown and others recognized what many voters refused to: that the state's situation had shifted and no number of small measures— like a state lottery—could supply the necessary funds to the degree that voters demanded. The voting public, however, was not inclined to believe such sobering messages. A member of the Delaware Gaming Commission summarized the situation in 1984, observing that states "are pursuing the glittering gold of the lottery dollar with all the intelligent foresight of the California gold rush."[50]

The possibility of a gold rush was exactly what Scientific Games wanted to convey. Once Proposition 37 made the ballot, the company ramped up its efforts to convince the public that a lottery could offset the lost revenue from the tax revolt and fix California's funding issues once and for all.

As it began its campaign, Scientific Games tried to cultivate pro-lottery grassroots political engagement. Despite the states' financial situation, little sprang forth organically. As a result, the company set up political committees to create the impression that its lottery initiatives were populist proposals. These groups bore euphemistic names: Californians for Better Education (CBE), Citizens for Economic Recovery (CER) in Oregon, and Arizonans for Tax Reduction (ATR)—with no acknowledgment that revenue from Arizona's lottery was designated for the state's general fund. The titles of these groups made no mention of the lottery, instead implying a cohort of activists interested in a specific cause, not the legalization of gambling. "Californians," "Citizens," and "Arizonans" marked the groups as local, concerned voters, obscuring that the lottery initiatives were the brainchild of a self-interested corporation headquartered on the other side of the country. Arizona lottery advocate William Adams claimed that ATR was "a group of ordinary citizens, taxpayers and business people who believe a lottery would be a good way to help reduce the ever-increased tax burden in our state."[51]

In truth, these organizations represented fronts for Scientific Games, part of the company's attempt to disguise its political operations. ATR, for

example, was set up by Michael Foudy, an executive for the political operations firm hired by Scientific Games. In an interview with the author, he
dubbed ATR a "façade," as most of its members had little or no involvement
in the lottery campaign.[52] In California, Fadem registered CBE as a nonprofit organization the day after he submitted the professionally gathered
Proposition 37 signatures. Though he maintains to this day that CBE was "real
grass" (as opposed to corporate astroturf), the group's registered headquar-
ters was the offices of McDowell and Woodward, the public relations firm
retained by Scientific Games for the campaign. Jack McDowell and Richard
Woodward, the company's eponymous executives, served as CBE's campaign
director and news director, respectively; Fadem was registered as its treasurer;
and two professional public relations specialists were listed as its deputy news
directors.[53] The group's leadership team was on the Scientific Games payroll.

Nonetheless, CBE officials insisted their organization was a grassroots
movement. Fadem claimed the group had over 5,000 supporters, and one CBE
spokesman put the number as high as 10,000.[54] These membership estimates
were built on mathematical sleight-of-hand by company spokespersons to
exaggerate the appearance of pro-lottery activism. Specifically, the company
sought to claim that anyone who approved of the lottery initiative was an
affiliate of their organization. Thanks in part to solicitation by Fadem and
others, Proposition 37 received the endorsement of 8 local school boards, 4
teachers' associations, over 50 city and municipal officials, and more than 100
school principals and administrators. Yet support for the lottery initiative was
not tantamount to membership in CBE. For example, five civil service groups
endorsed "Yes" on Proposition 37 though only one explicitly referenced CBE
in its endorsement. Despite this tepid affiliation, all five were included on a list
Fadem provided to a state legislator under the heading "Who Is Californians
for Better Education?"[55]

Even more significantly, almost all of the funding for these ostensibly
grassroots organizations came from the corporate coffers of Scientific Games.
According to newspaper reports, the company provided nearly every dollar
spent by CER (between $67,000 and $150,000) and ATR ($110,000) over
the course of their campaigns.[56] In California, at least $2.1 million of the
$2.4 million spent by CBE came from the company or one of its affiliates, as
only one California voter made a personal donation of over $100 to the or-
ganization. Six months after the election, campaign director McDowell was
unable to name a single member of CBE and Fadem was able to name only
two members of an organization that had ostensibly boasted 10,000 active
participants. In Oregon, state senator Dell Isham, whom Koza tapped to file

the lottery initiative with the state government, claims he was never involved in nor has he ever heard of CER.[57]

Operating through these citizens groups, Scientific Games sponsored pro-lottery advertising to convince voters of the potential panacea of lottery legalization. In Washington, DC, where citizens had put a lottery initiative on the ballot themselves, Scientific Games flooded proponents with funds to ensure the passage of a lottery referendum despite the intentions of local supporters to maintain a relatively inconspicuous campaign. Scientific Games donated $10,000 to the D.C. Committee on Legalized Gambling and established its own local political organization to sponsor $80,000 worth of radio and television commercials. The company made similar payments elsewhere, shelling out up to $90,000 in Colorado as well as $65,000 for a last-minute media blitz in Arizona in response to slipping poll numbers.[58]

The company's television commercials were designed to turn the debate over the initiative away from the lottery. Rather than appeal to voters by emphasizing access to legalized gambling if the initiative passed, Scientific Games told taxpayers that they faced a referendum over the government program slated to receive lottery revenue. These ads made emotional appeals. The company used a single commercial that it customized for the 1980 initiatives in Washington, DC; Colorado; and Arizona, likely the first television spot ever used to persuade voters to enact a lottery. In the ad, a voiceover explained how much money a lottery could produce in each area. In DC, a large pile of bills flew into a police officer's hat, a firefighter's helmet, and a graduation cap, warning that impending cutbacks in the city's budget could threaten education or emergency services. In Arizona, a cowboy hat, representing a tax cut, was added to this group, and in Colorado, where the lottery would support state parks, the hats were replaced by pictures of tracts of land. The narrator concluded ominously that these funds would not be available if the lottery did not pass.[59]

The message of Scientific Games' advertisements proved decidedly threatening, implying that states' public services faced certain doom without lottery funding. By excluding references to gambling, these commercials framed a lottery as a revenue measure that could make money for the state appear out of thin air. The ads, then, served as the complement to Jarvis's tax revolt campaign. While Proposition 13 promised tax cuts that would not entail reductions in services, these commercials drew their power from a political landscape where government programs were under fire but voters were reluctant to provide the necessary tax funding to prevent service cuts. The company placed those service reductions front and center, presenting the lottery as the only way to stave them off. In DC, an anti-lottery city council member said he was "mad as hell" that the advertisements were "playing up the city's financial crisis," admitting that this message "hits home to a lot of people."[60] Voters would undoubtedly support a measure that promised tax-free funding for education and police, especially when they were told that services might be cut if they rejected the initiative.

In California, advertisements weaponized education in a similar, albeit more positive, manner. Scientific Games' television spots used images of schoolchildren to dangle the prospect of a lottery as a means of improving school funding. One advertisement entreated voters to "Help our kids and have fun too! With a better education, everybody wins!"[61] Accompanied by pictures of children in a classroom, the commercial subtly hinted that the new revenue would come from gambling but assured viewers that gambling represented a good deed as, even if players did not win, the money from their losing wager would support education. Like the "hats" advertisement, this commercial did not present any details about how much revenue the lottery would raise. Instead, it focused on where the money would go, offering voters a simple proposition: if they supported education, they could supply an un-told sum to schools by voting for the lottery. A vote against the lottery was not a vote against gambling but against education.

Scientific Games' advertisements successfully convinced the public to support a lottery. In early September 1984, 37 percent of Californians said they had heard or seen an advertisement about the lottery initiative and 47 percent said they supported its passage. By late October, 93 percent of state residents said they had seen or heard an advertisement in favor or opposed to the lottery, and support had risen to 54 percent.[62] With a few weeks until election day, Proposition 37 looked like a shoo-in. Voters believed they had finally found their way out of the tax revolt morass, and John Koza believed Scientific Games had found its way to the grand prize of lottery contracts.

———◦—◦———

As election day neared, Scientific Games gradually realized its initiatives were in danger. Though it successfully evaded legislators and competing ticket firms, the company encountered a final hurdle: lottery opponents. Anti-lottery forces looked different in every state, but in the early 1980s they generally drew from the state's political elite and a cross-denominational cadre of religious leaders—especially conservative evangelical Protestants. Despite their connection to powerful officials, opponents' financing paled in comparison to Scientific Games' war chest. In Arizona, the Stop the Lottery

Committee raised $8,000 with an average donation size of $190, whereas Scientific Games spent $110,000. These groups understood the long odds they faced in overcoming Scientific Games' well-run campaign and its promises of new revenue. In California, the Coalition Against Legalized Lotteries (CALL) raised $100,000 to compete with the company's $2.4 million campaign fund. CALL's director, Methodist minister Harvey N. Chinn, framed the group' struggle in biblical terms: lottery opponents faced "a David-and-Goliath struggle."[63]

CALL represented the grassroots movement that CBE only claimed to be. The group was an independent entity that emerged out of the California Council on Alcohol Problems, an organization led by group of ministers—primarily Protestants—that fought to restrict alcohol, drugs, and gambling. CALL received endorsements from 10,000 churches statewide across 25 different denominations. As Chinn explained, "There is more agreement among Protestant groups on the adverse effect of gambling than on any other social issue, including the issues of abortion, alcohol, and homosexuality." Though it lacked the funds to compete with Scientific Games, CALL also received endorsements from a wide variety of educators, politicians, police officials, and district attorneys as well as Republican governor George Deukmejian, who agreed to serve as the group's honorary chairman.[64] While Deukmejian and the state's lieutenant governor and attorney general were highlighted in the group's limited newspaper advertising, its nucleus remained Protestant clergymen like Chinn and Jack M. Tuell, a Methodist minister and vocal opponent of same-sex marriage who held a leadership position with CALL. From advertisements to door-to-door campaigning, CALL was the means through which the states' evangelical Protestant leaders sounded the alarm about the lottery.

Opposition to Proposition 37 created strange bedfellows, as Chinn's coalition was joined in the fight by Californians Against the Eastern Lottery Fraud (CAELF), a political group set up by the state's horseracing interests. The long history of horseracing in California gave track operators tremendous power, and Koza and Fadem believe racing groups blocked Scientific Games' initial attempts to pass a lottery through the state legislature. After Proposition 37 qualified for the ballot, racetrack owners continued their efforts to prevent the enactment of a state lottery. In a letter to state racing officials, Charles Whittingham, president of the Horsemen's Benevolent and Protective Association, predicted that a lottery would "devastate" the sport of horseracing in California as a lottery would become the preeminent form of gambling statewide. Whittingham proposed a vigorous campaign so that the

"billion-dollar thoroughbred industry" could not "be threatened by a numbers game," simultaneously denigrating a lottery as a lesser form of gambling
while acknowledging the threat it posed to horseracing. Scientific Games' internal research indicated that lotteries had no effect on parimutuel betting.
Whittingham, though, was unconvinced. By the end of October, CAELF
had raised $2.6 million, almost all of its funding drawn from the state's major
racetracks and racing associations.[65] Though religious leaders opposed the
lottery and though CALL made significant public inroads, the campaign in
California was in many respects a battle between two interest groups, one
hoping to expand gambling and the other trying to preserve its monopoly
over legalized wagering.

Anti-lottery groups generally relied on three, often intertwined arguments
against Scientific Games' initiatives. First, opponents claimed the lottery
presented a way for organized crime to flood into the state. Due to the
long-standing connection between gambling and criminality as well as the
allegations against Bally, opponents painted Scientific Games as a front for
mafia interests. One CAELF ad, for example, deemed Proposition 37 the
work of "Eastern gambling promoters" with a history of "connections with
organized crime." Though CAELF's anti-lottery campaign was similarly self-
interested, the group alleged that Scientific Games represented a corrupt
criminal organization, which, by definition, was only concerned with making
money for itself, not helping California's education system. The campaign in
Arizona focused on a similar theme. "They'll get *profits* in Atlanta we'll get
organized crime in Phoenix," one advertisement warned.[66] Even three decades
after the Kefauver hearings, civic leaders hoped invoking the spirit of organized crime would make the anti-lottery message stick.

Accusations regarding organized crime were often accompanied by a
second concern, which focused on the harmful social effects of gambling,
particularly on children. This fear proved particularly resonant in California
where lottery revenue was designated for education. It was hypocritical,
opponents noted, to fund education with a practice that was antithetical to the
values of hard work that should be imparted to children. A Modesto woman
explained further that she did not want her "children and grandchildren
exposed to this temptation in public places such as grocery stores."[67] Not only
might a lottery entice children, but it could also take food out of their mouths
if irresponsible parents overspent on lottery tickets. In DC, the Committee
for Governmental Integrity, which had successfully organized against an initiative that would have allowed dog racing, claimed that the lottery vote
presented "an opportunity for D.C. citizens to show that they love children

as much as they love dogs. . . . Children suffer from numbers, lottery and bingo!"[68] This campaign likened children to abused animals, appealing to basic moral principles to protect them by rejecting the lottery. Both sides of the debate, then, employed children as symbolic champions of their cause. Opponents painted a grim picture of parents corrupted by gambling and youths unable to resist trying to make a quick buck through a game of chance. Meanwhile, Scientific Games presented needy schoolchildren whose education could be funded only through a new wellspring of lottery revenue.

Finally, opponents drew attention to Scientific Games itself, framing the initiatives as the work of an outside corporation exerting undue influence over state politics. Polls indicated the effectiveness of this line of argumentation. When asked to ignore all other considerations, 60 percent of Arizonans said they would oppose a lottery if they knew that "lottery proponents are primarily out-of-state interests." Ahead of the 1984 election, Arizona Governor Bruce Babbitt wrote in a letter to the Oregon media that "if the initiative is passed, it will be a lottery designed by and, for all intents and purpose, run by Scientific Games. It will surely not be a lottery for the citizens of Oregon."[69] Any proposal invested in this heavily by a private company could not be in the public interest. In a 1984 pamphlet entitled "Don't Gamble with California's Future," Harvey Chinn explained that "it was out-of-state money and out-of-state corporations that got Proposition 37 on the California ballot." Chinn condemned the "powerful Eastern gambling firms" who "see a river of gold flowing into their pockets," castigating Scientific Games for attempting to profit from Californians and for framing the lottery as a windfall for the state.[70]

However, voters also viewed the lottery as a river of gold, a new source of nontax revenue that would flow into the state's coffers. Scientific Games' promises of a cure-all for education or other state programs proved more tempting than the threats of organized crime or underage gambling. On November 6, 1984, the same day they overwhelmingly reelected Ronald Reagan to the White House, 57.9 percent of voters approved a lottery in California while 66.3 percent did so in Oregon.[71] It was a banner day for the company and for American legalized gambling, as West Virginia and Missouri also enacted lotteries (the latter thanks to the efforts of Scientific Games). These four states offered a definitive signal to lawmakers across the country that lotteries were no longer a novelty confined to the Northeast and Rust Belt.

Though all of Scientific Games' initiatives passed, the election results illustrated the effectiveness of the anti-lottery forces in dampening support for legalized gambling. In nearly every state, lotteries received fewer votes than had been predicted by initial company polling. Pre-campaign surveys had indicated over 70 percent support for a lottery in California, over 55 percent in Arizona, and up to 80 percent in favor of a lottery in Missouri. Proposition 200 in Arizona passed by less than 1 percent in 1980 and the 1984 Missouri referendum passed with 69 percent approval.[72] In California, the lottery found particular support in San Francisco and its surrounding suburbs (San Mateo and Solano counties), communities historian Robert O. Self labels as important bases of support for Proposition 13. Southern California, the erstwhile capital of the tax revolt, produced strong but not overwhelming support for the lottery initiative (56 percent and 58 percent in Los Angeles and Orange counties, respectively), as anti-gambling, evangelical Christians may have offset the support of their similarly fiscally conversative neighbors who set aside moral concerns in favor of a new source of state funding.[73]

While voters expressed a number of reasons for approving the lottery initiatives, the possibility of nontax revenue for the state represented the most important factor in Scientific Games' victories. In an exit poll in California, 70 percent of pro-lottery voters said they supported Proposition 37 because they believed it would help the state or the state's schools, and another 32 percent said they voted for it because they preferred a lottery to property taxes. Judie Rohde of San Pedro wrote to her assemblyman, "We just want our state back on its feet without the people being taxed to death. We want a choice, we want a lottery." She saw Proposition 37 as a means of restoring the revenue that had been lost in 1978. Speaking as a member of the silent majority of middle-class California taxpayers, Rohde continued that "rich people have loopholes, we the middle class people and voters need a break. . . . We want a lottery, we want to save our state."[74] The lottery was both relief for the state's beleaguered taxpayers and the savior of the state government. The middle class could finally receive the services they demanded without a reversal of the tax revolt.

The belief that a lottery would provide a panacea for the state was accompanied by the similar hope that a lottery offered voters the chance to win millions of dollars. The second largest driver of lottery support in California was the desire to participate in legalized gambling, as 18 percent of voters said they approved Proposition 37 because they wanted to buy lottery tickets. These voters wanted a lottery because of the odds—however small—that they would win a windfall. The lottery initiative campaign chairman for Washington, DC, noted, "People either wanted the revenue or thought they were going to win the lottery."[75] Both groups saw gambling as a jackpot, either for themselves or for their state. Whether driven by a will to gamble or a distaste for taxes, voters in California and across the nation ushered in a new wave of lottery legalization.

—•—

Scientific Games was not especially concerned with why voters had decided to pass a lottery. Koza and Bower simply wished to serve as states' instant ticket provider. They got what they wanted. The company secured the contract for every state where it participated in the initiative process. Scientific Games was the only eligible bidder in California—a bid from a Canadian firm was disqualified for failing to meet the disclosure requirements—and won the coveted contract to supply tickets to the nation's largest state. While the lottery commission emphasized that the company had not received any advantage during the bidding process, Scientific Games anticipated that it would receive the lucrative California contract. The company began construction on a $6 million factory in Gilroy, California, seven months before the passage of Proposition 37 to reduce manufacturing costs for a contract it was seemingly assured to win.[76]

In state after state, Scientific Games' investment in the initiative process paid off handsomely. The company's contract in California was worth $40 million and named the firm the provider of the state's first six scratch games (most state lotteries did not yet offer multiple instant games simultaneously). After spending approximately $2.4 million to pass Proposition 37, by 1987 Scientific Games had signed three contracts with the state worth $92 million. The company saw similar returns elsewhere. Scientific Games spent approximately $100,000 to pass an initiative and corresponding legislation in Colorado, and it anticipated $3 million in revenue from its Colorado Lottery contract for 1983 alone. In Oregon, the company was the only bidder on the contract and, after just four days of negotiation, signed a $4.3 million agreement for 1985.[77] Surveying Scientific Games' work on the Proposition 37 campaign and its prompt receipt of the contract, California state senator John Doolittle dubbed the company's operation "the most artful job that's ever been pulled off in California," implicitly likening the company's political campaign to a successful heist.[78]

Voters and state officials gradually realized, too, that an out-of-state firm had used the lure of state revenue to disguise its pursuit of profit. One Toledo, Oregon, voter wrote her governor two months after the initiative passed, "I resent that [the lottery] ballot measure[s were] drafted, campaigned and bankrolled by attorneys provided by Scientific Games, Inc. of Norcross,

Georgia, whose only interest was greed, appealing to our base instincts. . . . We fell for it," admitting that she, like other voters, had been swayed by unrealistic promises of state revenue. In Arizona, state senator Ray Rottas stated he had "misgivings" about the company supplying the state's tickets because "this is the first time in the state of Arizona that an initiative has been bought and paid for."[79] Noting the relative newness of moneyed intervention in state politics, he charged that for Scientific Games to receive the lottery contract—especially when the company that wrote the legislation represented the only eligible bidder—reeked of collusion.

Though not illegal, Scientific Games took full advantage of its status as states' instant ticket provider. The absence of competition in the bidding process allowed the company to inflate the prices of its tickets, which ultimately amounted to less revenue for states. In 1982, three years after voters passed a ballot initiative limiting tax increases, the Washington State legislature enacted a lottery as an emergency measure to generate revenue. Due to its urgency, the state turned directly to Scientific Games because a competitive process would delay the target ticket-sale date. However, when the Washington contract went on the open market two years later, the lottery commission realized its mistake by not opening up the contract to other bidders. Scientific Games charged the state 2.7 cents per ticket, 21 percent above typical market price, approximately the same cost the company offered to the Arizona Lottery in 1981. In 1984, Webcraft won the Washington contract at a cost of 2.2 cents. In Colorado, Scientific Games' status as the sole bidder allowed the cost of tickets to reach up to 3.7 cents. One Washington State contracting officer noted, "The more competition, the sharper the pencils get[.] I do think competition is healthy."[80] Healthy for the state, maybe, but not necessarily for Scientific Games' profit margin.

Most people did not care about the details of state lottery commission contracts. They were just eager for the opportunity to take a chance at a windfall. On October 3, 1985, California Lottery tickets went on sale (the state did not come close to meeting the 135-day startup requirement). As Scientific Games had hoped, tickets proved as popular in western states as they had been in the East. Californians bought 21.4 million tickets on the lottery's first day and 56 million in the first four days, almost equaling sales from Arizona for the entirety of 1983. In its first year, the California Lottery took in a total of $1.77 billion in sales, $70 million more than Scientific Games had projected.[81]

However, the promised windfall for education never materialized. Scientific Games had equated the lottery with education, and the state lottery commission saw no reason to disillusion voters of that idea. On the first day of lottery sales, a skywriting plane wrote "Lottery = School Support" in the skies over Orange County. The reality was not so simple. In its first year, the lottery raised $690 million for California's education fund. While the company had accurately predicted the sales total—and by extension the amount of money for education—it had greatly overstated the importance of this revenue in the context of the state's education budget. Lottery revenue amounted to 2 percent of total state income, roughly 5 percent of the state's education budget, and, by the early 1990s, less than 3 percent of most school districts' budgets.[82] In other words, it did not raise nearly enough to offset the 1978 tax cuts. As in the Northeast in the 1960s, visions of lottery riches proved more illusion than reality.

More problematic, though, was the fact that a legislative loophole meant state schools did not actually realize any additional funding from the lottery. While ticket sales generated millions in profits for the company, Scientific Games' initiative allowed California Lottery funding to feed into the general state budget rather than the education budget. As the *Los Angeles Times* noted in 1985, "Without some very strong and very precise legislative language, the idea of lottery money being a special bonus for schools will evaporate like the instant-riches dreams of most ticket-buyers." Bills were put forth to address the issue, to no avail. "Education was used to get the lottery passed," California superintendent of public instruction Bill Honig observed in 1988, "but education hasn't benefited from it."[83] In 1993, voters passed Proposition 172, a ballot initiative for a half-cent sales tax to bolster local budgets amid a restructuring of education finances. The long-dreaded tax increase arrived anyway.

In fact, the passage of Proposition 37 proved immensely troublesome for California schools in ways no simple follow-up legislation or ballot initiative could undo. As state officials had warned, the passage of the lottery and the rhetoric about all the money it would bring for schools created the misperception of a windfall that made it exceptionally difficult for advocates seeking actual additional funding for education. Policymakers were "under extreme pressure" during budget apportionment, Honig explained, pressure caused in large part by the aftereffects of Proposition 13. That pressure, combined with the illusion of lottery riches, amounted to problems for those concerned for the education budget: "What it's doing is conveying to people that schools are OK because the lottery's taking care of them," the president of a northern California community college complained. "That's not true." Even if all the proceeds had flowed directly into schools' pockets as intended, the impact would still be overstated. Honig estimated that it took the proceeds of 1,450 lottery tickets to buy a single microscope for a high school science classroom. If the state wanted to improve its declining education expenditure, it would need to recognize that legalized gambling was not the answer rather than assume that the lottery was meeting expectations. In 1992, one northern California newspaper dubbed Proposition 37 "a panacea gone sour."[84]

For its part, with the exception of a bid for an Oklahoma lottery initiative that was deemed constitutional in 1986, Scientific Games largely abandoned its political operations after 1984. Nonetheless, the company's initiatives and promises of revenue opened the floodgates for other states to pass lotteries. The four lotteries enacted in November 1984 signaled the seemingly inexorable march of legalized gambling across the country. Following the fiascos of the 1970s, high sales in the early 1980s and the apparent inescapability of gambling legalization made legislators increasingly receptive to lotteries. GTECH, another lottery firm which at the time specialized in lottery computer networks, particularly for lotto games, began lobbying state legislatures to expand their lottery offerings to include a wider variety of products. While Scientific Games was not responsible for the creation of any new lotteries after 1984, its campaigns set the stage for the massive spread of legalized gambling across the Midwest, West, and Upper South in the late 1980s and early 1990s.

The growing political power of lottery firms did not go unnoticed. "I am concerned that our elected officials have lost control over this industry," Minnesota senator David Durenberger presciently noted at a US Senate hearing on lotteries two months before Scientific Games' November 1984 victories. "We are not talking about a public charity any more, but about a private venture for the profit of a few large national corporations."[85] Lotteries had long been entangled with the private sector. Yet the political influence wielded by Scientific Games and GTECH over state legislators and voters was very different from the contractor role firms had assumed in the 1970s. The decision to pass lotteries was seemingly no longer up to states. It lay in the hands of the executives of major lottery companies.

The industry was out of control in other ways as well. Competition between firms turned fights over lottery contracts into bitter brawls replete with rumor mongering, legal challenges, and, in some cases, outright corruption. For decades, when lottery companies lost ticket contracts, they issued complaints or filed suit in court, alleging misbehavior by their competitor or by the state lottery commission. At times, these allegations had merit. In 1993, for example, a bribery trial of a lobbyist who had worked for GTECH revealed a tape in which the lobbyist referred to California's first and second lottery directors as "our guy" and "our gal," respectively. The recording and the subsequent resignation of the second lottery director implied that the state's highest lottery officials were in the pocket of GTECH, which had signed multiple contracts worth a total of $700 million to run the state's computerized lottery games. The tape appeared even more damning because—borrowing from Scientific Games' playbook—GTECH's competitors claimed that the call for proposals had been written in such a way as to make it effectively impossible for them to bid.[86] The nation had been warned in the 1950s that gambling was a dishonest industry but had ushered in lotteries anyway. "The legitimate and legal contemporary gambling business," historian Matthew Vaz observes, "proved to be the vast, corrupt, and organized conspiracy that the Kefauver Committee long ago imagined."[87]

The corporations that dominate the contemporary gaming industry represent the cause as well as the result of gambling legalization. Had it not been for Scientific Games, the lottery experiment may well have remained confined to the Northeast for a few more years—if not decades. Interest in lotteries had been growing nationwide. However, interest alone does not collect signatures, devise revenue projections, draft legislation, or purchase advertising. Despite the budgetary pressure put on states by the tax revolt, the spread of lotteries relied on the company's efforts, including its strategic partnerships with campaign professionals and its successful public persuasion about the benefits of a lottery.

The second wave of lottery expansion had broader consequences for the proliferation of American legalized gambling. Shortly after the passage of Proposition 37, California became the flashpoint in a brewing national fight over tribal gaming. In the early 1980s, Native American reservations faced terrible economic and social conditions, and threats from the Reagan administration to cut federal tribal aid only served to make things worse. Pushed by Reagan toward self-determination and self-reliance, tribal nations, like states themselves, turned to gambling. In the 1970s and 1980s, Native American reservations across the country began hosting bingo tournaments to raise revenue. In the 34 states where charitable bingo was legal, tribes reasoned that because they were not subject to state civil codes, they could offer larger prizes than were permitted off-reservation. Often to the chagrin of state governments—which did not receive their typical tax income from the games—these operations became huge moneymakers. Two tribes in California went to court to protect their bingo and card games, and the legality of tribal gaming was confirmed with the Supreme Court's 1987 *California v. Cabazon Band of Mission Indians* decision. The Court maintained that if a state legalized a type of gambling, tribes could operate that form of betting on reservations as they saw fit. "California itself operates a state lottery and daily encourages its citizens to participate in this state-run gambling," Justice Byron White wrote in his decision for the majority, reasoning that the state clearly endorsed gambling as a revenue source, so it had little standing to attempt to restrict it on tribal lands.[88]

Eventually, Congress passed the Indian Gaming Regulatory Act to codify the relationship between states and tribes wishing to profit from betting. The act laid out rules for three classes of games: Class I were traditional tribal games that tribes would self regulate; Class II comprised bingo, lotteries, and other games that did not require a "house"—these were to be initially overseen by the National Indian Gaming Commission; Class III comprised casino games, including slot machines. These required tribes to reach compacts with states, most importantly to settle the percentage of profits that tribes would pass along to states. Under these compacts, tribes built bigger casinos and, facing continued budgetary uncertainty from Washington, leaned further into the gambling economy. As of 2021, 29 states have some form of tribal gambling, and California, Oregon, and Arizona boast a combined 104 reservation casinos.[89]

Much to Scientific Games' relief, the rise of casinos has done little to harm lottery sales. In 2000, Autotote, Inc. purchased Scientific Games from Bally and the following year adopted Scientific Games' name. The company remains at the forefront of the lottery industry across the globe, and instant tickets serve as the backbone of the American lottery industry. Scratch tickets amounted to roughly 64 percent of total annual lottery sales in 2020, thanks in part to the introduction of word-search style games and the increase in the size of jackpots, such that some instant tickets offer seven- or eight-figure prizes. The most important change has been the advent of more expensive tickets. Massachusetts opened the nation's first instant game in 1974 with Scientific Games' $1 ticket. Over the years, states began introducing tickets at higher price points, culminating so far in the introduction of the first $50 scratch ticket in Texas in 2007, also designed by Scientific Games.[90] Of particular concern is that instant tickets remain among the most regressive of lottery games, a regressivity facilitated by the games' prize structure. The most common prizes are either a free ticket or small cash prizes, both of which are invariably reinvested in more tickets.

Today's scratch ticket gamblers have a lot in common with the voters who ushered in the second wave of state lotteries in the 1980s. Though not as hyperbolic as the promises that had enabled the passage of lottery laws in the 1960s, taxpayers believed Scientific Games' claims that lotteries were cure-alls for individual programs. Especially in the wake of the tax revolt, voters proved eager to support a measure they were told would provide a meaningful new source of revenue without any obligation on their part. However, many conveniently forgot that a similar promise had led them astray only a few years earlier. The tax revolt was based on the belief that voters could reduce their own taxes without any repercussions. When state services were cut, voters refused to recognize their flawed reasoning, turning instead to a new panacea to solve the panacea they had endorsed six years earlier. Like lottery players, western voters longed not just for a new source of income but their state's own river of gold.

4

Somebody's Gotta Win, Might as Well Be Me

LOTTOMANIA IN THE 1980S

GERALD WILLIAMS WAS captivated by dreams of a life-changing jackpot. In the late summer of 1985, the 73-year-old Harlem resident was one of millions of New Yorkers in line to buy tickets for the state's newest lottery game, lotto, in which grand prizes rolled over to create progressively bigger jackpots. Some of his fellow bettors were regular players. Others were first-timers. Some refused to give their names to reporters because they professed to oppose gambling. None could resist the chance to buy tickets for that month's $41 million jackpot. "It's got hold of me like a fever—I can't shake it," Williams stated of prize, at that point the largest in American history. Williams, who lived off his pension, spent $75 on tickets and had to resist the urge to spend his $50 emergency fund as well. He was far from alone in his enthusiasm, as the state was swept up by what journalists dubbed "lottomania." On August 20, New Yorkers spent $13.2 million on lotto tickets. The following day, they spent an additional $15 million, purchasing 21,000 tickets per minute in the final hours before the drawing.[1] Despite his nearly infinitesimal odds of taking home the jackpot—each set of numbers offered just a 1-in-12 million chance at the grand prize—Williams believed the lottery represented his best hope for unimaginable opulence. "The big difference between lotto and life," he explained, "is that in this game, everybody has the same chance." He may have had an equal chance, but luck was not on Gerald Williams's side. The August 22 drawing produced three winning wickets: a Brooklynite, a resident of Troy, and 21 Mount Vernon factory workers who shared a ticket.[2] Williams and millions of other gamblers would have to wait until the next massive jackpot for a shot at a windfall of their own.

In the 1980s, lotto fundamentally reshaped the place of lotteries in American society. Thanks to its periodically massive prizes, lotto attracted new gamblers, garnered widespread media attention, and captured the national imagination like no other game. The first state lottery drawings offered relatively small prizes, rarely in excess of $1 million. For lottery players in the 1960s and 1970s, six- and seven-figure jackpots paid out over multiple years represented financial stability—the ability to retire early, take a long-postponed vacation, or put the kids through college. Lotto was different. Lotto offered minuscule odds of winning but multimillion-dollar jackpots. These prizes offered a different form of mobility, one rooted not in middle-class security but in the chance to approach the highest echelon of American wealth.

Lotto emerged at the perfect cultural and economic moment. In the 1980s, the lives of the richest Americans became at once more lavish and more public. Following years of general distrust toward ostentatious extravagance and the concentration of wealth, the Reagan era was defined by the celebration and legitimization of luxury. Popular culture showed off wealth at every turn, and the decade made heroes out of Wall Street investors and men like Donald Trump, financial figures who embodied risk-taking and the unfettered pursuit of cold, hard cash. The new prominence of the ultra-rich changed standards for wealth and the definition of the American Dream. Instead of the dreams for a secure, middle-class lifestyle that had flourished in the immediate post–World War II period, many Americans began to see success as synonymous with becoming fabulously wealthy and achieving the type of affluence broadcast every Saturday night on a new television show that premiered in 1984: *Lifestyles of the Rich and Famous*.

This cultural current was especially powerful because of its sharp contrast with actual economic circumstances. In the 1980s, inequality surged and rates of downward mobility and insecurity grew. In a society increasingly bereft of economic opportunity, many Americans—especially African Americans like Gerald Williams—had few places to turn for economic advancement other than the lottery. Compared to other games, lotto promised not just incremental upgrades but immense, instantaneous wealth. For most Americans, a lottery jackpot was their only chance at the newest definition of the good life.

Large jackpots led to long lines at ticket retailers as hopeful gamblers waited for the chance to put down a few dollars for their dream. These lines, and the media frenzy surrounding lottomania, led reporters to conduct interviews with lottery players, asking average Americans what they would do if they won. Statements from hopeful gamblers reveal a cocktail of dejection and conviction, dejection that playing the lottery was their only chance at a windfall but a clear conviction that their numbers would come through, that everything they saw on TV would soon be theirs. Players vastly overestimated their odds of winning, but it did not matter. They dreamed and acted as if they would inevitably defy these odds, as if a win was a certain part of their future.

It quickly became clear to state lottery commissions, too, that gamblers did not care about the odds. They were after jackpots—the bigger, the better. Over the course of the decade, players' expectations for prizes grew, and, to appease money-hungry gamblers, state lottery commissions reduced the odds of winning and removed prize caps, allowing jackpots to rise from five to nine figures in the span of just over a decade. These increases bred interstate competition. In response to growing prizes in states like New York, smaller states banded together to offer massive jackpots of their own. This process drove lotto prizes even higher and eventually led to the birth of Powerball and MegaMillions, the multi-state, mega-jackpot games that continue to occasionally set off nationwide jackpot frenzies.

Lottomania over large prizes attracted many different types of lottery players. Regular bettors as well as infrequent players were caught up in the lottery craze. All players, rich and poor alike, approached lotto with similar hopes for instant wealth but the money spent on tickets—and the unfulfilled dreams that inevitably accompanied those tickets—ultimately proved more harmful to poorer players. The history of lotto is a history of shifting American attitudes toward wealth and offers an explanation as to why millions have turned to gambling as their best chance at being rushed to the top of the economic ladder.

For the first 14 years of the lottery era, states preferred games with reasonably good odds that granted small prizes to a relatively large number of winners. This sales strategy, however, did not sustain players' long-term interest. In the 1970s, as returns fell short of lawmakers' expectations, lottery commissions tried to boost revenue by adding three new games. First, states began selling instant, scratch-off lottery tickets. Second, in 1975, the New Jersey Lottery offered the nation's first legal numbers game. Designed to lure African American gamblers away from illegal operations, daily three-digit drawings became a stable moneymaker over the course of the late 1970s and 1980s as players gradually shifted to the better payouts offered by the state-run game. However, the steady revenue from these games quickly hit a ceiling. Daily numbers did not become popular beyond the core set of African American and white working-class gamblers, most of whom had previously patronized the illegal racket. Numbers games remain popular in the twenty-first century, particularly among black players, and account for roughly 13 percent of annual lottery sales nationwide.[3]

Finally, states introduced lotto, which had the greatest chance to replace passive games as the nation's premier drawing-based sweepstakes. With roots in a lottery game introduced in sixteenth-century Italy, lotto had long been popular among European bettors.[4] To play, bettors selected numbers (usually 6, sometimes 5 or 7) from a predetermined number range, such as 1 to 49. When the time period for play had closed, a representative of the lottery commission would draw the winning numbers randomly from that predetermined range. If a player correctly selected all of them, they would win the top prize. For example, in a standard lotto format, players select six numbers ranging from 1 to 49 (annotated as 6/49). If their six numbers matched the numbers selected by the lottery commission, they won the jackpot. This was easier said than done, of course, as a 6/49 game offered players 1-in-14 million odds at the grand prize, only slightly lower than the odds of giving birth to identical quintuplets. Lottery administrators determined lotto jackpots based on how much players bet, with around 30 percent of every dollar contributing to the top prize, though games varied in the number and size of secondary prizes. Players chose their own numbers and there was no guarantee that each drawing would produce a grand-prize winner. If no player correctly guessed every number, the jackpot would roll over, resulting in a bigger prize for the following drawing several days later. Lotto offered the possibility that multiple drawings without a winner would result in a jackpot many times larger than the base prize.

The advent of lotto was made possible by advancements in computer technology. Rather than simply walk up to a retailer and purchase a ticket, as with passive or instant games, players filled out a card with their lotto numbers and outlet employees would enter these numbers into a computer (in the mid-1980s, states began introducing the option of "quick picks," tickets with numbers randomly generated by the computer). The computer printed out a ticket for the player bearing their numbers and also stored the number combination. Because all players' numbers were entered into the computer, the lottery commission had a record of every number combination that had been sold statewide. Within a few hours of each drawing, officials could tell if someone had won the jackpot or if they should calculate how much to raise the grand prize for the following drawing.

As it had for instant tickets, the Massachusetts State Lottery provided the first American foray into lotto. The commonwealth introduced a 6/49 game in 1978, but sales began extremely slowly and never exceeded $100,000 in a single week. That year, the Massachusetts legalized numbers game grossed $94 million, its instant games recorded $32 million in sales, and its weekly, passive lottery took in nearly $25 million. The state's lotto game, on the other hand, barely topped $1 million in sales. As a result, the Massachusetts Lottery Commission terminated lotto after just 13 weeks. Officials believed the long odds of winning kept players away, yet the overwhelming success of the reinstated lotto game in the Bay State in the mid-1980s reveals that the small prize pool, rather than the long odds, made the game unappealing. When Massachusetts closed its first lotto operation, the jackpot had gone 13 weeks without a winner and had expanded to just $82,000, an unenticing sum given the bigger prizes and better odds offered in the state's passive game.[5]

Despite the misadventure in Massachusetts, New York instituted its own lotto game in 1978. For $1, players could pick 2 sets of 6 numbers between 1 and 40 (6/40), with each set of numbers offering a 1-in-3.8 million chance of winning a game with a base prize of $250,000.[6] As predicted based on results in the Bay State and Europe, New York's sales began slowly, grossing a total of $1.9 million in the first six weeks. New York Lottery director John Quinn maintained that lotto players had to get used to picking their own numbers and then waiting up to a week for the drawing rather than less than a day, as in numbers games. After six months, Quinn claimed lotto had "established a base of customers," and by 1980, sales reached approximately 1.3 million tickets per week, nearly matching the state's instant game as well as its new daily numbers game. Quinn had faith in lotto's future because "interest in [lotto] grows instead of dying, and with that growth of course prize money grows," promising that an increase in sales would raise the jackpot.[7] Quinn could have mentioned the crucial next step: high sales would drive up the jackpot, and then expanding prizes would attract new players whose sales would boost the jackpot further, in the process attracting even more players to what was quickly becoming the state's most popular lottery game.

After a sluggish start in the late 1970s, lotto took off and became the cornerstone of the lottery industry in the 1980s. By 1986, 21 of 23 state lotteries offered lotto (as did Washington, DC). The following year, lotto accounted for 40 percent of lottery sales nationwide. Massachusetts reintroduced lotto in 1983, and in 1986, approximately 70 percent of residents bought lotto tickets regularly and as many as 90 percent did so when the jackpot had grown over multiple drawings. "It's gone beyond a cycle. It's gone beyond a habit. It's become a mania. These people are obsessed," declared the overwhelmed owner of a Massachusetts lottery retailer. In 1980, nationwide lotto sales sat at $52 million. In 1990 sales hit $8.5 billion.[8] Lotto had become the nation's new game of choice.

Across the country, lotto sales were driven by lottomania (also dubbed "lotto fever"), periods when multiple rollovers created hysteria over huge jackpots. In the days before these drawings, some hopeful players purchased hundreds of dollars' worth of tickets and retailers reported long lines of gamblers at their stores. Like the lottomania that beset New York in August 1985, in the final hours before the drawing, sales often reached tens of thousands of tickets per minute as bettors rushed to buy a chance at the jackpot. "Can you believe Chicago today?" a Brighton Park, Illinois, resident remarked during a 1984 frenzy over a $34 million jackpot. "That money. People around here, that's all they can talk about."[9]

The fixation with massive lottery jackpots paralleled an obsession with wealth and celebrity that gripped American culture in the 1980s. This yearning for luxury offered a sharp departure from previous decades. The period from the 1940s through the 1970s was defined by economic egalitarianism. There were inequalities, to be sure, especially along lines of race and gender. But for white American men, the bounty of economic growth was shared relatively evenly, and the American Dream was as much a collective pursuit aimed at the common good as an individualistic one.[10] Organizational affiliations—including labor unions—reached an all-time high, and employers forged a social contract with workers, accepting responsibility for providing high wages and benefits to help make a middle-class life accessible to blue- and white-collar Americans alike. The ratio of CEO-to-worker compensation remained low—20-to-1 in 1965 and 30-to-1 in 1978—and skepticism with concentrated wealth and political power was not confined to the youth counterculture. Neither was wealth associated with the good life. A 1977 poll found Americans were increasingly concerned with "learning to get our pleasure out of nonmaterial experiences."[11] Given the always implicit contrast with Soviet communism, America celebrated itself as a land of plenty not because it created a few ultra-wealthy individuals but because of the opportunity and standard of living it offered to so many of its residents.

The 1980s ushered in a new ethos of showy opulence. The period from 1973 to 1982 was one of political, economic, and social upheaval that broke many of the rules of the postwar arrangement. Business gained more political power, conservatives ascended within the Republican Party, and the old industrial order came crashing down. In this context, wealth became part of the national culture, a culture ushered in from the White House by president and former Hollywood actor Ronald Reagan. Despite his populist campaign rhetoric, Reagan embodied the New Right's focus on the interests of the wealthy. From lavish inaugural galas to a tax plan that benefited the richest Americans, the extravagance of Reagan's tuxedoed administration contrasted sharply with the modesty of Jimmy Carter's sweater-clad Washington. "What I want to see above all," Reagan declared in 1983, "is that this country remains a country where someone can always get rich."[12] The New Right helped the personal quest for wealth evolve relatively quickly from selfish avarice to the natural result of American ambition, cloaked in the rhetoric of freedom, opportunity, and the righteousness of the free market. It was no longer taboo to collect a massive fortune; neither was it offensive to show it off. Wealth— not the prosperity of blue-collar workers but the fortunes of their bosses— became a means of reasserting the bounty of capitalism. In the aftermath of Vietnam, Watergate, the Iran hostage crisis, and a decade of cultural malaise, America could reassert its global machismo.[13] The rise of the super-rich was a sign that the United States was back.

Popular culture encapsulated the public's newfound appetite for opulence. In the 1970s, as the postwar economic order began to collapse, blue-collar America was center stage in both politics and culture.[14] But in the Reagan era, Americans seized any available chance to peer into the lives of the wealthy, both real and fictional. In 1982, *Forbes* published its inaugural list of the 400 richest Americans. Despite printing an additional 25,000 copies, the issue sold out instantly.[15] In a sharp departure from the sitcoms about middle- and working-class families that dominated television from the 1950s through the 1970s, the most popular programs of the Reagan era celebrated a life inaccessible to all but a small cadre of Americans. Shows that featured celebrities or focused on fictional wealthy individuals included *The Good Life*, *The Robb Report* (based on the luxury catalog of the same name), *Eye on Hollywood*, *Dallas*, *Falcon's Crest*, *Knot's Landing*, and *Dynasty*, which debuted the week before Reagan's inauguration and drew in 80 million viewers a week. On *Lifestyles of the Rich and Famous*, each week host Robin Leach took viewers on a tour of the home of a different celebrity, highlighting the person's material comforts and over-the-top purchases. At the end of each episode, Leach signed off with his catchphrase, "Champagne wishes and caviar dreams." The lyrics of the show's outro declared "It's a land of make believe / Dreams become reality," reminding viewers to preserve the hope that, one day, they might themselves live the lifestyle of the rich and famous.

Dreams of luxury took on particular importance amid the decade's economic climate. Though framed by Reagan's 1984 campaign advertisements as "Morning in America," the glitz and glamor of the 1980s were limited to those who had begun the decade wealthy. The Reagan years were defined by surging inequality. The ratio of CEO to worker pay began a rapid ascent, nearly doubling over the course of the decade, and, after decades of synchronous income growth, around 1980 the income of the top 5 percent began to increase at a much faster pace than the income of the rest of the population. By one estimate, the wealthiest 1 percent of Americans took in 70 percent of the total increase in family income between 1977 and 1989. Thanks in small part to lotto, in the 1980s, the number of American millionaires increased nearly 15-fold.[16] However, the increase in millionaires reflected a growing concentration of wealth, not a sudden increase in upward mobility.

Closely tied to surging inequality, the decade's other defining economic trends were stagnating mobility and a rise in financial insecurity. Poverty rates hit double digits for the first time since the 1960s, and American manufacturing continued to decline, a trend that further hastened a drop in private-sector labor union membership. A growing number of Americans began relying on the low-wage service industry for their livelihood, and entire communities—especially urban black communities and Rust Belt industrial centers—had little to no access to the financial stability of middle-class life. By the end of the decade, just 8 percent of those born into the bottom 40 percent of household wealth reached the top 20 percent.[17] For many Americans, the United States was losing its status as a land of opportunity.

These conditions created fertile soil for the public fascination with the rich and famous, a fascination that bred new definitions of success. Unlike the wealth from Reagan's tax cuts, the decade's new standards of affluence successfully trickled down. Shows like *Lifestyles of the Rich and Famous* may have become popular as part of a national quest to feel good, but an important consequence of their popularity was the changing ambitions of the general public. Even as opportunities for middle-class stability began to evaporate, many Americans began to set their sights higher, defining success against the visions of extravagance on display in Washington and on popular sitcoms. "*Dynasty* and *Knots Landing*, that's what you aspired to," one Baltimore resident recalled. "I could never have afforded any of those things. I was working in a low-end retail job. There was just this big disconnect."[18] Despite the disconnect between economic aspiration and economic reality, rising inequality did not lead to a growing desire for the increasingly elusive comforts of a middle-class life. Instead, many Americans rested their hope on joining the super-wealthy elite, accepting the growing gap between rich and poor partly out of an expectation that, one day, they would also be rich. *Newsweek* theorized that the public's obsession with the super-wealthy was driven by "the possibility that we could be them."[19]

Coupled with the culture of opulence, the financial crunch forced Americans to focus on the bottom line, as people gradually realized that the financial stability that many had taken for granted in the 1950s and 1960s was fading away. The percentage of college freshmen who stated that their life goal was "to be well off financially" rose from 40 percent in 1972 to over 70 percent in 1985, while the percentage who said their chief aim was to develop a "meaningful philosophy of life" declined precipitously, a shift emblematic of the cultural chasm between the metaphysical 1960s and the corporate 1980s. Wealth was no longer seen as immoral or a hollow path to happiness. In 1990, roughly 70 percent of Americans between the ages of 18 and 49 said they wanted to be rich—though men were much more likely to want to be rich than women—and 62 percent of all Americans said the country benefited from having a rich class of people.[20] Following a decade of rhetorical assault, popular culture in the 1980s helped legitimize affluence and scale up regular Americans' definitions of the good life. As the mid-century promise of opportunity disappeared, more Americans turned their attention to money as a means of providing happiness at the precise moment that money became increasingly hard to come by.

——•——

Lotto was the perfect game for this economic and cultural climate. Unlike passive, instant, or numbers games, lotto prizes could expand into multiple millions of dollars. Players' aspirations for luxury were, to a large extent, a byproduct of its new visibility, buoyed by centuries-old rhetoric celebrating the United States as a place where someone's ambitions need not know any bounds. For many, 1980s dreams of wealth became inextricably tied up with lotto. Author Taylor Branch observed in 1990 that while scratch games offered the fun of chasing small rewards, "lotto cultivates yearnings at the opposite extreme—pleasure drenched Hollywood fantasies."[21] Americans liked *Lifestyles of the Rich and Famous* because they thought that celebrities were like them and that there was a chance, however small, that what they saw on television could one day be theirs. Lotto worked the same way and offered the best chance for a quick rise to the stratosphere of wealth. The California Lottery recruited *Lifestyles* host Robin Leach to appear in 1987 commercials for lotto, the ad's creative director explained, because Leach "represents the life styles that people who play the lotto want to have."[22] Especially as growing numbers of Americans began to grapple with insecurity and downward mobility, lotto represented a ticket to a financial fortune.

As a testament to the power of the decade's culture of wealth, gamblers already knew how they would live when they won the lottery. Homes, in particular, represented a common focus for dreams. But a four-bedroom house in the suburbs with a white picket fence would not suffice for these would-be multimillionaires. In the 1980s, aspirational dreams of home-ownership centered around the types of extravagant estates showcased on *Dynasty*. A Brooklyn man pictured "a big house, a mansion on Long Island. It would have a gymnasium, two swimming pools, the works." A new home represented a new neighborhood, new friends, a new school for one's kids, a new life. So, while some players knew exactly how many pools their mansions would have, others just knew that they wanted to get out of their current lifestyles. Retired hotel worker Claudette Fields bought tickets for a $22 million jackpot in New York in 1986, vowing that when she won, "the first thing I'll do is get out of the projects."[23] Winning the lottery meant leaving the old life behind.

Luxurious cars were the other primary object of fixation, an embodiment of players' new life atop the class ladder. Private detective Ed White bought a chance at the same $22 million jackpot that captured Claudette Fields's imagination: "I normally play a few tickets, but this week I'm buying 65. Why? So I can live like I was born to live—with a Mercedes Benz."[24] A fancy car offered a stereotypical luxury good and represented throwing away the functional in favor of the flashy. While a mansion represented new social standing, a fancy car embodied a new attitude. As Bruce Springsteen sings in his 1982 ballad "Used Cars," "Mister the day the lottery I win, I ain't ever gonna ride in no used car again." Written from the perspective of a young boy who sees his embarrassed working-class father purchase yet another used vehicle, a new car served as a defiant statement of a new approach to money. Cars had long represented the open road, and an expensive car bought with lottery winnings symbolized leaving budget crunching behind, a highway to a new mindset paved by a windfall.

Ed White's comment that he was "born to live" with a Mercedes reveals the entitlement toward jackpots that many players brought with them to lotto. White implied that his modest living situation was a mistake, merely a temporary stepping stone to his proper birthright. Thanks in part to the decade's popular culture, gamblers like him had a preconceived idea that they would get rich. Lotto presented simply the most convenient way for them to make it happen. "I have a dream and I feel one day I'm going to be a millionaire," one Brooklyn lotto player declared, "and the only way that will happen is if you take chances."[25] Lotto players had no doubt that it was worth a few dollars for a chance to make their dreams come true.

Fantasies of mansions, fancy cars, and other luxuries represented a crucial dimension of the lotto experience. Players bought tickets not merely for the chance to win a jackpot but for the opportunity to imagine what they would do if they won. The lottery served as a vehicle of escapism. A Vermont woman explained her mindset and that of her fellow lotto players: "A dollar or two invested in a lottery gives us the opportunity to fantasize about a hopefully better life, an easier life. . . . That kind of dreaming, of how things could be, if only—that's got to be worth the small cost of the ticket." Rather than watch celebrities and fictional families on television parade around in the lifestyle they coveted, lotto provided players the opportunity to imagine their own life as the next instant millionaire. As cultural theorist Ien Ang argues, the pleasure of a fantasy does not lie in the possibility that the fantasy will become a reality but in the fantasy itself, the chance to envisage a world in which one's dreams have come true without any adverse consequences.[26]

The dynamics of lotto helped facilitate these dreams. Unlike numbers games, which offered fairly small prizes on a daily basis, or scratch games that instantly revealed whether someone won a prize, lotto players had to wait up to a week between when they purchased their tickets and when numbers were drawn. In that period, players were left to fantasize about how they would spend their windfall. "Hope springs eternal," a New York restaurant owner noted after the numbers were drawn for the $41 million prize in 1985. "For a few hours, millions of New Yorkers were multimillionaires." Purchasing a lottery ticket allowed gamblers to feel that they had taken action in pursuit of their dreams, and until the numbers were drawn, they could feel that they had actually won. The fantasies of mansions and Mercedes were not side effects of lottery gambling. The fantasies were the point. As the director of the Michigan Lottery admitted in 1982, "It all comes down to the fact that we're the purveyor of dreams."[27]

These dreams were especially significant because many players perceived the lottery as one of the only ways to change their lives or strike it rich. The economic environment of the 1980s meant that more and more Americans were facing the prospect of moving down, not up, the class ladder. And in the 1980s, middle-class security was no longer enough. For those struggling to get by, and for those who had achieved financial stability but wanted more, the lottery offered a unique chance to shoot to the top. Becoming middle class did not necessarily require a jackpot. Fabulous wealth did. Harlem gambler Millie Scott noted that she played for large jackpots because "being a cleaning lady, I know I'm not gonna be sitting on Park Avenue when I retire." Scott knew that a life of wealth and ease would always remain out of reach, that her job might allow her to get by, but it would never grant her access to everything she dreamed of: "If I did ever win a big one, I could live in a nice house about anywhere I wanted."[28] Her future was set in stone, unless she won the lottery.

Every American had better odds of making incremental moves up the economic ladder through traditional means—or of getting struck by lightning—than they did of winning the lottery. However, many perceived that they had no chance of mobility, not to mention mobility into the wealthiest of the wealthy. Millie Scott's job was never going to get her to Park Avenue. But with sufficient wages, benefits, and job training opportunities, low-wage employees in the 1970s and 1980s had some chance at moving up the ladder. Nonetheless, because of the decline in jobs that offered a secure middle-class life and the concentration of economic opportunities in certain parts of the country, even this type of life seemed more distant than a lottery jackpot. "When you have no money you are forced to rely on ridiculous things," one Brooklyn gambler admitted. "I still have hope for the ridiculous."[29]

The relationship of the social ladder and lottery sales was acknowledged by no less than Victor Markowicz, vice chairman of GTECH, the nation's predominant lotto vendor. In a 1988 article for a gaming industry magazine, Markowicz admitted that trends in corporate consolidation and downward mobility would be a boon for lotteries. "The business opportunities that once allowed people in America to get rich are shrinking," he wrote. "Everybody needs a dream. The lottery is a vehicle for the realization of that dream. Because of the downward trend in self-made wealth, there [is] less and less competition with the lottery to be the potential provider of the dream."[30] An unlikely jackpot represented the most reliable means of accessing the United States' promise as a land of opportunity.

The lottery was a particularly important mechanism of upward mobility for black Americans. The economic crises of the 1970s and the slowdown of the 1980s hit urban black communities especially hard. African Americans lost fragile entry into labor unions as manufacturing declined,

service cuts reduced the number of public sector jobs just as they were finally opening to black workers, the war on drugs wreaked havoc on black
communities and the black labor force, and private sector investment in black
neighborhoods remained low. Over the course of the 1980s, the percentage of
African Americans with incomes below the poverty line increased 44 percent
(compared to a 31 percent increase for white Americans). Young black men
suffered in particular. In 1987, one-third of black men between the ages of 25
and 34 had incomes that were below the poverty line, twice the percentage of
white men in the same age bracket.[31]

Many black gamblers saw little choice but to turn to the long odds of the
lottery. An unemployed black bulldozer operator in Camden, New Jersey,
said he made sure to bet $5–$10 per week on the lottery, "The way things are
now, I've got to try something." For African Americans and others, the lottery
exemplified a democratic means of wealth distribution. Lotteries did not dis-
criminate on the basis of race or class or gender or education. A win might be
unlikely, but at least everyone had the same odds. The inherent impartiality
appealed to anyone who had lost faith in the traditional economic ladder but
had not lost faith in their chance of striking it rich. By buying tickets, lottery
players—and black gamblers in particular—implicitly acknowledged that the
meritocracy, long central to politicians' claims about the American Dream,
was not as equitable as proponents claimed. Even New York Lottery director
John Quinn admitted that a central feature of his job was providing "a little
hope" to players without other options.[32]

Lotto became an object of fantasy and fascination even though its massive prizes were only possible because of nearly impossible odds. Most
players understood the unlikelihood that a ticket would provide them with
a windfall. Despite an abstract grasp of the improbability of winning, however, they still viewed the lottery as providing a shot at a new life because
they had some chance of winning, however small. "The odds are one million
to something. I don't know," a Maryland player admitted. The actual odds
were one in almost 4 million, though he made it clear that the precise probability did not matter: "It only takes one ticket. Just one ticket. Then a new
house, a new car . . ."[33] He acknowledged the long odds but at the same time
downplayed their importance, focusing instead on just how life-changing a
win would be. Even after months or years of losses, lotto players remained optimistic, retaining faith that their numbers would come through. This ethos
was summarized in a common saying, an adapted version of which has since
become the slogan of the Kentucky Lottery: "Somebody's gotta win, might
as well be me."[34] "Might as well" conceded that the lottery had no logic or

reason, but the "somebody" suggested that *someone* would win the lottery. If *someone* was going to win, and if every player had an equal shot of winning, then every gambler could reason that it was worth buying tickets to make sure they were that someone.

Players' focus on the distant chance of winning, rather than the far more likely possibility of losing, represents a common psychological bias. Daniel Kahneman and Amos Tversky call this phenomenon "Prospect Theory," namely, an overestimation of the probability of rare, positive events (and an underestimation of the odds of negative outcomes). Regardless of how distant the odds, lottery advertising or news stories about winners meant gamblers could visualize some possibility of winning. Coupled with many Americans' certainty that they were destined for a life of riches, players retained the belief that they would win, ignoring what they may have logically understood deep down as their actual, nearly impossible mathematical chances. "So what" if the odds are 1-in-2 million, a Maryland lottery player asked in 1985: "If I don't play at all, my chances are zero in two million, right? Somebody's got to win, right?" Her friend standing behind her in line to buy tickets responded, "And that's going to be me."[35] Players bought tickets for the chance to dream, but that dream was enhanced by the genuine belief that they could—and would— win. This dream and this belief let players keep the faith, and when a drawing failed to produce a winner, that faith kept them coming back again and again.

Even as they displayed undeserved confidence in their seemingly inevitable win, players took action to try to influence their luck and shape the odds in their favor. The most common manifestation of players' illusion of control was the careful selection of lottery numbers. Lotto allowed gamblers to do what numbers players had done for decades, namely, choose meaningful digits based on birthdays, anniversaries, or current events. This widespread strategy rested on the causal belief that numbers with special meanings were more likely to hit—that a loved one's birthday, for instance, could invite a jackpot, or that a prize would be more meaningful if it was won with personally significant numbers. Lottery commissions were happy to encourage faith in lucky numbers as this strategy could lead to entrapment—a commitment to a set of numbers and an inability to stop playing them out of the fear that they would eventually win. As late as 1986, some states, including Massachusetts, New York, and Pennsylvania, did not offer the option of computer-selected numbers, meaning every player had to pick their lotto numbers by hand for every ticket (which helps explains the long lines during lottomania). Gamblers also preferred betting at stores that had recently sold a winning ticket. Even though every outlet could sell tickets with the same numbers, gamblers were buoyed by the belief that certain vendors were more likely than others to sell a winning ticket.[36]

Some gamblers resorted to other means of asserting control, and they made plans for their winnings that they hoped would increase their odds. In addition to describing the lavish homes and expensive cars they would buy after hitting the jackpot, many players explained the good deeds they would perform with their winnings. One California office worker joked that everyone she talked to had made the same plans for when they won the lottery: "They're going to buy houses for themselves, or their mothers or their sisters or their brothers. And they're going to give a lot to charity. Charity is going to be so well off." Players made philanthropic promises partly out of the desire to help others but also, problem gambling scholar Durand F. Jacobs explains, because of the belief that "altruistic thinking" would "enhance their chances of winning."[37] The selection of specific numbers, lucky retailers, and promises of donations in the hope of karmic reward indicate the wishful thinking underlying gamblers' behaviors. When speaking to reporters, players were quick to acknowledge that the game was pure luck and they had only a small chance of winning. But when it came time to buy tickets, many players acted as if they could control their luck. Somebody was going to win, and gamblers took steps premised on the idea that they could increase the odds that that somebody would be them.

The lottery was not the only way to make a quick million without working for it. The growing popularity of lotto mirrored the rising prominence of Wall Street and its seemingly miraculous generation of wealth. For decades, Wall Street was a staid place, defined by risk aversion and relatively little innovation. Amid the economic tumult of the 1970s, the percentage of households with assets in the stock market plummeted. The Dow Jones lost three-quarters of its value between 1968 and 1982.[38]

After the 1981–1982 recession, however, the investment environment changed rapidly into a fast-paced world of money mania, and Wall Street assumed a place at the center of American culture. The Reagan administration made big business a top priority and oversaw a deregulation of the financial sector that allowed for the creation of new investment commodities. The combination of deregulation, low interest rates—which were pushed down even at the expense of rising unemployment—and a strong dollar helped lead to a mid-decade bull market. In August 1982, the Dow sat at 788. In December 1986 it was 1,908, and even after a market crash in 1987, at the dawn of the

1990s it hit 2,810. "All in all," Reagan declared as he signed a bill deregulating mortgage lending, "I think we hit the jackpot."[39] Market growth was also fueled by a growing trend of mergers and acquisitions, companies sold or combined, often in the name of financial efficiency and investor profits. In many cases, these deals entailed downsizing, especially of manufacturing facilities, which had been the financial backbone of the American working class for decades. This trend was part of a broader financialization of the global economy, which increasingly hinged more on the whims of Wall Street than on industrial capacity. British scholar Susan Strange concluded in 1986 that "the Western financial system is rapidly coming to resemble nothing as much as a vast casino."[40]

As with more traditional casinos, a central element of this new Wall Street atmosphere was a veneration of risk. Investing had always entailed some chance, though speculation and deal-making took on added importance in the 1980s. Risk was seen not as a necessary evil but as an inherent good. Anyone not taking chances lacked faith in the market or, even worse, in themselves. Deal-making was tied up with the reassertion of American machismo, and Wall Street titans and dealmakers became unlikely folk heroes. Chrysler CEO Lee Iacocca's autobiography was the nation's bestselling non-fiction book in 1984 and 1985, and Donald Trump and Tony Schwartz's *The Art of the Deal* spent 48 weeks on the *New York Times* bestseller list, including 13 at the top. There was a fine distinction between risk and chance, and these businessmen painted themselves as the product of the former and not the latter. "I believe that you make your own luck," Trump told Oprah Winfrey in 1988, four years after opening a casino in Atlantic City where Americans could put their own luck to the test.[41] When Iacocca or Trump gambled and won, it seemingly affirmed the connection between merit and money, not the influence of luck. The strong and the savvy won because they made good bets. Taking chances with money was a way for all Americans to prove their worth and grab success for themselves.

But not everyone had access to the Wall Street bonanza where money could be multiplied overnight. Firms like Charles Schwab and Merrill Lynch tried to bring investments to the people, and the rise of mutual funds and the advent of 401(k)s tied the wealth of more Americans to the market than ever before. Nonetheless, most remained shut out of the world of finance. In 1989, 33 percent of American households had a retirement account and just 19 percent owned stocks.[42] Many admired Trump and Iacocca. Few, though, had opportunities for deal-making of their own. Especially as finance, investment, and real estate replaced manufacturing as the driving forces of the economy, the gains of Wall Street were increasingly disconnected from life on Main Street.

Lotto offered an alternative mechanism of risk for anyone who wanted to make a quick buck but could not afford entry to the Wall Street game. Investing and speculating bear many similarities to gambling, so much so that over the course of American history regulators have had difficulty distinguishing among the three.[43] For gamblers, lottery tickets were less like a mutual fund than a hot stock—a high-yield, high-risk investment opportunity with long odds of astronomical growth. Many Americans were befuddled by headlines of the massive profits on Wall Street, particularly given the disconnect with economic conditions in many parts of the country. Lotteries capitalized on the apparent ability of money to magically multiply. In 1990, Washington State began selling "Wall Street" themed scratch tickets, where players scratched numbers labeled "buy" and "sell." If the number in the "sell" column was higher than that in the "buy" column, they won the prize listed under a third column, labeled "profit."[44] Lottery tickets could, through seemingly mysterious, odds-defying means, make a set of numbers on a small slip of paper worth millions, much in the same way that Wall Street seemed to every day.

Even non-themed games like lotto were treated by players as analogous to Wall Street. Gamblers saw betting as an investment strategy and explicitly described their wagers in terms one would expect to hear regarding a stock portfolio. Emulating the culture of risk on Wall Street, gamblers justified their bets on the grounds that any activity that entailed spending money with the promise of making money constituted an investment. Notwithstanding the likelihood that their lotto ticket would become worthless immediately after the drawing, anyone locked out of Wall Street finance could take solace in the fact that they, too, were taking a chance with their money. Cynthia Harris, an employee at a Camden, New Jersey, convenience store, said she bought $10 in tickets per week in the New Jersey Lottery and $12 per week in the Pennsylvania Lottery, spreading her bets around to cover different opportunities for returns. Harris bought tickets because she saw the lottery as "a good investment. If I hit the lotto game, I could retire at 22."[45] What made the lottery a good investment for Harris was the size of the jackpot at stake, regardless of her actual odds of winning.

Like Wall Street stockbrokers, lottery players chased the big score. When jackpots rolled over multiple times, regular players bought more tickets, sometimes to a dramatic extent. Then, because lotto prizes were tied to sales, players' increased investment pushed jackpots up even further, which in turn drove sales up again, a cycle that repeated until someone guessed the right numbers. For example, on August 20, 1984, the Illinois Lottery sold approximately 500,000 lotto tickets for a $9 million jackpot. After five days with millions of tickets sold per day but no winners, the jackpot reached $19 million on August 25, with 6 million tickets sold on that day alone. Sales slowed the following day as players waited to hear if anyone had won the grand prize. When news came through that no one had, sales shot back up in dramatic fashion. On August 28, gamblers spent almost $5 million on tickets, pushing the jackpot to $30 million. Then, between August 28 and September 3, players spent almost $31 million on lotto (82 percent of the total amount spent on lottery tickets in this period), driving the jackpot up to $40 million for the September 1 drawing, making it the largest lottery prize in American history until the $41 million New York jackpot the following year.[46]

Players purchased more tickets for massive jackpots because large prizes offered the most dramatic changes in financial standing. The bigger the prize, the better suited it was to fulfill the decade's new standards of wealth. Accordingly, players were willing to spend more to make it happen. They could bet at lucky stores or pick meaningful numbers, but many players recognized that the only way to actually increase their odds was to buy more tickets. If someone saw a jackpot as their only means of striking it rich, then it should not be surprising that they were willing to make a big bet. "I'd better win," one Pennsylvania lotto player stated in 1989, "because this is the mortgage money," claiming, perhaps jokingly, that they were forgoing paying off their loans in favor of the distant possibility of winning a sum that could pay off their mortgage many times over.[47]

Though technically mathematically effective, buying extra tickets rested on the miscalculation that a few additional tickets would provide significantly better odds. Gamblers vastly underestimated the probability that they would lose and seemed unable or unwilling to comprehend the sheer mathematical improbability they were up against. In 1988, Californian Harvey Ah Sam bought 65 tickets instead of his weekly 5 in hopes of taking home a $40 million jackpot.[48] His extra 60 tickets increased his odds by only a minuscule amount. Assuming Sam was the only player, if he bought 5 tickers per week for a 6/49 lottery (1-in-14 million odds of winning), it would take him 37,280 years to have a 50 percent chance of winning the top prize. By buying 65 tickets per week, it would still take 2,868 years to have just a 50 percent chance of winning.

These miscalculations were not limited to poor and working-class regular gamblers. Large jackpots encouraged habitual players to up the ante and also attracted first-time bettors, many of them middle and upper class. The riches promised by lotto appealed even to those with comfortable financial futures. In fact, given the wide range of players who tend to play for large jackpots, lotto is the least regressive lottery game. In 1985, a Connecticut marketing executive said he felt "ridiculous" waiting in line for 45 minutes at a Manhattan retailer to buy a ticket. His feeling of ridiculousness implied that he judged the lottery as a typically lower-class enterprise that he would not normally participate in and also one that was so improbable it should not have been worth his time. Nonetheless, he played for the same prize as working-class gamblers: "How many chances do you get to win $41 million?" the executive asked.[49] His use of the word "chance" took on two meanings, referring to the rare opportunity to gamble on such a large sum as well as the fact that winning a jackpot was inherently based around luck, that anyone, even someone who was already well-off, could strike it really rich.

Lottomania brought infrequent and regular gamblers together, facilitating camaraderie around the shared pursuit of elusive jackpots. Far from regarding other players as competitors, the infinitesimal odds of winning led to solidarity among gamblers, irrespective of their background or how frequently they played. This accord rested on the implicit admission that gamblers could not predict or control the outcome of the drawings. Despite most bettors' rudimentary understanding of probability, they recognized that other people purchasing tickets did not reduce the odds that they would win (though it did increase the odds that they would have to split the jackpot if multiple tickets won). The social element of gambling has facilitated the emergence of office lottery pools, in which individuals opt into spending a few dollars a week or a month on the understanding that any winnings will be shared among the group, an activity as much about the collective gambling experience as the actual chance of splitting a massive jackpot 20 or 50 ways. So too, standing in lines to buy lotto tickets was a social activity centered around discussions of fantasies of imminent windfalls. An affluent New York filmmaker recalled standing with "down-and-outers, the local drunks or people looking anxiously for a dream." They would discuss their lucky numbers and wish each other good luck. Regardless of the differences in life circumstances, the filmmaker recognized that they were all equal in the face of the lottery odds and that they were playing for the same reason: "We were all the same, of course, all dreaming."[50]

They may have shared dreams of winning, but well-off bettors like this New York filmmaker took a different approach to gambling from that of their poor neighbors. While every ticket buyer saw the lottery as a means of entering the world of the ultra-rich, many middle- and upper-class players could gamble knowing their financial stability did not rest on the result of the lottery balls that states used to select the winning lotto numbers. These players often emphasized that they were playing purely for entertainment, not for the money, partly as a way to try to distinguish themselves from the game's working-class player base. A 1986 *Los Angeles Times* poll found that poorer players were more likely to buy tickets strictly "For Money," while richer players were more likely to say they played "For Fun" or for both equally.[51] As jackpots grew and became media events, infrequent players wanted to participate as much for the chance to take part in a cultural phenomenon as for the chance to dream of wealth. Buying a ticket served as a signal that a middle- or upper-class individual was not at the top of the mountain yet. In this sense, they had more in common with working-class gamblers than they thought. Lotto represented a tool of investment for just about anyone. The jackpots were big enough to hold everyone's dreams.

For state lottery commissions, lottomania represented the ultimate jackpot. Big prizes drew media attention, attracted new players, and led regular gamblers to buy more tickets, so lottery officials had every incentive to let prizes grow. Nonetheless, states did not start off with eight-figure jackpots. New York began its lotto game with a ceiling, preventing grand prizes from exceeding $5 million. However, competition between states drove prizes upward. When New Jersey removed its $10 million lotto prize cap in 1982, New York Lottery director John Quinn was compelled to raise his state's cap to prevent a flow of jackpot-hungry players into the Garden State. In 1984, Quinn stated that he would tentatively limit jackpots to $25 million, though the following year he acknowledged that "the key factor in selling a lottery is a big prize." Eventually, he moved New York's ceiling to $50 million, leading to lottomania over jackpots of $41 million in 1985, $30.5 million in 1986, and $45 million in 1988. The new cap was still only provisional. "I'm not locked in concrete on the $50 million figure," Quinn admitted. "If states all around us go higher, we'd have to, too."[52]

The other way lottery commissions could facilitate large jackpots was reducing players' chances of winning. By adding more numbers for players to choose from, states could make jackpots harder to win and therefore more prone to roll over. Over the course of just 10 years, for example, the odds of winning New York's lotto game ballooned from 1-in-3.8 million to 1-in-26 million. Fearing its players would devote their lottery dollars to New York's surging prizes, in 1986 New Jersey lowered the odds of its lotto game from 1-in-1.9 million (6/36) to 1-in-3.8 million (6/40).[53] When it launched lotto in 1980, New Jersey had sought to lure players from New York by offering better odds of winning (6/36 compared to New York's 6/40), as the Garden State had a smaller pool of numbers to choose from. By the middle of the decade, it became clear that players were attracted to worse odds and correspondingly larger payouts. New Jersey expanded its number pool to compete with the bigger prizes—and lower odds—offered on the other side of the Hudson River.

Players appreciated the larger jackpots that resulted from states' lotto arms race. Brooklynite Zachary Berman wrote in 1987 that despite the long odds, he played the 6/48 game because "the potential dividends—multimillion-dollar prizes—are mind boggling." Such prizes represented "the possibility of fulfilling the American Dream" of wealth and independence, and "for such a dream, no odds are too long." Berman explained that he "invest[ed]" $100 a year in the lottery with the hope of winning a jackpot, "the bigger, the better."[54] Berman did not acknowledge, though, that these prizes were only possible thanks to the lottery commission's gradual worsening of his chance of winning. Nonetheless, an apparent proponent of the decade's new standards of wealth, he enjoyed the dream of winning and the hope that he could overcome the odds.

As states increased the size of grand prizes, players' sense of what constituted a large jackpot changed. By the second half of the 1980s, top prizes that had sparked lottomania in the early part of the decade could no longer attract casual players. In 1986, Ricardo Diaz of Queens explained why he played only when jackpots got really big: "If it's one million, you can spend that in a day if you buy a big house or something."[55] Diaz implied that he could win a $1 million prize if he wanted to, but that it was not worth the effort to compete for what he regarded as a paltry sum. Diaz believed he could pick and choose which jackpot to win, that he was bound to win a jackpot and did not want to waste his good fortune on a measly $1 million. The odds were the same regardless of the size of the prize, of course, and Diaz was almost certainly not going to win a major payout of any kind. But Diaz is emblematic of lottery players' shifting mindset over the course of the decade. One million dollars, which had been the top prize for the first 15 years of American state lotteries' existence, was, by 1986, no longer worth a second glance. That year, in a survey of Illinois lottery players, 54 percent said a "big jackpot" had to be at least $10 million.[56]

Table 4.1 The Changing Odds of New York Lotto

Year Introduced:	Format:	Odds of Winning Jackpot:	Roughly Equivalent Odds:
1978	6/40	1-in-3.8 million	Being killed by a shark attack in the United States
1983	6/44	1-in-7 million	Being killed in a US commercial jet airline accident (1987–2003)
1985	6/48	1-in-12 million	Becoming an astronaut
1988	6/54	1-in-26 million	Two golfers in the same group hitting a hole-in-one on the same par 3 hole
1999	6/51*	1-in-18 million	Becoming canonized
2001	6/59	1-in-45 million	Being killed by a venomous snakebite in the United States

Some games ran concurrently. New York began selling tickets for MegaMillions in 2002 and Powerball in 2010. In the 1990s, the state also began adding smaller, lower-odds lotto games to supplement the larger jackpot games.

*Until 1999, every New York Lotto ticket provided two number combinations, so the odds of winning were half of those listed in the table. For example, in 1978, each set of numbers had 1-in-3.8 million odds of winning. For $1 players received a ticket with two sets of numbers, meaning each ticket had total odds of 1-in-1.9 million. When the state lowered the range of numbers from 54 to 51 in 1999, it also switched from two to one set of numbers per ticket. While the odds of each set of numbers improved, players' effective odds of winning with each ticket dropped from 1-in-13 million to 1-in-18 million. The state returned to two numbers per ticket when it expanded the range in 2001.

Eventually, $10 million began to feel small too. In 1990, the *Chicago Sun-Times* asked gamblers why so many more people bought tickets for $50 million jackpots than for $10 million jackpots. Chicagoan John Orlando explained, "We play for the huge jackpots because we don't want to be merely as rich as the average rich person. We all want to be richer than the Donald." Orlando scoffed at the merely life-changing sum of $10 million, holding out for a prize five times as large, one that, he assumed, would make him as rich as Donald Trump. Notwithstanding that Trump was worth between $400 million and $600 million in 1990 (though he claimed to be worth multiple billions), Orlando envisioned $50 million as sufficiently large to make him an equal of Trump, a paradigmatic figure in the decades' new standards of wealth.[57] Therefore, a $50 million prize was worthy of a large ticket investment whereas a $10 million prize was not. Lottery players' desires for wealth centered around a clear sense of precisely how big a jackpot needed to be to catapult them into the upper echelons of inequality. Even if they underestimated exactly how much money it would take, they knew the jackpot would have to be massive.

So, while lottomania initially presented a huge boon, large rollover prizes ultimately represented a double-edged sword for state lottery commissions. In the short term, big jackpots increased sales and attracted new players. Yet massive payouts also led to what lottery officials deem "jackpot fatigue," in which jaded players expect bigger prizes in future drawings. "We've had so many people who've won a million or more, it now takes a pot of $10 million to generate the interest that $5 million did once," a Michigan Lottery spokeswoman explained in 1988. John Quinn noted a similar phenomenon among ticket retailers in New York City who told him, "Players like to stick their heads in the door to check on the size of the jackpot. The [cashier] says '$3 million' and they say, 'Aw, heck, is that all? I'll wait until it goes up.'"[58] Thanks to the losses of regular gamblers—who were disproportionately poorer and nonwhite—the jackpot would eventually go up. And then, only after millions or tens of millions had been poured into the drawing, it would start to catch the eye of richer players who decided to throw in a few dollars for a lark.

Though aspirations for wealth were widespread, standards for large jackpots were not uniform across the country. Because each state operated its own lottery and because lotto prizes were determined by the number of tickets sold, players' definition of a lottomania-worthy prize varied based on where they lived. Jackpots that captured headlines and led to long lines in one state could be ignored as routine in another. A $6 million prize could spark lotto fever in Iowa but pass without a second glance across the border in Illinois.

Lottery commissions in populous states were happy to oblige players' desire for massive jackpots. Because of their large player base—as well as the players who flooded in from across state lines during lottomania—lotteries in states like New York, California, and Florida could offer prizes worth tens of millions of dollars, and by the early 1990s, over $100 million. Smaller states, however, did not have enough players to offer such magnanimous windfalls, as their games had much smaller base prizes and rolled more slowly. To compensate, smaller states began to band together. In 1985, after years of watching players flock to retailers in Massachusetts, the states of New Hampshire, Vermont, and Maine formed the Tri-State Lottery, a venture likely inspired by the formation in 1982 of the Interprovincial Lottery Corporation in

Canada, North America's first multi-jurisdictional lotto game. The Tri-State Lottery started as a 6/30 lotto game contracted out to Scientific Games—the company's first venture into lotto—with jackpots that periodically exceeded $1 million and advertisements featuring *Lifestyles* host Robin Leach. After conceding to players' desires for bigger prizes by expanding to a 6/36 format, the jackpot reached $9.6 million in June 1986, a far larger prize than any of the three states could have offered on their own. In a reversal of fortune, the prize was won by a Massachusetts woman who happened to buy a ticket while passing through New Hampshire, unaware that she was playing for a prize that had transfixed gamblers across northern New England.[59]

The success of the Tri-State Lottery inspired further cross-border collaboration among small lottery states. In 1987, the District of Columbia and six states—Iowa, Kansas, Oregon, Rhode Island, Missouri, and West Virginia, five of which bordered a larger lottery state—formed the Multi-State Lottery Association (MUSL). The following year, MUSL introduced Lotto America, which offered a $2 million base prize for a 7/40 game (1-in-18 million odds of winning) that later became 6/54 (1-in-26 million). Forty-five percent of every ticket went to prizes, while 40 percent was shared among the states as revenue (the remaining 15 percent went to the retailer and to administrative costs). By 1992, MUSL had expanded to nine additional states and replaced Lotto America with Powerball, a 5/45 game in which players selected one additional "Powerball" number between 1 and 45 (1-in-55 million total odds of winning, the lowest odds of any lotto game to that point).[60] Though Powerball jackpots rolled more slowly—with a higher percentage of sales going to secondary prizes—the small odds meant potentially massive jackpots. About a year after its formation, the Powerball jackpot reached $110 million, the fourth nine-figure prize in American history and the first available to residents of small states without crossing state lines (the previous three had been in California, Pennsylvania, and Florida). In 1996, a separate consortium of larger states—Georgia, Illinois, Maryland, Massachusetts, Michigan, and Virginia—formed their own multi-state operation, "The Big Game," which later became known as MegaMillions. In 2010, MegaMillions and Powerball reached a cross-sales agreement, allowing both games to be sold in every lottery state, promising jackpots that could reach new heights by drawing in gamblers from across the country. In 2016, after 18 consecutive drawings without a winner, Powerball offered the nation's first $1 billion jackpot.

Not everyone approved of the trend toward games with lower odds and larger jackpots. Some players called for a return of smaller lottery prizes with better odds. Harkening back to the economic egalitarianism of the mid-twentieth century, critics chastised the new obsession with wealth and criticized lotto for feeding into these new desires. "I'm glad New York has decided to put a lid on the maximum for lottery prize [*sic*]," Antonio Carloni of New Hampshire wrote to New York governor Mario Cuomo in 1984: "Anything over $10 [million] is obscene." Carloni suggested that no single gambler needed to win that much money. In a critique that hinted at opposition to the inequality on the rise across the nation, Carloni implied that it was immoral for anyone to receive an eight-figure windfall. In 1988, Zachary Berman railed against New York's new 6/54 game. Berman complained that the game's "insurmountable" odds will "drive away players like myself who would be satisfied with a few million."[61] The previous year, Berman had praised New York's 6/48 game for providing access to the American Dream, though just a few months later he complained that the reduced odds made the game impossible to win. Berman's comments represented his desire for the impossible: jackpots that were relatively easy to win but could fulfill his desire for social mobility into a life of luxury. At a certain point, Berman suggested, jackpots did not need to expand further, as his dream could be satisfied with

FIG 4.1 Even as the lottomania of the 1980s faded, massive jackpots continued to spark periods of lottery frenzy. In May 1998, the grand prize for multi-state lotto game Powerball reached $195 million, the largest in American history to that point. At the Kwik Stop Gas & Groceries in Malad, Idaho, hundreds of people—many of them from Utah, a state with no lottery—waited in line for several hours to buy tickets. AP Photo/Standard-Examiner, Kort Duce.

tens of millions—rather than hundreds of millions—of dollars. However, Berman drastically misunderstood the odds involved. He painted a 6/48 game (1-in-12 million odds) as a winnable, long-shot possibility whereas a 6/54 drawing (1-in-26 million) was somehow a sheer impossibility.

Opponents of large jackpots were against the expansion of top prizes because they viewed the lottery as a vital tool of wealth redistribution for lower-income gamblers. Long odds were not purely an issue of keeping players entertained. Rather than offer giant, improbable jackpots, these players believed lotteries should feature better odds in order to return money to more players, many of whom were desperate for profits from their lotto investment. Occasional lottery player Joseph Carbonell opposed John Quinn's expansion of New York's lotto from 6/40 to 6/44 because "a lottery is the one hope of many small people to acquire enough money to pay off debts and maybe live just a little better." Ignoring the low probability of winning even the smallest of five- and six-figure lotto prizes, Carbonell proposed a $100,000 limit on jackpots: "This would provide for many, many more of us having a chance to improve our daily living." Players "just want a reasonable chance at a windfall, not 'Pie-in-the-Sky' millions."[62]

However, ticket sales indicated that "Pie-in-the-Sky millions" was exactly what players wanted. As jackpots expanded, states routinely broke sales records, and sales increases tied to large jackpots continued even after someone won the jackpot, suggesting that lottomania attracted first-time players, some of whom became reliable gamblers. Players recognized that bigger jackpots entailed reductions in their odds of winning. Most welcomed the chance to compete for massive prizes. A West Virginia Lottery official admitted in 1989, "Lottery players nationally really aren't so interested in odds as they are in the size of the jackpot."[63] Bettors could hardly notice the difference between 1-in-4 million, 1-in-14 million, or 1-in-40 million odds of winning. Though far more unlikely, the initial prize was already so implausible that the marginal difference felt inconsequential. By contrast, gamblers could easily notice the difference between a $4 million, $40 million, or $104 million jackpot, even if larger prizes were possible only because of lower odds. Due to their hope that they would win, gamblers did not see an increase in the jackpot as a reduction in their chances of winning. Instead, it represented an increase in how much they would take home when their numbers finally came through.

——◆——

Eventually, the nation's lotto fever broke. In state after state, within a few years of the introduction of lotto, sales began to stagnate or decline. Officials identified numerous culprits. Most attributed the drop to players' unsustainable thirst for bigger prizes. Some explained that reducing the odds of winning might discourage players initially and that it would take some time—and a big jackpot—to entice them back. Others explained that big prizes were becoming more infrequent because players were getting smarter and picking random numbers. Players originally had to pick their own numbers, and most picked numbers between 01 and 31, which were associated with birthdays and anniversaries. But because most people picked numbers in that range, fewer players selected numbers in the 30s and 40s. Once gamblers start using random numbers, a larger percentage of possible combinations were accounted for, increasing the odds that someone would win and preventing rollovers. Some blamed the slowdown on the opening of new riverboat casinos and tribal bingo games, though studies have found only modest cannibalization of revenue between lotteries and other forms of gambling.[64] Others pointed to the slowing economy, despite the fact that the stuttering economy of the 1980s had propelled lotto sales in the first place. One Illinois official even blamed the stock market, claiming that as the market soared in the 1990s, "people might want to invest their money more aggressively," gambling on the Dow Jones and not at their local lottery retailer.[65]

The game had simply lost its novelty. Players' expectations for prizes remained high, and it was becoming harder and harder for states to avoid jackpot fatigue. In response to the demand for smaller jackpots that were easier to win, states introduced separate lotto games with lower odds, an especially important addition as MegaMillions and Powerball spread across the country and began dominating the long-odds lotto market. In the 1990s and into the 2000s, lottomania persisted but became gradually more infrequent. It also increasingly became a national phenomenon rather than one concentrated in a particular state, especially after Powerball and MegaMillions began cross-sales in 2010. Both games capture headlines roughly every two years with the latest record-breaking jackpot, and relative to the state-level games that siezed gamblers' imagination in the 1980s, multi-state games today offer unfathomably long jackpot odds: 1-in-292.2 million for Powerball and 1-in-302.6 million for MegaMillions as of 2021. For reference, hitting the MegaMillions is the equivalent of releasing an ant onto an area the size of roughly four football fields, randomly sticking a pin into the ground, and hitting the ant. Nonetheless, in 2019, Powerball and MegaMillions brought in a combined $7.4 billion in gross sales, while all other lotto games brought in an additional $3.6 billion, a combined 13 percent of nationwide lottery sales.[66]

Lotto's heyday has passed, but the fantasies endure. The growth of lottery jackpots and the decline in the odds of winning offer an apt metaphor for the economic changes of the last four decades, particularly the growing concentration of wealth and the declining odds of climbing the economic ladder. Since the 1980s, lotto has helped acclimate Americans to these economic conditions. As scales of wealth increased, many Americans' hopes shifted accordingly. With more and more Americans left behind economically, rather than breed anger against the wealthiest Americans, the widening chasm between the rich and the poor fostered widespread desire to enter the increasingly exclusive upper echelon. Even before the introduction of lotto, many Americans assumed that they were bound for an inevitable life of wealth. The rich getting richer was acceptable in part because many gamblers believed that they would one day join the gated community of the rich and famous. Lotto offered the best and quickest way to get there.

Citing the infinitesimal odds of hitting the Powerball or MegaMillions, critics frequently chastise American lottery players for throwing down even a few dollars on the dream of a new life. These criticisms often target low-income gamblers, though for 40 years, lotto—and lottomania in particular—has tapped into a cultural vein that cuts across class, race, gender, age, ability, and education. Millions of Americans, rich and poor alike, are drawn to lotto for the same reasons. As one lottery retailer noted in 1987, "Everybody has hopes and dreams, no matter how much money they have."[67] It should hardly prove surprising that in a culture defined by downward mobility and the valorization of wealth, millions would risk a few dollars on a chance to transform their lives, no matter the odds.

5

This Could Be Your Ticket Out

THE PARADOX OF LOTTERY ADVERTISING

ON JANUARY 20, 1986, Josephine McCord stepped out of St. Malachy Roman Catholic Church on the West Side of Chicago onto Washington Boulevard. A pastoral associate at the church, McCord had been attending a special service for a new federal holiday: Martin Luther King Jr. Day. Twenty years earlier, she had worked with King on his campaign against housing and employment discrimination in Chicago. Since 1966, though, many of the problems King encountered on the West Side had only gotten worse. African American neighborhoods in Chicago had been deprived of public- and private-sector investment for decades, and the West Site was beset by unemployment, violence, drug abuse, poverty, and police brutality. The situation was so dire that in 1983, Mother Teresa sent a group of nuns to provide aid to the community out of the church gymnasium.[1]

Because of the conditions on the West Side, McCord was appalled by what she saw on her way out of St. Malachy on January 20. A giant advertisement featuring nine words in white writing on a green background had been plastered to the side of a building across the street from the church: "How to get from Washington Boulevard to Easy Street." Emblazoned below this phrase was a familiar symbol identifying the source of the advertisement, a symbol ubiquitous on billboards across the state and on the ticket stubs that lined the sidewalks around St. Malachy: a pot of gold at the end of the proverbial rainbow, the logo for the Illinois State Lottery.

McCord was furious that the lottery had put up a sign specifically designed to entice members of her community to buy lottery tickets in pursuit of a quick path to Easy Street. She was no stranger to gambling, having worked as a child selling slips for policy, the illegal daily lottery game in Chicago.[2]

But between the barrage of advertising, the vastly lower odds of winning, and the imprimatur of state legitimacy, the Illinois Lottery operated at a different level than the gambling racket that had dominated the Windy City. The ad hit home for Josephine because her son Leo (whose story opens this book), had played the lottery consistently since 1974, even after he lost his job driving a taxi and fell on hard times. Leo took responsibility for his poor decision-making, though he noted that promotions like the Easy Street billboard worsened his situation: "I've been poor all my life, both by circumstance and out of my own mistakes," he told the *Chicago Tribune*. "I shouldn't be seeing that pot of gold at the end of the rainbow around most every corner I turn in this neighborhood, big billboards and signs on the sides of buses telling me that if I just play the lottery, I can get to Easy Street." This type of marketing lured desperate people into thinking a lottery ticket might be their ticket out. "Around here, that's powerful advertising. A psychological gun to my forehead, telling me to reach into my pocket because I might be able to change my life. I might win."[3] St. Malachy's pastor, Father Thomas O'Gorman, had also been incensed by the sign, particularly that the children who attended school at the parish should have to walk past a billboard that implied their best chance at a new life was not through education or hard work but gambling. Josephine and O'Gorman made repeated calls to the state lottery office to complain. When their pleas went unanswered, the two of them and Leo took action, covering the offending advertisement with a new message: "Boycott the Lottery."

Lottery officials were stunned by the response to their advertisement on Washington Boulevard. The Easy Street campaign had been suggested by a previous jackpot winner, and the the lottery commission put up over 200 posters and billboards around Illinois, each customized to its location. A billboard in northern Chicago marked the lottery as the path "from Clark Street to Easy Street," while posters on public buses proclaimed, "Easy Street: This bus won't take you there, but playing the lottery can." After receiving multiple complaints from across the state, Illinois Lottery director Rebecca Paul recognized that the site-specific nature of the ads had been misunderstood and that many residents felt belittled. "Our ads are not intended to imply," she wrote to one angry Calumet Park resident, "that the neighborhood in which they appear is inferior to the mythical Easy Street."[4] Rather, the billboards sought to personalize the lottery's message, to tell everyone, no matter where they lived, that a ticket offered a chance at a life of ease, regardless of whether or not they moved away from their current neighborhood. Nonetheless, as soon as Paul got word of the trouble the campaign was causing on the West

Side, she moved the Washington Boulevard sign 10 blocks away, out of sight of St. Malachy. It was replaced with a message promoting the preservation of Illinois wildlife.

Given the ubiquity of lottery advertising on the West Side, Josephine, Leo, and Father O'Gorman were not satisfied with the relocation of one billboard. To investigate the pervasiveness of lottery playing in the community, O'Gorman closed his sermon on February 23 by asking parishioners to bring their losing tickets from the past week in lieu of collection for the following Sunday. He was astounded by the results. St. Malachy, with a membership of 300 families and parishioners, handed in over $5,000 worth of ticket stubs. Assuming every ticket had been purchased in the last week—and even if every family was actually in attendance—the average St. Malachy household spent almost $17 on lottery tickets every week. This amounted to $867 every year (the equivalent of $2,000 in 2020 dollars), nearly 10 times the average amount spent on tickets per person in lottery states nationwide and almost 8 times the average in Illinois. O'Gorman continued his weekly collection of tickets, and garbage bags filled with stubs quickly filled his office. As Josephine McCord observed, playing the lottery "has become like a national pastime for the poor."[5]

Armed with evidence of the problem state-run gambling posed for the West Side, St. Malachy embarked on a campaign against the Illinois Lottery. O'Gorman dubbed the lottery a "victimizer" of poor and black people who were tempted to gamble "because they have so few options for the future." Many of his parishioners, he claimed, had little discretionary income or relied on welfare. Nonetheless, they were "the target of heavy advertising which promises to move them into the middle class." O'Gorman remembers that he heard rumors that some executives at the Illinois Lottery's advertising firm knew the Easy Street ad would lure in desperate gamblers but that they did not care because their job was to increase sales as much as possible.[6] In a letter to Governor James Thompson, the priest acknowledged the importance of gambling as a source of revenue for Illinois but argued, "The Lottery must not be of more value than our citizens who live in the grip of poverty and hardship." In its search for extra revenue, the government should not entice these people to gamble. "It makes me feel even more angry," he later contended, "that the culprit in this is the State of Illinois."[7] Calling for an investigation into its effect on the poor, O'Gorman wanted the lottery to act less like a profit-hungry business and more like an arm of the state concerned for the well-being of its citizens.

St. Malachy's campaign against the lottery reached its apex in March. Following a meeting at the church with 100 parishioners and two city aldermen, O'Gorman, Josephine and Leo McCord, and a group of supporters marched downtown to a state government building, the State of Illinois Center (since renamed the James R. Thompson Center), where the Illinois Lottery had a claims office and occasionally hosted live drawings. Some community members stopped outside to picket, bearing signs declaring "Lottery Is a Con Game," "Stop the Lottery," and "Lottery Is Unfair to Poor and Blacks." Meanwhile, other protestors—mostly children and older black women who were less likely to be hassled by security—went to each of the building's 17 stories carrying piles of the losing lottery stubs collected at the church. At a designated moment, they released thousands of tickets from the balconies into the building atrium, showering the state employees below.[8] Illinois officials may not have realized how prevalent the lottery was in poor black communities, or they may have known or suspected but not cared. The protest put proof into their laps that the state's lottery revenue came from its most vulnerable residents.

While the boycott proved short-lived, two West Side state representatives passed legislation creating the investigative panel O'Gorman had demanded. In December 1986, a special report of the Illinois Economic and Fiscal Commission (IEFC) concluded that predominantly black and lower-income zip codes accounted for a disproportionate share of lottery sales and that the simplicity of lottery ads "may be misleading the poor and un-educated into spending substantially greater portions of their incomes on dreams." Echoing O'Gorman, the report concluded, "State government has responsibilities towards all of its citizens; it should not put the best interests of these individuals against one of its revenue-producing efforts." While O'Gorman called for Illinois Lottery director Paul to resign following the IEFC's revelations, in June 1986 the National Association of State Lotteries awarded Illinois its annual prize for best lottery advertising in the country. The following year, Illinois Lottery annual advertising expenditure surpassed $10 million for the first time and ticket sales hit a record $1.35 billion.[9]

The Easy Street advertisement on Washington Boulevard was unique for the attention it garnered but remarkably unexceptional in its placement, its message, and the contradiction it revealed about government-run gambling. In Illinois and across the country, lottery commissions have long relied on advertising to generate sales. Most lottery ads are built on messages that encourage players to believe in luck, chance, and the possibility of defying the odds. It is reasonable to dream of Easy Street, marketing tells players, because the lottery is a vehicle of miraculous transformation. A new life is just around the corner. These promotions are designed to persuade people to play a game whose odds are stacked against them and to tell them they were missing the opportunity of a lifetime by not buying a ticket.

These enticements are especially significant because they are the work of state governments. Lottery commissions represent unique state agencies. Like private-sector companies, they are tasked with raising as much revenue as possible, an undertaking that often butts up against the broader purpose of government: acting on behalf of the greater good. When it comes to legalized gambling, though, public officials are often only concerned about the bottom line, even when raising that bottom line means promoting a product that preys on the poor or creating advertisements that denigrate hard work or education. Facing budgetary pressure from tax-averse citizens, lawmakers took action to open the floodgates for lottery advertising. Gambling promotions were initially limited by a series of federal regulations until lawmakers overturned these restrictions in the 1970s on the grounds that they hampered lottery profitability. Policymakers in Illinois and elsewhere made numerous attempts to rein in lotteries' promotional capabilities in the 1980s and 1990s, but these efforts were unsuccessful. Even after thousands of ticket stubs were rained down into a state office building, hard-luck gamblers like Leo McCord were out of sight and out of mind. It was imperative that lotteries be free to rake in as much money as possible.

In their efforts to maximize revenue, lottery officials in Illinois and other states targeted their advertisements at communities they expected would buy the most tickets. Invariably, this resulted in a disproportionate concentration of ads in lower income and African American neighborhoods. Though the Easy Street ad was not unique to Washington Boulevard, like many other state lotteries, the Illinois Lottery exhibits a long history of utilizing advertising and sales tactics that target black communities. It should hardly be surprising, then, that black residents of Illinois felt enticed by lottery marketing, as state officials made consistent efforts to ensure they were hooked on dreams of a jackpot. The popularity of lottery tickets in these communities is not simply the result of bettors' poor financial decision-making or a natural result of economic conditions but the purposeful product of state-funded promotions that painted gambling as a reliable path of upward mobility.

Lotteries' hard-sell tactics were a response to hopes for a different kind of windfall, namely, unrealistic expectations for gambling as a source of state revenue. Even as lotteries—and other forms of gambling—fell short of initial expectations, state lawmakers demanded steady increases in revenue. Left with few other mechanisms to improve sales, lottery officials turned to advertising. When revenue failed to meet lawmakers' and taxpayers' projections, ads played an important role in maintaining the illusion that gambling represented an important source of state income. Since 1986, the Illinois Lottery has promoted itself not just as a way to get rich but as a benefactor of education to impart the message that buying a lottery ticket is both a philanthropic act and one that can catapult someone to unfathomable riches.

For Leo McCord and countless other players, the promise of a windfall has proven illusory. The same is true for the states themselves, no matter how much they advertise or how many forms of gambling they legalize. A lottery ticket was not the path off of Washington Boulevard, nor was it a bountiful fountain of revenue for government. "We need to be honest about life, about who we are and what we want to be," Father O'Gorman noted in 1987. "There is no easy street."[10]

Advertising has always been crucial to the success of lotteries. More so than other forms of gambling, lotteries rely on mass participation, on as many tickets as possible being sold to large numbers of players. In the American colonial period, lotteries were advertised on handbills, on street posters, and in newspapers. Promotional materials detailed all pertinent information: jackpot size, ticket cost, locations to buy tickets, the date of the drawing, and who or what the lottery was raising money for. In some cities, lottery ads were even more ubiquitous than they are today. A New York City grand jury wrote in the early 1830s that "some of our principal streets are literally disfigured by [lottery] advertisements." These were no mere informational inducements. In 1833, a Pennsylvania lawmaker described "hand-bills of the most insidious and seductive character" thrust into the hands of Philadelphia residents. "Powerfully appealing" images were used for "deceiving the credulous and alluring the unwary. A prize is always promised."[11]

As states cracked down on lotteries in the nineteenth century, legal and political debates over sweepstakes gambling centered around the question of advertising. By the 1880s, the nation's lone remaining sweepstakes was the Louisiana State Lottery Company, which was notorious for its reach into states that had barred gambling. With state governments helpless to stop the flood of promotions from Louisiana and from nascent illegal gambling operations, Washington took action. Congress passed a series of laws restricting the interstate transportation of lottery tickets as well as the distribution of gambling promotions through the mail. The lottery ticket restriction was upheld by the Supreme Court in *Champion v. Ames* (1903), a groundbreaking ruling that affirmed Congress's ability to regulate interstate commerce.

Seven decades later, these laws presented a serious stumbling block for states seeking to publicize their newly established government-run lotteries. Newspapers were uncertain about what exactly constituted promotional material. Because of the restrictions on the interstate transmission of gambling information, papers could not send lottery news or advertisements to readers across state lines, meaning the *New York Times* would have to remove lottery ads in order to legally deliver to customers in Connecticut. Shortly after its founding in 1934, the Federal Communications Commissions (FCC) extended the ban on broadcasting lottery information, a policy that the agency decided in 1967 also applied to government-run games. Television and radio stations were prohibited from airing lottery drawings or even showing winning numbers, and ABC and NBC initially refrained from broadcasting any information about the lottery altogether, even in news reports.[12] These restrictions severely hampered the games at a vulnerable point in their development. If early lottery winners were unable to attend drawings in person, they found out they had won only when they were contacted directly by lottery representatives or if they called a hotline set up by the lottery that read the winning numbers. Unsurprisingly, prizes frequently went unclaimed. In 1974, the New Jersey Lottery needed to seek special permission from the FCC to broadcast a limited number of radio spots to let residents know about unclaimed prizes.[13]

Lottery officials railed against the federal regulations impeding their industry. Ralph Batch, the first director of the Illinois Lottery and former head of the New Jersey Lottery, testified to a US Senate subcommittee in 1974 that lotteries were simply revenue-producing agencies. The prohibition on televised drawings, he argued, limited their ability to operate transparently. Illinois voters expected lottery revenue to stave off a tax increase but these restrictions harmed sales because the public could not be assured that the games were conducted fairly.[14] The New Jersey Lottery—with backing from Pennsylvania and New Hampshire—sued the FCC in 1973, and two years later, Congress and President Gerald Ford exempted state-run lotteries from federal restrictions on gambling promotions. A 1976 law, sponsored by Illinois Republican representative Paul Findley, deregulated lottery advertising further, allowing newspapers to contain lottery information and advertisements and permitting the distribution of these materials to neighboring states that had also enacted a lottery.[15]

Even before the federal restrictions were lifted, the Illinois Lottery had advertised to help sell tickets, which first became available on July 30, 1974. Most of the lottery's first advertisements were informational, instructing prospective gamblers how to play and explaining the two types of tickets. The goal was to create awareness, to "make the Illinois state lottery tickets as familiar to Illinois residents as a $1 bill," Batch explained. Marketing surveys indicated the success of these efforts. In the two weeks before tickets went on sale, over 90 percent of the population was aware of the Illinois Lottery, and 68 percent stated that they planned on buying a ticket. By September 1975, 83 percent of Illinois residents had bet at least 50 cents on the dream of a jackpot.[16]

From the outset, the lottery's first newspaper, transit, and billboard ads were not distributed evenly throughout the state. The state spent much more on advertising in areas with larger black populations, especially East St. Louis, which was almost 70 percent African American and where ad spending was double per capita compared to some primarily white downstate metro areas.[17] Given the ubiquity of numbers games—Chicago players continued to prefer the earlier version, policy—in urban black communities, officials presumed that tickets would be especially popular with black gamblers, regardless of the fundamental differences between the first lottery games and policy, which offered daily drawings and cheaper tickets. When the state did introduce a daily numbers game in 1980, its advertising was even more precisely targeted. In an internal memo, an Illinois Lottery official "anticipated that the game will be very favorably accepted by the ethnic communities," presumably based on the popularity of policy. "Therefore, during the introductory period, special emphasis will be placed against these communities."[18] Though the content of the ads did not target any specific demographic, before tickets went on sale officials projected that poor and black communities would provide a strong market for tickets. Then, thanks in part to a flood of advertising, these areas recorded disproportionately high sales. Consequently, the lottery justified targeted advertising in these communities on the grounds that they bought large numbers of tickets. Assumptions about black gamblers led to targeted advertising. Ad placement then begot sales, which begot more advertising, which begot more sales, and so on.

In Illinois and other states across the Northeast and Midwest, public interest in the first wave of lottery games waned over time. In its first few years, Illinois could meet its sales goals by attracting new players curious about state-run gambling. The novelty wore off quickly, and sales remained low as African Americans in Chicago, whom officials had counted on as a key player base, remained loyal to policy outfits. The Illinois Lottery recorded sales of $129 million in its inaugural year, though revenue fell for the next four years, bottoming out at just $68 million in 1979. While the lottery advertised to support its games, budget restrictions limited the scope of these promotions, and a contractor report later concluded that this lack of advertising contributed to the drop-off in sales.[19]

The Illinois Lottery's first tactic to boost revenue was to add new games, including instant games in 1975, daily numbers in 1980, and lotto in 1983. These efforts increased annual sales, which climbed to $200 million in 1980, hit nearly $500 million in 1983, and surpassed $1 billion for the first time in 1985. The popularity of the new games was partly the result of more consistent, better-financed marketing, as lottery spending on advertising increased almost 300 percent between 1980 and 1986. Initially, many of these ads were expository, similar to the 1970s introductory campaigns. Commercials to announce the start of the numbers game, for example, featured a convenience store owner explaining how the game worked, telling players that they would be able to pick their own numbers and reminding them that, if they won, they could receive their money the same day.[20]

Introductory ads could not sustain appeal over the long term, and lotteries could not rely on players experimenting with new games. Starting in the early 1980s, lotteries in Illinois and other states had to consider how to attract those who had not bought a ticket and how to maintain a market of stable, reliable gamblers. As they sought to expand their player base, lotteries turned to a different kind of message to entice players to take a chance at a jackpot.

———

Lottery tickets are unlike nearly every other retail good. Most consumer products offer some demonstrable benefit. Even if a purchaser pays for something impermanent—like a concert ticket or a meal—the transaction is rooted in the prior knowledge of what they are buying. Lottery tickets are anything but predictable. Their value lies in the possibility that the money spent on tickets will transform into a much greater sum. The only guaranteed value from a lottery ticket is the entertainment—the chance to dream, for a few moments or a few days, about a life of wealth. Even if many are willing to pay for this period of fantasy, most players experience failure after failure, purchasing what ultimately amount to slips of paper with losing numbers printed on them. As Illinois Lottery director Sharon Sharp explained in 1991, the lottery "is not just soap. It is not tangible. You're selling dreams."[21]

In the 1980s, the Illinois Lottery set out to do just that, to sell tickets by selling the dream of winning the lottery. As players grew more familiar with the games, the lottery shifted toward promotions centered around the possibility of winning. In a study of 101 lottery commercials from 13 states in 1987,

63 percent of ads concentrated on the themes of "You Could Win/Winning Could Change Your Life," "Jackpot/Growing Money," or "Wealth/Elegance." By contrast, just 23 percent offered an informational-based sales appeal, and only 15 percent focused on the fun and excitement of playing. The 1986 IEFC report observed that Illinois's lottery commercials "do not concentrate on the game-playing aspect, but rather on the possibility that individuals can actually change their lifestyles by winning."[22]

These depictions of instant, life-altering jackpots reflect the promises of instantaneous transformation that have long proven central to American advertising. As cultural critic Raymond Williams writes, advertising represents "a highly organized and professional system of magical inducements and satisfactions." Advertising, he contends, is a process of attaching social meanings to material objects. Williams and historian Jackson Lears trace modern advertising's origins to traveling medicine men, mercurial merchants who peddled potions and other goods as miraculous cures for physical, mental, and spiritual ailments. As the advertising industry professionalized, Lears writes, it developed a disdain for this informal economy. Nonetheless, advertisers "remained wedded to its principal strategy: the promise of magical self-transformation through the ritual of purchase."[23]

No product offered the promise of magical self-transformation more than a lottery ticket. With a jackpot, bettors could become just about anyone they wanted to be. States were happy to encourage players to fantasize about a life of wealth and to consider the lottery as their best chance of making that life a reality. In case a potential gambler was not prone to fantasizing or did not have a clear dream in mind, lottery ads offered examples—actor portrayals of regular lottery players imagining how they would spend their lottery riches. One 1985 campaign featured people sharing what they would do if they won: an elderly woman dreams of going on safari, a couple bicker about whether to move to the mountains or near the ocean, and a woman dreams of going on a shopping spree.[24] Audiences were meant to see themselves reflected by these actors, who, as stand-ins for the viewer, had dreams of trips or new homes or new goods. These people were trying to make those dreams a reality with a jackpot. Anyone who had similar dreams should do the same.

Ads like these played on the gap between how people lived and how they wanted to live. The lottery represented different things for different people, and ads wanted to make it clear that the examples offered in commercials were just that: examples from which players should craft their own ideas. "What does being a 'big winner' mean to people?" one advertising firm wrote in a marketing proposal for the Illinois Lottery, "Clearly, it's just not the money but what the money buys. Vacations. Clothes. Jewelry. A new car. Financial security."[25] Reflecting the 1980s culture of wealth, the commercials acknowledged that most Americans wanted to be rich and desired goods that were effectively unattainable. The goods themselves were in some way immaterial, as they embodied what players really wanted: a new life. Lottery marketing is exemplary of what Lears calls the "therapeutic ethos" of advertising, promoting a product not by focusing on the product itself but on the promise of a certain lifestyle the product would bring.[26] Any fantasy, lottery ads suggested, could be made a reality by taking a chance on a ticket. Lottery advertising helped solidify wealth as central to any definition of the good life.

The promise of a transformational windfall went hand in hand with the other major theme of lottery advertising: that everyone who bought a ticket could win. Players were safe to dream about winning, ads implied, because playing the lottery would almost inevitably lead to bountiful riches. One 1987 campaign, entitled "Millionaire," featured poster advertisements with a reflective surface framed by a top hat and tails, allowing pedestrians to stop in front of the ad and picture themselves as a jackpot winner (though the clothes were clearly designed for men). If it was not enough for gamblers to see themselves figuratively reflected by actors in commercials, the "Millionaire" poster let them see themselves literally reflected as a member of high society. The ad acted as a funhouse mirror, a window into a world where the lottery had made their dreams come true.[27] This ad and others painted the lottery as a simple transaction: buy a ticket, receive a fortune. Some ads made pointed critiques of hard work, suggesting that the lottery was an easier—and, ironically, more guaranteed—way of striking it rich than education or meritocratic achievement. A windfall stood as an inevitable reward for anyone who seized the chance. For players who had not won yet, it was their own fault for not buying enough tickets.

Of course, lottery administrators knew that only a handful of gamblers would actually ride their tickets into wealth. They understood that if marketing promised a jackpot, players would be disappointed when prizes proved far more elusive than advertised. As a result, around the early 1990s, the Illinois Lottery adopted a new, softer message. "We want to stress the fun, the joy of playing versus 'You're going to win,'" director Desiree Rogers explained in 1992. "We want to keep it light and not promise more than we can deliver."[28] For decades, state lottery commissions have successfully kept it light, incorporating surrealism or wackiness into their campaigns. This tone encourages a view of lotteries as a less than serious enterprise, a casual venture that is fun to play regardless of outcome. Per these ads, the lottery remains, above all, a game. And the silliness of the game's advertising conceals the serious money being paid into it by poorer and minority players.

Even as advertising shifted away from promising a jackpot, one long-standing theme remained. To paint the lottery as a democratic, random, and fair method of upward mobility, advertising celebrated jackpot winners. In the 1987 sample of commercials, 70 percent of ads that showed lottery players also showed at least one winner.[29] Lotteries focused so heavily on past winners because they offered living proof that regular people could win. The lottery worked, these ads said, offering as evidence examples of regular people whose lives had been changed. Winning the lottery was implied to be a common occurrence. Of course, the lack of any reference to the odds of winning helped obscure just how lucky these winners had gotten. Players were encouraged to reason that if it had happened to someone like them, then it could happen to them too.

Especially when it came to winners, lottery commissions were helped in their publicity campaigns by the media. More than any private company, lotteries can count on massive amounts of free exposure through news coverage. Because such a large proportion of the population plays the lottery and because it is a state agency, most lottery-related events are considered news-worthy, from the introduction of new games or a change in game structure to the winner of the latest seven-figure jackpot. In addition to drawings for lotto and numbers games, lottery coverage is a near daily staple for state and local media. In August 1985, for instance, stations across Illinois broadcast 26 radio or television stories about the lottery, many of which ran on the same stations the lottery paid to air its commercials.[30] More important, human-interest reports about winners echoed lottery advertising and contributed to players' confidence that they were destined for a windfall. After a local woman's lottery win captured headlines statewide in 1986, a Decatur newspaper explained the impact of these types of stories: "Such tales tend to rejuvenate interest in playing the lottery. People tell themselves that lightning can strike, that it can happen to them, an attitude fostered by lottery advertisements. Why bother to work? Play the lottery. Easy Street is just around the corner."[31] While commercials at times made lottery winners out to be comedic caricatures, organic news broadcasts captured the ordinary quality of lottery winners, and by extension the ordinariness of a lottery win.

No matter their subject matter, lottery advertisements were designed to implant the belief in the possibility—if not the inevitability—of hitting the jackpot. Advertising kept players in pursuit of ever-elusive prizes, causing them to overestimate the odds of winning while showing how great winning would be. Like many players, lottery officials knew how unlikely it was that gamblers would win. Yet they clearly felt that promising a prize was their best bet. A 1998 study of marketing materials from 22 states showed that the move away from guaranteeing a jackpot was short-lived both in Illinois and in other states. That year, 56 percent of ads emphasized the fun of playing and/or the size of the jackpot, while slightly less than half mentioned or featured lottery winners.[32] All of these ads were built around the message that while the odds were stacked against bettors, it was smart to play the lottery. The lottery was not a gamble but a path to a new life for anyone willing to bet a few dollars on their dream.

Lottery advertising was ubiquitous throughout Illinois in the 1980s and 1990s. In a 1987 survey, three-quarters of Illinois residents said they had seen a lottery ad in the last two months, half said they saw the ad in question more than once a week, and one-third said they saw it daily.[33] Though both sales and advertising expenditure generally grew year over year, it is difficult to draw a direct correlation between advertising and lottery revenue. For the Illinois Lottery, the biggest increases in ticket sales appeared to be the result of massive lotto jackpots or the introduction of new games, not specific marketing campaigns.

Many Illinois residents, however, worried about the effects of lottery advertising on the poor. One 1988 study of Illinois found that the lottery was "extremely regressive," that nonwhites spent a disproportionate share of their income on tickets, and that Chicago households, in particular, spent $5.50 more per week on the lottery than those in the rest of the state ($286 per year, $655 in 2021 dollars). For critics, advertising offered an especially egregious manifestation of the lottery's adverse effects on the poor, a vital agent in deepening the inequity of state-run gambling. "Lottery commercials," one Chicago comedian wrote in 1987, "are big electronic biscuits helping to sop up the meager resources of the nation's neediest families."[34]

As it had been for Josephine McCord, stopping the lottery came to be synonymous with limiting its advertising. Critics believed poor bettors would be particularly vulnerable to portrayals of instant wealth because their lives contrasted most sharply with those of lottery winners. Nora Zaring from Mattoon, Illinois, wrote to Governor Thompson that she was "concerned" about advertisements "which portray gambling as a good investment. These ads prey on those people who can least afford to waste their money.... Please don't exploit the lower class people to raise your funds."[35] Zaring assumed that "lower class people" did not understand the odds of winning and would be duped easily. She implied that if the lower-income Illinoisans were not subjected to aggressive advertising, they would not buy as many tickets. Since the days of Thomas Jefferson, lotteries had been championed as a form of voluntary taxation. However, according to critics, in the face of indoctrinating marketing, the poor had seemingly no choice other than to buy tickets.

Illinois Lottery officials denied that their ads were directed at any specific population and refuted the accusation that their games subsisted on the money of the poor. Michael Jones, a former advertising executive who became Illinois Lottery director in 1981, contended that advertising was not designed to increase how much people spent on gambling. Instead, it served to "broaden the base of players." Rather than entice lower-income or black gamblers or tempt anyone into betting more than they could afford, advertising served to attract new players or turn infrequent, occasional gamblers into regular bettors. Jones and his successors claimed that their ads were meant to appeal to all Illinois residents, that lottery tickets were simply a consumer good competing for the public's discretionary entertainment dollar. "Without relatively constant reminders as to the existence of Lottery products, revenues would rapidly shrink," one lottery administrator wrote in 1986, framing ads as "reminders" to play rather than enticements.[36] In fact, a 2005 study found no evidence that advertising was responsible for the disproportionate gambling among low-income people, as the group most impacted by advertising were middle-income lotto players.[37] But lottery officials relied on tenuous logic. They insisted that their marketing was vital to sustaining sales but also that it was effectively benign. It was crucial to convincing people to play but would not convince the poor to bet more than they could afford.

Anger over lottery advertising persisted. Critics were particularly frustrated that these promotional materials came at the behest of the state and that it was a government agency enticing people to gamble. In a 1995 hearing, Illinois US Senator Paul Simon invoked the common comparison of gambling and smoking to shed light on states' inconsistent approach to advertising: "If the state of Illinois had a billboard promoting the smoking of cigarettes to get revenue, we would be offended." Though the state profited from a cigarette tax, it would never advertise smoking because of the adverse health effects. Nonetheless, "the state of Illinois will have a billboard . . . in impoverished areas . . . that says 'this is your way out' and advertising the lottery," Simon declared. The "this is your way out" billboard in question—also cited occasionally as "this could be your ticket out"—was a common misquotation of the Easy Street ad that had drawn the ire of the St. Malachy congregation in

1986. Like cigarettes, Simon reasoned, an increase in lottery sales may be in Illinois's short-term financial interests but would be deleterious to the health and morality of the state. "That is not our way out. Our way out is education. Our way out is hard work. Those are the things that we ought to be stressing."[38] Simon drew a key distinction between the values fostered by lottery advertising—gambling and luck—and "our" values, an ostensibly American commitment to hard work and education. Lottery ads promising a new life would convince gamblers to abandon these values and the traditional economic ladder. Instead, bettors would buy all the lottery tickets they could afford and hold out hope for instant riches through gambling. No one should promote this message, Simon suggested, least of all state governments.

Though critics were genuinely concerned about the effects of the lottery, their class- and race-based view of lottery bettors served an ulterior rhetorical function. By condemning lotteries' inducements to the poor, critics distinguished themselves from gamblers, marking themselves as rational thinkers who could not be swayed by such simplistic promises. In 1987, one Chicago state senator noted that while low-income, uneducated people were vulnerable to lottery advertisement, "people with educations do not believe in miracles."[39] Faith in jackpots was strictly the preserve of the poor, he argued, ignoring the widespread popularity of lotto tickets among upper- and middle-class people during lottomania as well as the hopes for a financial miracle that inspired Illinois politicians and taxpayers to enact a lottery in the first place.

Criticism of lottery advertising also rested on the legal grounds that state-funded promotions were misleading. Lottery marketing frequently made two types of claims that could be considered deceptive or false. First, many ads promised a windfall of a certain amount. In fact, federal and state income taxes reduced how much winners actually took home, and most large jackpots would only be paid out over multiple decades through an annuity (lotteries did not begin offering winners the option of a single lump-sum prize payment until the early 1990s). Second, ads often misrepresented the probability of winning. In addition to using language that implied that every gambler had a good chance to win, in the rare event that ads actually mentioned any odds, these odds typically referred to the chances of winning any prize, including a free ticket. Ads almost never included the specific likelihood of winning a grand prize, therefore implying that players had much better odds than they actually did.

Lotteries are able to make misleading claims because of the lack of external oversight over their advertising. Especially when it comes to federal regulation, lotteries operate in a legal gray area. The Federal Trade Commission

(FTC) levels restrictions on promotional material for privately run lotteries, contests, and other sweepstakes, restrictions designed to limit precisely the type of deceptive assertions prevalent in state-lottery marketing. So too, while many lottery ads promised viewers that they would win, guarantees of instant, transformational wealth are banned from promotions for the financial services industry.[40] Nonetheless, because lottery advertisements are state run, they are exempt from these regulations. Most notably, state lotteries are not bound by FTC truth-in-advertising laws.

The FTC loophole has left state lotteries to self-regulate their advertising practices. In 1975, the National Association of State Lotteries (NASL)—a membership organization made up of state lottery commissions since renamed the National Association of State and Provincial Lotteries—adopted an advertising code of ethics in an effort to "insure [*sic*] truth in advertising." The original version of the code—which was updated in 1999 and remains in use—is a 500-word document replete with seemingly strict but ultimately vague and highly subjective language. The 1975 code prohibits "false, misleading, or otherwise deceptive" advertising, bans suggestions of "greed or avarice" as a reason to buy a ticket, and forbids any misrepresentation of players' odds of winning. Based on the ads that appeared in Illinois in the 1980s, this code was clearly not followed closely. More than likely, it was ignored completely. And yet, as one Maryland advertising executive admitted in 1984, the NASL code of ethics "contains the most comprehensive guidelines for advertising state lotteries."[41] With the exception of individual state laws, lottery advertising is overseen by administrators whose official duty is to maximize lottery sales.

On the surface, the lack of federal oversight of lottery advertising is in line with a broader late twentieth-century trend of deregulation. Beginning in the late 1970s and into the 1980s—around the time Congress spared lotteries from FCC restrictions—Washington rolled back regulations on a variety of business sectors, from airlines and oil to finance and utilities. Amid the rise of laissez-faire economics, deregulation was meant to unshackle the magic of the free market. Initially, the FTC provided a paradigmatic example of government's efforts to get out of business's way. After a highly activist period in the 1960s and 1970s, the agency was disempowered under the Reagan administration, particularly in the area of deceptive advertising, which Reagan's first chairman allegedly told staff to stop enforcing. However, the FTC returned to strength in the 1990s.[42] The renewal of the agency's focus on misleading marketing makes the continued lack of oversight on deceptive lottery marketing even more notable.

The FTC loophole and lottery industry self-regulation are also unique because of the sharp contrast with restrictions on the promotion of tobacco and
alcohol. Over the course of the twentieth century, alcohol producers and cigarette companies adopted advertising codes of their own to try to ward off federal intervention. Nonetheless, under pressure over public health concerns,
lawmakers considered additional advertising restrictions. In 1969, Congress
passed the Public Health Cigarette Smoking Act, placing warning labels on
cigarette packaging and banning all television and radio cigarette advertising.
Restrictions on alcohol advertising faced an even tougher fight. After failed
attempts in previous decades, in 1988, a bipartisan coalition finally enacted
legislation requiring warning labels on alcohol packaging. In the 1990s, multiple attempts to mandate the addition of warning messages about the effects
of alcohol stalled in Congress.[43]

Legislators pointed to numerous similarities between lotteries, cigarettes,
and alcohol, especially their shared addictive potential, their regressivity, and
their adverse health effects. Yet, in the 1990s, two attempts to close the FTC
lottery loophole failed in Congress. A 1996 bill, sponsored by Representative
Pete Geren (D-TX), would have subjected lotteries to FTC regulations and
required the odds of winning to appear in every advertisement. He noted that
if a medical company offered one-in-multimillion odds of curing baldness,
the FTC would not allow it to be promoted as a treatment. "If a State is going
to be in the numbers business and use the Nation's airwaves to market the
chance of living the life style of the rich and famous," Geren declared, "it has
the duty to tell those people their chances of winning that lifestyle."[44] More
than private companies, state governments had a responsibility to advertise
prudently. If states needed gambling to raise revenue, they did not need to
engage in advertising that debased government in the process. Geren's bill
gained little support on Capitol Hill. Tobacco and cigarette companies relied
on national advertising campaigns, so the regulation of these industries was
generally understood to be Congress's responsibility. Lotteries, on the other
hand, were confined within the borders of individual states and, more importantly, were run by state governments. Even as evidence of misleading advertising and regressivity mounted, since 1975, Congress has largely stayed out of
the lottery game.

———

With Washington reluctant to act, the only possible source of advertising
regulation was the same state governments that counted on a steady stream
of lottery revenue. Unsurprisingly, states generally declined to impose any

onerous constraints. In a few states, advertising restructions were included in the lottery's enacting legislation, stipulating that the lotteries must rely entirely on informational advertising. Missouri, for instance, forbade advertising "designed to induce persons to participate" and required every ad to include pay-out ratios.[45] Though the definition of what constituted an inducement was subject to interpretation, these states generally tended toward relatively cautious promotional tactics, avoiding promises of winning. However, when politicians' prudishness interfered with revenue, the desire for tax-free income took precedence. In a 1988 public referendum, Missouri voters removed the advertising restriction because it was hampering sales.

In states like Illinois that had enacted lotteries in the 1970s, lawmakers concerned about the effect of lotteries focused on restricting advertising. No state has ever repealed an operational lottery, so the best that could be hoped for was a check on advertising that might induce the public to play. In 1984, Republican state representative Sam Vinson proposed a ban on any ad suggesting that lottery tickets offered a better path to financial success than hard work, savings, investment, or technological innovation. It was one thing for the Illinois Lottery to promote itself as a way to get rich but another for its advertising to disparage the benefits of individual initiative. For Vinson, this message should never have the stamp of state legitimacy: "I believe that it is truly, truly a preposterous situation," he told the state House of Representatives, "when the State of Illinois, with public funds, denigrates the work ethic." Vinson's fellow legislators did not share his concern. His proposal was fairly limited in scope, and still three attempts were required for it to pass the Illinois House before failing in the state Senate. Other efforts gained even less traction. In 1987, inspired by the Easy Street protest, Democratic state representative Monique Davis proposed a bill to require the lottery to track its advertising and sales by zip code and to print the odds of winning on every ticket. The bill failed to make it out of committee. A 1990 bill similar to Vinson's also went nowhere.[46]

Advertising restrictions were nonstarters because economic conditions in Illinois and across the Rust Belt made states desperate for revenue. The recessions of the 1970s and early 1980s hit the nation's traditional industrial center especially hard and caused severe budgetary problems for state governments. In Illinois, the steel, automotive, and equipment manufacturing sectors laid off thousands of workers and an agricultural crisis struck downstate producers. Pointing to a $400 million shortfall in his proposed 1984 budget, Republican James Thompson lamented that for the first time in his seven years as governor, the moment had come for a major tax increase: "The same cruel recession which has been punishing so many of our citizens has taken its toll on the ability of your state government to maintain a standard of decency in the delivery of human services, of excellence in education, and a new standard of achievement in economic development." Though Illinois had relatively low expenditure and revenue compared to other states, old tax levels were no longer sufficient as the state's economy faced a tighter crunch. The legislature approved a temporary income tax increase in 1983, which eased some of these issues temporarily. However, the state entered a new period of fiscal peril in the 1990s.[47]

The economic troubles that pulverized the Rust Belt and the Farm Belt led to gambling fever across the region for lawmakers and bettors alike. Illinois experimented briefly with lottery video games to appeal to younger and more affluent customers, and the state legalized off-track horserace betting parlors in 1987.[48] Meanwhile, midwestern states that had not already enacted a lottery did so in rapid succession, including Missouri and Iowa (both with help from Scientific Games) in 1984 and 1985, respectively, and then Wisconsin, South Dakota, and Kansas in 1987, Minnesota in 1988, Indiana in 1989, and Nebraska in 1992. As they had in other parts of the country, lotteries helped legitimize gambling as a source of government revenue. While commercial casinos remained too disreputable, the Midwest soon became one of two national hubs of riverboat casinos—the other being Mississippi and Louisiana. The nation's first riverboat casinos set sail in Iowa in 1991 and Illinois opened its own later that same year after legislators approved this new form of gambling as a source of economic development for downstate areas. Missouri and Indiana sanctioned riverboats of their own in 1992 and 1993, and, amid the opening of Native American tribal casinos across the country, South Dakota permitted limited non-tribal casino betting in 1988. Detroit, with its crumbling tax base and economy, opened three new casinos in 1999.[49] In response to a troubled economy, midwestern states went all in on gambling.

Between lottery tickets, off-track betting, and riverboats, $3.7 billion was wagered in Illinois in 1994, nearly double the total from 1984. All this gambling yielded $717 million in revenue for the state, the majority of it from the lottery. Although it accounted for roughly 3.5 percent of general income, the Illinois Lottery represented the fourth-largest source of state revenue, after income, sales, and public utility taxes.[50] On the hunt for nontax revenue, legislators were in no mood for advertising regulations that might remove the pot of lottery gold from the end of the rainbow. In 1992, Democratic state representative John Matijevich proposed legislation that would have banned any ad promoting lottery tickets as a way out of financial trouble. Opposition was swift. "The State of Illinois needs revenue," Republican representative William Black responded to Matijevich. "This Bill limiting the advertising ability of the lottery will have a negative impact on our sales," which were apparently a higher priority than preventing desperate Illinoisans from forking over their last few dollars for a ticket. The state legislature had authorized a lottery, Black noted, and "the least we can do now is to maximize the profits," suggesting that the state had no choice but to take in as much money as possible. Without any new games to introduce, legislators like Black were especially hesitant to restrict advertising because states had few other ways to increase sales. As one advertising executive noted amid a slowdown in 1991, "Any time sales are flat, you have to look at advertising." Matijevich's proposal was defeated 93–10.[51]

Illinois lawmakers were reluctant to impede the flow of revenue even though they knew full well where lottery money came from. Studies and anecdotal evidence like the St. Malachy protest illustrated the regressivity of lotteries, and proposals to regulate advertising were rooted in the belief that the disproportionate spending on gambling in poor communities was due, at least in part, to the heavy-handed advertising targeting these neighborhoods. In fact, though most ad campaigns—including the Easy Street billboard— ran statewide, promotions were not distributed evenly across Illinois. The 1986 IEFC report, for instance, concluded that the lottery commission engaged in a "deliberate" practice of targeting African Americans, specifically through outdoor advertising. The commission acknowledged the practice, which it attributed to a miscommunication with its advertising firm.[52] While the deliberate targeting was apparently discontinued, advertising in Chicago remained high relative to its share of the state's population. Lottery officials claimed that the availability of transit advertising and the cost of advertising on sports broadcasts accounted for the extra expenditure, but community leaders like Thomas O'Gorman were not so sure. In 1992, 74 percent of all lottery billboards statewide were located in either Chicago or East St. Louis.[53] The concentration of lottery advertising—especially billboards—in lower-income and nonwhite communities paralleled contemporary tobacco and alcohol marketing practices. A 1989 investigation found that both alcohol and cigarette advertisements were more plentiful—and accounted for a much higher percentage of overall billboard advertising—in Detroit's African American urban areas compared to the surrounding suburbs. More recent studies from California, St. Louis, and Boston have identified a similar concentration of tobacco advertising in nonwhite and lower-income neighborhoods.[54]

For the Illinois Lottery, some types of ads were easier to target than others. The IEFC argued that the lottery's overall marketing strategy could not be egregious in its targeting because the majority of advertising expenditure went to television commercials. In Illinois between 1981 and 1986, on average 58 percent of the lottery's advertising budget went to television commercials, which, the IEFC concluded, were the worst ad format for targeting specific demographics. However, a Scientific Games report for the Illinois Lottery explained that the company's data analysis meant "even time-buying for the electronic 'mass' media can, in fact, be targeted to [specific] demographic groups."[55]

Though the Illinois Lottery faced public criticism and the threat of regulation for these tactics, the targeting of black and low-income gamblers suited the desires of black media executives eager for a cut of the lottery's marketing budget. Regardless of their audience or their medium, media companies cannot survive without revenue from advertisers. In 1987, Horace Livingston Jr., publisher of *The Voice*, a black Central Illinois newspaper, wrote to lottery director Rebecca Paul asking her to consider advertising in his paper. Livingston maintained that marketing in *The Voice* would "greatly enhance" ticket sales and would "show a fair share [*sic*] concern by returning revenues to communities on a fair and equal basis."[56] The publisher acknowledged that a large proportion of lottery sales came from the black community but that African Americans did not receive their proper share of gambling revenue. In return—and with a keen eye for self-interest—he proposed that the lottery take out ads in his paper. Seemingly unperturbed by the amount being gambled in his community, Livingston saw a lottery advertisement in a black newspaper not as targeting black readers but as a public service in support of a community institution. In 1991, the Illinois Lottery spent roughly $5,000 on advertisements in *The Voice*, and in 1993, a combined 63 percent of the lottery's Chicago newspaper advertising budget went to black or Latino outlets.[57] These marketing practices were similar to the heavy advertisement of cigarettes in black newspapers. Historian Keith Wailoo posits that newspapers' dependence on this advertising revenue stifled criticism of the tobacco industry in these outlets.[58] The steady stream of revenue to *The Voice* and other publications may have similarly prevented criticism of lotteries' practice of heavy-handed advertising in black and Latino communities.

In addition to advertising placement, the lottery carefully distributed lottery retailers to ensure their prevalence in communities with a high rate of gambling. In the 1970s, states sold tickets in a wide variety of retail businesses and nonprofit organizations. Gradually, lottery commissions shifted their

agent portfolio toward convenience, liquor, and grocery stores, partly in response to changes in the urban business environment. Of particular importance was the rapid proliferation of convenience stores. In 1959, there were
just 900 convenience stores across the entire United States. By 1977 there
were 27,000 and in 1990 there were 71,000.[59] A number of factors contributed
to the quick rise of quick shopping. Convenience stores aimed to beat out
grocery stores by opening earlier and closing later. As more women entered
the workforce, households compensated by making fewer grocery trips and
picking up goods at convenience stores, even if the prices were somewhat
higher. But, as historians Bryant Simon and Marcia Chatelain note, framing
decisions around food as a matter of individual choice obscures the financial pressures that drive gastronomic decision-making, especially for the
working class and for people of color.[60] The spread of convenience stores
coincided with the consolidation of the grocery store industry and the shut-
tering of small grocery stores in favor of superstores, which followed white
homeowners from urban areas into the suburbs. In Chicago, the number of
grocery stores declined from over 13,000 in 1954 to 3,600 by 1987.[61] One result of this trend was the emergence of entire communities, especially in rural
areas and nonwhite urban neighborhoods, where residents had little access
to healthy food, locales often referred to as "food deserts." Convenience and
liquor stores are more common in predominantly minority and lower-income
neighborhoods, and in the 1980s, they were an increasingly ubiquitous part
of the urban American landscape.[62] For many, the choice to patronize these
businesses was less a choice than a last resort born of financial and logistical
necessity.

The spread of convenience stores was especially significant because these
retailers shared a primary customer base with state lotteries. Convenience
store clientele consisted primarily of blue-collar men, many of whom were
drawn to the stores' prepared foods, their expanded operating hours, their
large number of locations, and their sale of alcohol and tobacco. Nationwide,
as many as 70 percent of 7-Eleven's customers in the late 1970s were men, and
the industry's gender imbalance was so pronounced that in the late 1980s,
chains engaged in a conscious effort to renovate their stores and add new
products in order to attract women patrons.[63] Similarly, while the imbalance
is not as severe, studies show that in the 1980s, as had been the case the previous decade, men were more likely than women to play the lottery, and, on
average, they gambled more. It should come as no surprise, then, that lottery tickets were a major convenience store item. By 1997, roughly 65 percent of convenience store customers nationwide purchased lottery tickets at

least occasionally, and 55 percent said the availability of lottery tickets was important to their choice of shopping destination. As recently as 2020, nearly 70 percent of total lottery sales nationwide were made at convenience stores (including convenience stores attached to gas stations).[64]

For their part, retailers were more than happy to add lottery tickets to their inventory. Stores receive a cut on each ticket sold, generally around 5 percent. While the margin on lottery tickets is lower than for most other products, and though periods of lottomania created havoc at overwhelmed ticket counters, lottery players typically purchased other goods when they bought their tickets. In some states, convenience store chains even helped lobby for the passage of lottery legislation. The profits explain why. In the mid-1990s, convenience stores in the nation's 37 lottery states sold $18 billion worth of lottery tickets. By contrast, tobacco sales at convenience stores across all 50 states totaled $17 billion.[65]

The spread of convenience stores was a major boon for state lottery commissions. Convenience stores had a built-in appeal to likely lottery players and were already located in gambling-heavy communities. As lottery agencies shifted their retailer base more firmly toward convenience and liquor stores, then, a result was the concentration of outlets in certain neighborhoods. In 1984, administrators from nine state lotteries were asked their preferences for type of lottery retailer. Liquor and convenience stores were the most preferred, followed by drug stores and newsstands.[66] State officials distributed licenses to sell tickets accordingly. Lotteries are careful in how they choose their agents, examining stores' foot traffic, annual and weekly sales, and distance from other retailers when considering retailer applications. States make these decisions with the aim of maximizing sales, without considering whether lottery agents are distributed in such a way as to disproportionately target certain communities, which is exactly what happened in Chicago. A 1981 study of numbers game terminals in Chicago found one terminal per 6,600 residents in predominantly black neighborhoods, one per 6,700 people in Latino areas, and one per 11,000 in predominantly white neighborhoods. More recent studies have not found severe concentrations of lottery outlets in lower-income or nonwhite neighborhoods. Initially, though, officials showed no hesitation in flooding certain—minority—communities with outlets to create a player base for the lottery and to inculcate gambling as a daily habit. As Leo McCord noted, "Tickets are as easy to buy as drugs on the corner or alcohol in the store."[67]

The popularity of lottery tickets among convenience store shoppers was not just a matter of demographic and geographic destiny. It was also the result of on-the-spot enticement. States made a conscious effort to help retailers maximize profits, and they periodically sent newsletters to retailers with advice on how to increase sales. Convenience stores featured various types of lottery promotions: signs on the door displaying the size of the current lotto jackpot or advertising that tickets were sold inside, tickets displayed prominently above or under the counter, and cards for filling out lotto or numbers game tickets conspicuously placed on a stand near the register. While gas stations, liquor stores, grocery stores, and other businesses also sold lottery tickets, one Ontario study found that convenience stores boast much more point-of-sale lottery marketing than other retailers, regardless of store location or socioeconomic makeup of customers. Many lottery players have a ticket-buying routine, but a Missouri Lottery administrator estimated that 80 percent of instant tickets were purchased spontaneously.[68] The goal of in-store promotions was to remind shoppers to grab a few lottery tickets along with their milk, beer, cigarettes, or newspaper, to take a chance on a jackpot as they picked up goods at their newly opened corner store.

The strategic placement of retailers and the use of targeted advertising were the result of the unique priorities of lotteries as a branch of government. State agencies have a range of tasks, from wildlife preservation to banking regulation, all generally devoted to some definition of the common good. "What is the purpose of government?" Chicago mayor Jane Byrne asked an audience in 1979: "The purpose of government is to serve the people."[69] While every arm of the state serves the people in a slightly different fashion, none serves it like lottery commissions, the only agency charged with raising money by selling a product to the public. In an era of opposition to bureaucracy and big government, officials were quick to maintain that lotteries were more like a private company than a state agency. To prepare for a mid-1970s meeting with the editors of the *Chicago Tribune*, for instance, the Illinois Lottery's public relations firm advised director Ralph Batch to emphasize that the "Lottery is a business, a living game . . . with a consumer product. . . . What other state agency is providing $1 million per week to the General Revenue Fund?"[70] Lotteries serve the people by inducing sales, regardless of any harm caused to those players tempted to put in more money than they can afford.

So the Illinois Lottery, like every other state lottery, continued to place tickets in convenience and liquor stores and strategically advertise in ways administrators knew would reach lower-income and minority players prone to gambling. While their actions were not part of a conspiratorial quest to extract revenue from nonwhite gamblers, as some scholars have claimed, neither were state legislators or lottery officials concerned that a disproportionate share of sales came from these communities.[71] Driven by an organic quest for sales, lotteries' unique charter as a state agency facilitated targeted appeals of black and lower-income gamblers to raise revenue for cash-strapped state governments.

⸺◆⸺

Not all lottery advertising relies on promises of an imminent windfall. The other major genre of advertising promotes lotteries as a source of government revenue, encouraging bettors to think of buying a lottery ticket as a civic good. These soft-sell appeals seek to boost lotteries' reputation while maintaining the fiction that gambling provides a vital, bountiful source of revenue for the state. Even as lottery commissions act like private businesses, they use their stature as a government agency to generate goodwill and encourage players to consider exactly where the money goes.

Between 1974 and 1985, Illinois Lottery advertising did not emphasize the benefits the lottery provided to the state because all profits fed into the state general fund. While lottery officials frequently boasted that they operated one of the largest sources of revenue for the general fund—and though the general fund was used to pay for a variety of popular public programs—the lottery could not gain much traction with claims that it benefited the state budget. Then, in 1985, though he had vetoed similar legislation twice in the past, Governor Thompson agreed to redirect the state's lottery funding to the Common School Fund, making Illinois one of three midwestern lotteries established in the 1970s that switched beneficiaries to education between 1981 and 1985.[72] Thompson was right to have been skeptical. Once the bill went into effect, one dollar of standard appropriation from the General Fund was removed for every lottery dollar that flowed into the Common School Fund. As had occurred in California and other states, the lottery supplanted, rather than supplemented, state spending on education.

Nonetheless, the fact that revenue ostensibly benefited Illinois schools offered a public relations bonanza for the lottery. The agency sought to make itself synonymous with education and utilized a new type of promotion to do so, marketing itself as a vital source of school funding. In one prominent campaign from 1989 to 1991, the lottery ran commercials featuring Chicago Bulls superstar Michael Jordan, who *Sports Illustrated* in 1991 called "unquestionably the most famous athlete on the planet and one of its most famous citizens of any kind." A commercial concept pitched by the Illinois Lottery's ad firm, Bozell & Jacobs, titled "School Is Cool," proposed that Jordan explain: "It happens every day. Every time we buy an Illinois Lottery ticket, some

of that money goes to our schools. And our kids' dreams come a little closer
to coming true," reminding players "Whether you win or not, they do."[73]
Playing the lottery was synonymous with investing in education. Lottery
players were not selfish, money-hungry bettors but astute altruists concerned
for the common good. By utilizing the inclusive "we," Bozell wanted Jordan
to mark himself as a lottery player, not just an advocate for education or an
NBA star but someone who bought tickets because he cared about Illinois
schoolchildren. For the lottery's disproportionately black and male player
base, the use of "we" by a black spokesman would be seen as a pitch to think
about the positive impact of their betting. Although in his private life Jordan
was a notorious gambler, his public reputation and the content of the commercial made no association between the lottery and gambling. Director
Desiree Rogers wrote to Jordan about aligning the Illinois Lottery with the
"wholesome, athletic, All-American image that you represent."[74] Much like
the players he sought to encourage on behalf of schoolchildren, his endorsement was not tied to selfishness or greed but was simply a philanthropic concern for the students of Illinois.

Commercials focused on the civic value of the lottery were designed to
steel gamblers against the inevitability that, time and again, they would come
away empty-handed. Even as they lost, the ads encouraged players to consider where their money went and to keep betting. In one commercial concept pitched by Bozell, a Jordan voiceover explains, "Each year the Illinois
Lottery helps to make alot [sic] of dreams come true. . . . Not of traveling the
world, having a big house or a new car. But those of being a doctor, a lawyer,
or a teacher." This ad admitted what many others sought to obscure: a lottery ticket was not a guarantee of an instant fortune and was far more likely
to leave a gambler poorer than richer. The lottery entailed risk, but only for
players, not for the state. These ads effectively told bettors that the house always wins, but did so in a reassuring way, as the profits went to schools, not
a private company. This type of ad created a permission structure for bettors.
While jackpot-based ads convinced gamblers to keep playing because a win
might lie in their future, these campaigns were designed to help players justify
their continued losses on the grounds that the money they spent on lottery
tickets went to good cause. As Jordan reminded Illinoisans in a proposed 1991
ad: "There are no losing tickets."[75]

The Illinois Lottery used education-focused ads in part because of the gap
between the revenue it brought in and what it had been expected to produce.
As in New Jersey in 1969, when Illinois passed a lottery in 1974, lawmakers
and voters expected immediate help paying for a wide variety of state services,

particularly education and highway repair. Ten years later, voters were uncertain if it had actually raised any money, and letters poured in to Thompson's office asking how the state was spending its lottery riches. "Enough taxes," one Metamora resident wrote. "What has become of all the money from the lottery that was supposed to be the answer to all our problems in education?"[76] Even before lottery funds were actually directed to education in 1986, Illinois voters expected legalized gambling to be a quick and painless answer to the state's financial issues.

Lottery officials were not as concerned about how to best help Illinois schools as they were with the possibility that Illinois residents might not buy tickets if they thought the state was squandering its lottery riches. Their school-focused ads with Jordan reinforced the idea that the lottery pumped money into the education budget. Lottery money may not be enough to offset taxes but the money was going to the right place. While advertisements trumpeted the millions raised by the lottery, they made no mention of this sum in relation to the state education budget. The Illinois Lottery recorded $1.6 billion in sales in the 1992 fiscal year, $610 million of which went to education, roughly 6 percent of overall state spending on elementary and secondary education. Soft-sell ads served to dispel the belief, expressed by one Lake Villa high school student, that while the state lottery "was started in order to help the financial system in the schools . . . so far none of these profits have been distributed to any of the schools." By advertising its contributions to education, the lottery sought to recapture some of the hopes for a windfall that had propelled its passage. These promotions assured voters that the lottery did help education, even if they could not see its effects. Nationwide, roughly 28 percent of lottery ads in the late 1990s focused on the civic good of this type of gambling.[77]

Lotteries did what they could to prolong the impression that they were a wellspring of tax-free state revenue. "The perception is that the lottery can solve education's problems," Lee Milner, assistant to the Illinois state superintendent of education, bemoaned. "It's a sore point for local educators that the lottery may have a giant billboard of a third-grade class saying that the lottery is helping to prepare our future." The lottery had every incentive to convince voters that it created a windfall for the state, regardless of the anger that might come against politicians when they needed to raise additional funding for education. For gamblers and for taxpayers, the lottery made an unlikely revenue windfall seem like a sure thing. But Milner wondered about the consequences: "Where you step over the line from providing information to distortion, I don't know."[78]

According to one recent estimate, Americans encounter hundreds or even thousands of advertisements every day.[79] While the promise of magical transformation—the notion that a product offers more than its functional value—sits in some form at the heart of nearly all advertising, lottery promotions are unique for inculcating a belief in the possibility of getting something for nothing. The fundamental goal of most lottery advertisements is to entice people to gamble, to foster belief in the possibility of hitting a jackpot.

A curious feature about lottery advertising is not its content—which has remained remarkably consistent for the last 300 years—but the fact that an arm of state government encourages faith in an unlikely windfall. Revenue-hungry politicians want lotteries to produce as much money as possible, and advertising represents one of the only available means of increasing sales. Though lottery officials maintained that their ads do not target any specific demographic, the message and, at times, the actual placement of marketing indicates a tactical focus on black and poor gamblers. Even if these ads ran against some of the values that politicians wanted to nurture, soft-sell ads could go only so far in convincing gamblers to part with their money for the benefit of education. With legislators eager for new revenue, lotteries needed to behave like businesses. Though jackpot-focused messaging led critics to propose state-level regulations, these threats proved futile. For voters and for politicians, the benefits of tax-free revenue outweighed the largely diffuse costs that lotteries inflicted at the grassroots. Even if lotteries generate only a fraction of a fraction of state revenue, legislators are hooked on the money they bring in. Like bettors themselves, lawmakers continue to play the gambling game, hoping for a jackpot.

In Illinois, the tension over the state lottery agency acting like a private business reached its logical conclusion with the privatization of the lottery. In the 1970s and 1980s, the rise of anti-government rhetoric led to calls for government to relinquish some of its duties to the private sector. Companies' profit-driven mindset, the theory went, would allow them to offer services more cheaply and efficiently, especially at the local level. The same budgetary pressures that compelled states to legalize gambling also accelerated momentum for privatization, which promised to generate short-term revenue as the state sold off its services and to produce long-term savings due to a reduction in the size of the government. Illinois—and the city of Chicago in particular—sat at the forefront of the nation's privatization movement.

Between 2004 and 2009, the city privatized a major toll road, four parking garages, and its entire parking meter system while also looking seriously into selling off Midway International Airport.[80] The turn to privatization was emblematic of a broader shift of government away from protecting economic security and toward enabling the marketplace to provide for the common good. Other areas of government were starting to behave more like businesses, as state lotteries had for decades.

As the first step in the privatization process, Illinois governor Rod Blagojevich commissioned Goldman Sachs to study the lottery's potential value in 2006. A privatized lottery was especially appealing because, as the head of Goldman's gaming division noted, a sweepstakes overseen by a private company could push the envelope in ways a state-run game could not. It could utilize even more specifically targeted advertising, for example, or find new ways to turn young people into dedicated lottery players. For decades, the Illinois Lottery had sought to maximize revenue but had at least somewhat moderated its advertising. A privately run game could be much less sensitive and thus much more profitable. However, a 2008 memo from the US Department of Justice put an end to dreams of outright privatization. Despite the George W. Bush administration's support for privatization, the Justice Department's Office of Legal Counsel maintained that states could contract with firms for the operation and management of the lottery but that states had to have "actual control" over lotteries' significant business decisions. Profits, too, had to flow directly to the state.[81]

In 2009, Illinois opted for a more modest lottery privatization plan, the first such agreement of the modern lottery era. Northstar Lottery Group assumed daily operation of the state's lottery, including management, advertising, and game development. The state would pay Northstar an annual fee (roughly $15 million) in addition to a percentage of sales. If anyone could make privatization work, it was Northstar, as the company represented a consortium of the two biggest lottery firms—GTECH (which owned 80 percent of the company) and Scientific Games (20 percent)—in partnership with Energy BBDO, a Chicago advertising firm. Northstar won the bid with promises of generating additional revenue: $4.8 billion in profits over five years, more than $1 billion above what the state projected it would make under its own management.[82]

Northstar quickly implemented a series of innovations designed to increase sales. Most notably, the company made Illinois the first state to allow the sale of lottery tickets over the internet. Yet Northstar failed to deliver on its promises. It missed revenue projections in each of its first three years, creating a total shortfall of $500 million. Northstar maintained it was held back by state regulations, but in 2014 Governor Pat Quinn terminated Northstar's contract, though the company fought the decision and the state did not name a replacement operator until 2017.[83] Around this time, New Jersey and Indiana experimented with privatized lotteries with similar results. Privatization initially appeared to be the latest frontier in states' quest for a lottery windfall. Once again, lawmakers were left sorely disappointed. They were not the only ones. Amid an Illinois budget crisis, in 2015 lottery officials announced they would not pay out prizes over $25,000 until further notice. Tickets continued to be sold as usual even as the state's budget problems— which stemmed in large part from continuing questions about education funding—trickled down to an arm of the state designed to fight those very issues. The general assembly eventually passed a bill allowing for a backlog of nearly 4,000 prizes to be paid out, but not before a drop of nearly $70 million in sales.[84]

The budget problems affecting lottery payments offer a stark reminder of the costs of lotteries in misleading politicians and voters into thinking of gambling as a windfall. No matter how much they advertise, lotteries cannot solve state budget problems. Any arrangement that would allow a lottery to serve as a source for a significant proportion of state revenue would require an intense regime of marketing and player targeting, one that would surely draw protest from players and legislators alike. Even under the current, largely unregulated system, advertising carries a significant cost to many gamblers lured to bet more than they can afford. Many of these advertising practices run counter to the stated mission of nearly every other branch of government. Nonetheless, in 2013, Northstar adopted a new slogan to entice Illinois gamblers to buy tickets. The simple phrase, paired with the Illinois Lottery's longtime logo of a pot of gold at the end of the rainbow, captured gamblers' faith in a jackpot as well as the role of the lottery in promoting a belief in luck, chance, and life-changing transformation: "Anything's possible."

6

Selling Hope

LOTTERY POLITICS IN THE SOUTH

ON OCTOBER 4, 1998, with 88 days remaining in his final term as governor of Georgia, Zell Miller delivered the keynote address at the convention of the North American Association of State and Provincial Lotteries. A devout Methodist from the Deep South might have seemed a curious choice to address a room full of gambling executives, but few of the attendees doubted the governor's credentials. Miller had been one of the nation's most adamant lottery advocates since 1989 and had been instrumental in the passage of a lottery in Georgia in 1992. In his address, Miller detailed Georgia's famous lottery-funded education programs, in particular a college scholarship that had been replicated by the White House, become the envy of other southern states, and even landed the governor on the cover of *Lotto World* magazine. He ended his remarks by noting the similarities between Georgia's students and the gamblers who funded their education. "For many of its players, the lottery represents the chance for their dreams to come true," he observed. "In Georgia that is true not only for the players, but also for our children. They are the real winners of the lottery."[1] Georgia gamblers bet on the long odds of a jackpot. However, the Georgians who would actually see returns from the lottery, its "real winners," were the children who counted on it to fund their education. Both bettors and students depended on the lottery for a better future. According to Miller, only the latter would see their dreams come to fruition.

The will to gamble that Zell Miller associated with lottery players paralleled the hopes that inspired voters in Georgia and across the South to enact state lotteries in the 1990s and early 2000s. In Georgia, taxpayers and politicians—including Zell Miller himself—approached legalized gambling as a panacea.

As in other states in previous decades, voters believed a lottery would have immediate, dramatic effects on state finances without new taxes. However, Miller updated the fiscal promise of legalized gambling. The governor tied lottery funding to scholarships for high-achieving students and to a pre-kindergarten program. Unlike New Jerseyans in the 1960s who believed a lottery would balance the state budget or Californians in the 1980s who hoped it would bolster the education system as a whole, in the 1990s Georgians expected the lottery to benefit their pocketbooks directly. Miller designed new, lottery-funded education programs to help students go to college and access early childhood education. By giving nearly every Georgia household with children a stake in the lottery, Miller ensured that bettors were not the only ones who would turn to the lottery with the hope of a jackpot.

The specific beneficiaries of Miller's lottery proposal proved particularly important in the political atmosphere of the 1990s. In the 1994 mid-term election, suburban, Sun Belt conservatism made waves in Washington when Georgia's Newt Gingrich led a Republican takeover of Congress, the first time the GOP had controlled both chambers since 1955. In Gingrich's "Contract with America," Republicans marked their commitment to family values, the free market, and a rejection of Great Society welfare politics. But opposition to welfare was not synonymous with opposition to government spending that benefited the white middle class. Most prominently, the new conservatism entailed extravagant spending on the military-industrial complex, spending that apparently did not contradict celebrations of a free market meritocracy.[2] Education offered a similar contradiction within suburban Sun Belt politics. Over and over, voters who claimed to be hostile to government solutions supported a growing government role in education, and they supported lotteries with the hope of creating new education revenue. Yet, unlike military spending, middle-class support for a lottery divided the Silent Majority from the state's religious community. White evangelical Georgia churches mobilized against the lottery and tried to defeat a measure that religious leaders deemed anti-biblical, inequitable, and idolatrous.

Suburban southern voters, though, put their finances over their faith. In Georgia, South Carolina, Louisiana, and elsewhere in the South, conservative voters broke from evangelical leaders. Three times Georgia voters faced a choice between legalizing gambling to fund new education programs and protecting family values by rejecting a lottery. All three times they voted for the lottery, opting to legalize a sinful activity provided they benefited from the revenue. The lottery, then, exposes a fault line in the seemingly harmonious marriage between the economic and religious values of Sun Belt conservatism.[3]

Miller's lottery-funded education programs were carefully designed to suit the political moment. In the 1990s, voters, especially in the South, were concerned about education, were comfortable with more government spending on education, but were wary of anything that looked like welfare. Georgia's lottery scholarship, named HOPE (Helping Outstanding Pupils Educationally), fit conservative suburban voters' ideas about the role of government as an agent of economic development. Instead of aiding the state's poorest citizens through a need-based program, the scholarship was based around merit, helping deserving students who needed a leg up. Similarly, pre-kindergarten would be universal rather than only for those in need. The design of these programs marked Miller's commitment to the new, conservative Democratic Party politics of the 1990s, which focused on color-blind appeals to "opportunity." Though not the first southern state to pass a lottery, Georgia provided a model for the enactment of lotteries throughout the region, and HOPE represented the first in a wave of state-funded merit scholarships enacted in the 1990s. As social scientists have illustrated, HOPE is utilized primarily by richer, white students, while it draws its funding from the lottery habit of poor, less-educated, and nonwhite gamblers.[4]

From jackpot recipients to the parents who benefited from subsidized tuition, the Georgia Lottery had many winners, perhaps none bigger than Zell Miller himself. Miller viewed the lottery as a singular issue that could shape his political future. After decades in Georgia politics, he staked two gubernatorial campaigns on the lottery. His gambling proposal allowed him to propose a grandiose education agenda that would not require a cent in new taxes. In the 1990 and 1994 gubernatorial races, Miller ensured that the lottery superseded every other major policy question, and he framed himself as the only candidate who supported the immediate, immense benefits it would provide. Even as a Republican wave swept over the South, the lottery represented a nonpartisan alternative to taxation that won the Democratic Miller—and Democratic governors in other southern states—support from both sides of the aisle. Voters equated Miller with the lottery. Hoping for an education windfall, they elected him twice. Miller's lottery campaigns reveal the origins of a lottery system that draws from the poor and benefits the rich, how desires for an educational windfall and one politician's electoral strategy brought doubly regressive lotteries to the South.

Located in the heart of the Bible Belt, Georgia represented an unlikely home for legalized gambling. Lotteries had been permitted in Georgia until the drafting of the state's 1868 constitution, and subsequent revisions to the constitution sustained the state's lottery ban. Beginning in 1977, the same year Georgia permitted nonprofit organizations to host bingo games, state representative John D. White made an annual habit of submitting a lottery bill to the state legislature. Only in 1982, however, did his proposal even make it to the floor, where it was soundly rejected. As White continued his futile effort to introduce gambling bills, lotteries made their first inroads in the South, as voters passed referendums allowing them in neighboring Florida in 1986, in Virginia in 1987, and in Kentucky in 1988.

As he completed his fourth term as lieutenant governor and prepared to run for the state's highest office, Zell Miller renewed the push for a Georgia lottery. A former history teacher, Miller had served as the mayor of his hometown of Young Harris, Georgia; as state senator; and as chief of staff to segregationist governor Lester Maddox. Miller proposed a constitutional amendment to revise the state's lottery prohibition in 1989, securing the necessary two-thirds vote in the state senate for a bill that would put the question before voters in 1990. Despite Miller's optimism, and despite lobbying from the lottery industry and state horseracing interests—which hoped a lottery would pave the way for parimutuel betting—the Georgia House of Representatives rejected the proposal in February 1989.[5]

The House setback ultimately helped Miller's cause. After serving 16 years as lieutenant governor, Miller entered a crowded 1990 Democratic gubernatorial primary. A familiar face in Georgia politics, Miller searched for a defining issue that could boost his campaign. The lottery was popular and, thanks to the House, its fate remained up in the air. Polls at the time registered support for the lottery ranging between 70 and 80 percent, with over 90 percent of Georgians in favor of letting the public vote on the issue.[6] Still, Miller was the only candidate to embrace the lottery wholeheartedly. Every other gubernatorial candidate—Democrat and Republican alike—came out either against the lottery or in favor of the public's right to vote on the issue without explicitly endorsing the lottery itself. For a politician who had been a part of Georgia politics for decades, the lottery made the lieutenant governor appear innovative rather than a stale product of the state's power structure. Miller framed the lottery as a democratic repudiation of Georgia's elected politicians, warning that the state's "old guard"—which apparently did not include himself—was opposed to legalized gambling. "The only way Georgia is going to get a lottery," Miller claimed, "is if Zell Miller is elected governor," betting his campaign on an unlikely but promising political proposal.[7]

After he adopted the lottery as his signature issue, Miller sought to convince voters that a lottery represented a painless and significant windfall for Georgia's schools. Miller had been a staunch education advocate as lieutenant governor, so his credentials as a champion for education were well established. At the time, the idea of tying a lottery to education funding was still fairly novel. Though Georgia-based Scientific Games had attached the lottery to school funding in California's 1984 initiative, most of the nation's first lotteries directed their revenue toward states' general funds or to a variety of beneficiaries. In 1989, 10 of 27 state lotteries raised money for education.

Miller's proposal to tie the lottery directly to education came at the right time. In the 1980s and 1990s, Georgians and other Americans were alarmed over the state of the nation's schools. In the aftermath of a damning Reagan administration report on academic underachievement, *A Nation at Risk* (1983), education became a focal political issue across the country. The report sparked widespread unease among legislators and helped launch the first of many waves of education reform that would sweep the nation over the following three decades. The report also staved off Republican calls to eliminate the Department of Education. For many voters, the solution to improving education was more government, not less. In 1994, 73 percent of Americans said they approved of additional spending on education, with just 5 percent opposed. Though the George H.W. Bush administration's major education initiative, *America 2000*, failed in Congress, the plan represented voters' broader concern about education policy and the fear that the nation would fall behind other countries in the new millennium.[8]

Southerners had particular reason to be concerned about education. In the mid-1980s, partly in response to *A Nation at Risk*, Secretary of Education Terrell Bell began issuing "wall charts," collections of state education statistics, to assess the progress states had made (or not made) since the publication of the 1983 report. Though lawmakers and educational groups objected to the charts—claiming the figures were misleading, unrepresentative, or blatantly false—the diagrams proved popular in the media, part of a growing emphasis on comparative state education data. Unfortunately for southerners, these comparisons invariably showed that, by almost any available metric, the region had the nation's worst educational systems, as decades of segregated schools and limited government investment hampered educational progress. On the 1987 wall chart, for example, 8 of the 10 states with the lowest expenditure per pupil were in the South. South Carolina, North Carolina, and Georgia registered the lowest average SAT scores in the nation while Mississippi and Louisiana had the lowest ACT scores.[9]

Like other southerners and like voters nationally, Georgians turned to government as the solution to their schooling woes. State spending on public schools in Georgia more than doubled during the 1980s and then increased another 47 percent between 1989 and 1995. The state had one of the highest increases in local school revenue over the course of the decade and restructured its education financing system in 1985.[10] Even this additional expenditure did not assuage public concern. In a 1990 survey of undecided Georgia Democratic primary voters, 47 percent stated that education was the most important issue in the gubernatorial election, more than any other issue (11 percent said the lottery was the biggest). Miller was well suited for this political environment, and he hoped to join a cohort of gubernatorial candidates who dubbed themselves "education governors" or "higher-education governors." In a 1990 letter to the president of DeKalb College, Miller wrote that his top priorities were "education, education, education."[11]

The lottery was central to Miller's education-focused campaign. Rather than dwell on the details of school reform, Miller made the lottery synonymous with education and vice versa. His campaign focused on maximizing the state's potential, closing the distance between "the Georgia that is" and "the Georgia that can be." Education represented the linchpin of Miller's plan to close that gap, and the lottery sat atop his education platform, the first of nine education proposals in his official campaign booklet. Miller detailed a host of new programs that the state could offer with lottery revenue, including an in-school anti-drug initiative, solutions for teacher shortages, after-school programs, leadership training for educators, summer enrichment programs, and voluntary pre-kindergarten.[12]

For Miller, the lottery represented a financial panacea that would fund a political panacea. He projected between $250 million and $400 million in annual profits for the state, using the highest possible estimates to exaggerate the lottery's potential. However, the amount of money was not as important as how the state could spend it. In a speech at a pre-school a few days before the election, the lieutenant governor declared that education, especially early intervention education, represented the "best solution to the drug problem, the best solution to prison overcrowding, the best solution to teen pregnancy, drop-outs, and welfare dependency."[13] Miller echoed education reformers nationwide by claiming that education was a cure-all for a range of social problems. Notably, in media representation and political discourse, the social issues Miller mentioned were all highly racialized and were associated particularly with African Americans, some specifically with black women.[14] The issues facing Georgia, Miller implied, were especially acute in the state's black community. And he had an answer. The lottery would address all of the problems that apparently threatened Georgia's future.

These ambitious projections were particularly important in the partisan environment of the early 1990s American South. Dating back to the nineteenth century, Democrats had dominated southern politics. With the flowering of the civil rights movement and the Lyndon Johnson administration's support for the Civil Rights and Voting Rights Acts, however, white voters increasingly flocked to the GOP and its racially coded allegiance to "states' rights" and "law and order." Southern support for Democratic presidential candidates never again approached the 80 percent approval garnered by Franklin Roosevelt in the 1930s, and, after 1964, no Democratic candidate received more than 50 percent of the southern vote with the exception of Georgia governor Jimmy Carter in 1976.[15] Democratic dominance endured a bit longer at the state level, though in the 1990s a well-organized GOP gained strength throughout the region. When Zell Miller assumed the governorship in 1991, Newt Gingrich was the lone Republican among Georgia's 10-member House delegation. By the time Miller left office in 1998, Georgia sent eight Republicans and just three Democrats to Washington (the state added a congressional seat in 1993).

Republicans made inroads in the South despite changes to the political makeup of the Democratic Party. Miller belonged to a new generation of Democrats, a conservative cohort that adopted the market-oriented, small government solutions of Reagan Republicans. This centrist Democratic ethos was embodied by Miller's friend and fellow southern governor Bill Clinton. Clinton took a leading role in the Democratic Leadership Council (DLC), an organization founded in 1985 on the belief that the Democratic Party needed to reorient itself away from Great Society liberalism to remain competitive in a nation that had taken a step to the right. The group was focused on winning back white middle-class voters who had abandoned the Democrats in the 1960s and 1970s. One way it promised to do so was to promote the use of state power to spur investment in education and economic development rather than to address social inequality. Because of its demographic makeup, the DLC was occasionally derided as the "Southern white boys' caucus," or "Democrats for the Leisure Class" according to Jesse Jackson, who finished second in the party's 1988 presidential primary.[16] Though the ranks of the DLC gradually gave way—Miller would become one of the most prominent

southern defections to the GOP in the early 2000s—the group dominated
national Democratic politics in the 1990s.

Despite the DLC's embrace of elements of moderate conservatism,
Democratic politicians in the South struggled to stave off a surging Republican
Party. In Georgia, Miller faced a GOP that, for the first time in decades, had
a chance of seizing the governorship. To win the 1990 election, he turned to
the lottery, a tactic that had already proven effective in Kentucky. There, with
the help of campaign adviser James Carville, businessman Wallace Wilkinson
surged from an early deficit in the Kentucky Democratic primary to win the
1987 gubernatorial election, largely on the basis of his support for a lottery.
Inspired by Wilkinson's victory, Miller hired Carville for his 1990 campaign,
hoping the lottery would prove equally effective in the Peach State.

The lottery became particularly important to Miller's gubernatorial campaign because it enabled him to propose new education initiatives without
the threat of tax increases. In a 2003 memoir, Miller wrote, "If I had any hope
of realizing my big dreams for education, I'd have to pull a rabbit out of a
hat," so he "turned to the lottery as the hat." Notwithstanding voters' concern about education, it would prove difficult amid a brewing state budget
crisis and the national political climate to suggest new programs that might
require new taxes. The lottery offered an alternative. As the "hat" in Miller's
magic trick, the lottery provided the cover out of which the rabbit (education funding) would appear, seemingly out of thin air. Carville explained that
Miller could talk about his extensive education platform "and he could do
so without talking about raising taxes because of the lottery."[17] Regardless of
how much money the lottery would raise or how much his proposals cost—
Miller was not always clear about the latter—the very presence of the lottery
on his platform allowed him to propose more state spending.

Voters wanted more government, particularly for education. They just did
not want to pay for it. "A lottery is neither a tax nor another big-spending liberal program," Miller insisted in 1989. "It is a tried and true means of raising
revenue without raising taxes, and to me that is not liberal or conservative—
it's just good sense."[18] Miller claimed the lottery was above the fray of partisan
politics. He assured voters that he had identified a distinctive source of revenue and that they could expect something for nothing.

—◆—

In addition to concerns about education, the other major inspiration for a lottery in Georgia was the apparent success of a lottery in neighboring Florida. In
1986, Florida became the twenty-third state to enact a lottery and the first in

the former Confederacy. Tickets went on sale in January 1988, shattering early projections with $1.6 billion in sales in the lottery's inaugural year. Though nearly every state saw significant second-year sales drop-offs, Florida's initial results bolstered Miller's assertion that a lottery could provide a windfall for Georgia. A Macon city counselor wrote in 1989, "Success in other states, particularly Florida, prove lotteries to be a viable revenue source at a time when alternative revenues are being sought."[19]

From a personal standpoint, Miller claimed that the Florida Lottery represented a crucial turning point in his support of a lottery. The lieutenant governor was a devout Methodist, and he fused his faith and his politics throughout his time in office. However, the Methodist Church took a strict approach to gambling. Its 1980 doctrinal handbook maintains, "Gambling is a menace to society . . . and destructive of good government." The church held that Methodist organizations and individuals should prevent the spread of gambling, including "public lotteries," which represented "undesirable and unnecessary . . . means of producing public revenue." Correspondingly, as lieutenant governor, Miller did not support a lottery. As opponents would later point out gleefully, he wrote in 1977 that he was "unalterably opposed" to the legalization of gambling. In 1988, he argued that a lottery would attract poor players "lured by the search for the lucky pot at the end of the rainbow," insinuating that Georgia should not enact a lottery because it would promote wishful thinking among the state's most vulnerable residents.[20]

Yet, in 1989, after witnessing the revenue raised in Florida, Miller began his own search for gold at the end of the rainbow, as he hoped a lottery could both win him the governor's race and solve Georgia's educational problems. Miller set his concerns about gambling aside. By contrast, he became such an evangelist for the lottery that his advocacy invoked religious undertones. Miller likened his conversion on the lottery to Paul's conversion on the road to Damascus from the book of Acts, equating his change of heart on legalized gambling to a religious experience and the acceptance of salvation.[21]

Miller shifted his beliefs about the lottery in large part because of the torrents of Georgians who traveled to Florida to buy lottery tickets. Georgians won a number of multimillion Florida Lottery jackpots in the late 1980s, and Miller estimated that Georgians spent $20 million on Florida tickets in 1988 alone. According to a Florida Lottery official, 9 of Florida's top 10 ticket retailers, and 23 of its top 25, were located near the Georgia border, and at least 50 percent of players at these locations came from Georgia. Historically, southern Georgia was one of the poorest parts of the state. In the 1990 census, 9 of the 11 Georgia counties along the Florida border had higher poverty rates than the state average.[22] The popularity of lottery tickets in these counties could have been an indication to Miller of how regressive a Georgia lottery would be. Instead, he chose to focus on the game's moneymaking potential, regardless of where the money came from. Miller argued that lottery tickets were already popular in Georgia and that gambling was unavoidable. Echoing proponents of the 1960s, he implied that a lottery would not increase the prevalence of lottery tickets. It would simply ensure that money already spent on gambling remained in Georgia.

To emphasize the revenue available for the Peach State, in July 1990 Miller made a campaign stop at a convenience store in Jennings, Florida, a small town directly over the Georgia border. Amid lottomania over a $27 million jackpot, Miller stated that voters were "sick and tired of spending Georgia dollars to educate Florida children."[23] The lieutenant governor suggested that the real reason gamblers bought tickets was to provide money for education and that the primary impact of the lottery was improvements to Florida schools. He also purchased a lottery ticket himself, legitimizing lottery gambling and illustrating how easy it was to provide money for the state. Miller's decision to buy a lottery ticket served an apt parallel to the gamble at the heart of his gubernatorial campaign. As lottery players hoped, despite the odds, that their gamble would secure a jackpot, so too Miller bet his campaign on his ability to convince voters that a lottery represented Georgia's financial savior. Florida seemed to offer proof that lotteries could successfully produce revenue in the South and that legalized gambling was the issue that could sweep Miller into the governor's mansion.

Other candidates' sober messages of fiscal responsibility could not compete with Miller's bountiful promises of lottery beneficence. Roy Barnes, a lottery opponent who came in third in the Democratic gubernatorial primary, recalled that he told voters that they have "some hard choices to make" to balance the state budget. But voters "don't want to hear that. We would rather win a million bucks from buying a dollar lottery ticket." The lottery offered a simple solution to the complex issues facing the state and its desire for education funding. The lottery was a "siren song," Barnes observed, and "it was a very effective song."[24]

Ultimately, Miller succeeded in turning the gubernatorial race into what he dubbed a "referendum on the lottery." After winning 41 percent of the vote in the first round of the primary, he faced Atlanta mayor Andrew Young in a runoff election. A former congressman and civil rights leader, Young was vying to become the state's first African American governor. While his popularity in Atlanta made him a contender, his work as an aide to Martin Luther

King Jr. in the 1960s "will make it so some whites would never consider voting for him," one Savannah farmer admitted. Miller did not harp on the race issue. He did not need to. As the *Atlanta Journal-Constitution* reported, talk about the lottery dominated the election cycle: "Lottery fever swept aside abortion, taxes and environmental protection to become virtually the only issue of the campaign."[25] Thanks to the lottery—and white voters' unwillingness to support a black candidate—Miller captured a resounding 62 percent of the vote in the primary runoff.

The lottery was once again the biggest issue in Miller's race against Republican Johnny Isakson, the seven-time state representative for eastern Cobb County. Like Young, Isakson had initially supported letting the public vote on the lottery question, but neither Young nor Isakson embraced it as wholeheartedly as Miller. In the final weeks before the election, Isakson tried to reverse his previously tepid position and seize the lottery for himself. However, the simplification of the race into a competition over the lottery suited Miller, as it remained his signature issue. One poll found Miller had a 2 to 1 advantage among lottery supporters, which at this point accounted for as much as 70 percent of the electorate. In a survey a few days before the election, the lottery was the biggest reason Georgians gave for backing the lieutenant governor. Twenty-five percent of Miller supporters said they would vote for him because of the lottery, more than said they would do so because he was a Democrat (15 percent) or because of his stand on education (13 percent).[26] As a result, Miller secured a close but decisive victory (53–45). One journalist concluded, "Zell Miller won the game of issues on a one-run single scored in the first inning. The lottery may not be such a great reason for electing a governor, but it's one more than his opponent gave, and . . . it was enough." Miller believed his lottery proposal offered a windfall for state education, and voters did too. "More than any one single thing," Miller told his biographer, "it elected me."[27]

For state lawmakers in Atlanta, Miller's victory provided definitive proof that Georgians wanted the chance to vote on a lottery. Miller pushed for a bill specifying the lottery's structure and its beneficiaries in the first months of his term in order to put a constitutional amendment on the ballot as quickly as possible. The bill passed both houses of the legislature, setting up a statewide referendum for voters to decide alongside the 1992 presidential election.

The 1992 campaign for the lottery championed it as a civic good that would raise crucial funding for education. Miller established a committee to promote the passage of the referendum, Georgians for Better Education (GBE), a group whose name, like Scientific Games' Californians for Better Education, implied concerned citizens rather than proponents of legalized gambling. The organization's title also obscured the fact that most of GBE's funding came from the Georgia Association of Convenience Stores and other retailers eager to profit from selling lottery tickets.[28] In his address announcing the formation of GBE, Miller remarked that the state needed to "take innovative approaches to educating our children," framing the lottery as a creative and forward-thinking policy. Lotteries had been common fundraising tools in the United States since the eighteenth century, so the "innovative" dimension of Miller's proposal was not the use of gambling to raise revenue but the possibility of raising money for education without taxes. A GBE fact sheet explained the particulars of Georgia's education problems, including "overcrowded, dilapidated" classrooms, "outdated" textbooks, and the thirty-eighth highest per-pupil expenditure in the nation.[29] The organization sought to dramatize the state's educational woes, to take advantage of a climate in which voters were already concerned about school quality and were desperate for a solution, especially one that did not require taxes.

Miller and GBE claimed that the future of the state was on the line in the lottery referendum. They envisioned disastrous consequences if the state rejected the proposal. "Unless bold steps are taken and substantial changes are made now," one GBE document argued, "our state will not be a contender in the next century." Like Bill Clinton, Miller envisioned a new millennium in which economic growth was tied to a well-educated workforce. In the face of deindustrialization—which in the South particularly affected rural areas and small towns—and the growth of white-collar employment, "there is one way we can give our teachers . . . and our kids and their parents the tools they need to prepare for the 21st century. That is to pass the constitutional amendment this fall authorizing a lottery for education." Referring to Miller's proposal to use a portion of lottery funds on pre-kindergarten programs, GBE concluded, "As goes the education of 1992's four-year-olds, so goes Georgia's prospects for future growth, prosperity and security."[30] The lottery represented seemingly the only way to improve education and for Georgia to embrace the rapid pace of technological and economic change sweeping the nation.

Georgians for Better Education relied on simple messaging. One poster, shaped like a lottery ticket, claimed the lottery represented "The Ticket to a Better Education" while bumper stickers dubbed the lottery "Georgia's Newest Cash Crop."[31] The "Cash Crop" designation harkened to the state's agricultural bounty to portray the lottery as a financial bonanza, suggesting that it would be a major moneymaker. Neither ad mentioned gambling explicitly, instead framing the lottery as a painless source of revenue for the state. In notes to prepare Miller for a 1992 press conference, aides reminded the governor to "pirouette back to our message: that this is about education, it's about our kids, it's about giving them the tools to compete in the new world economy . . . without increasing taxes."[32] The last thing the lottery was about was gambling. Instead, it was a simple tax-free revenue measure that Miller promised would catapult the state into the new millennium.

—•—

Miller and GBE's advocacy was crucial to the lottery's passage. The referendum sparked ferocious opposition, and anti-lottery activity in Georgia—and across the South—was stronger and more effective than the campaigns in other states. This was primarily because of the size and prominence of the region's evangelical community. The governor had been warned that churches would put up a tough political fight. According to Miller, James Carville estimated that the lottery "will poll 67–33, but that 33 percent will beat you to death" due to the intensity of their opposition.[33] Evangelical Christians in Georgia had been active in the 1990 gubernatorial campaign and had written angry letters to their elected officials when Miller first suggested a lottery. As the debate reignited during the 1992 referendum campaign, the state's conservative Protestant voters staged their last stand in the lottery wars.

The outpouring of evangelical opposition to the lottery represented part of a broader wave of religious political engagement in the 1980s and 1990s over issues including abortion, gay marriage, and school prayer.[34] While many of these fights took place at the national level, gambling remained a state-level issue. As a result, the campaign against the lottery in Georgia was organized by state- and local-level groups that mobilized voters at the grassroots.

Georgia's evangelical community went all in to fight state-run gambling. Across Georgia, anti-lottery activity was led by the heads of rural white Methodist and Baptist churches. Without the help of national organizations, ministers took it upon themselves to preach against gambling, broadcast anti-gambling messages on Christian radio stations, host voter registration drives on church property, and organize rallies, some of which attracted Georgians who had not been involved in politics previously.[35] An undecided voter from Mableton reported that his local United Methodist church told members that a vote for the lottery was the equivalent of selling one's soul to the devil and that some churches were considering boycotts against businesses that supported the passage of the referendum. As political scientists Michael

Nelson and John Lyman Mason observe, however, white evangelical leaders failed to engage the black clergy in their campaign, which ultimately enabled the passage of the referendum.[36]

Opponents leveled a variety of arguments against the lottery. They claimed that legalized gambling represented an immoral, regressive, and ineffective venture. While some opponents based their opposition on what they interpreted as biblical injunctions against gambling, the most common charge against the lottery relied on its social consequences. In particular, opponents highlighted the lottery's regressivity, which they claimed made it an unethical enterprise. Members of a Methodist church in Woodstock wrote that they opposed a lottery because of their Christian compassion for the poor. People "would spend their last dollar on a lottery ticket hoping to strike it rich, when that dollar should go for food for the family."[37] The lottery was ungodly and anti-family, not necessarily because gambling was inherently sinful but because of its harmful social impact. For his part, Miller vociferously denied that lotteries harmed anyone. But the Christian community was not convinced. J. Emmett Henderson, executive director of the Georgia Council on Moral and Civic Concerns, maintained, "Like the money changers in the temple, state lottery turns the state capitol, meant to be a house of justice, into a den of thieves."[38] Henderson likened Miller's money obsession to the contamination of holy spaces, utilizing a biblical metaphor to make a political case about the impropriety of the state's role as a gambling promoter.

Concerns about the poor were tied into Christians' fears that the proliferation of gambling would lead to a spread of immorality and ungodliness, especially the degradation of the value of hard work. "The lottery has been promoted as a cure-all for education," wrote an elementary school teacher from Tifton, but these projections ignored the belief that "children will suffer" because their parents spend too much on lottery tickets and because gambling "negates all that we teach our children."[39] Echoing a critique raised during nearly every lottery debate across the country, opponents charged that gambling would entice players to hope for the long odds of a jackpot instead of striving to get ahead through traditional meritocratic means. Just as Miller saw the lottery as a financial miracle—a "cure-all" for education—so too lottery players would try to bypass the traditional meritocracy through betting. Miller confirmed to opponents that the lottery bred wishful thinking. Gamblers, like the governor, would turn to the long odds to earn a quick buck.

Yet religious opponents exhibited their own wishful thinking when it came to the lottery amendment. A July poll highlighted the difficult fight facing the state's evangelical community: 68 percent of Georgians, including 85 percent of non-churchgoers and 45 percent of churchgoers, said they favored establishing a Georgia lottery.[40] As they ramped up their campaign with rallies, billboards, and sermons, Georgia evangelicals turned to prayer to defeat the lottery. Roy Smith of Jonesboro noted that as a Christian, he could not stand for the passage of a lottery, "I just want you to know that myself and a lot of others are praying about this," Smith wrote; "I know that the power of prayer has moved a lot bigger mountains." Requests of the heavens could stop the lottery when conventional politics could not, he suggested, as defeating a political referendum proved a small task compared to the immense potential power of prayer. Christians retained faith that divine intervention would overturn the referendum. "We are the people of miracles," Henderson told the crowd at an anti-lottery rally in Smyrna; "come Nov. 3, headlines all across the state will say, 'Church people have worked a miracle. Lottery has been defeated.'"[41] Christians worried that poor gamblers would ignore the long odds of winning and buy lottery tickets hoping for a miracle, and they criticized Miller for depicting the lottery as a miraculous new source of state revenue. However, they exhibited their own beliefs in the miraculous as they prayed for divine intervention to overcome the long odds in their fight against the lottery.

Georgia evangelicals did not think they were overdramatizing the significance of the lottery referendum by turning to the heavens for help. Rather than simply an immoral vice, gambling was so pernicious that it threatened to upend the religious order altogether. Margaret Scandrett of Warrenton wrote that a lottery "promotes an idolatrous belief in luck rather than faith in the sovereignty of God."[42] While Scandrett unwittingly pointed to the similarities between religion and gambling—both entailed ceding control to an invisible, abstract force—she argued that luck was "idolatrous" and therefore not a proper locus of belief. Because of the lottery's religious implications, the legalization of gambling signaled not merely the spread of an ungodly vice but a fundamental change in the state's divine standing. "NOTHING LESS THAN OUR WAY OF LIFE IS AT STAKE!" one north Georgia Methodist wrote.[43] His letter reflected the urgency felt by lottery supporters and opponents alike. Both Miller and evangelicals viewed the referendum in religious terms, and both believed that the enactment of a lottery would result in rapid, massive, and fundamental changes in their state. Whereas supporters imagined a land of high-quality, accessible education without taxes, opponents envisioned a measure that sacrificed divine protection in exchange for 30 pieces of silver for government revenue.

Opponents also utilized economic arguments to counter Miller's promise that the lottery represented a surefire path toward improved education. Ironically, the most popular economic argument focused on Florida, which had not seen any material improvement in education funding since the passage of its lottery. When Miller tried to use the Sunshine State as proof of the importance of lottery revenue, opponents, such as Benjamin Dille from Albany, retorted by asking the governor to "look south of the Georgia/Florida line." "Lottery backed education in that state is in a shambles thanks to the 'panacea' called lottery."[44] Opponents rebuked the hopes that had surrounded the Florida lottery proposal and sought to prevent the proliferation of similar projections in Georgia.

Dille was right that Florida offered a cautionary tale regarding the effects of lottery legalization. By 1992, Florida's lottery faced serious problems that threatened to tarnish Miller's projections of a windfall. Six years earlier, Floridians had passed their lottery referendum with the aim of helping education. "Don't Fail Our Kids," one bumper sticker read, entreating voters to approve the "Florida Education Lottery," the start of a southern trend of inserting the beneficiary directly into the name of the lottery agency.[45] However, a legislative loophole, previously exploited by officials in California, New York, and Illinois, prevented the state's education system from realizing any benefits whatsoever. For every dollar of lottery revenue added to the state's education fund, legislators removed one dollar from the state's standard education appropriation. As a result, the lottery supplanted, rather than supplemented, school spending. Even as sales exceeded $1 billion per year, general fund education expenditure per K-12 student slowed and, in 1991, actually began to decrease. Floridians who had hoped for major benefits to public schools quickly turned on the lottery. As one teachers' union official explained, voters believed that "a fraud and a scam have been perpetuated on the people of Florida."[46] Despite the passage of an amendment ostensibly designed to provide a jackpot for schools, Florida continued to rank near the bottom of the nation in education funding and quality.

Miller acknowledged the issues in Florida and insisted that Georgia could replicate the lottery bounty of its southern neighbor without duplicating the funding structure that had siphoned revenue away from schools. A fact sheet distributed by GBE highlighted the specific passages in Georgia's lottery bill that would prevent the supplanting scheme executed by the Florida legislature. Nonetheless, Georgians were understandably skeptical of Miller's claim that their state should emulate the Sunshine State. A Marietta eighth-grader wrote that initially she was "convinced that the lottery would be wonderful for education in Georgia" but had recently become concerned because she did not "want a repeat of Florida."[47]

GBE spent $100,000 in the final weeks of the campaign to convince voters that Georgia's lottery would not enact a similar arrangement.[48] Despite assurances that the state would handle its lottery windfall differently, Miller tried to have it both ways. As he castigated the mistakes made in Florida, he continued to promote its high sales figures, hoping that Georgians would focus on the funding raised by other states without focusing on how these states had mismanaged the revenue. The lottery, he insisted, could still be a panacea.

———————

The governor had one more rabbit to pull out of his hat to convince voters to support a lottery. To demonstrate that Georgia would avoid Florida's appropriation issue, Miller tied lottery funding to particular education initiatives. Rather than let revenue get lost in the legislative budget process, Miller proposed that the state use lottery income for three brand-new programs: a merit-based college scholarship, voluntary pre-kindergarten, and technological upgrades for Georgia's schools. Because the legislature passed the enabling legislation before the referendum, voters knew how lottery money would be spent before they voted on it. While the technology funding exemplified Miller's claim that the lottery would allow Georgia to embrace the new millennium, pro-lottery advocacy focused primarily on the scholarship and pre-kindergarten provisions. These programs were aimed at attracting distinct groups of Georgians to vote for the referendum, namely, white middle-class suburban parents and African American households, respectively.

Miller announced the HOPE (Helping Outstanding Pupils Educationally) Scholarship in September 1992. Although the governor took credit for what became the centerpiece of his gubernatorial legacy, the first concrete proposal for a lottery-funded, merit-based scholarship had originated three years earlier with Miller's chief of staff Steve Wrigley.[49] Borrowing elements from Wrigley's memos, Miller helped settle on the final terms of the scholarship in 1992, and he chose a name that not only evoked the hope it would provide to Georgia students but also rode the coattails of Bill Clinton's presidential campaign. In a film debuted at the 1992 Democratic National Convention— where Miller was the keynote speaker—Clinton was touted as "The Man from Hope," a reference to his birthplace of Hope, Arkansas, that embodied the message of hope and change the young, outsider candidate would bring to Washington.

More important than a distinctive title, the initial criteria for HOPE were purposefully simple and broad based so that, as Wrigley explained, even those who did not like the lottery could support its passage.[50] All Georgia high school students with family income under $66,000 and a GPA over 3.0 would be eligible to receive free tuition at a Georgia public college or university for their first year of study. If they maintained a 3.0 GPA as freshmen, the scholarship would extend to their sophomore year, but not further. A central goal of the scholarship was to keep Georgia's high school students in-state, so smaller grants were also available for students to enroll in Georgia's private universities, technical institutes, and GED programs.

To build support for the lottery, Miller framed HOPE as a silver bullet for Georgia's middle-class families. The median household income in Georgia in 1991 was $27,212, so most families fell under the $66,000 income cap, a figure chosen by Miller because it represented the combined income of two public school teachers with doctorates.[51] This decision reflected his image of a prototypical scholarship recipient: the child of middle-class parents, both of whom were educated and in the workforce. Miller framed the typical Georgia household not as economically prosperous but in need of state assistance. "Sadly," he noted, "too many of our families are realizing that their savings have left them too rich to qualify for most college aid, but too poor to actually pay the high cost of college," as their income could exclude them from eligibility for a federal Pell Grant. Tuition costs had, in fact, soared in recent years. In 1990, paying for public university tuition required 13 percent of household income for those in the fiftieth income percentile; private college tuition required nearly 36 percent. Though these percentages were nearly doubled for households in the twenty-fifth income percentile, Miller suggested that the Georgians deserving of aid were the middle tier of families, not the poor who, to his mind, could receive money elsewhere. Miller maintained that the "only way we can pay for the HOPE program is to pass . . . the amendment authorizing a lottery for education."[52] HOPE was important, the governor implied, though not so important that he would be willing to raise taxes to pay for it. Voters could have this new scholarship only by passing this referendum.

With HOPE, Miller distilled the benefits of the lottery in terms of what each individual family would receive. Rather than promise to balance the entire state budget or provide funding for the education system as a whole, the lottery would channel benefits directly into the pockets of Georgia families. This shift away from collective education policies paralleled Miller's embrace of charter schools, which also entailed a departure from a broad-based education system by providing parents the choice to opt out of traditional public schools. After Minnesota passed the nation's first charter school legislation in 1991, Georgia became one of six states—and the only one in the South—to pass a similar bill in 1993. By 1998, nearly 16,000 Georgia students were enrolled in charter schools.[53]

Charter schools and HOPE embodied the central tenets of Miller's vision for education policy. "When it comes to education," the governor noted in 1993, "I want opportunity to be the by-word for this administration." "Opportunity" was more than just a buzzword; it represented Miller's embrace of the conservative Democratic politics of 1990s. Al From, founder and CEO of the Democratic Leadership Council, insisted that Democrats needed to orient themselves around both "growth and fairness," claiming that in the 1960s and 1970s, the party had ignored growth in favor of fairness through its support for welfare programs and affirmative action. The DLC "gradually moved away from fairness to opportunity," From explained, "because fairness meant to people, 'We're going to take from you to give to somebody else.' Opportunity meant that everybody had a chance to get ahead." In coded language, "fairness" implied government assistance to poor and black families while "opportunity" offered a market-oriented, colorblind approach. The new Democrats viewed the economy as a relatively fair playing field and thought government should ensure every individual's chance to compete rather than address historical or present inequities. Clinton's famous "New Orleans Declaration" for the DLC emphasized that "the promise of America is equal opportunity, not equal outcomes."[54] To win back white middle-class voters, the DLC wanted to use government as a tool of economic development, not social justice.

For Clinton and Miller, education represented an important terrain to demonstrate this new approach. By claiming that HOPE would create "opportunity" for Georgia's students, Miller rhetorically incorporated the scholarship into this new Democratic ethos. The scholarship was not designed to aid poor or minority families, and it would not interfere with the nominally free and competitive market. Instead of ensuring that poor students had access to college—which, per Al From, might have been the goal of the 1960s, fairness-focused Democrats—Miller wanted a scholarship that was available to everyone and that subjected every student to the same standards. With HOPE, Miller assured middle-class families that the state would reward their children for their achievements. This assurance relied on a vision of education as a meritocracy and purposefully did not take into account factors such as school quality or familial need for tuition assistance. The lottery would benefit the state through rewards to particular students for individual achievement.

Miller was careful not to paint HOPE as a welfare program or a government handout. In the 1990s, this might have doomed the lottery's electoral chances. Alongside the lottery amendment on the ballot was the presidential ticket of Clinton and Al Gore, two southern Democrats who pledged to "end welfare as we know it." In cooperation with congressional Republicans, Clinton later fulfilled this pledge in 1996 with the Personal Responsibility and Work Opportunity Reconciliation Act, which shifted the federal welfare system toward payouts contingent on proof of employment. Miller took a similar approach. Throughout his governorship, he emphasized personal responsibility while cutting the duration of recipients' welfare eligibility in order to force them back to work.

In the lottery referendum campaign, the governor emphasized the scholarship's merit requirements to draw a careful distinction between HOPE and a government handout. As he would later explain, HOPE was based on a single premise: "You study and you work hard in school, and HOPE will be there to help you go to college. You give something, you get something."[55] HOPE could not be welfare, he implied, as its recipients were students who had worked hard and therefore deserved aid from the government. Thus, Miller fought off the popular accusation that the lottery would subvert the ethic of hard work. Because HOPE was based around merit rather than need, Miller argued that the lottery would promote hard work, as students would be motivated to study to earn a scholarship.

HOPE's emphasis on merit was expressed in a nickname for the scholarship, "the GI Bill for college students," so labeled by Stephen Portch, who became chancellor of Georgia's university system in 1994.[56] In this comparison, like educational aid for veterans through the GI Bill, HOPE represented an individualized government program that was contingent on a transaction. For example, after serving three years in the Marines in the Korean War, Zell Miller used GI Bill funding to receive his bachelor's and master's degrees from the University of Georgia. Just as the GI Bill provided university scholarships in recognition of military service, HOPE rewarded students' academic success in high school with free college tuition.

The GI Bill provided a more apt parallel to HOPE than Portch intended. The 1944 GI Bill avoided associations with the welfare state in large because of the race and class of its recipients. The scholarship component of the GI Bill was primarily utilized by those who would have gone to college regardless, namely, white middle-class men. Especially in southern states like Georgia, black veterans were often barred from exercising their benefits.[57] Nonwhite students were by no means explicitly prevented from accessing HOPE, but it was clearly designed with white suburbanites in mind. Like the GI Bill, HOPE ultimately fostered racial and economic inequality, an unsurprising feature of a scholarship constructed to convince middle-class parents to pass a lottery to subsidize their children's college tuition.

———✦———

The other pillar of Miller's lottery pledge was voluntary pre-kindergarten for four-year-olds. In contrast to the advocacy around HOPE, GBE and Miller's campaign made it clear that they intended the pre-kindergarten program to entice the state's poor and African American voters to support the lottery. Early childhood education had in fact been a priority for Miller since the beginning of his administration. Echoing a national focus on early schooling in the 1990s, Miller established pre-kindergarten for at-risk children in 20 communities in his first years in office. The governor vowed that a lottery would allow him to expand the program statewide and make Georgia the only state in the nation to offer free, universal pre-kindergarten.

As he had during the 1990 campaign, Miller made a series of appearances in schools to highlight the need for pre-kindergarten. "The only way we can expand pre-kindergarten across this state is to pass the lottery amendment," Miller told the assembled media at a federally funded pre-school in Decatur. He did admit that "the only other way I suppose would be an increase in taxes."[58] Following dramatic budget cuts early in his term and anger over the Bush administration's 1990 tax increase, Miller did not consider taxes a legitimate way to pay for pre-kindergarten. Rather, as with HOPE, he claimed that the state could offer this service only by passing a lottery. Georgians jumped at the promise of free pre-school. One Dunwoody voter wrote that "as a working mother, I understand the value in sending a child to prekindergarten instead of paying for another year of expensive day care. As a taxpayer, I find it intolerable that our public schools are next to last in the country. . . . We need the Georgia lottery."[59] For her, the lottery was synonymous with pre-kindergarten and vice versa. The propriety of state-run gambling was not part of her calculus or, if it was, it was secondary to the immediate benefit a pre-kindergarten would provide her family.

While Miller proposed making pre-kindergarten a statewide program, many of the children he posed with on his pre-school tour were black, such as a group of girls with whom he played "kitchen" before addressing the media in Decatur. Miller was not subtle about dangling free pre-kindergarten in front of black voters to lure them into casting a vote for the lottery. In 1992, Earlene Hicks of Macon wrote to the state's African American community via her local newspaper: "Black people, do you see what Gov. Zell Miller is trying to do to you? He's posing with 4-year-old black children . . . to try and con you into voting in favor of the lottery." Specifically, she chastised Miller for painting the lottery as the answer to black financial desperation. "He thinks that by playing up to black people, as if we were the only ones who needed financial help, we will jump at the chance to have a lottery in Georgia," cautioning black voters not to support the lottery out of the belief that it presented a cure-all for economic and social issues.[60] African Americans were not the only ones who needed state aid, and the aid they did need should not arrive in the form of a Trojan Horse lottery proposal.

Especially because its beneficiaries were presumed to be black and because of its resemblance to the Great Society's Head Start program, Miller's pre-kindergarten proposal, more so than HOPE, resembled a welfare program. To deflect from accusations that lottery funds would be given as a handout to poor African Americans, Miller presented early intervention education in financial terms. He claimed that pre-kindergarten was an "investment" by the state that would be repaid many times over in the coming years. In his 1990 campaign, Miller hailed early intervention as "the most cost-effective form of education," as it could prevent children from dropping out, winding up on welfare, or getting caught up in the criminal justice system: "It's a whole lot cheaper to teach a child when he's four than to incarcerate a man when he's 24."[61] Pre-kindergarten—and, by extension, a lottery—represented an apparent alternative to the nascent mass incarceration complex. Given the disproportionate concentration of African Americans in the state's penal system, by connecting the two issues, Miller made it clear that even though the program would be universal, he saw pre-kindergarten as a way of garnering support from the state's black population for the lottery referendum. Additionally, in an age characterized by what sociologist Randy Martin calls the "financialization" of daily life, the economic argument for pre-kindergarten proved especially useful.[62] Miller's rhetoric justified aid to the poor not because they deserved assistance or because they lived in areas where educational systems still bore the inequities of slavery and Jim Crow. Rather, providing help to the poor was important because pre-kindergarten would be cost-effective for the state over the long term.

By early November, however, it remained unclear if support for HOPE and pre-kindergarten would be enough to pass the lottery. Polls indicated that the popularity of the lottery had slipped, and it sat at 57 percent approval two weeks before the election.[63] On election night, Miller celebrated his friend Bill Clinton's election to the presidency, including a victory in

Georgia, where Clinton won by less than 1 percent of the vote, the smallest margin between the candidates of any state. News appeared grim on the lottery, however, as initial results indicated that it might be defeated. Ultimately, support in the state's urban areas secured a 100,000-vote margin of victory (52–47 percent). Of Georgia's 159 counties, only 53 voted in favor of the lottery, and only half of these counties approved it by a margin greater than 3 percent.[64] Fulton County, which includes most of Atlanta, boasted the second highest approval percentage statewide (65.7 percent), and the lottery won comfortable majorities in most of the state's affluent white suburban counties, including Clayton (58.7 percent), Cobb (54.5 percent), and Gwinnett (53.2 percent). All three of these counties had voted for Isakson over Miller in 1990, and Cobb and Gwinnett both went heavily for George H.W. Bush in the presidential election, indicating that the lottery picked up a significant number of suburban Republicans. Exit polls showed that African Americans supported the lottery by a 2–1 ratio and voters with incomes under $30,000 favored it as well. A slight majority of white voters and those with incomes over $50,000 rejected the measure, though opposition was concentrated among conservative Christians and those 60 and older, a demographic that may not have been enticed by the lure of college scholarships or free prekindergarten. Combined, Asian Americans, Latinos, and Native Americans constituted roughly 3 percent of Georgia's population but were not included in exit polling, so their degree of lottery support remains unclear.[65]

Nonetheless, Miller had successfully convinced a majority of voters that a lottery represented a bountiful source of revenue for them and for their state. After passage of the referendum, the governor sprang into action, appointing lottery commissioners who signed a contract with Norcross-based instant-ticket manufacturer Scientific Games. After three years of advocacy from one of the state's most important politicians, Georgia prepared to join the gambling nation.

When Georgia Lottery tickets went on sale on June 29, 1993, they were an immediate sensation. The state's 5,100 vendors sold 13 million instant tickets on the first day and 52 million the first week. On average, this amounted to $7.80 spent on lottery tickets per person in Georgia—including children—a figure that broke Florida's record for highest startup per capita sales in American lottery history. The Georgia Lottery introduced a daily numbers game in August and lotto in September, garnering total sales of $1.128 billion in its inaugural year, or $164 for every Georgia resident.[66] Not all of the money came from in-state, though. Just as Georgians had patronized the Florida Lottery, gamblers from South Carolina, Tennessee, and Alabama flooded over the state border for their chance to buy tickets.

After initial enthusiasm settled down, it became clear that just as evangelicals had feared, dreams of a quick jackpot were particularly popular among low-income Georgians. In a 1993 poll, 33 percent of those who bought a lottery ticket at least once a week made less than $25,000 per year. As in other states, education and race were also predictors of lottery play. Over 50 percent of weekly players had less than a college degree, and 67 percent of those surveyed with less than a college degree played the lottery at least once a week. By 2000, one study found African Americans three times more likely to bet at least $10 per week and someone without a high school diploma was four times more likely.[67] Gamblers without education were paying for tuition and pre-kindergarten for Georgia college students and four-year-olds.

Other than the occasional jackpot recipient, the biggest winners of the Georgia Lottery were its beneficiaries, particularly those who could not have pursued a college degree without HOPE. In its first year (1993–1994), HOPE sponsored scholarships for over 55,000 students. For some, the program made it possible to pursue higher education. After completing her first quarter at Albany Technical College, La Sonda Clyde noted, "When I found out about HOPE, I decided that I no longer had a reason not to go to school."[68] Miller frequently told Clyde's story during his final years as governor because it embodied the new opportunity created by the scholarship: HOPE provided opportunity to someone who would not have gone to college otherwise. The scholarship had added one more educated worker to the state's employment pool. HOPE proved to be Miller's crowning achievement. Even after he was appointed to Paul Coverdell's vacant US Senate seat in 2000, the former governor regularly received letters from students expressing their gratitude. One Waycross College student thanked him for the scholarship, which she dubbed "the greatest thing. I would have never gotten to go to college if it wasn't for [HOPE]."[69]

As he completed his first term as governor, Miller celebrated the results of the scholarship. "We are taking this state from among the bottom in some areas of education," Miller declared, "and putting—almost instantly— Georgia among the leaders."[70] Just as the lottery offered lucky gamblers an immediate windfall, students and the state were reaping immediate rewards for the enactment of the lottery. Because of initial ticket sales, Miller sought to expand the scholarship. Instead of providing more money to students who qualified under the $66,000 household income cap or adding a need-based component, he broadened the income eligibility. In 1994, Miller applied the scholarship to all four years of college and increased the income cap to $100,000, extending eligibility to 95 percent of state households. "I want to make this scholarship as universal as possible," Miller stated. "There will be nothing else like it in the United States."[71] The justification for the program lay in the fact that it provided opportunity to almost every student, even those who did not need the aid. In 1995, Miller removed the income ceiling altogether, allowing any Georgia high schooler, no matter how wealthy, to receive four years of free tuition at an in-state university provided they met the high school and college GPA requirements. "Now you don't have to be the next [Atlanta Hawks star] Dominique [Wilkins], Mozart, or Einstein to get a scholarship in Georgia," one HOPE brochure proudly proclaimed. Scholarships were no longer the preserve of the gifted or the poor. HOPE was an agent of opportunity for any Georgia student willing to work for it.[72]

Especially following these changes, HOPE redistributed the lottery losses of Georgia's low-income residents to middle- and upper-class families. While the scholarship provided some students with the opportunity to go to college, because it was based on merit rather than need, the majority of its recipients were high achieving students from the state's best public high schools or private institutions. College attendance in Georgia increased 7 percent thanks to HOPE, largely because the scholarship succeeded in its mission of incentivizing students to enroll in-state. At historically black Spelman College and private Emory University, every single in-state freshman was a HOPE Scholar by 1999. The director of the Georgia Student Finance Commission happily reported that "the brain drain from Georgia has slowed down to a drip."[73]

However, the scholarship widened the gap between black and white students as well as between rich and poor students. Approximately 80–85 percent of HOPE Scholars could have pursued higher education without the subsidy, meaning only one of roughly every five HOPE recipients needed the program in order to attend college.[74] Studies indicate that enrollment increased for both black and white students, though the black enrollment increase was concentrated primarily at less-competitive four-year institutions, and the black share of enrollment at the state's top public universities—the University of Georgia and Georgia Tech—generally declined after 1995.[75] Additionally, in order to qualify for HOPE, students with family incomes under $50,000 were required to fill out Free Application for Federal Student Aid (FAFSA) paperwork.[76] For recipients of external aid, such as Pell Grants, federal funding was applied to their tuition first, leaving HOPE to cover the remainder. The federal government subsidized the scholarships of the state's poorest residents, and HOPE went to those too rich to qualify for other aid.

Miller showed no interest in expanding need-based education scholarships. After enacting HOPE, Georgia absolved itself of providing assistance specifically designed to help poor students on the grounds that they qualified for the scholarship. HOPE catapulted the state from twenty-first to seventh in the nation in proportion of students who received state aid, and, by 2003, Georgia led the nation in aid per undergraduate student. Yet the state was third-to-last in the nation in need-based assistance. Only one-third of 1 percent of all financial aid in Georgia was distributed solely based on need rather than merit or a combination of need and merit.[77] Such were the politics of providing equal of opportunity instead of equal outcomes.

Parents of HOPE recipients, especially the 80 percent whose children could have gone to college without the scholarship, largely accepted the reality that the state's poorest residents were underwriting their children's tuition. Many middle-class parents felt that HOPE provided them with a long overdue government windfall. David Moulton from Evans planned to attend Augusta College on a HOPE Scholarship, a program that, his mother Candy raved, "gives the good old middle class a break for once."[78] Candy Moulton framed HOPE as middle-class restitution, acknowledging the regressivity of the lottery but suggesting that neither poor nor wealthy Georgians paid taxes and that state services did not aid the middle class. She drew a distinction between middle-class families—implicitly hardworking and taxpaying—and welfare recipients—implicitly lazy and living off the tax dollars of the middle class. She painted a picture of all government benefits flowing exclusively to poor and black people, in the process ignoring the often-obfuscated state subsidies for the middle-class, from tax credits and airport appropriations to mortgage deductions and military industrial complex funding. For Moulton, the lottery would turn the tables: while the middle class aided the poor through taxes, the poor could return some of that money by buying the lottery tickets that funded HOPE.

Georgia's middle-class families celebrated HOPE even though it quickly became clear that some recipients did not need the money. The popularity of the scholarship among Georgia's wealthiest families led to the infamous phenomenon of the "HOPE Mobile." If their child received good grades in high school and chose to attend an in-state college, some parents bought them a car with the funds set aside for tuition. One study found the practice so common that HOPE was directly responsible for an increase in car sales in the richest 25 percent of Georgia counties in 1994 and 1995.[79] In a letter to

Miller's successor, one Athens resident fumed: "I have a problem with Hope scholarship [*sic*] paying for wealthy kids to go to school free.... It is disgusting seeing rich kids drive around Athens in their $35,000 SUV's that their parents can afford since college is free."[80] The HOPE Mobile, then, paralleled the popular image of a "welfare Cadillac," a symbolic stand-in for welfare cheaters living luxuriously on undeserved government benefits. While the Cadillac was associated with African American welfare recipients, anger against the HOPE Mobile was directed less at the individuals who received government funding and more at the design of a lottery revenue system that benefited the wrong people. Because HOPE recipients were predominantly white and wealthy, frustration with their ill-deserved government benefits was not inflected with racial animus. The HOPE Mobile inspired anger because most of the lottery's inequity was hidden, taking the form of scholarships to the state's middle- and upper-class students. An SUV rolling through the campus in Athens offered a unique, visible, and egregious example of the regressivity of state lottery spending.

The second pillar of Miller's lottery programs, pre-kindergarten, offered benefits to parents across the state, but it was not the particular boon for African American families that the governor had implied in 1992. The program succeeded in expanding early education access, as the percentage of Georgia students enrolled in pre-kindergarten increased rapidly, from around 8 percent to over 50 percent. Nonwhite families and single mothers were slightly more likely to use the program, and while the largest effects of the program were in rural areas, the popularity of pre-kindergarten bore no major correlation to race, income, or education at the county level. Like the scholarship, pre-kindergarten was designed to be universal, benefiting any family in Georgia that wanted to take advantage of it. The program served a wide swath of Georgia families and children, though it did little to close pre-existing class or racial gaps in early education access.[81]

Other uses of lottery revenue were more obviously regressive. Most of the lottery technology grants funded school computer labs for elementary schools and satellite dishes for schools, colleges, and technical institutes.[82] However, some of these grants further deepened class and racial inequality in Georgia by helping fund Miller's escalation of the war on crime. Borrowing from two decades of Republican rhetoric about "law and order," Miller, Clinton, and other DLC lawmakers instituted a series of tough-on-crime laws in the 1990s. Miller dubbed crime "the number one problem in this country" and "the number one problem in this state" in 1994. That year, Georgia enacted a "two strikes" law, mandating life imprisonment for two violations of a series of violent crimes. Lottery funds paid for other escalations of the war on crime in Georgia—for example, video cameras in Cobb County schools, state-wide "Safe Schools, Safe Streets" programming, and metal detectors for 70 schools.[83] These funds helped create what scholars have designated a school-to-prison pipeline, a system that integrates law enforcement into schools and funnels students from classrooms into the penal system. Like other forms of policing, this pipeline disproportionately targeted African Americans, a population that bought a large share of lottery tickets, accounted for a large percentage of those caught up in the state's prison system, and constituted a disproportionately small share of HOPE Scholars. Despite Miller's frequent appeals to opportunity, lottery funding helped take away opportunity from the black students whose parents were the biggest lottery players. In 1998, Georgia voters approved a referendum that limited lottery revenue to funding HOPE and pre-kindergarten, removing technology funding as a beneficiary.

Overall, while the lottery appealed disproportionately to the poor, none of its education programs were specifically aimed at giving lower-income Georgians or nonwhite households a leg up. Though Miller couched the scholarship and pre-kindergarten programs in universality, in practice, HOPE especially benefited the white suburban middle class, while pre-kindergarten benefited those who needed it and those who did not. Meanwhile, many students reaped the benefits of school technology grants, but the program also exacerbated the criminal justice issues roiling the black community. All of this was exactly how the lottery had been designed. For better or worse, it reshaped the education landscape in Georgia.

As his education programs came into effect, Miller championed the lottery—and HOPE in particular—as a crucial source of financial assistance for the state's beleaguered middle class. While the governor did not celebrate the lottery's regressivity, neither was he apologetic that his signature program primarily benefited students already on track to attend college. Instead, Miller continued to emphasize that the scholarship provided "opportunity." Speaking in White County in 1994, Miller explained that due to rising tuition costs, in other states "a college degree is out of reach for the families of many middle-class students. But not in Georgia. If a student is willing to work hard in school, we are willing to help them further their education."[84] The governor reiterated that the role of government was not to enforce equality. As long as every student had the opportunity to access education—regardless of whether they received the same resources to develop those opportunities—then the onus of success lay with the individual student. By claiming HOPE was about teaching students the value of hard work, Miller justified the fact that even the state's richest students could receive the scholarship. All students deserved the chance to be rewarded for their efforts.

Miller's speech about HOPE in White County was one of his many appearances around the state in 1993 and 1994 to celebrate the benefits the lottery brought to Georgia. Gradually, these events set the stage for the governor's 1994 reelection campaign. Miller decided to run again even though he had promised in 1990 that he would only serve a single term and despite the fact that he had lost political points in a failed attempt to remove the Confederate Stars and Bars from the state flag ahead of the 1996 Atlanta Olympics. As he had four years earlier, Miller placed the lottery at the center of his campaign. In the 1994 election, he attempted to take full credit for the passage of the lottery and for its dramatic impact on Georgia education. In his speeches, Miller announced the implementation of school technology funding—the first lottery revenue spent by the state—and, when speaking at colleges or universities, he highlighted the number of HOPE Scholars on each campus. Some of Miller's campaign promotions were indistinguishable from lottery advertisements. A draft of a newspaper ad listed every HOPE Scholar in the local county, declaring that the students were "The _REAL_ Winners of the Georgia Lottery." The "Zell Miller for Governor" logo appeared directly under the list of names, reminding voters precisely who was responsible for the new scholarship program.[85]

Georgia Republicans were upset that Miller was able to draw on a deep well of lottery goodwill to connect with voters. They knew they could not compete with the fact that HOPE was Miller's signature program and that it was providing Georgians with millions of dollars in education subsidies. One Republican state representative grumbled, "This lottery money is being doled out like Christmas money to buy votes." Another Republican legislator used a similar metaphor, informing voters, "Yes, Georgia, there is a Santa Claus and he's running for governor."[86] Though meant to disparage Miller, the Santa Claus comparison proved appropriate. If the promise of lottery-funded education programs had been a rabbit-in-a-hat trick in 1990, four years later, HOPE, pre-kindergarten, and school computers resembled toys on Christmas morning, presents bestowed by Miller that appeared seemingly out of nowhere, without any additional costs for taxpayers. Though Republicans aimed their derision at Miller, the comparison implicitly criticized Georgia voters, as the legislators equated them with children hoping for a Christmas miracle. The early success of HOPE presented tangible evidence of Miller's

Santa Claus–like powers. The governor embraced the role of gift-giver, and he hoped Georgians would repay him on election day.

Voters did, in fact, give Miller credit for the lottery and the education programs it funded. The mother of a University of Georgia HOPE Scholar remarked that she was not sure if she had voted for Miller in 1990 but said she would "definitely vote for him" in 1994 because the "HOPE [S]cholarship is helping out my son and it's helping a lot of other kids go to school." Miller bet that the families who had benefited from the lottery would associate these benefits with him personally. "All voters with children or grandchildren under the age of 18 should be out campaigning for Miller," the Rome, Georgia, *News-Tribune* concluded, explaining that citizens could express their gratitude for the new education programs by reelecting the governor.[87] In a survey of Democratic voters, most respondents associated Miller with the lottery and praised him for following through on his promise but hoped his campaign would shift gears. One respondent noted of the lottery, "He has already got that passed, he needs more to run on." The surveyors concluded, "In 1990 Zell Miller was able to fashion a win from a hot issue.... It seems, presently, unlikely that any single issue will emerge as the single key to the electoral lock in '94."[88]

Miller had other plans. The governor turned his 1994 reelection campaign into yet another referendum on the lottery, claiming that the new educational initiatives were under threat. By doing so, he framed his campaign not as a reversal of his pledge not to run again but as an altruistic act of political service to protect the programs he had fought for in 1990 and 1992. Miller's opponent, Republican Guy Millner, had voted against the lottery referendum and, like other Georgia Republicans, supported a statewide referendum on the lottery every four years. Miller claimed Millner wanted to replicate the supplement/supplant Florida scheme, thereby draining money from HOPE and pre-kindergarten. "The reason I'm running for reelection," Miller told a crowd at Georgia Southwestern College in late September, "is to protect HOPE and the other lottery programs from being sabotaged by those who want to put the lottery funds into the general treasury to be used for other things."[89] Georgians were still concerned about education. Though HOPE had not improved the state's education ranking as instantly as Miller had promised, it did provide benefits to individual families, and the governor warned that the scholarship would disappear if Millner won. One Roswell voter wrote that HOPE "has been touted as a panacea for students," summarizing Miller's reelection message as "No Zell, No HOPE."[90]

Miller's accusations against Millner proved sufficient to derail the Republican's campaign. Millner insisted that he wanted to improve HOPE rather than discard it, but Miller successfully removed any nuance from Millner's position, painting him as a lottery opponent. At an October debate, Miller stated, "No where [*sic*] is there a greater difference of opinion on any issue than between Guy Millner and Zell Miller than on [*sic*] the lottery issue."[91] While the candidates bickered over crime, welfare, the state flag, and other topics, questions about education continued to center on the lottery. Millner insisted to no avail that he supported HOPE. On election day, Miller defied the Republican Revolution that swept the nation. Led by Cobb County's Newt Gingrich, 10 previously Democratic governorships around the country and three of Georgia's congressional seats flipped to the GOP. Meanwhile, Miller once again rode the lottery to a narrow victory.[92]

HOPE proved so innovative that it drew national attention and spawned a wave of imitators. On June 4, 1996, President Bill Clinton delivered the commencement address at Princeton University and, with Miller seated on the dais, announced the formation of "America's Hope Scholarship," a tuition tax credit for high-achieving students aimed at making the first two years of college as universal as high school. As Miller's invitation to Princeton indicates, Hope purposefully built on the success of HOPE, and Miller joked at a press conference that "since I borrowed the President's name of his birthplace [*sic*] for my program . . . now he is [able] to take it back."[93] Clinton mirrored Miller's HOPE messaging, framing Hope as a crucial measure to allow the nation's students to access the education that would let them step into the internet age. By providing tax credits to students paying college tuition, the Hope Scholarship represented one of DLC Democrats' main efforts to embrace the rhetoric of opportunity, colorblind meritocracy, and the use of government to aid economic development. Mired in his own reelection campaign, Clinton also used Hope to seize the mantle as a proponent of education and to do so by providing assistance to middle-class families through the tax code rather than through a new, expensive government program.

Clinton was not the only politician eager to replicate Georgia's HOPE and Miller's electoral formula. In the late 1990s and early 2000s, Democratic gubernatorial candidates across the South borrowed from the Miller playbook and staked their election chances on lottery proposals. In the 1998 midterms, Alabama's Don Siegelman and South Carolina's Jim Hodges were the only two Democrats to unseat incumbent Republican governors, and both did so by placing the lottery at the center of their campaigns. The lottery allowed Siegelman to frame himself as a stalwart education advocate; incumbent Fob James could not compete with the promises of new, tax-free revenue for the state's children. In South Carolina, incumbent David Beasley had initially

appeared unbeatable, but Hodges exploited the lottery issue to secure an unlikely victory. One notorious Hodges commercial depicted "Bubba," a convenience store owner wearing a University of Georgia T-shirt, who noted that
Georgians "appreciated" South Carolinians buying over $100 million worth
of lottery tickets to benefit Georgia education. "Here in Georgia," Bubba
concludes with a sly smile, "we loooooove David Beasley." Hodges argued, as
Miller had before him, that with a lottery, voters could stem the tide of money
flowing out of state. The only impediment to a windfall for education, Bubba
implied, was the obstinacy of South Carolina's Republican governor.[94]

As Siegelman and Hodges depended on the electoral benefits of lotteries
in Alabama and South Carolina, Miller's education programs provided a
model for lottery revenue distribution throughout the South. In his campaign, Siegelman proposed utilizing lottery funds for a merit-based college
scholarship, pre-kindergarten, and school technology funding, explicitly

FIG 6.1 After the passage of the lottery in Georgia, Alabama held a lottery referendum
in October 1999. As in other southern states, evangelical Christians in Alabama opposed
the referendum. However, in Alabama—unlike in Georgia—white evangelicals brought
black church leaders into the anti-gambling campaign. The day before the referendum,
Bishop Richard Thompson of the central district of the AME Zion Church (above, *front
right*) held a press conference at the Alabama State House urging voters to oppose the lottery. The referendum was defeated 46–54. AP Photo/Dave Martin.

mimicking the three components of Miller's lottery proposal, and Miller even administered Siegelman's oath of office at his inauguration. An advertisement supporting Alabama's subsequent lottery referendum explained that the measure offered a "once in a lifetime chance to change education in Alabama forever," similar to the promises that had passed the lottery in Georgia in 1992.[95] Yet, following a vigorous campaign by conservative Christians, Alabama voters defeated the lottery, only the third time voters had rejected a lottery proposal nationwide since 1979.[96] For their part, South Carolina (2001), Tennessee (2003), and Arkansas (2008, after a 2000 initiative was defeated) all enacted lotteries and promptly utilized the revenue to fund an in-state merit scholarship program, which, in Tennessee, was even named "HOPE." Florida, which had been a model of the mismanagement of lottery funds, also copied Georgia's education initiatives, adding a "Bright Futures Scholarship" in 1997. HOPE inspired the spread of merit-based scholarships more generally. As of 2021, 19 states offered large scale, merit-based scholarship programs that do not account for need, and 8 states used some or all lottery revenue to fund higher education scholarships. Studies from other states have found their merit scholarships as regressive as Georgia's, with poor and minority students far less likely than other students to be awarded a scholarship.[97] Despite embracing the rhetoric of equal opportunity, merit scholarships widen the gap between the nation's richest and poorest students.

Beginning in 2003, Rome millworker William Griffin spent $1 every week on a ticket for Lotto South, a 6/49 jackpot game run by the Georgia, Kentucky, and Virginia lotteries. On New Year's Eve 2005, Griffin's gambling habit paid off. Defying 1-in-14 million odds—and his wife Rita, who chastised him for wasting the family's money on lottery tickets—Griffin won $27 million, the largest jackpot in Lotto South's five-year history. Rita disclosed how important the newfound fortune would be for the family. Their eldest son, Tristan, was about to start his final semester of high school and the threat of paying college tuition had been "hanging over our heads." With little saved for Tristan's tuition, William had counted on his son receiving a HOPE Scholarship, but, as he cashed his ticket and received his lump-sum $15 million payout, William sheepishly joked, "I don't think we'll need that anymore."[98] Though Georgia raised the grade requirements for HOPE in 2000, Tristan was still eligible for the scholarship. In the first years of the Georgia Lottery, players had sought jackpots that would place their income far above the $66,000 cap, but Zell Miller had removed the income maximum in 1995. As a result, even the child of lottery multimillionaires could take advantage of HOPE, a scholarship funded by gamblers who, unlike William Griffin, would almost certainly never have their financial troubles solved by a jackpot.

The history of the Georgia Lottery reveals that the inequity of HOPE is not a flaw in the program's implementation but an intended consequence of an education initiative designed to aid middle-class families.[99] In the 1992 referendum, Zell Miller claimed that by voting for a lottery—and only by voting for a lottery—white suburbanites could receive free in-state college tuition. Out of the desire for a scholarship or a genuine belief that a lottery would improve education in Georgia, the state's middle class, and its poor residents attracted by expanded pre-kindergarten, provided the votes to pass a lottery.

These programs passed over strenuous objection from the state's sizable and powerful evangelical community. Churches ran an effective anti-lottery campaign. However, family values politics resonated with suburban voters only to the degree that they did not interfere with the possibility of tax-free government services. Miller knew education-minded voters would prove susceptible to his exaggerated promises because he himself viewed the lottery as a winning political strategy. The lottery secured him an electoral victory in 1990—when he proposed programs to increase education spending without increasing taxes—and again in 1994, when he was reelected by claiming that these new programs were under threat from anti-lottery Republicans.

Georgia illustrates the final evolution of the promises that facilitated lottery legalization in the United States. After lotteries failed to bring about balanced state budgets in the 1960s and 1970s and then did not meaningfully aid education finances in places like California and Florida in the 1980s, by the 1990s even lottery advocates like Zell Miller recognized that any promise of an immediate, visible benefit for the state education budget was not realistic. Instead, Miller geared the lottery around dividends for individual families. However, since a lottery could not produce enough revenue to fund tuition for all of Georgia's students, Miller opted to create a merit-based program that would limit accessibility to the scholarship in an educational environment increasingly oriented around competition. Tying HOPE to grades meant that only the deserving few would receive a scholarship. The lottery was not a handout to these students but compensation for their hard work.

This emphasis on individual achievement emerged from and served the political culture of the 1990s. Amid the rise of charter schools, a bipartisan assault on welfare, and a growing rhetorical disdain for large government, an education initiative designed around need rather than merit could have been associated with the welfare state. By making the scholarship merit-based, by allowing even the richest families to qualify, and by providing funding to individuals rather than the entire education budget, HOPE fit a growing Democratic focus on opportunity for the best students rather than aid for every student. Georgia helped set off a trend of merit scholarships in the South and nationwide in the 1990s. In their pursuit of a panacea, Zell Miller and Georgia parents deepened the regressivity of the nation's state lottery system, creating a new set of winners and losers.

Conclusion: Jackpot

ASHANI ACQUAVIVA BEGAN paying attention to the lottery when she was 19, after she started working at a gas station near her hometown in central Georgia. She still remembers the regulars who would come in for cigarettes, beer, and a tank of gas. And lottery tickets. Always a ticket or two. Or 10. Almost every convenience store or gas station, she learned, has a community of lottery players, regulars who talk strategy, favorite games, recent wins, and near misses. The person behind the counter handing out the tickets and scanning winners gets to hear about all of them. Pretty soon, Ashani started having lottery dreams of her own. Across the street from the gas station was a billboard advertising the size of various rollover jackpot games, usually in the tens or hundreds of millions of dollars. On her break she would step outside and stare at the billboard, imagining what it would be like to have that kind of money. Eventually, she tried the lottery for herself. Her first ticket was one she shared with her roommates during a period of lottomania—each of them put in about 33 cents with the promise of splitting the winnings. There weren't any to split, but it was a fun experience, and she reasoned that you can't dream if you don't play. So she started playing.

It has been 20 years since the lottery first caught Ashani's eye. She is now a committed lottery player and spends roughly $400 on tickets every month (around $5,000 annually). She tries to be strategic about her gambling, using tactics she insists have helped: she plays certain numbers when she thinks they are "due" or has a good feeling about them. She buys scratch tickets in specific quantities—usually spending $75 at a time when the mood strikes. She also refrains from buying tickets if she doesn't think luck is on her side, sometimes for multiple weeks in a row. One of the times I talked to her, she had recently come back from the store having spent $120 on tickets when she had planned to spend $100. She did not feel bad about the extra $20, she told me, because if she lost, she knew the money would help fund the HOPE Scholarship.

Ashani worked for a few years as a flight attendant, and around 2010 she got a job teaching high school in rural Georgia. After a trying year during the COVID-19 pandemic, though, she quit, and she and her husband live on their savings and his income. When she was teaching, imagining a win was her escape on a bad day. Since leaving her job, she acknowledges, she thinks about the lottery a lot more. When I asked what prize would make her stop her lottery habit, she first says $30,000. Then she admits that she meditates on $1 million. Of course, she dreams of winning a whole lot more, and the sums of $10, $50, or $80 million comes to mind. Whenever she drives past a sign bearing the lotto jackpot, she waves, smiles, and says she'll see it in her bank account soon. For two decades, the lottery has been a source of entertainment, a subject of reflection, and, most of all, a chance to dream. Playing the lottery "is about the possibility of financial prosperity or abundance," she observes. "It's all about hope."[1]

Every week, one in eight American adults buys a lottery ticket, holding on to their own hope for a life-changing jackpot. For players like Ashani, the lottery is a pastime but also a serious venture that represents their best chance at a new life. Gambling, and lotteries in particular, have long served as mechanisms of social mobility in the United States. In the late twentieth and early twenty-first centuries, economic circumstances ensured that lottery tickets were more than just a gambling game. As the old industrial order collapsed, as rates of absolute economic mobility declined, and as government shifted its focus away from protecting economic security for the middle and working classes, lotteries offered a chance, however slim, of catapulting winners near the highest reaches of American inequality. "Stuck in jobs that are going nowhere, faced with a future that is ever less certain," one Winona, Minnesota, journalist explained in 2019, "winning the lottery has replaced the union pension plan for millions of working men and women."[2] The lottery has become the quickest path to the modern American Dream.

The sheer existence of the lottery means that those who have little hope elsewhere tether their dreams to an unlikely jackpot. The lottery is the sole mechanism by which many Americans think their fortunes might change, the only way they can imagine a significant upgrade to their class status and standard of living. One Oregonian wrote his governor in 1982 to explain why he wanted the state to start a lottery: "I would like to have a chance, even a small chance to attain a lifestyle that as a common working citizen I can see coming no other way."[3] While stories of rags to riches have long been a part of American culture, actual opportunities for instant wealth have rarely been so easy to come by. Today's lotteries are better managed, better marketed, and more ubiquitous than lotteries at any point in American history, providing everyone with at least a few dollars and a dream a chance at a windfall. As the California Lottery reminded players in a 2013 advertising campaign: "Believe in something bigger."

The proliferation of lotteries has had profound consequences for how Americans think about wealth. In an essay reflecting on her mother's decades-long lottery habit, journalist Leah Muncy dubs the lottery a "beacon of false hope" for its players, a beacon that, for many, is "blinding." Without such a blinding beacon, more Americans might be willing to think critically about the economic forces that have degraded access to social mobility and have made it more difficult for people to attain financial security. This is not to say that lotteries are the opiate of the proletarian masses—as George Orwell and other have painted them to be.[4] There is a lot more preventing a class war than lottery tickets. But lotteries do provide false promises of imminent opulence, promises that may prevent people from pursuing other opportunities. Lotteries also uphold the idea that a life of wealth—not just financial stability but outright opulence—is the pinnacle of success, a vision that disparages other, more achievable, and potentially more satisfying versions of the good life. At the very least, lotteries can foster problem gambling and take money that, in many households, would be better saved or spent on essentials.

Sales results from recent years indicate just how blinding the lottery beacon has become. In 2006, nationwide lottery sales hit roughly $60 billion, where they plateaued for the following five years. After 2011, though, sales took off, hitting $70 billion in 2014, $80 billion in 2016, and crossing the $90 billion threshold in 2020. The 2020 sales figure is particularly astonishing. At the onset of the COVID-19 outbreak, states expected massive drop-offs in sales as businesses closed and many white-collar Americans began working from home. The result, though, was just the opposite. Despite—or because of—the layoffs and economic slowdowns, state after state posted record sales figures. In Texas, the lottery saw sluggish sales in March 2020. Sales shot back up again the following month when families started receiving their first round of stimulus checks from the federal government.[5] Amid a disruption to many areas of the national economy, Americans were not going to stop taking chances on a jackpot.

The lottery has become such a cultural touchstone that "winning the lottery" serves as an essential metaphor for describing any positive but unlikely occurrence. One can win the lottery in seemingly any arena—the job lottery, the apartment lottery. Ashani reports that among other black women—even those who do not gamble—meeting a bachelor with good prospects is described as "hitting the jackpot." These expressions acknowledge the uncertain odds that determine so much in life, from health to wealth. But, like the lottery, these odds can be overcome. The lottery represents an organizing principle of how Americans reckon with uncertainty, a measuring stick against which they explain their good fortune.

For many Americans, the lottery remains just that, a metaphor. In many households— including the upper-class white Jewish suburban home in which I grew up—lottery tickets are purchased only during periods of lottomania or perhaps as a gift during the winter holidays. Whenever the MegaMillions got big, one of my parents would buy a few tickets, which were never taken seriously but of course did breed fantasies, as they do for millions of other American dreamers, regular and non-regular gamblers alike. Still, for people from households like mine, lotteries are an afterthought. During each of the billion-dollar jackpots that occurred over the course of my work on this book (2016, 2018, 2021), friends and relatives would ask if I had bought a ticket and how many they should buy. Few had any experience playing the lottery or knew much about how the games worked. I would explain how to play, methodically detail the infinitesimal odds of winning, and admit that, yes, I had bought a ticket (usually more than one). I am by no means a regular lottery player. However, even years of writing about lotteries has not shaken the dreams that take hold in the moments before lotto drawings.

To Americans like Ashani, the lottery is a lot more than a metaphor and a lot more than a biennial lark. It is a daily or weekly habit, one worthy of reflection, of commitment, and, oftentimes, of prayer. The nation's most committed lottery players are disproportionately lower income, nonwhite, and less educated. They are the ones whose lotto losses pile up to create the rollover jackpots that eventually get on the news. They are the ones scratching away at instant tickets and putting their small wins immediately back into more tickets. They are the ones who faithfully play the same digits in the daily numbers. They believe in something bigger every single day.

Critics on both sides of the aisle—particularly the Christian right and a certain class of political commentator—have long been befuddled by the nation's gambling habit. Especially since the emergence of lottomania in the late 1980s and early 1990s, they cannot believe the popularity of lottery tickets in the United States. What happened to the work ethic, they wonder (ignoring the reality that luck has always presented a countercurrent to the meritocracy). Why are Americans these days obsessed with trying to get rich quick?—notwithstanding the popularity of lotteries since the eighteenth century. Aren't people rational economic thinkers? (Decades of behavioral economics research has proven they are not.) "The lottery business," author Kurt Andersen writes, "is all about selling ridiculous long shots to magical thinkers."[6] To be certain, many lottery players are what Andersen would call magical thinkers. They pray to win. They play certain numbers on certain days. They are committed to strategic systems that have no actual mathematical bearing on their odds of winning.

Nonetheless, these critiques of lottery players are laden with class-based judgments. Is a lottery ticket that much more irrational than a ticket to the opera? The lottery player and the opera aficionado both spend money on a form of entertainment. Like the stub of a past performance, the lottery ticket will likely be worthless once it has been used, but for a few minutes or a few hours it provided the chance to dream of a windfall, to fantasize about a different life. The condemnation that the lottery is irrational—at times leveled by those much more likely to attend an opera than buy a scratch-off ticket—may be correct in terms of pure probability. However, it takes a limited view of rationality and it does not account for the value that players derive even from losing tickets.

Denigrations of lottery players also fail to consider all of the factors that go into gamblers' decision to buy a ticket. To be sure, most lottery players do not know their precise odds of winning. Many reason, though, that they have absolutely no chance of getting rich if they do not play the lottery. If they buy a ticket, they will have some chance, no matter how small. In the economic climate of the last few decades, it is not hard to imagine why millions of lower- and middle-income Americans feel even a small chance is worthwhile. As the former tagline for the New York Lottery maintains: "You gotta be in it to win it."

Part of the reason millions of Americans play the lottery rests on the shifting standards of wealth since the 1980s. For the very poor spending whatever they can scrape together on a cheap scratch ticket or a shot at the daily numbers, the lottery is the best way to get some quick cash. Many of these gamblers are not playing for the pie-in-the-sky multimillion-dollar payout. They are looking to turn $1 into $100. Most players are like Ashani though, and they dream a lot bigger. Not only has the amount of money needed to maintain a middle-class lifestyle increased, but the goalposts of becoming rich have shifted as well. Even for those like Ashani who are financially stable, the lottery represents the only chance at modern definitions of material success.

Disparaging lottery players, then, verges on victim blaming. Yes, lottery tickets are an ill-advised financial decision and an imprudent retirement strategy. And yes, the stereotype that lotteries are the preserve of the poor and the working class has some statistical merit. However, the demographics of lottery players should not be used to condemn lower-income Americans or justify policies that penalize the poor. Lotteries serve as a barometer of the health of the nation's economic system. The popularity of lottery tickets should cause reflection on the conditions that have compelled tens of millions of Americans every single week to reason that their best hope for a new life lies in the luck of the draw.

———

For gamblers, lotteries represent an old solution to an old problem. The nation's history is replete with people who felt they were due more than what they were born with or what they could earn in the traditional economy. For centuries, these Americans have turned to gambling, hoping that some combination of luck and grace could work for them in ways other endeavors could not.

For states, too, lotteries represent an old solution, though to a new version of an old problem. State and local governments used lotteries in the eighteenth and nineteenth centuries to raise funds without leveling taxes. In the twentieth century, states legalized lotteries for the same reason, though in response to specific historical circumstances. The first modern lotteries represented attempts to preserve the post–World War II social compact between taxpayers and state governments. These were not small governments that offered few services but relatively robust states that for over a decade had been able to expand while keeping taxes low. As this arrangement ground to a halt in the 1960s, voters and legislators in the Northeast and Rust Belt turned to lotteries with the hope of bolstering state services without raising the taxes that might be expected to pay for them.

The something for nothing ethos that drove lottery legalization endured, even as political and economic circumstances changed the precise nature of that ethos. In the 1960s, states hoped lotteries would balance their entire budgets. When Scientific Games got involved in the initiative process in the 1980s, these promises had been proven untenable. Additionally, sources of revenue that fed into state general funds clashed with the era's growing distrust of bureaucracy and big government. As a result, the company framed lotteries as panaceas for specific state programs, particularly those threatened in the aftermath of the tax revolt. When even these promises proved too

ambitious, in the 1990s and early 2000s southern politicians tied lottery revenue to specific education programs that would be created with lottery revenue. Amid even louder concerns over big government, a decades-long crisis
of education policy, and skepticism of welfare, these programs were designed
to suit contemporary ideas about opportunity and the role of the state as an
agent of economic development.

The spread of lotteries slowed in the new millennium but only because
they had already saturated the nation. As of 2021, there are only five lottery
holdouts: Alabama, where legislators have been toying with lottery proposals
for over two decades; Nevada, where a powerful casino lobby has blocked a
lottery as a potential source of competition; Alaska, which has a few bingo
halls and slot machines but little other legalized gambling; and Hawaii and
Utah, the only two states without any form of legalized betting. These are the
only parts of the country that have abstained from entering the lottery age.

Lotteries remain popular among legislators despite the fact that they
continue to provide relatively small proportions of state revenue. In 2020,
lotteries accounted for 2.3 percent of all tax revenue generated by the 45
states with lotteries.[7] Nonetheless, the hope for a windfall that brought
lotteries to these 45 states has persisted. When the need arises, lawmakers
continue to turn to lotteries as seemingly endless wells of revenue that can
singlehandedly solve budgetary problems. In 2014, for example, Republican
state legislators in North Carolina proposed paying for schoolteacher raises
by lifting the cap on lottery advertising, a move they insisted—over the objection of state lottery officials—would bring in an additional $106 million
in sales. "My first thought, they need to call the gambling hotline," one state
senator declared of his fellow legislators. "They seem to have a gambling
problem."[8]

Incidents like the one in North Carolina aside, state lawmakers overall
do appear to have a better sense of the relatively small share of revenue provided by gambling. Yet they still find the lure of tax-free revenue too hard
to resist. Aided by lotteries' legitimization of state-run gambling and inspired by the success of tribal gaming, 32 states offered commercial casinos
as of 2021. Advocates hail casinos as job creators, as development tools for
blighted areas, and as fonts of state revenue. These lofty expectations are often
unrealized.[9] In addition to casinos, sports betting represents the new fron-
tier of American gambling. In 2018, the Supreme Court's *Murphy v. National
Collegiate Athletic Association* decision overturned a congressional restriction
on sports gambling, thereby allowing states to decide the issue for themselves.
States began looking into legalization immediately, and Delaware governor

John Carney made his state's first legal sports bet less than a month after the ruling. In many states, calls for sports gambling gained additional momentum in 2020 as the COVID-19 pandemic threatened to decimate states' tax income. By the end of 2021, 30 states had legalized or were in the process of legalizing sports betting.[10]

States have plunged further into the gambling economy in large part because lawmakers choose not to look too closely at where—or whom—the revenues come from. Despite frequent attempts by state and industry officials to frame the data in a more flattering light, it is common knowledge that lotteries are regressive. Yet lawmakers have come to accept that their states make money from a lottery and that they will continue to do so. Most have decided that they do not want to question even this relatively small source of state income, especially if the alternative is a tax increase. This intentional ignorance is eased in part by the demographics of lottery players, a population that is disproportionately poorer, less educated, and nonwhite, and therefore easier to overlook. Gamblers are out of sight and out of mind. But their bets add up.

Lawmakers' lack of deliberation on the source of lottery revenue is reflective of a general inattention to gambling policy. Lottery regulation was a recurring issue in Congress in the 1960s and 1970s as the federal government decided the degree to which it should regulate state-run sweepstakes. In 1976, the Commission on the Review of the National Policy Toward Gambling released a major report, *Gambling in America*, that offered a sweeping set of recommendations on gambling policy—from horseracing and bingo to lotteries and Nevada casinos. Lotteries were also sufficiently important in the 1980s to warrant a dedicated 1984 US Senate hearing, and over the course of the decade multiple proposals for a federally administered national lottery circulated around Capitol Hill. In 1996, Congress created the National Gambling Impact Study Commission on the assumption that the recommendations in *Gambling in America* were outdated. In its final report, released in 1999, the commission recommended an immediate pause to the expansion of legalized gambling until Washington and state governments could assess the consequences of continued proliferation.[11] No such pause ever occurred. In the 23 years since the release of the 1999 commission report, the gambling landscape in the United States has changed just as dramatically as it did in the 23 years between 1976 and 1999. From the continued ascent of internet gambling to experiments with lottery privatization to the spread of sports betting, state and federal guidance on gambling is lacking and unsuited for the modern day.

Oversight of lotteries is sorely needed because for decades the industry has been a runaway, revenue-seeking machine. Lotteries were enacted because they were painted as panaceas, whether for the entire state or middle-class households whose children could go to college for free. As a result, legislators came to expect ever-greater sums of lottery revenue. Any decline in sales is deemed unacceptable.

These expectations compel lottery administrators and their private-sector allies to engage in ever-more aggressive sales and marketing tactics. Charged not only with raising revenue but also with working budgetary miracles, lottery commissions gradually added more games, spent more on advertising, and sought to appeal to more and more players. In the process, they created new, successive generations of gamblers. Many states justified their initial pursuit of lottery revenue on the grounds that residents were already gambling, so the state might as well capture that money for itself. This argument has served legislators and voters from the 1960s, when northeasterners assumed that black numbers players would become legal lottery bettors, to the 2000s, when pro-lottery lawmakers in Wyoming pointed to residents buying tickets across state lines as a justification for the state to enact a game of its own.[12] Once lotteries were in place, though, they did a lot more than capture sales from those already gambling elsewhere. They ramped up marketing to appeal to a broad base of players and adopted new games to attract young people. When Georgia Lottery tickets went on sale in 1993, for example, Ashani was just 11 years old. Through its advertising and its ubiquity, the state lottery turned her into a regular player, one who, by her own admission, will keep playing until she hits a jackpot.

The quest for younger players has long been a concern of lottery commissions. This quest was behind the introduction of scratch-off games in the 1970s and is behind a great deal of lottery advertising. Attempts to appeal to younger players are also the reason for lottery commissions' current push to sell online lottery tickets as well as their increased efforts to advertise on social media platforms. As state gambling officials are painfully aware, indications are that millennials and Gen-Z are less interested in lottery tickets than older generations.[13] Facing pressure from revenue-hungry legislators and the unsustainable expectation that revenue should grow every year, lotteries are currently in the process of trying to hook young gamblers on the dream of an instant jackpot.

Lotteries' unfettered quest for revenue has been in place for nearly 60 years. States need to consider how much they truly value gambling revenue and the incentives that should guide the behavior of their lottery commissions. Voters, bettors, and policymakers should reflect on whether the continued expansion of gambling is in the best interests of players, states, or the common good.

———

Since I started work on this book, a question I have been asked frequently is, simply, whether lotteries are good or bad. In other words: should lotteries exist in twenty-first-century America?

Proponents would stake their case on the amount of revenue raised for states. According to the National Association of State and Provincial Lotteries, between 1964 and 2019, lotteries raised a total of $502 billion for their designated beneficiaries.[14] While this represents a small sum relative to total state revenues from this period, lotteries have helped keep taxes down in some states, if only by a small amount. In southern states, they bankrolled new scholarship and pre-kindergarten programs that, given the political circumstances of the 1990s and 2000s, would surely not have been enacted without lottery funding. Lotteries are a rare opportunity for states to raise revenue without placing a compulsory burden on taxpayers.

The case against lotteries is easy to make based on the material covered in this book. Lotteries were enacted for specific purposes in specific contexts and have generally failed to meet these expectations. They appeal disproportionately to less-well-off gamblers who stake their hopes for wealth on the promise of a jackpot with infinitesimal odds. Whether intended this way or not, lottery advertising and the growing size of jackpots have helped foster an unhealthy obsession with opulence and the idea that the only successful life is one lived in luxury. And the ubiquity of lotteries can lead to unhealthy play, including problem gambling. As state agencies, lotteries appear to run counter to the purpose of all other branches of state government: to promote the greater good, not to sell a product to the public. Additionally, lotteries have warped the public's ideas about taxation. Promotions about all the good lotteries do for states have fed the idea that states can increase services without additional tax revenue because states have hit the gambling jackpot.

Weighing these considerations, state lotteries should not exist in the modern United States. Despite the revenue raised, a proposal for a new tax with the demographic distribution of a state lottery would be rejected out of hand for its regressivity. The state services funded by the lottery should be models not just for how states can make the best use of gambling revenue but the relatively inexpensive nature of government programs that can make a significant difference in the lives of millions of Americans.

Economists and others might argue that removing the state monopoly on lotteries would inevitably lead to a return of the regime of illegal lotteries. Unlike state-run games (for the most part), these operations would be ripe for infiltration of crooked management, unfair rules, and deceiving practices. As with the war on drugs or even Prohibition a century ago, laws against certain vices only push them underground. They do not eradicate them. There is some merit to these claims, and the return of illegal lotteries might—but should not—entail the criminalization of gambling, which would invariably affect people of color disproportionately.

However, lotteries differ from narcotics in one important respect. The popularity of lotteries rests on mass participation. The more people who play—and the bigger the bankroll of the person or entity organizing the games—the larger the prizes can be, which attracts more people to play, which allows for bigger prizes, which attracts more players, and so on. Without the involvement of major corporate entities or state governments, no illegal lottery could come close to the prize size, ticket variety, and ubiquity of outlets offered by state-run games. If state lotteries were disbanded, the most committed players would begin playing illegally or in overseas games via the internet. However, the total amount spent on lotteries under these circumstances could not begin to approach the $91 billion bet legally on lotteries every year in the United States. This would leave more money in the hands of the people who could use it most and would help reframe how Americans think about wealth, luck, and success.

I am under no illusions that any state will seriously consider repealing its lottery. None has done so since the nineteenth century. Most lawmakers who rely on lottery revenue would be unlikely to entertain such legislation. Meanwhile, the process of passing a state constitutional amendment to repeal lottery legislation is expensive and would require agreement from a majority of voters. If they are not gamblers themselves, most voters—like their elected representatives—have come to accept the lottery as a way that their state raises money. Especially if neighboring states keep their games, voters are unlikely to repeal lottery laws.

Nonetheless, states should consider significant reform to lottery operations, particularly to prevent the popularization of tickets among younger generations. A few possible reforms stand out, such as imposing strict regulations (or outright bans) on the online sale of lottery tickets, limiting the cost of scratch tickets, and placing a cap on the size of lotto jackpots. Perhaps most effective would be limits on lottery advertising. Some states have laws that regulate the content of these promotions, and while it is difficult to assess their impact on sales, these types of protocols offer a good starting point. Helpful in these efforts would be closing the loophole that excludes state lottery promotions from Federal Trade Commission regulations on false advertising. At the very least, lottery operations and marketing should be subject to oversight from an entity that does not have a direct stake in the revenue that lotteries generate.

Lotteries were a worthwhile experiment in public finance that continued a long tradition of legalized gambling in the United States. However, they have exceeded their mandate, have vastly disappointed as a means of raising revenue, and have done untold damage to gamblers who still play for the unlikeliest of windfalls. Despite raising money for state governments, they have also bred the idea that complex budgetary problems can have simple answers. Gamblers and lawmakers alike need to confront the fact that for decades they have been entranced by hopes for a windfall. Now is the time to consider the consequences of the nation's embrace of lotteries, before a new generation of Americans starts believing that a jackpot presents their last, best, or only chance to change their luck.

Notes

LIST OF ABBREVIATIONS

ASA   Arizona State Archives, Phoenix, Arizona
CAC   Carl Albert Congressional Research and Studies Center, Norman, Oklahoma
CSA   California State Archives, Sacramento, California
CSL   California State Library, Sacramento, California
CTSA   Connecticut State Archives, Hartford, Connecticut
DPL   Denver Public Library, Denver, Colorado
GAA   Georgia Archives, Morrow, Georgia
ISA   Illinois State Archives, Springfield, Illinois
NJSA   New Jersey State Archives, Trenton, New Jersey
NJSL   New Jersey State Library, Trenton, New Jersey
NYSL   New York State Archives, Albany, New York
NYSL   New York State Library, Albany, New York
OSA   Oregon State Archives, Salem, Oregon
RAC   Rockefeller Archives Center, Sleepy Hollow, New York
UGA   Richard B. Russell Library for Political Research and Studies, University of Georgia, Athens, Georgia
UNLV   Special Collections and Archives, University of Nevada, Las Vegas, Las Vegas, Nevada

INTRODUCTION

1. Author interviews with Leo McCord, March 13 and July 15, 2021; Bonita Brodt, "Lottery's Down Side: Road to Easy Street Littered with the Poor," *Chicago Tribune*, May 25, 1986, A1.

2. Zac Auter, "About Half of Americans Play State Lotteries," *Gallup*, July 22, 2016; Pew Research Center, "Gambling: As the Take Rises, So Does Public Concern," *Social Trends Report*, May 23, 2006, 21; National Association of State and Provincial Lotteries Resource Index, "United States Lotteries," https://www.nasplmatrix.org/nri; Richard Hoffer, *Jackpot Nation: Rambling and Gambling Across Our Landscape of Luck* (New York: HarperCollins, 2007).

3. Jackson Lears, *Something for Nothing: Luck in America* (New York: Viking, 2003).

4. Consumer Federation of America and the Financial Planning Association, "How Americans View Personal Wealth Vs. How Financial Planners View This Wealth," January 9, 2006, https://consumerfed.org/pdfs/Financial_Planners_Study011 006.pdf; Robert Frank, "How to Get Rich? Luck Ties Savings in Poll," *Wall Street Journal* Blog, January 14, 2010.

5. John L. Mikesell, "State Lottery Sales and Economic Activity," *National Tax Journal* 47, no. 1 (March 1994): 165–171; Garrick Blalock, David R. Just, and Daniel H. Simon, "Hitting the Jackpot or Hitting the Skids: Entertainment, Poverty, and the Demand for State Lotteries," *American Journal of Economics and Sociology* 66, no. 3 (2007): 545–570; Csilla Horváth and Richard Paap, "The Effects of Recessions on Gambling Expenditures," *Journal of Gambling Studies* 28 (2012): 703–717; Charles A. Lyons, "Gambling in the Public Marketplace: Adaptations to Economic Context," *Psychological Record* 63 (2013): 309–322.

6. Raj Chett et al., "Is the United States Still a Land of Opportunity? Recent Trends in Intergenerational Mobility," NBER Working Paper 19844 (January 2014); Raj Chetty et al., "The Fading American Dream: Trends in Absolute Income Mobility Since 1940," *Science* 356, no. 6336 (2017): 398–406; Julia B. Isaacs, Isabel V. Sawhill, and Ron Haskins, "Getting Ahead or Losing Ground: Economic Mobility in America" (Washington, DC: Brookings Institute and Pew Charitable Trusts, 2008) ; Board of Governors of the Federal Reserve, "Adults who would cover a $400 emergency expense using cash or its equivalent," Survey of Household Economics and Decisionmaking, 2013-2020, https://www.federalreserve.gov/ consumerscommunities/sheddataviz/unexpectedexpenses.html. .

7. Jacob Hacker, *The Great Risk Shift: The Assault on American Jobs, Families, Healthcare, and Retirement and How You Can Fight Back* (New York: Oxford University Press, 2006); Paul Delaney, "For State Lotteries, Business Is Booming," *New York Times*, March 16, 1975, 49.

8. Charles T. Clotfelter, Philip J. Cook, Julie A. Edell, and Marian Moore, "State Lotteries at the Turn of the Century," Report to the National Gambling Impact Study Commission (1999), https://govinfo.library.unt.edu/ngisc//reports/lotfi nal.pdf; .Todd A. Wyett, "State Lotteries: Regressive Taxes in Disguise," *Tax Lawyer* 44, no. 3 (1991): 867–883; Mary Herring and Timothy Bledsoe, "A Model of Lottery Participation: Demographics, Context, and Attitudes," *Policy Studies Journal* 22, no. 2 (1994): 245–257; Donald I. Price and E. Shawn Novak, "The Tax Incidence of Three Texas Lottery Games: Regressivity, Race, and Education," *National Tax Journal* 52, no. 4 (1999): 741–751; John W. Welte, Grace M. Barnes, William F. Wieczorek, and John Parker, "Gambling Participation in the U.S.— Results from a National Survey," *Journal of Gambling Studies* 18 (2002): 313–337; Kathryn L. Combs, Jaebeom Kim, and John A. Spry, "The Relative Regressivity of Seven Lottery Games," *Applied Economics* 40 (2008): 35–39; K. Brandon Lang and Megumi Omori, "Can Demographic Variables Predict Lottery and Pari-Mutuel

Losses? An Empirical Investigation," *Journal of Gambling Studies* 25, no. 2 (2009): 171–183; Skip Garibaldi, Kayla Frisoli, Li Ke, and Melody Lim, "Lottery Spending: A Non-Parametric Analysis," *PLOS One* 10, no. 2 (2015).

9. Larry Hollowell to Kenneth W. Thorson, October 17, 1991, Folder "Public Opinion— 1991," Box 3, Lottery Department, Office of the Director: Correspondence 1988– 1992, Virginia State Library, Richmond, Virginia.

10. Elaine Tyler May, *Homeward Bound: American Families in the Cold War Era* (New York: Basic Books, 2008 [1988]); Jim Cullen, *The American Dream: A Short History of an Idea that Shaped a Nation* (New York: Oxford University Press, 2003).

11. Pete Earley, *Super Casino: Inside the "New" Las Vegas* (New York: Bantam Books, 2000), 372.

12. *Frontline*, "Betting on the Lottery," Show #904, Written, directed, and produced by Marian Marzynski, WGBH-TV, November 6, 1990, Special Collections & Archives, University Libraries, University of Nevada, Las Vegas, Las Vegas, Nevada.

13. Richard Leone, "Personal Statement of Richard Leone," June 7, 1999, National Gambling Impact Study Commission, Appendix 1: Commission Members' Statements, https://govinfo.library.unt.edu/ngisc/reports/fullrpt.html.

14. Jefferson Cowie, *The Great Exception: The New Deal and the Limits of American Politics* (Princeton, NJ: Princeton University Press, 2016).

15. Lizabeth Cohen, *A Consumers' Republic: The Politics of Mass Consumption in Postwar America* (New York: Vintage, 2003); Molly Michelmore, *Tax and Spend: The Welfare State, Tax Politics, and the Limits of American Liberalism* (Philadelphia: University of Pennsylvania Press, 2012); *Jacob Hacker and Paul Pierson, American Amnesia*: *How the War on Government Led Us to Forget What Made America Prosper* (New York: Simon and Schuster, 2016).

16. George L. Pinkham, "State Lottery," Letter to *Asbury Park Press* (Asbury Park, NJ), March 4, 1964, 19.

17. *Wall Street Journal*, "An Educational Gamble," September 28, 1966, 14.

18. Bryant Simon, *The Hamlet Fire: A Tragic Story of Cheap Food, Cheap Government, and Cheap Lives* (New York: New Press, 2017).

19. For example, Bethany Moreton, *To Serve God and Wal-Mart: The Making of Christian Free Enterprise* (Cambridge, MA: Harvard University Press, 2009); *Darren Dochuk, From Bible Belt to Sunbelt: Plain-Folk Religion, Grassroots Politics, and the Rise of Evangelical Conservatism* (New York: W. W. Norton, 2011); *Matthew Avery Sutton, American Apocalypse*: *A History of Modern Evangelicalism* (Cambridge, MA: Harvard University Press, 2014); Frances Fitzgerald, *The Evangelicals: The Struggle to Shape America* (New York: Simon and Schuster, 2017).

20. Joshua Schwartz, "Jews at the Dice Table: Gambling in Ancient Jewish Society Revisited," in *Envisioning Judaism: Studies in Honor of Peter Schäfer on the Occasion of His Seventieth Birthday*, ed. Ra'anan S. Boustan, Klaus Herrmann,

Reimund Leicht, Annette Y. Reed, and Giuseppe Veltr (Tübingen: Mohr Siebeck, 2013), 129–146; David G. Schwartz, *Roll the Bones: The History of Gambling* (New York: Gotham Books, 2006), 16–17; Chevalier Louis de Jaucourt, "Roman lotteries," *The Encyclopedia of Diderot & d'Alembert*, Collaborative Translation Project (Ann Arbor: University of Michigan Library, 2004), http://hdl.handle.net/2027/spo.did2222.0000.321), originally published as "Loteries des Romains," *Encyclopédie ou Dictionnaire raisonné des sciences, des arts et des métiers*, 9:695 (Paris, 1765).

21. Cecil L'Estrange Ewen, *Lotteries and Sweepstakes: An Historical, Legal, and Ethical Survey of Their Introduction, Suppression, and Re-Establishment in the British Isles* (New York: Benjamin Blood, 1972 [1932]), 25–27, 36; Evelyn Welch, "Lotteries in Early Modern Italy," *Past & Present* no. 199 (May 2008), 87.

22. Alexander Brown, *The First Republic in America* (Boston: Houghton, Mifflin, 1848 [1624]), 395.

23. Neal E. Millikan, *Lotteries in Colonial America* (New York: Routledge, 2011), 7, 12, 23–24, 71; Lucius Wilmerding Jr., "The United States Lottery," *New York Historical Society Quarterly* 47, no. 1 (January 1963): 5–39; Thomas Jefferson, *The Works of Thomas Jefferson*, vol. 12 (New York: G. P. Putnam's Sons, 1905), 435–444.

24. John Samuel Ezell, *Fortune's Merry Wheel: The Lottery in America* (Cambridge, MA: Harvard University Press, 1960), 178.

25. *New York Times*, "John A. Morris, Lottery King," *New York Times*, February 11, 1894, 17; G. W. McGinty, "The Louisiana Lottery Company," *Southwestern Social Science Quarterly* 20, no. 4 (1940): 329–348; Howard O. Rogers, "The Lottery in American History," *Americana Illustrated* 13, no. 1 (1919): 40–54; Ezell, *Fortune's Merry Wheel*, 242–270.

26. Commission on the Review of the National Policy Toward Gambling, *Gambling in America* (Washington DC: US Government Printing Office, 1976), 1.

CHAPTER 1

1. Elizabeth Hinton, *America on Fire: The Untold History of Police Violence and Black Rebellion Since the 1960s* (New York: Liveright, 2021), 7–8, 313–338.

2. Governor's Select Commission on Civil Disorder, State of New Jersey, *Report for Action* (February 1968), 2, 16–18, 45–52, 55; Lizabeth Cohen, *A Consumers' Republic: The Politics of Mass Consumption in Postwar America* (New York: Vintage Books, 2003), 373–378; Kevin Mumford, *Newark: A History of Race, Rights, and Riots in America* (New York: New York University Press, 2007).

3. Governor's Select Commission on Civil Disorder, *Report for Action*, 20; Max Arthur Herman, *Summer of Rage: An Oral History of the 1967 Newark and Detroit Riots* (New York: Peter Lang, 2017 [2013]), 73; National Advisory Commission on Civil Disorders, *Report of the National Advisory Commission on Civil Disorders* (Washington, DC: US Government Printing Office, 1968), 31.

4. Kevin Flynn, *American Sweepstakes: How One Small State Bucked the Church, the Feds, and the Mob to Usher in the Lottery Age* (Lebanon, NH: ForeEdge, 2015).

5. New Jersey Council of County (Community) Colleges, *New Jersey Community Colleges: The First Ten Years, 1963–1973* (Trenton: New Jersey Office of Community College Programs, 1975), 8; Wilbur Smith and Associates, *Needs and Finance for the New Jersey State Highway System,* (Columbia, SC: Wilbur Smith and Associates, 1966); Commission on State Tax Policy, *Tenth Report: Increased State Aid to Public Schools and Distribution of the Cost of Expanding Public Service* (Trenton: State of New Jersey, 1963), 10; Barbara G. Salmore with Stephen A. Salmore, *New Jersey Politics and Government: The Suburbs Come of Age* (New Brunswick, NJ: Rutgers University Press, 2013), 256–260.

6. Molly Michelmore, *Tax and Spend: The Welfare State, Tax Politics, and the Limits of American Liberalism* (Philadelphia: University of Pennsylvania Press, 2012).

7. Lyndon B. Johnson, Remarks at the Smithsonian Institution at a Ceremony Marking the 200th Anniversary of the *Encyclopedia Britannica*, December 14, 1967, American Presidency Project, https://www.presidency.ucsb.edu/node/237 928; Hobart Rowen, "LBJ Melts Some Butter to Provide More Guns," *Washington Post*, January 30, 1968, A1.

8. Randall G. Holcombe and Russell S. Sobel, *Growth and Variability in State Tax Revenue: An Anatomy of State Fiscal Crises* (Westport, CT: Greenwood Press, 1997), 6; United States Bureau of the Census, *Statistical Abstract of the United States: 1952* (Washington, DC: US Government Printing Office, 1962), 366; United States Bureau of the Census, *Statistical Abstract of the United States: 1962* (Washington, DC: US Government Printing Office, 1962), 426; United States Bureau of the Census, *Statistical Abstract of the United States: 1972* (Washington, DC: US Government Printing Office, 1972), 423.

9. Associated Press, "Some States Cut Services in Fiscal Pinch," *Chicago Tribune*, December 16, 1970, B16; Council of State Governments, "Gambling: A Source of State Revenue" (Lexington, KY: Council of State Governments, 1973), 1.

10. David Broder, "7 of 9 Biggest States Face Money Crisis," *Washington Post*, December 6, 1970, A1; United States Bureau of the Census, *Statistical Abstract of the United States: 1974* (Washington, DC: US Government Printing Office, 1974), 249; United States Bureau of the Census, *Statistical Abstract of the United States: 1965* (Washington, DC: US Government Printing Office, 1965), 422; Associated Press, "House Committee Cuts State Budget," *Fitchburg Eagle* (Fitchburg, MA), April 25, 1972, 5.

11. United States Bureau of the Census, *Census of Governments, 1967: Compendium of Government Finances* 4, no. 5 (Washington, DC: US Government Printing Office, 1969), 44.

12. Richard Hughes, "Budget Message of Richard J. Hughes Governor of New Jersey Transmitting to the One Hundred and Eighty-Seventh Session of the Legislature Recommendations for State Expenditures for the Fiscal Year Ending June 30, 1964"

(Trenton, n.p., February 11, 1963), 22a, New Jersey State Library, Trenton, New Jersey (hereafter NJSL); Cohen, *Consumers' Republic*, 227–240; United States Bureau of the Census, *Statistical Abstract of the United States: 1971* (Washington DC: US Government Printing Office, 1971), 411.

13. Governor's Select Commission on Civil Disorder, *Report for Action*, 48; Advisory Commission on Intergovernmental Relations, *State Aid to Local Government* (Washington, DC: US Government Printing Office, 1969), 10; United States Bureau of the Census, *Statistical Abstract of the United States: 1970* (Washington, DC: US Government Printing Office, 1970), 383–384.

14. Commission on State Tax Policy, *Tenth Report*, xvii, 15; *New York Times*, "State Taxation: Jersey Tries to Hold Line as Expenses Mount," January 28, 1962, 140.

15. Barry B. Bushell, "The Drive for a Broad-Based Tax in New Jersey" (MA Thesis, Newark State College, 1969); Richard Leone, "The Politics of Gubernatorial Leadership: Tax and Education Reform in New Jersey" (PhD dissertation, Princeton University, 1969), 58.

16. *Trenton Times,* "They Still Have to Pay," January 27, 1964, 10.

17. William Musto testimony to New Jersey Legislature, State Assembly, Judiciary Committee, *Public Hearing on A.C.R. 2 (Off-Track Betting) and A.C.R. 4 (State Lotteries)* (n.p., 1964), NJSL, 5–6.

18. Associated Press, "Jersey Is Weighing State Lottery Again to Build Up Funds," *New York Times*, July 7, 1965, 39; *Courier-Post* (Camden, NJ), "Straw in the Lottery Wind," July 5, 1967, 14.

19. Ronald Sullivan, "Jersey Assembly Approves Lottery Referendum," *New York Times*, May 21, 1968, 40; Governor's Commission to Evaluate the Capital Needs of New Jersey, *A Capital Program* (n.p., April 1968), 129; Economic Policy Council and Office of Economic Policy, *First Annual Report* (State of New Jersey, Department of the Treasury, April 1968), 13–14.

20. *Courier-Post*, "Lottery Balloon Holes," February 12, 1968, 14; Richard Hughes, Budget Message for the Fiscal Year Ending June 30, 1969, delivered February 13, 1968, Trenton, New Jersey, NJSL.

21. Franklin Kistner, testimony to New Jersey Legislature, Senate Judiciary Committee, in *Public Hearing on Senate Concurrent Resolution No. 7* (n.p., June 1, 1966), NJSL, 47.

22. William Musto testimony to New Jersey Legislature, State Assembly, Committee on Taxation, in *Public Hearing on Assembly Concurrent Resolution No. 32*, March 5, 1969 (Trenton, NJ: Division of State Library, 1969), NJSL, 10; Cornelius Gallagher to Harry Sears, December 31, 1969, Folder 89, Box 31, Cornelius Gallagher Papers, Carl Albert Congressional Research and Studies Center, Norman, Oklahoma (hereafter CAC); William Musto testimony, *Public Hearing on A.C.R. 2 (Off-Track Betting) and A.C.R. 4 (State Lotteries)*, 5–6.

23. E. Kornish, "Advice for C-P, Hughes and State," Letter to *Courier-Post*, January 17, 1966, 20.

24. Orin Wilcox to Altee Marshall, March 6, 1970, Reel 42, Subseries 3: Third Administration, Series 37: Office Subject Files, Nelson A. Rockefeller Gubernatorial Files, Rockefeller Archives Center, Sleepy Hollow, New York (hereafter RAC).

25. E. A. Pettersen to William Cahill, July 22, 1970, Folder 1, "Treasury—Lottery 1970," Box 25, Subject Files, 1970–1974, William T. Cahill Gubernatorial Papers, New Jersey State Archives, Trenton, New Jersey (hereafter NJSA).

26. Joseph Diaz testimony, *Public Hearing on A.C.R. 2 (Off-Track betting) and A.C.R 4 (State lotteries),* 34a.

27. Jon C. Teaford, *The Rise of the States: Evolution of American State Government* (Baltimore: Johns Hopkins University Press, 2002), 217–218; Elizabeth Pearson, "Saying Yes to Taxes: The Politics of Tax Reform Campaigns in Three Northwestern States, 1965–1973," *American Journal of Sociology* 119, no. 5 (2014): 1281.

28. John B. Wefing, *The Life and Times of Richard J. Hughes: The Politics of Civility* (New Brunswick, NJ: Rivergate Books, 2009), 132; John O. Davies, "Hughes Hits Assembly No-Tax Stand," *Courier News,* April 24, 1969, 1.

29. United Press International, "Hughes Outlines Budget Cut," *Morning Call* (Paterson, NJ), March 26, 1966, 3.

30. Ronald Sullivan, "Jersey Sales Tax Signed by Hughes," *New York Times,* April 28, 1966, 1; *New York Times,* "New Jersey Decides," April 27, 1966, 46.

31. Associated Press, "Lottery Vote Uncertain," *Red Bank Register* (Red Bank, NJ), February 8, 1968, 1.

32. Special Committee to Investigate Organized Crime in Interstate Commerce, *Third Interim Report* (Washington, DC: US Government Printing Office, 1951), 2.

33. *Life,* " 'It Is Positively the Most Wonderful Thing I Ever Saw,' " April 2, 1951, 22.

34. Richard Nixon, "Special Message to the Congress on a Program To Combat Organized Crime in America," *Public Papers of the Presidents of the United States: Richard Nixon, 1969* (Washington, DC: US Government Printing Office, 1971), 165; Lyndon B. Johnson, "Special Message to the Congress on Law Enforcement and the Administration of Justice," March 8, 1965, *American Presidency Project,* https://www.presidency.ucsb.edu/node/242223; President's Commission on Law Enforcement and Administration of Justice, *The Challenge of Crime in a Free Society* (Washington, DC: US Government Printing Office, 1967), 298–299; on the beginning of the war on crime during the Johnson administration, see Elizabeth Hinton, *From the War on Poverty to the War on Crime: The Making of Mass Incarceration in America* (Cambridge, MA: Harvard University Press, 2016).

35. Richard Nixon, "Executive Order 11534—Establishing the National Council on Organized Crime," June 4, 1970, *American Presidency Project,* https://www.preside ncy.ucsb.edu/node/306520; Public Law 91–452, "Organized Crime Control Act of 1970," October 15, 1970; Commission on the Review of National Policy Towards Gambling, *Gambling in America* (Washington, DC: US Government Printing Office, 1976), 48.

36. Public Law 90–351; 82 Stat. 197, "Omnibus Crime Control and Safe Streets Act of 1968," (June 19, 1968); United Press International, "Assembly Passes State Wiretap Law," *The News* (Paterson, NJ), January 15, 1969, 8; *New York Times*, "Excerpts from Governor Cahill's Inaugural Address," January 21, 1970, 33.

37. Governor's Committee on Gambling, *Final Report* (n.p., n.d.), Box A-256, John Dempsey Gubernatorial Papers, Connecticut State Archives, Hartford, Connecticut (hereafter CTSA), 14, 18; Wayne Phillips, "Rockefeller Asks Gambling Curbs," *New York Times*, March 16, 1960, 1; National Association of Attorneys General, Committee on the Office of Attorney General, *Organized Crime Control Units* (Raleigh, NC: National Association of Attorneys General, January, 1974), 4–7.

38. Sidney Kingston to William Cahill, June 14, 1970, Folder 3, "Treasury—Lottery 1970," Box 26, Subject Files, 1970–1974, William T. Cahill Gubernatorial Papers, NJSA.

39. David G. Schwartz, "No End in Sight: How the United States Became a Gambling Nation, 1950–2000," in *All In: The Spread of Gambling in Twentieth-Century United States*, ed. Jonathan D. Cohen and David G. Schwartz (Reno: University of Nevada Press, 2018), 152–153; Commission on Law Enforcement, *The Challenge of Crime in a Free Society*, 189; Ronald Sullivan, "New Jersey's Proposed Lottery," *New York Times*, October 17, 1969, 41; United Press International, "Major Rackets Run by Crime," *Courier Post*, December 27, 1968, 11.

40. Cornelius Gallagher to Harry Sears, December 31, 1969, CAC.

41. David G. Schwartz, *Roll the Bones: The History of Gambling* (New York: Gotham, 2006), 151.

42. Shane White, Stephen Garton, Stephen Robertson, and Graham White, *Running the Numbers: Gambling in Harlem Between the Wars* (Cambridge, MA: Harvard University Press, 2010), 13, 19, 40, 121.

43. Fund for the City of New York, *Legal Gambling in New York: A Discussion of Numbers and Sports Betting* (New York: Fund for the City of New York, 1972), 2; Malcolm X with Alex Haley, *The Autobiography of Malcolm X* (New York: Ballantine Books, 1999 [1964]), 88.

44. Colin Powell with Joseph E. Persico, *My American Journey* (New York: Ballantine Books, 1995), 30.

45. LaShawn Harris, *Sex Workers, Psychics, and Numbers Runners: Black Women in New York City's Underground Economy* (Urbana: University of Illinois Press, 2016); Bridgett M. Davis, *The World According to Fannie Davis: My Mother's Life in the Detroit Numbers* (New York: Little, Brown, 2019).

46. Matthew Vaz, *Running the Numbers: Race, Police, and the History of Urban Gambling* (Chicago: University of Chicago Press, 2020), 6.

47. Dana Stevenson, "Public Confused but Leans to 'Yes' in State Lottery Vote," *Trenton Times*, October 5, 1969, 3.

48. Eugene Doleschal, "Victimless Crime" (Hackensack, NJ: National Council on Crime and Delinquency, 1971); Matthew Vaz, "'We Intend to Run It': Racial Politics, Illegal Gambling, and the Rise of Government Lotteries in the United States, 1960–1985," *Journal of American History* 101, no. 1 (2014): 79. On marijuana decriminalization in the 1970s, see Emily Dufton, *Grass Roots: The Rise and Fall and Rise of Marijuana in America* (New York: Basic, 2017).

49. Floyd J. Fowler Jr., Thomas W. Mangione, and Frederick E. Pratter, *Gambling Law Enforcement in Major American Cities* (Washington, DC: National Institute of Law Enforcement and Criminal Justice, Law Enforcement Assistance Administration, US Department of Justice, 1978), 83; Testimony of Dominick A. Spina to the New Jersey Legislature, Special Joint Legislative Committee to Study Crime and the System of Criminal Justice in New Jersey, Public Hearing, March 29, 1968, vol. 4, NJSL, 140–142.

50. Fowler, Mangione, and Pratter, *Gambling Law Enforcement in Major American Cities*, 76–77.

51. I. Gutstein, "An Alternative to a State Sales Tax," *Letter to Asbury Park Press*, January 25, 1963, 18.

52. Neal E. Millikan, *Lotteries in Colonial America* (New York: Routledge, 2011), 11; John Samuel Ezell, *Fortune's Merry Wheel: The Lottery in America* (Cambridge, MA: Harvard University Press, 1960), 206–214.

53. Ronald Sullivan, "Lottery Referendum Approved in Jersey," *New York Times*, May 2, 1969, 1; Oliver Quayle and Company, "A Study of the Numbers Game in New York City," Study #1458-A (Bronxville, NY: Oliver Quayle and Company, 1972), 13.

54. Reverend Samuel A. Jeanes testimony, *Public Hearing on A.C.R. 2 (Off-Track betting) and A.C.R 4 (State lotteries)*, 54, 57.

55. Francis M. Lordan, "Lottery Referendum Stirs Dispute in GOP Assembly," *Courier-Post*, January 21, 1964, 3; Samuel Jeanes, "The Lottery," Letter to *Trenton Times*, May 24, 1963, 18.

56. New Jersey Secretary of State, "Results of the General Election Held November 4, 1969," https://nj.gov/state/elections/assets/pdf/election-results/1920-1970//1969-general-election.pdf.

57. On the mob in Hudson County, see Scott M. Deitche, *Garden State Gangland: The Rise of the Mob in New Jersey* (Lanham, MD: Rowman and Littlefield, 2018); "Public Questions, 1969," Box 190, Department of State, Division of Elections, Election Returns, 1911–1997, NJSA.

58. Theodore R. Morgan, "Cahill Is Given Ideas on Lottery," Letter to *Asbury Park Press*, November 18, 1969, 10.

59. Governor's Select Commission on Civil Disorder, *Report for Action*, 2; "Public Questions, 1969," Box 190, Department of State, Division of Elections, Election Returns, 1911–1997, NJSA; data on Bergen and Middlesex Counties, found in State of New Jersey, *Results of the General Election Held November 4, 1969*, https://www.

state.nj.us/state/elections/assets/pdf/election-results/1920-1970//1969-general-election.pdf; Vaz, " 'We Intend to Run It.' "

60. *New York Amsterdam News*, "Hope and the Lottery," September 2, 1967, 17.

61. Ronald Sullivan, "Jersey Lottery Exceeding Expectations," *New York Times,* March 8, 1971, 1; Bob Sykes, "State Got $31.8 Million from Lottery in Year, Half of Estimated Return," *Glen Falls Times* (Glen Falls, NY), June 19, 1968, 9; William M. Ham to Joseph Murphy, "Lottery Sales, Prizes, Winners," June 24, 1969, Folder "Lottery Statistics," Box 2, Lottery Correspondence and Regulations, Records of the New York State Department of Taxation and Finance, Law Bureau, New York State Archives, Albany, New York.

62. New Jersey Lottery, *Milestones: 1995–96 Annual Report* (November 1995), NJSL; *Central New Jersey Home News*, "Lottery Is Odds-On Favorite," April 18, 1972, 32.

63. Errolette M. Flynn to Thomas J. Meskill, January 25, 1971, Folder "Lottery," Box A-844, Special Revenue Commission: Subject Files, Agency Files, Thomas J. Meskill Gubernatorial Papers, CTSA.

64. Maisie Brown, "Reactions Mixed Locally to Lifting Lotteries Ban," *Hillsdale Daily News* (Hillsdale, MI), March 17, 1972, 1; Kelly Goodman, "Tax the Rich: Teachers' Long Campaign to Fund Public Schools" (PhD dissertation, Yale University, 2021).

65. Richard Boudreaux, "N. Jersey Lottery Attracts 5 Others," *Washington Post*, April 30, 1972, E6; State of Connecticut Auditors of Public Accounts, "Auditors' Report: Commission on Special Revenue," January 9, 1973, Folder "Special Revenue, M-Z," Box A-843, Agency Files: Special Revenue Commission, Thomas Meskill Papers, CTSA; *Concord Monitor* (Concord, NH), "The Selling of the Lottery," May 31, 1973; Fredrick D. Stocker, "State Sponsored Gambling as a Source of Public Revenue," *National Tax Journal* 25 (1972), 437.

66. Robert R. Douglass to Howard P. Miller, "State Lottery Ticket Price," July 23, 1971, Reel 37, Subseries 4: Fourth Administration, Series 37: Office Subject Files, Nelson A. Rockefeller Gubernatorial Files, RAC.

67. Christopher Z. Mooney, "Modeling Regional Effects on State Policy Diffusion," *Political Research Quarterly* 54, no. 1 (2001): 103–124.

68. Alok Kumar, Jeremy K. Page, and Oliver G. Spalt, "Religious Beliefs, Gambling Attitudes, and Financial Market Outcomes," *Journal of Financial Economics* 102 (2011): 671–708.

69. President's Commission on Law Enforcement, *Challenge of Crime in a Free Society*, 192.

70. James H. Rubin, "Sales Tax Hike Certain," *The Herald-News*, January 13, 1970, 1; *Philadelphia Inquirer*, "15 Days Left Until Tax Jumps," February 14, 1970, 1.

71. *Trenton Times*, "Numbers Runners Needn't Fear Lottery," November 18, 1969, 6; Statement of Senator William Musto of Hudson County on ACR 32 of 1969, *Public Hearing on Assembly Concurrent Resolution No. 32*, 43.

72. Edna I. Vincent, "Income Tax Unnecessary," Letter to *Asbury Park Press*, April 10, 1976, 11.

73. Charles E. Schropp, "Income Tax Issue," Letter to *The Courier-Post*, August 8, 1975, 14.

74. David M. Goldberg, "Lottery Opening Door to N.J. Casinos?," *The Courier-News* (Bridgewater, NJ), December 28, 1970, 26; Bryant Simon, *Boardwalk of Dreams: Atlantic City and the Fate of Urban America* (Oxford: Oxford University Press, 2006), 175; Ronald Sullivan, "Legal Gambling Sought in Jersey," *New York Times*, February 11, 1972, 40.

75. Anita Bellin, "Gaming Revenue Questioned," Letter to *Asbury Park Press*, October 30, 1974, 18.

76. Richard Benfield, "Tax Reform Defeated," *The Record* (Hackensack, NJ), July 18, 1972, 1; *Asbury Park Press*, "Vote in Assembly Kills Tax Reform," July 18, 1972, 1; Neil A. Lewis, "A Hot, Emotional Day," *The Record*, July 18, 1972, 1.

77. George Sternlieb and James W. Hughes, *The Atlantic City Gamble* (Cambridge, MA: Harvard University Press, 1983), 50.

78. Massachusetts State Lottery Commission, *1974 Annual Report*, State Library of Massachusetts, Boston, Massachusetts; no author, "Projections for Rhode Island: Weekly Sales," Folder "Gambling Legalization: Lottery (Miscellaneous)," Box 250, Philip Noel Papers, University of Rhode Island Special Collections, Kingston, RI.

79. Stanley Penn, "Federal Strike Forces Get Lots of Headlines, But Do They Work?," *Wall Street Journal*, March 16, 1982, 1.

80. *Robinson v. Cahill*, 118 N.J. Super. 223, 287 A.2d 187 (L. Div. 1972); Deborah Yaffe, *Other People's Children: The Battle for Justice and Equality in New Jersey's Schools* (New Brunswick, NJ: Rivergate Books, 2007).

81. *Trenton Times,* "State Lottery Offers Gamble That Can't Win," February 13, 1969, 14.

CHAPTER 2

1. *Lottery Player's Magazine*, "Cinderella Millionairess Finally Surfaces" 1, no. 1 (1981); Associated Press, "$2.8-Million Lottery Winner Finally Shows Up," *Los Angeles Times*, July 3, 1981, A4.

2. *Pando v. Fernandez*, 127 Misc.2d 224, 485 N.Y.S.2d 162, (1984); Christopher Pando, "Affidavit of Christopher Pando," *Appendix to Brief of Plaintiff-Appellant,* Pando v. Fernandez, *118 A.D.2d 474* (N.Y. App. Div. 1986), New York State Library, Albany, New York (hereafter NYSL).

3. *Weekly World News,* "She Gives God Credit for Lottery Win," August 11, 1981, 4.

4. *Pando v. Fernandez,* 127 Misc.2d 224 (1984).

5. *Pando v. Fernandez*, 118 A.D.2d 474 (1986).

6. Jack Alexander, "Bachelor Wins 7-Year Battle with Neighbor for Share of Lottery Payoff," *Weekly World News*, May 17, 1988.

7. James M. Henslin, "Craps and Magic," *American Journal of Sociology* 73, no. 3 (1967): 316–330; Ellen Langer, "The Illusion of Control," *Journal of Personality and Social Psychology* 32, no. 2 (1975): 311–328; Stuart A. Vyse, *Believing in Magic: The Psychology of Superstition* (New York: Oxford University Press, 1997).

8. Robert P. Weller, "Matricidal Magistrates and Gambling Gods: Weak States and Strong Spirits in China," *Australian Journal of Chinese Affairs* 33 (1995): 107–124; Ilana van Wyk, "Prosperity and the Work of Luck in the Universal Church of the Kingdom of God, South Africa," *Critical African Studies* 7, no. 3 (2015): 262–279; Pasi Falk and Pasi Mäenpää, *Hitting the Jackpot: Lives of Lottery Millionaires* (Oxford: Berg, 1999).

9. On the American meritocracy, see Nicholas Lemann, *The Big Test: The Secret History of the American Meritocracy* (New York: Farrar, Straus and Giroux, 2000); Michael Sandel, *The Tyranny of Merit: What's Become of the Common Good?* (New York: Farrar, Straus and Giroux, 2020); Daniel Markovits, *The Meritocracy Trap: How America's Foundational Myth Feeds Inequality, Dismantles the Middle Class, and Devours the Elite* (New York: Penguin, 2019).

10. Sandel, *The Tyranny of Merit*, 40; Max Weber, *The Protestant Ethic and the Spirit of Capitalism* (New York: Charles Scribner's Sons, 1958 [1904–05]).

11. Jackson Lears, *Something for Nothing: Luck in America* (New York: Viking, 2003), 3.

12. Rhonda Byrne, *The Secret* (New York: Atria Books, 2006), 28.

13. Lears, *Something for Nothing*.

14. Jon Butler, *Awash in a Sea of Faith: Christianizing the American People* (Cambridge, MA: Harvard University Press, 1990); Alexis de Tocqueville, *Democracy in America*, trans. Harvey C. Mansfield and Delba Winthrop (Chicago: University of Chicago Press, 2000), 594; Jonathan Levy, *Freaks of Fortune: The Emerging World of Capitalism and Risk in America* (Cambridge, MA: Harvard University Press, 2012); Lears, *Something for Nothing*.

15. Jim Cullen, *The American Dream: A Short History of an Idea that Shaped a Nation* (New York: Oxford University Press, 2003), 161–162; Ann Fabian, *Card Sharps and Bucket Shops: Gambling in Nineteenth-Century America* (Routledge: New York, 1999 [1990]), 115–117.

16. Edwin G. Burrows and Mike Wallace, *Gotham* (Oxford: Oxford University Press, 1999), 978; Mitchell Zuckoff, *Ponzi's Scheme: The True Story of a Financial Legend* (New York: Random House, 2005).

17. Thomas Piketty and Emmanuel Saez, "Income Inequality in the United States, 1913–1998," *Quarterly Journal of Economics* 118, no. 1 (2003): 1–39; Tables and Figures updated February 2020: https://eml.berkeley.edu/~saez/TabFig2018.xls.

18. H. Roy Kaplan, *Lottery Winners: How They Won and How Winning Changed Their Lives* (New York: Harper & Row, 1978), 6.

19. Illinois State Lottery Press Release, October 4, 1975, folder "Attitude Studies 1975–1976," Box 22, and Scientific Games Inc., "Preliminary Analysis of Sales Data of

Illinois State Lottery," version I, June 19, 1981, Box 71, Lottery Records, Office of the Director, Illinois State Archives, Springfield, Illinois (hereafter ISA); ; H. Roy Kaplan, "Lottery Winners: The Myth and Reality," *Journal of Gambling Behavior* 3, no. 3 (1987), 174; Kaplan, *Lottery Winners*, 6.

20. Jacob Hacker, *The Great Risk Shift: The Assault on American Jobs, Families, Healthcare, and Retirement and How You Can Fight Back* (New York: Oxford University Press, 2006); Jefferson Cowie, *Stayin' Alive: The 1970s and the Last Days of the Working Class* (New York: New Press, 2010); for an economic history of the 1970s, see Judith Stein, *Pivotal Decade: How the United States Traded Factories for Finance in the Seventies* (New Haven, CT: Yale University Press, 2011).

21. Tom Wolfe, "The 'Me' Decade and the Third Great Awakening," *New York*, August 23, 1976; Robert Nisbet, *Twilight of Authority* (New York: Oxford University Press, 1975), 23; Ellen Goodman, "The '70s Obsession—Me . . . My . . . Myself," *Boston Globe*, October 17, 1976, I1; Peter Marin, "The New Narcissism," *Harper's* 251, no. 1505, October, 1975, 46.

22. Christopher Lasch, *The Culture of Narcissism: American Life in an Age of Diminishing Expectations* (New York: W.W. Norton, 1979), 28; Cowie, *Stayin' Alive*, 217–219.

23. Public Opinion Surveys, Inc., "The Public's View of the New York State Lottery" (Princeton, NJ: Public Opinion Surveys, Inc., 1967), NYSL; Mathematica, Inc., "Lottery Background and Information" (n.d., probably 1977), Box 64, Lottery Records, Office of the Director, ISA; Alice Kessler-Harris, *Out to Work: A History of Wage-Earning Women in the United States* (New York: Oxford University Press, 2003 [1982]); Elaine Tyler May, *Homeward Bound: American Families in the Cold War Era* (New York: Basic Books, 2008 [1988]); Robert O. Self, *All in the Family: The Realignment of American Democracy Since the 1960s* (New York: Hill and Wang, 2012).

24. George Gallup, "Lottery Stirs Controversy," *Los Angeles Times*, June 2, 1963, M2; Maureen Kallick et al., "Survey of American Gambling Attitudes." Appendix 2 to Commission on the Review of the National Policy Toward Gambling, *Gambling in America* (Washington, DC: US Government Printing Office, 1976), 277, 362; Mike Vogel, "Nuns Hope to Beat Odds on Pennies from Heaven," *Buffalo Evening News*, January 17, 1980, C1; *Buffalo Courier-Express*, "Nuns Clinch 3rd in Lottery," January 22, 1980, 7.

25. *Catholic Encyclopedia,* "Gambling," http://www.newadvent.org/cathen/063 75b.htm.

26. Commission on the Review of the National Policy Toward Gambling, *Gambling in America* (Washington, DC: US Government Printing Office, 1976), 160–161; Dan Judson, "Sanctity, Pragmatism, and Paying the Bills: The Controversial Use of Bingo in Synagogues," in *All In: The Spread of Gambling in Twentieth-Century United States*, ed. Jonathan D. Cohen and David G. Schwartz (Reno: University of Nevada Press, 2018), 202–219; Illinois Legislative Investigating Committee, "Bingo

in Illinois: A Report to the General Assembly" (Chicago: Illinois Legislative Investigating Committee, 1982); United Press International, "Catholic Bingo More Profitable Than Ohio Lottery," *News-Journal* (Mansfield, OH), November 18, 1979, 14A.

27. Jack Tucker, "Latin Teacher Drawn in Lottery," *Democrat and Chronicle* (Rochester, NY), August 17, 1967, B1.

28. Ben Johnson, *The Lottery Book: Play to Win!* (New York: Avon Books, 1991), 167; Kaplan, *Lottery Winners*, 84.

29. Robert Frank, *Success and Luck: Good Fortune and the Myth of Meritocracy* (Princeton, NJ: Princeton University Press, 2016), 57.

30. Bruce Schulman, *The Seventies: The Great Shift in American Culture, Society, and Politics* (Boston: Da Capo Press, 2002), 100.

31. Jerry LeBlanc and Rena Dictor LeBlanc, *Suddenly Rich* (Englewood Cliffs, NJ: Prentice-Hall, 1978), 35.

32. Kathryn Tanner, "Grace and Gambling," in *Gambling: Mapping the American Moral Landscape*, ed. Alan Wolfe and Erik C. Owens (Waco, TX: Baylor University Press, 2009), 228; Lears, *Something for Nothing*, 33.

33. Susan Heller Anderson, "$5 Million Fantasy Becomes a Reality in New York Lotto," *New York Times*, December 1, 1982, B1.

34. Beverly Keel, "What Are the Odds?," *The Tennessean* (Nashville, TN), November 10, 2002, 11; Paul D. Colford, "You Ain't Seen Nothin' Yet," *Newsday*, September 1, 1987, II.3; Trudy Moore, "The Man Who Won $5 Million," *Ebony* 38, no. 6 (1983): 56.

35. Kaplan, *Lottery Winners,* 43.

36. Max Weber, "The Social Psychology of the World Religions," in *From Max Weber: Essays in Sociology*, ed. H. H. Gerth and C. Wright Mills (New York, Routledge, 2009), 271.

37. John T. Flynn, *God's Gold: The Story of Rockefeller and His Times* (New York: Harcourt, Brace, 1932), 401.

38. Richard Nixon, "Labor Day Message," September 3, 1972., American Presidency Project, https://www.presidency.ucsb.edu/node/254864.

39. Barry Bluestone and Bennet Harrison, *The Deindustrialization of America: Plant Closings, Community Abandonment, and the Dismantling of Basic Industry* (New York: Basic Books, 1982), A1. For case studies of deindustrialization, see John Hoerr, *And the Wolf Finally Came: The Decline and Fall of the American Steel Industry* (Pittsburgh, PA: University of Pittsburgh Press, 1988); Howard Gillette Jr., *Camden After the Fall: Decline and Renewal in a Post-Industrial City* (Philadelphia: University of Pennsylvania Press, 2006).

40. Katherine Newman, *Falling from Grace: The Experience of Downward Mobility in the American Middle Class* (New York: Free Press, 1988), 198.

41. Kaplan, *Lottery Winners*, 42; Nixon, "Labor Day Message. On the dehumanizing nature of blue-collar work in this period, see Ruth Milkman, *Farewell to the*

Factory: Auto Workers in the Late Twentieth Century (Berkeley: University of California Press, 1997).

42. Michael Lewis, *The Culture of Inequality* (Amherst: University of Massachusetts Press, 1978), 146.

43. Neal E. Millikan, *Lotteries in Colonial America* (New York: Routledge, 2011), 37–38.

44. Kate Bowler, *Blessed: A History of the American Prosperity Gospel* (Oxford: Oxford University Press, 2013), 68, 75–76, 78, 82.

45. Schulman, *The Seventies*, 131–140; Louis Hyman, *Debtor Nation: The History of America in Red Ink* (Princeton, NJ: Princeton University Press, 2012), 220–280; Bowler, *Blessed*, 99–100; Thomas E. Ludwig et al., *Inflation, Poortalk, and the Gospel* (Valley Forge, PA: Judson Press, 1981), 17.

46. Tony Tian-Ren Lin, *Prosperity Gospel Latinos and Their American Dream* (Chapel Hill: University of North Carolina Press, 2020), 10–11; Bowler, *Blessed,* 97, 98.

47. Nicholas Purcell, "Literate Games: Roman Urban Society and the Games of *Alea*," *Past and Present* 147, no. 1 (1995): 19 n. 70; Eric D. Huntsman, "And They Cast Lots: Divination, Democracy, and Josephus," *Brigham Young University Studies* 36 (1996–1997): 365–377.

48. Robert A. Orsi, *Thank You, St. Jude: Women's Devotions to the Patron Saint of Hopeless Causes* (New Haven, CT: Yale University Press, 1996), 49.

49. Emphasis in the original, Kaplan, *Lottery Winners*, 39–40.

50. Jon Van, "Pair Get $300,000 Answer to Prayers," *Chicago Tribune,* August 23, 1974, 3.

51. Alfred Gruen, "What's He to Do?," letter to *Herald and Review* (Decatur, IL), September 5, 1974, 6.

52. A 1967 crime commission estimated that loan sharking was the second largest source of revenue for organized crime after gambling; President's Commission on Law Enforcement and Administration of Justice, *The Challenge of Crime in a Free Society* (Washington, DC: US Government Printing Office, 1967), 189.

53. It is not clear what game Pulaski played. If he indeed picked his own numbers, then he had played a daily numbers game and must have bet much more than $1. If he played a scratch off or raffle-type game, he would not have had the opportunity to pick his own numbers. Kaplan, *Lottery Winners*, 37.

54. *Catholic Encyclopedia,* "Prayer," https://www.newadvent.org/cathen/12345b.htm.

55. Joseph P. Chinnici, "The Catholic Community at Prayer, 1926–1976," in *Habits of Devotion: Catholic Religious Practice in Twentieth-Century America*, ed. James M. O'Toole (Ithaca, NY: Cornell University Press, 2004), 9–88.

56. *The Evangelist* (Albany, NY), "Lottery Winners Count Blessings," October 21, 1976, 1.

57. James H. Bowman, "Can You Win the Lottery with Prayer?," *Chicago Daily News,* September 21–22, 1979, 20.

58. Bowler, *Blessed*, 233; Kaplan, *Lottery Winners*, 36.

CHAPTER 3

1. Leo McCarthy, Press Release: "Lieutenant Governor Voices Opposition to State Lottery Initiative," June 25, 1984, included in *State Lotteries: An Overview*, Hearing before the Subcommittee on Intergovernmental Relations of the Committee on Government Affairs, United States Senate, Ninety-Eighth Congress, Second Session, October 3, 1984 (Washington, DC: US Government Printing Office, 1985), 225.

2. William Endicott, "Wrong Number? Religious Groups Planning 'David-and-Goliath' Battle," *Los Angeles Times*, July 6, 1984, A3.

3. Beth Moncure Winn and Marcia Lynn Whicker, "Indicators of State Lottery Adoptions," *Policy Studies Journal* 18, no. 2 (1989–1990): 293–304; Frances Stokes Berry and William D. Berry. "State Lottery Adoptions as Policy Innovations: An Event History Analysis," *American Political Science Review* 84, no. 2 (1990): 395–415; John Lyman Mason and Michael Nelson, *Governing Gambling* (New York: Century Foundation Press, 2001); Denise Von Herrmann, *The Big Gamble: The Politics of Lottery and Casino Expansion* (Westport, CT: Praeger, 2002); Jason L. Jensen, "Policy Diffusion Through Institutional Legitimation: State Lotteries," *Journal of Public Administration Research and Theory* 13, no. 4 (2003): 521–541.

4. System Operations Inc., "Lottery Background and Information," and Mathematica Inc., "State Lotteries: A Viable Alternative to Increased Taxes" (n.d.), Folder 37, LP121, Assemblyman Leon Ralph Papers, California State Archives, Sacramento, California (hereafter CSA); *Hartford Courant*, "Two Men Helped Start Lotteries in 11 States," February 15, 1976, 27A.

5. Lee Smith, "An Instant Success Story," *Dun's Review*, December 1978, 56; George Lardner Jr., "Betting Business Booms and Seeks to Get Bigger," *Washington Post*, October 18, 1976, A1.

6. Edward Dodd, "The Brains Behind the Games," *Lottery Players Magazine* 1, no. 3 (November 1981), 9.

7. Tom Stevenson, "Mastermind of the Instant Lottery," *New York Times*, January 2, 1977, 85; Charles Connolly, "Illinois State Lottery Survey," September 1986, page 16, Box 31; Illinois State Lottery, "New Lottery Game! Win up to $10,000 Instantly," October 9, 1975, Folder "Promotional Materials," Box 73; Scientific Games, "Working Papers for 'Lottery Mile' (Instant Game No. 14)," June 17, 1980, Box 1, Lottery Records, Office of the Director, Illinois State Archives, Springfield, Illinois.

8. Massachusetts State Lottery, "Announcing the Instant Game" (n.d., probably 1974), found in the records of the Massachusetts State Lottery, Braintree, Massachusetts; Tom Stevenson, "Mastermind of the Instant Lottery," *New York Times*, January 2, 1977, 85; *Hartford Courant*, "Ajello Approves New Lottery Game," June 28, 1975, 38; New Jersey Lottery, *Annual Report: 1976*, New Jersey State Library, Trenton, New Jersey; Peter Kihss, "Instant Lotteries Prove to Be Popular, with 12 States Besides New York Operating or Organizing Them," *New York Times*, September 8, 1976, 12.

9. Michael Philip Davis, "Scientific Games: Lobbying for Lotteries as Art," clipping from unknown publication, n.d. (probably 1981), Folder "Lottery: Gen. Correspondence 1981 (File 1)" Box 207, Bruce Babbit Papers, Governor's Office, Records, Arizona State Archives, Phoenix, Arizona (hereafter ASA); *Public Gaming*, "The Economic Potential of State Lotteries," January 1982, 46.

10. Daniel W. Bower to George C. Anderson, February 2, 1982, Folder "Lottery Commission, Arizona State General Correspondence 3," Box 384, Subseries 1, Series 7, Governor Bruce Babbitt Papers, ASA; Charles Storch, "Bally Plans to Buy a Lottery Game Firm," *Chicago Tribune*, October 24, 1981, N6; Jube Shiver Jr., "D.C. Lottery Rights Given to Ga. Firm," *Washington Post*, May 25, 1982, C1.

11. Kathleen Deveny, "McWorld?," *Business Week,* October 13, 1986, 79.

12. Tom Little interview with the author, February 1, 2017, recording in the possession of the author; Kenneth Bredemeier, "Jai Alai Group Heavily Backs Legal Gambling in Referendum," *Washington Post*, April 27, 1980, B1.

13. Paul Silvergleid interview with the author, February 1, 2017, recording in the possession of the author; Scientific Games Inc. (advertisement), "Is Your State Losing Its Share of $2,500,000,000?," *State Legislatures*, October 1983, 1; Scientific Games Inc. (advertisement), "Scientific Games Has Been Selected as Consultant and Ticket Supplier for all 6 of the New Lottery Start-Ups in the United States Since 1976," *State Legislatures*, January 1984, back cover; John R. Koza, "The Myth of the Poor Buying Lottery Tickets," *Public Gaming*, January 1982, 31–40.

14. Testimony of Martin Puncke, Hearing Before the Subcommittee on Intergovernmental Relations of the Committee on Governmental Affairs, U.S. Senate, 98th Congress, 2nd Session, October 3, 1984 (Washington, DC: US Government Printing Office, 1985), 5; Jim Carney interview with the author, January 30, 2017; Lee Ann Osbun, "Of Chance and Finance: Passage and Performance of the Iowa Lottery," in *Issues in Iowa Politics*, ed. Lee Ann Osbun and Steffen W. Schmidt (Ames: University of Iowa Press, 1990), 218–220.

15. David Magleby, "Direct Legislation in the American States," in *Referendums Around the World: The Growing Use of Direct Democracy*, ed. David Butler and Austin Ranney (Washington, DC: AEI Press, 1994), 233.

16. Daniel A. Smith, *Tax Crusaders and the Politics of Direct Democracy* (New York: Routledge, 1998), 70–83.

17. Mark P. Petracca, "Political Consultants and Democratic Governance," *PS: Political Science and Politics* 22, no. 1 (1989): 12; Todd Donovan, Shaun Bowler, and David McCuan, "Political Consultants and the Initiative Industrial Complex," in *Dangerous Democracy? The Battle over Ballot Initiatives in America*, ed. Larry J. Sabato, Howard R. Ernst, and Bruce A. Larson (Lanham, MD: Rowman and Littlefield, 2001), 101–134.

18. California Commission on Campaign Financing, *Democracy by Initiative: Shaping California's Fourth Branch of Government* (Los Angeles: Center for Responsive Government, 1992), 264, 283; on the professionalization of political consultants

and the technological improvements of the 1970s and 1980s, see Larry J. Sabato, *The Rise of Political Consultants: New Ways of Winning Elections* (New York: Basic Books, 1981); David McCuan, Shaun Bowler, Todd Donovan, and Ken Fernandez, "California's Political Warriors: Campaign Professionals and the Initiative Process," in *Citizens as Legislators: Direct Democracy in the United States*, ed. Shaun Bowler, Todd Donovan, and Caroline J. Tolbert (Columbus: Ohio State University Press, 1998), 55–79.

19. Barry Fadem interview with the author, February 27, 2017; Tracy Wood, "Odds Leaning Toward OK of State Lottery This Year," *Los Angeles Times*, February 22, 1984, A15.

20. Bill Jones, *A History of the California Initiative Process* (Sacramento: California Secretary of State, 1998), 101; Bill Behm interview with the author, January 26, 2017, recording in the possession of the author; John Koza interview with the author, March 2, 2017, recording in the possession of the author; Vic Pollard, "California Ponders Lottery to Aid Cancer," *Reno Gazette,* January 28, 1980, 40; State Lottery California Initiative 242 (1980), https://repository.uchastings.edu/ca_ballot_in its/404.

21. Bill Meek interview with the author, February 14, 2017, recording in the possession of the author; John Leach, "Drive Begun to Create State-Operated Lottery," *Arizona Republic*, May 1, 1980, A1; John Koza interview with the author, May 9, 2017; Tracy Wood and Bud Lembke, "Consultants for Prop. 9 in Debt," *Los Angeles Times,* October 8, 1980, B3.

22. Davis, "Scientific Games."

23. Associated Press, "Bally Corp. Has Stake in Lottery Vote," *St. Louis Post-Dispatch,* October 9, 1984, 6B.

24. Emphasis in the original; Daniel Hays Lowenstein and Robert M. Stern, "The First Amendment and Paid Initiative Petition Circulators: A Dissenting View and a Proposal," *Hastings Constitutional Law Quarterly* 17, no 1 (1989): 198; Sue Hill, "State Lottery Backers Over-the-Top on Names," *Statesman Journal* (Salem, OR), July 4, 1984, 1; John Leach, "Ticket Firm Spent $300,000 to Push Lotteries," *Arizona Republic,* November 16, 1980, B1; Bill Meek interview.

25. John Koza to Irv Babson (n.d., probably 1985), Folder "Scientific Games Development Corp," Box 20, Eugene Martin Christiansen Papers, Special Collections & Archives, University of Nevada, Las Vegas, Las Vegas, Nevada (hereafter UNLV); "Measure No. 5, State of Oregon" in *Voters' Pamphlet: State of Oregon General Election*, November 6, 1984, http://library.state.or.us/reposit ory/2010/201003011350161/; California Voter's Pamphlet, "Proposition 37: State Lottery, Initiative Constitutional Amendment and Statute," *California Ballot Pamphlet: 1984 General Election*, November 6, 1984, UC Hastings Scholarship Repository, University of California, Hastings College of Law, https://repository. uchastings.edu/ca_ballot_inits/509/; Barry Fadem Interview, February 27, 2017.

26. Bethany MacLean, *Democracy in Chains: The Deep History of the Radical Right's Stealth Plan for America* (New York: Penguin, 2017); liberal efforts to build organizations comparable to ALEC sputtered, making little headway outside of already liberal states; see Alexander Hertel-Fernandez, *State Capture: How Conservative Activists, Big Business, and Wealthy Donors Reshaped the American States—and the Nation* (New York: Oxford University Press, 2019).

27. John Hurst, "Lottery Ticket Supplier to Win Biggest Jackpot of All," *Los Angeles Times*, May 16, 1985, B3; State of New Jersey, Casino Control Commission, "Application by Bally's Park Place, Inc. for a Casino License and Application by Bally Manufacturing Corporation for a Casino Service Industry License" (n.d., approximately 1980), Folder 48, Box 6, Series 3, Gerald Kopel Papers, Denver Public Library, Denver, Colorado (hereafter DPL).

28. Dewey Knudson, "Lottery Service Clash Erupts on Eve of Debate," *Des Moines Register*, February 13, 1985, 2; John Van De Kamp to Richard Alatorre, "PROPOSITION 37—Fadem Lottery Initiative," August 22, 1984, Folder 1, Box 446, Lottery Commission Records, Subject Files, Richard Floyd Papers, CSA; Jeff Mapes, "Lottery Wording Viewed as Effort to Exclude Rivals" *Oregonian*, September 19, 1984, A1.

29. Koza Interview, May 9, 2017.

30. California explicitly required the lottery to start within 135 days; in Oregon, the bill allotted 30 days for the appointments and stipulated that the lottery had to start 105 days after the appointment process was completed; Barry Fadem testimony, Senate Committee on Governmental Organization, *Interim Hearing on the California State Lottery*, September 10, 1984, 32, California State Library, Sacramento, California.

31. William Endicott, "Lottery: '82 May Yield Better Odds," *Los Angeles Times*, January 13, 1982, 1.

32. Davis, "Scientific Games"; Meek, Foudy, and Zimmerman, Inc., "Arizona Statewide Survey on a State Lottery Proposal," Folder "Lottery," Subseries 3, Series 3, Box 180, Bruce Babbitt Papers, ASA;

33. Ronald Reagan, "Inaugural Address," January 20, 1981, https://millercenter.org/the-presidency/presidential-speeches/january-20-1981-first-inaugural-address.

34. Stanley Steingut to William Haddad, "Preliminary Report on the New York State Lottery," November 3, 1975, Folder "Lottery," Box 3, Correspondence and Subject Files, New York State Legislature, Assembly, Office of Legislative Oversight and Analysis, New York State Archives, Albany, New York; Marvin R. Brams, "The Failure of the Delaware Lottery," *Proceedings of the Annual Conference on Taxation Held Under the Auspices of the National Tax Association*, vol. 68 (1975): 271–275; Report of the Joint Standing Committee on Performance Audit, *Study of the State Lottery Commission,* House Paper 2173 (State of Maine, January 3, 1977), Harvard Law Library, Cambridge, Massachusetts; *Cincinnati Enquirer*, "Lottery Scandal Intensifies with Additional Charges," October 15, 1978, A4; Philip W. Noel to Allie

Volpe, July 29, 1974, Folder "Gambling Legalization, Lottery," Box 250, Phillip W. Noel Gubernatorial Papers, University of Rhode Island Special Collections Library, Kingston, Rhode Island; Commonwealth of Pennsylvania, Press Release, September 19, 1980, Folder 18, Container 88, Administrative Correspondence, Governor Victor Atiyeh Administration Records, Oregon State Archives, Salem, Oregon.

35. Meek, Foudy, and Zimmerman, Inc., "Arizona Statewide Survey"; Barry Fadem interview with the author, January 6, 2017, recording in the possession of the author.

36. Richard Demmer, Letter to *Los Angeles Times,* March 3, 1983, F6.

37. J. Beckwith, Letter to *San Bernardino County Sun*, "See Lottery as Painless Answer," June 9, 1984, B12.

38. Barry Fadem testimony to Senate Committee on Governmental Organizations, *Interim Hearing on the California State Lottery Initiative*, September 10, 1984, 33, 43, CSL.

39. Scholars have debated *Serrano*'s impact on Proposition 13; see William A. Fischel, "Did *Serrano* Cause Proposition 13?," *National Tax Journal* 42, no. 4 (1989): 465–473; Kirk J. Stark and Jonathan Zasloff, "Tiebout and Tax Revolts: Did *Serrano* Really Cause Proposition 13?" *UCLA Law Review* 50 (2003): 801–858.

40. California Constitution, Article XIII: A [Tax Limitation], Section 1–Section 7, https://leginfo.legislature.ca.gov/faces/codes_displayText.xhtml?lawCode= CONS&division=&title=&part=&chapter=&article=XIII+A; Bruce Schulman, *The Seventies: The Great Shift in American Culture, Society, and Politics* (Boston: Da Capo Press, 2002), 205–212; Robert Kuttner, *Revolt of the Haves: Tax Rebellions and Hard Times* (New York: Simon and Schuster, 1980), 96; Theo Wilson, "Calif. Taxpayer Revolt Spreading like Wildfire," *Daily News* (New York, NY), June 5, 1978, 20; on Proposition 13 as a conservative white suburban backlash, see Lisa McGirr, *Suburban Warriors: The Origins of the New American Right* (Princeton, NJ: Princeton University Press, 2002); Becky M. Nicolaides, *My Blue Heaven: Life and Politics in the Working-Class Suburbs of Los Angeles, 1920–1965*; Darren Dochuk, *From Bible Belt to Sunbelt: Plain-Folk Religion, Grassroots Politics, and the Rise of Evangelical Conservatism* (New York: W. W. Norton, 2012).

41. David O. Sears and Jack Citrin, *Tax Revolt: Something for Nothing in California* (Cambridge, MA: Harvard University Press, 1982), 43, 195.

42. Conrad C. Jamison, *Before and After Proposition 13: Expenditure by State and Local Government in California* (Los Angeles: Security Pacific Bank, March 1982), A-9, B-37–38; Jack Citrin, "Introduction," in *California and the American Tax Revolt: Proposition 13 Five Years Later*, ed. Terry Richardson (Berkeley: University of California Press, 1984), 7; David G. Savage, "Public School Decline Predates Prop. 13 Vote," *Los Angeles Times*, June 12, 1983, 29; James Ring Adams, *Secrets of the Tax Revolt* (San Diego: Harcourt Brace Jovanovich, 1984), 173; George Neill, "Loss of Funds Cited in Deterioration of California Schools," *Education Week*, February 24, 1982.

43. Congressional Research Service, "Federal Grants to State and Local Governments: A Historical Perspective on Contemporary Issues," R40638 (Updated May 2019), https://fas.org/sgp/crs/misc/R40638.pdf; White House Office of Management and Budget, "Summary Comparison of Total Outlays for Grants to State and Local Governments: 1940–2026," Table 12.1, https://www.whitehouse.gov/omb/historical-tables/; Edward Dodd, "The Brains Behind the Games," *Lottery Players' Magazine* 1, no. 3 (November 1981): 29.

44. John L. Mikesell, "The Path of the Tax Revolt: Statewide Expenditure and Tax Control Referenda Since Proposition 13," *State & Local Government Review* 18, no. 1 (Winter 1986): 5–12.

45. Arnold Powelson to Victor Atiyeh, February 24, 1984, Folder 22, Container 88, Administrative Correspondence, Governor Victor Atiyeh Administration Records, OSA; Jerry Gillam, "Cline to Resurrect State Lottery Plan," *Los Angeles Times,* June 14, 1978, A23.

46. Ken Feldman, "Legalized Betting in California," letter to *Los Angeles Times,* July 7, 1983, E4; Isaac William Martin, *The Permanent Tax Revolt: How the Property Tax Transformed American Politics* (Stanford, CA: Stanford University Press, 2008), 169.

47. Lynn Thompson testimony, *Interim Hearing on the California State Lottery Initiative,* 152–155.

48. *Los Angeles Times,* "Arizonans Will Vote on State-Run Lottery," October 26, 1980, 5; John Leach, "Businessmen to Campaign Against Tax-Cut Initiative," *Arizona Republic,* September 23, 1980, B1.

49. Ronald L. Soble, "Prop 36: A Rescue Net for Prop. 13 or Legal Morass?," *Los Angeles Times,* September 17, 1984, B1; Nancy Jenkins testimony, Senate Committee on Government Organization, "Interim Hearing on the California State Lottery Initiative," 121–122, CSL.

50. Endicott, "Lottery: '82 May Yield Better Odds"; Gerard Fulcher testimony, *State Lotteries: An Overview,* 119.

51. John Leach, "Backers of State-Lottery Initiative Are Revealed," *Arizona Republic,* August 9, 1980, A1.

52. Michael Foudy interview with the author, February 6, 2017; among the names of Arizonans for Tax Reduction (ATR) members provided to newspapers by William Adams was Phoenix advertising executive Mary O'Hanlon, who claims she was never involved in ATR or the lottery campaign, nor had she ever met Adams; Mary O'Hanlon, email correspondence with the author, January 25, 2017.

53. Fadem Interview, January 6, 2017; Californians for Better Education, Press Release, n.d. (probably 1984), Folder "Lottery Commission, Arizona State General Correspondence 3," Box 384, Subseries 1, Series 7, Governor Bruce Babbitt Papers, ASA.

54. Barry Fadem testimony, "Fadem Lottery Initiative Proposition 37," August 22, 1984, 53, CSL; Paul Jacobs, "Supporters of Lottery Link Foes to Jockeys and Racehorse Owners," *Los Angeles Times*, October 4, 1984, 24.

55. Barry Fadem to Richard Alatorre, "Californians for Better Education: Partial List of Endorsements" and "Who Is Californians for Better Education?," n.d. (probably August 1984), Folder 1, Box 446, Lottery Commission Records, Subject Files, Richard Floyd Papers, CSA.

56. *Statesman Journal*, "Groups Contribute to Ballot Measures," October 31, 1984, 7; John Leach and Bill Waldrop, "Most Financial Backers in Proposition 106 Battle Will Remain Secret," *Arizona Republic*, October 31, 1980, A2; Jeff Mapes, "Petitions for Lottery Over Top" *Oregonian*, July 4, 1984, D3.

57. Carl Ingram and Jerry Gillam, "Lottery Initiative Backers Given $1.5 Million in Funds," *Los Angeles Times* September 27, 1984; B19; Hurst, "Lottery Ticket Supplier to Win Biggest Jackpot of All"; Dell Isham interview with the author, January 20, 2017, recording in the possession of the author.

58. Some reports indicate that the entire Colorado campaign—not just advertising—cost $90,000; though the Colorado lottery initiative passed in 1980, Scientific Games had to spend an additional $10,000 in 1982 to lobby state legislators to formally create the lottery agency and set up its guidelines; Maria Garcia Berry interview with the author, April 18, 2017; Keith B. Richburg, "Lottery Company Starts $80,000 Blitz in District," *Washington Post*, October 29, 1980, A1; John Leach, "Ticket Firm Spent $300,000 to Push Lotteries," *Arizona Republic*, November 16, 1980, B1; Ray Flack, "Gamble Wins Lottery Coup," *Denver Post*, n.d. (approximately 1983), Folder 1, Box 39, Series 11, Gerald Kopel Papers, DPL.

59. Koza interview, March 2, 2017; Leach, "Ticket Firm Spent $300,000"; Peter Zimmerman interview with the author, February 9, 2017.

60. Keith B. Richburg and Ron Shaffer, "Progambling Ads May Turn Tide on Vote in D.C.," *Washington Post*, October 30, 1980, A1.

61. *CBS Evening News*, "California Vote / Lottery," October 21, 1984, Record 293950, Vanderbilt Television Archives, Nashville, Tennessee.

62. Mervin Field, "Ads Push Initiatives into Public Spotlight," *Sacramento Bee*, November 2, 1984, A13.

63. Albert J. Sitter, "Lottery Opponents Identify Group's Financial Backers," *Arizona Republic*, October 25, 1980, 27; United Press International, "Church Groups Plan to Defeat Lottery Proposal," *Napa Valley Register*, July 6, 1984, 1.

64. Author interview with Mark Pruner, May 25, 2021; Susan Britton, "The Prophets May Frown, but the Profits Can Tempt," *Sacramento Bee*, December 8, 1985, A21; *Los Angeles Times*, "The State," September 13, 1984, A2.

65. Steve Wiegand, "Odd Coalitions Fight over a Lottery," *San Francisco Chronicle*, October 18, 1984, 4; Scientific Games, "Lotteries and the Parimutuel Industry" (May 1983), Folder "Scientific Games Development Corp.," Box 20, Eugene Martin

Christiansen Papers, UNLV; Jerry Gillam and Carl Ingram, "Racing Industry's $2.6 Million Fights Lottery," *Los Angeles Times*, October 30, 1984, B13.

66. Paul Jacobs, "Anti-Lottery Ads Charge Backers Have Had Ties to Organized Crime," *Los Angeles Times*, September 29, 1984, A29, emphasis in the original; Stop the Lottery Committee (advertisement), "If the Lottery Passes . . .," *Arizona Republic*, November 3, 1980, 2.

67. Dorothy Salander to Gary Condit, February 1, 1984, Folder 2, Box 446, Subject Files, Lottery Commission Records, Richard Floyd Papers, CSA.

68. Committee for Governmental Integrity (advertisement), "The Committee for Governmental Integrity Urges the Citizens of Washington, D.C. to vote against D.C. Initiative #6 on November 4, 1980," *Washington Post*, October 30, 1980, DC6.

69. EdB/BRH (no full name provided), "Internal Report (Not for Release)," August 25, 1980, Folder "Lottery Commission, Arizona State General Correspondence 3," and Bruce Babbitt to "Editor," October 30, 1984, Folder "Lottery Commission, Arizona State General Correspondence 2," Box 384, Subseries 1, Series 7, Governor Bruce Babbitt Papers, ASA.

70. Harvey N. Chinn, "Don't Gamble with California's Future: An Analysis of Proposition 37: The State Lottery Initiative" (Sacramento: Coalition Against Legalizing Lotteries, n.d., probably 1984), Folder 4, Box 515, Subject Files, Series 2, Tim Leslie Papers, CSA.

71. March Fong Eu, *State of California: General Election, November 6, 1984*, (n.d, n.p.), CSA; "Oregon State Lottery: Chronology of Events," attached to Robert W. Smith to Victor Atiyeh, August 6, 1985, Folder "Lottery," Box 117, 89A-15, Issue Research Correspondence Collection, Governor Victor Atiyeh Administration Records, OSA.

72. Meek, Foudy, and Zimmerman, Inc., "Arizona Statewide Survey on a State Lottery Proposal"; Fred W. Lindecke, "Strength in Numbers for Lottery Vote," *St. Louis Post-Dispatch*, February 29, 1984, 1A; Barry Fadem to Richard Alatorre, August 15, 1984, Folder 1, Box 446, Subject Files, Lottery Commission Records, Richard Floyd Papers, CSA; *St. Louis Post-Dispatch*, "County by County Election Results," November 8, 1984, 20A.

73. Robert O. Self, *American Babylon: Race and the Struggle for Postwar Oakland* (Princeton, NJ: Princeton University Press, 2003), 323–324; Fong Eu, *Statement of Vote: General Election, November 6, 1984*, 32.

74. Ed Salzman, "State Lottery's 'Pot of Gold' Brings Variety of Uncertainty," *Sacramento Bee*, November 7, 1984, A4; Judie Rohde to Gary Condit, July 1, 1983, Folder 2, Box 446, Subject Files, Lottery Commission Records, Richard Floyd Papers, CSA.

75. *Sacramento Bee*, "How Voters Felt About Propositions," November 7, 1981, A4; Eugene Robinson and Keith B. Richburg, "D.C.: Carter, Lottery, Statehood Win Easily," *Washington Post*, November 5, 1980, A1.

76. *Los Angeles Times*, "The State," June 6, 1985, A2; Behm interview.

77. John A. Bolt, "Scientific Games Reign as King of State Lotteries," *The Courier* (Waterloo, IA), September 8, 1987, B6; Tom Witosky and Dewey Knudson, "Pinball Firm Lobbies for Iowa Lottery," *Des Moines Register*, February 20, 1983, 1; "Oregon State Lottery, Chronology of Events," attachment to Robert W. Smith to Governor Victor Atiyeh, "Oregon State Lottery Report as of August 6, 1985," August 6, 1985," Folder "Lottery," Box 117, Issue Research Correspondence, Victor Atiyeh Papers, OSA.

78. Michael Michalko testimony, State of California, Senate Rules Committee, Hearing, Sacramento, California, August 28, 1985, CSL, 15–16.

79. Attachment to Margaret Rowland to Victor Atiyeh, January 16, 1985, Folder 21, Container 88, Administrative Correspondence, Governor Victor Atiyeh Administration Records, OSA. Frank Turco, "Lottery Turns 1 on July 1; Success Is 'Almost Unreal,'" *Arizona Republic*, June 28, 1982, B1.

80. In 1975, Scientific Games charged the New Jersey Lottery just 1.7 cents per ticket for its first batch of instant tickets; Robert A. Boyd to James S. Rennie, August 9, 1982, Box 2U 09 066, Policy Files, Chief of State, John Spellman Gubernatorial Papers, Washington State Archives, Olympia, Washington; Mapes, "Lottery Wording," ; Flack, "Gamble Wins Lottery Coup"; Don G. Campbell, "Arizona Goes into the Lottery Business," *Los Angeles Times*, June 19, 1981, I1; Beatrice S. Tylutki, "Instant Lottery," August 26, 1975, Folder "Lottery 1974–1975," Box 10, General Files, Executive Secretary/Chief of Staff Papers, Brendan Byrne Gubernatorial Papers, New Jersey State Archives, Trenton, New Jersey.

81. Associated Press, "California Lottery Sells 21 Million Tickets in 1 Day," *Reno Gazette-Journal*, October 5, 1985, 3A; Steve Gibson, "56 Million Lottery Tickets Sold in Four Days," *Sacramento Bee*, October 8, 1985, B2; Californians for Better Education," Questions and Answers about the Proposed California State Lottery" (n.d., probably 1984), Folder "Lottery Commission (1 of 5), Subject Files, Richard Floyd Papers, CSA; California State Lottery, First Annual Report, 1985–1986, CSL.

82. Lanie Jones and Nancy Skelton, "Fanfare, $1 Fantasies Herald State's Lottery," *Los Angeles Times*, October 4, 1985, OC1; Mary Laine Yarber, "The Inside Story of Schools and the State Lottery," *Los Angeles Times*, August 20, 1992, LBJ3; *Los Angeles Times*, "Text of Gov. Deukmejian's State of the State Address," January 10, 1986, A26; David Roberti and Willie L. Brown Jr., "The 1985–1986 Budget: Perspectives and Issues," Report of the Legislative Analyst to the Joint Legislative Budget Committee (n.d. probably 1984), https://lao.ca.gov/analysis/1985/pandi_85.pdf.

83. *Los Angeles Times*, "A Gamble for Education," August 27, 1985, B4; Louis Freedberg, "California Educators Assert Lottery Has Failed to Pay Off for the Schools," *New York Times*, October 4, 1988, A18; Steve Gibson, "Educators Fear School Will Be Lottery Losers," *Press Democrat* (Santa Rosa, CA), December 2, 1985, 7A.

84. David Streitfeld, "What the Lottery Won't Buy," *Washington Post*, November 4, 1988, B5; Michelle Quinn, "The Lottery Lemon," *California Journal*, December

1, 1991; *Appeal-Democrat* (Marysville, CA), "Let's Scratch the Lottery," April 9, 1992, D6.

85. David Durenberger opening statement, *State Lotteries: An Overview*, 2.

86. Virginia Ellis and Carl Ingram, "Secret Recording Brags of GTECH Influence With Lottery Directors,," *Los Angeles Times*, October 22, 1993, A3; Virginia Ellis and Daniel M. Weintraub, "Embattled Director of State Lottery Resigns," *Los Angeles Times*, November 9, 1993, A1.

87. Matthew Vaz, *Running the Numbers: Race, Police, and the History of Urban Gambling* (Chicago: University of Chicago Press, 2020), 160.

88. *California v. Cabazon Band of Mission Indians*, 480 U.S. 202 (1987); David G. Schwartz, *Roll the Bones: The History of Gambling* (New York: Gotham, 2006), 433–439; Dean J. Kotlowski, "From Backlash to Bingo: Ronald Reagan and Federal Indian Policy," *Pacific Historical Review* 77, no. 4 (2008): 617–652.

89. Schwartz, *Roll the Bones*, 436.

90. Nelson D. Schwartz, "The $50 Ticket: A Lottery Boon Raises Concern," *New York Times*, December 27, 2007.

CHAPTER 4

1. Margot Hornblower, "$41 Million Jackpot Has New Yorkers Burning with Lotto Fever," *Washington Post,* August 22, 1985, A3.

2. Melinda Beck, "The Lottery Craze," *Newsweek,* September 2, 1985, 16.

3. National Association of State and Provincial Lotteries, "NASPL Resource Index," accessed February 6, 2021, https://www.nasplmatrix.org/nri.

4. David G. Schwartz, *Roll the Bones: The History of Gambling* (New York: Gotham Books, 2006), 389.

5. Massachusetts Lottery Commission, *Annual Report: 1978* (Massachusetts Lottery Commission, 1979), Massachusetts State Library, Boston, Massachusetts; *New York Times,* "Lotto, a Failure, Is Discontinued by Massachusetts State Lottery," January 8, 1979, A15; Associated Press, "Bay State's 'Lotto' Loses to Competition," *Burlington Free Press* (Burlington, VT), January 8, 1979, 1.

6. Associated Press, "Lottery Turns to 'Lotto,'" *Journal News* (White Plains, NY), October 25, 1978, 10B; Bill Beeney, "New Lottery Lets You Pick the Numbers," *Democrat and Chronicle* (Rochester, NY), November 2, 1978, C1.

7. New York State Lottery, Press Release, April 20, 1979, folder "Lottery (Legislation), Taxation and Finance" and John D. Quinn to Robert Morgado, "Update on Daily Numbers/Automated Lotto," November 17, 1980, folder "Lottery (Miscellaneous Data) Taxation and Finance," Box 138, Subject Files, Records of the New York State Department of Budget, New York State Archives, Albany, New York (hereafter NYSA); Associated Press, "Efforts Under Way to Boost Lotto," *Poughkeepsie Journal*, December 21, 1978, 24.

8. Illinois Economic and Fiscal Commission, *The Illinois State Lottery: A Special Report* (State of Illinois, December 1986), 22; Charles T. Clotfelter, Philip J. Cook, Julie A. Edell, and Marian Moore, "State Lotteries at the Turn of the Century: Report to the National Gambling Impact Study Commission" (April 23, 1999), 26, https://govinfo.library.unt.edu/ngisc/reports/lotfinal.pdf Bruce Mohl, "Why the Mass. Lottery Is a Big Winner," *Boston Globe,* January 28, 1986, 25; US Census Bureau, *Statistical Abstract of the United States: 1999* (December 1999), 333, https://www.census.gov/library/publications/1999/compendia/statab/119ed.html.

9. Lauren Silverman, "Cubs? Weather? No, City's Buzzing About Lotto," *Chicago Tribune*, August 31, 1984, A1.

10. Jefferson Cowie, *The Great Exception: The New Deal and the Limits of American Politics* (Princeton, NJ: Princeton University Press, 2016); Nicholas Lemann, *Transaction Man: The Rise of the Deal and the Decline of the American Dream* (New York: Farrar, Straus and Giroux, 2019); Robert D. Putnam with Shaylyn Romney Garrett, *The Upswing: How America Came Together a Century Ago and How We Can Do It Again* (New York: Simon & Schuster, 2020).

11. Lawrence Mishel and Alyssa Davis, "CEO Pay Continues to Rise as Typical Workers Are Paid Less," Economic Policy Institute, *Issue Brief* #380 (June 2014), 3; Barbara Ehrenreich, *Fear of Falling: The Inner Life of the Middle Class* (New York: Twelve, 2020 [1989]), 282.

12. Ronald Reagan, "The President's News Conference," June 28, 1983, https://www.reaganlibrary.gov/research/speeches/62883f.

13. Gil Troy, *Morning in America: How Ronald Reagan Invented the 1980s* (Princeton, NJ: Princeton University Press, 2005), 56–63, 115–135, 204–234; Steve Fraser, *Every Man a Speculator: A History of Wall Street in American Life* (New York: HarperCollins, 2005), 540, 556–557; Kurt Andersen, *Fantasyland: How America Went Haywire, A 500-Year History* (New York: Random House, 2018), 253–254.

14. Jefferson Cowie, *Stayin' Alive*: *The 1970s and the Last Days of the Working Class* (New York: New Press, 2010).

15. Larry Samuel, *Rich: The Rise and Fall of American Wealth Culture* (New York: AMACOM, 2009), 184–185.

16. Fraser, *Every Man a Speculator*, 555; Chad Stone, Danilo Trisi, Arloc Sherman, and Jennifer Beltrán, "A Guide to Statistics on Historical Trends in Income Inequality," Center on Budget and Policy Priorities (Updated January 13, 2020), https://www.cbpp.org/research/poverty-and-inequality/a-guide-to-statistics-on-historical-trends-in-income-inequality; Sylvia Nasar, "Who Paid the Most Taxes in the 80's? The Superrich," *New York Times*, May 31, 1992, 3.4; Paul Farhi, "Number of U.S. Millionaires Soars," *Washington Post*, July 11, 1992.

17. Lisa A. Keister, *Getting Rich: America's New Rich and How They Got That Way* (New York: Cambridge University Press, 2005), 57.

18. Sabrina Tavernise, "Will the Coronavirus Kill What's Left of Americans' Faith in Washington?," *New York Times*, May 23, 2020.

19. Harry F. Waters, "An Embarrassment of Riches," *Newsweek,* April 2, 1984, 74.

20. Cooperative Institutional Research Program, "New Report Tracks 20 Year Shift in Freshman Attitudes, Values and Life Goals" (American Council on Education/ University of California, Los Angeles, n.d.), http://digitalcollections.library.cmu. edu/awweb/awarchive?type=file&item=672500; Frank Newport, "Americans Like Having a Rich Class, as They Did 22 Years Ago," Gallup, May 11, 2012, https://news.gallup.com/poll/154619/americans-having-rich-class-years-ago. aspx; George H. Gallup Jr. and Frank Newport, "51% of Americans Say They Have a Shot at Making Big Bucks," *Star-Tribune* (Minneapolis, MN), July 1, 1990, 1E; on Americans' long-standing aspirations for wealth, see Michael Mechanic, *Jackpot: How the Super-Rich Really Live—and How Their Wealth Harms Us All* (New York: Simon and Schuster, 2021).

21. Taylor Branch, "What's Wrong with the Lottery?," *New England Monthly* (January 1990), 43.

22. Charles A. Johnson, "The Poor Get Richer," *Los Angeles Times*, June 28, 1987, 29; California State Lottery, *Lotto Lines* 2, no. 4 (July/August 1987), 2, Folder 2, "Lottery Commission," Subject Files, Richard Floyd Papers, California State Archives, Sacramento, California; on the parallels between the lottery and celebrity culture, see Karen Sternheimer, *Celebrity Culture and the American Dream: Stardom and Social Mobility* (New York: Routledge, 2015), 11.

23. Associated Press, "Did You Win $24 Million Last Night?" *Asbury Park Press* (Asbury Park, NJ), November 9, 1986, A2; Amy Pagnozzi and Jim Nolan, "Lotto Fever: $22M and Rising," *New York Post,* November 7, 1986.

24. Pagnozzi and Nolan, "Lotto Fever: $22M and Rising."

25. Associated Press, "Did You Win $24 Million Last Night?," *Asbury Park Press*, November 9, 1986, A2.

26. Lynn L. Wiley, "Daydream Is Worth MegaBucks Ticket Price," Letter to *Burlington Free Press* (Burlington, VT), June 24, 1986, 8; Ien Ang, "Melodramatic Identifications: Television Fiction and Women's Fantasy," in *Television and Women's Culture: The Politics of the Popular*, ed. Mary Ellen Brown (London: SAGE, 1990), 83–84.

27. Maureen Dowd, "Just in Case You Missed It," *New York Times,* August 22, 1985, A1; Louise Cook, "Billions of Dollars Pour into Gambling Despite Fluctuations in U.S. Economy," *Los Angeles Times,* June 18, 1982, D4.

28. *Asbury Park Press*, "'84 Lotteries in U.S. to Gross $6 Billion," September 2, 1984, B12.

29. Though not necessarily representative, the case of Gail Evans, a janitor at Kodak in the 1980s who rose to be the company's chief technology officer, is instructive in the opportunities available to service workers at the time that have since disappeared; Neil Irwin, "To Understand Rising Inequality, Consider the Janitors

at Two Top Companies, Then and Now," *New York Times*, September 3, 2017; David Bird, "After Years of Growth, Lotto Hits First Slump," *New York Times*, August 10, 1985, 25.

30. Victor Markowicz, "The State of State Lotteries (Part II)," *Public Gaming International* 16, no. 8 (1988).

31. Bennett Harrison and Lucy Gorham, "Growing Inequality in Black Wages in the 1980s and the Emergence of an African-American Middle Class," *Journal of Policy Analysis and Management* 11, no. 2 (Spring, 1992), 243–246.

32. Ronald Alsop, "State Lottery Craze Is Spreading, but Some Fear It Hurts the Poor," *Wall Street Journal*, February 24, 1983, 31; Nancy Skelton, "'Good Luck' for Sale: Lotteries: What Comes with Them?" *Los Angeles Times*, September 5, 1985, A1.

33. Paul Daggan, "3,800,000 to 1 to Win $15 Million," *Washington Post,* May 14, 1988, B4.

34. The first appearance of this phrase dates back to the early twentieth century; Edgar A. Guest, "At the Yankee Circus," *Detroit Free Press*, January 20, 1907, 4.1; *Washington Times* (Washington, DC), "Woman Receives $10; Writes Ten Words," August 9, 1908, 5.

35. Daniel Kahneman and Amos Tversky, "Prospect Theory: An Analysis of Decision Under Risk," *Econometrica* 47, no. 2 (1979), 263–292; Sue Anne Pressley, "$12 Million Pot Draws Dreamers Galore," *Washington Post*, April 13, 1985, B1.

36. Illinois State Lottery, "History of U.S. Lotteries' Lotto" (n.d., probably 1986), Folder "January–December 1986 Lottery Control Board Meetings," Box 10, General Information Files, Department of Revenue: Lottery, Illinois State Archives, Springfield, Illinois (hereafter ISA); Jonathan Guryan and Melissa S. Kearney, "Gambling at Lucky Stores: Empirical Evidence from State Lottery Sales," *American Economic Review* 91, no. 1 (2008): 458–473.

37. Laura Kurtzman, "Lotto Lines Get Longer," *Los Angeles Times*, October 29, 1988, V3; Carol Krucoff, "Money: The Biggest Game in Town," *Washington Post*, August 25, 1982, B5.

38. William Cohan, *Why Wall Street Matters* (New York: Random House, 2017), 86–88; Fraser, *Every Man a Speculator*, 536.

39. Tom Petruno, "A Look Back at a Great Bull Market," *Los Angeles Times*, August 13, 2002, OCC4; John Crudele, "Stocks Retreat Again; Dow Off 3.51," *New York Times*, December 31, 1986, D6; Security Exchange Commission, "Dow Jones Industrial Average," accessed February 7, 2021, https://www.sec.gov/Archives/edgar/data/357298/000035729801500016/dowjones.html; Ronald Reagan, Remarks on Signing the Garn-St. Germain Depository Institutions Act of 1982, October 15, 1982, American Presidency Project, https://www.presidency.ucsb.edu/node/244729.

40. Susan Strange, *Casino Capitalism* (Manchester, UK: Manchester University Press, 1997 [1986]), 1; on the beginnings of financialization in the 1970s, see Judith Stein,

Pivotal Decade: How the United States Traded Factories for Finance in the Seventies (New Haven, CT: Yale University Press, 2011).

41. Edwin McDowell, "'Iacocca' and 'Wobegon' Top-Selling Books of '85," *New York Times,* January 6, 1986, C15; Oprah Winfrey Network (OWN), "Donald Trump: 'There's No More Important Word Than "Luck"'" | The Oprah Winfrey Show | OWN, March 16, 2019 (clip from 1988), https://www.youtube.com/watch?v=1-SEMV_leAE.

42. Arthur B. Kennickell and Janice Shack-Marquez, "Changes in Family Finances from 1983 to 1989: Evidence from the Survey of Consumer Finances," *Federal Reserve Bulletin* 78 (January 1992), 4.

43. Stuart Banner, *Speculation: A History of the Fine Line Between Gambling and Investing* (New York: Oxford University Press, 2017).

44. *The Pantagraph* (Bloomington, IL), "'Wall Street' Lottery Off to a Good Start," April 16, 1990, D1.

45. Alsop, "State Lottery Craze Is Spreading."

46. Rebecca Paul to Lottery Control Board Members, "'Best Days' Illinois," February 21, 1986, Folder "January–December 1986 Lottery Control Board Meetings," Box 10, General Information Files, Department of Revenue: Lottery, ISA; Silverman, "Cubs? Weather? No, City's Buzzing About Lotto."

47. Sylvia Porter, "The World's Worst Investment: State Lotteries," *Midlands Business Journal*, May 18, 1989.

48. Carol McGraw, "$45-Million Jackpot Sparks 'Lottomania,'" *Los Angeles Times*, June 4, 1988, P1.

49. Harriet Stranahan and Mary O. Borg, "Separating the Decisions of Lottery Expenditures and Participation: A Truncated Tobit Approach," *Public Finance Review* 26, no. 2 (1998): 99–117; Emily Oster, "Are All Lotteries Regressive? Evidence from the Powerball," *National Tax Journal* 57, no. 2 (2004): 179–187; Kathryn L. Combs, Jaebeom Kim, and John A. Spry, "The Relative Regressivity of Seven Lottery Games," *Applied Economics* 40 (2008): 35–39; Margot Hornblower, "$41 Million Jackpot Has New Yorkers Burning with Lotto Fever," *Washington Post,* August 22, 1985, A3.

50. Skelton, "'Good Luck' for Sale."

51. Roxane Arnold, "Scratching for Ticket to Big Spin," *Los Angeles Times*, June 22, 1986, A1.

52. Joseph F. Sullivan, "Jackpot $11 Million in Jersey Lottery Drawing," *New York Times*, December 3, 1982, A1; William R. Greer, "Retiree Wins Record $20 Million Lotto Prize," *New York Times,* July 27, 1984, A1; New Jersey Lottery, *New Jersey Lottery: Milestones, 1995–1996 Annual Report* (n.d., n.p), NJSL; David Bird, "After Years of Growth, Lotto Hits First Slump," *New York Times*, August 10, 1985, 25; on the relationship of jackpot size and lotto sales, see Philip J. Cook and Charles T. Clotfelter, "The Peculiar Scale Economies of Lotto," NBER Working Paper No. 3766 (Cambridge, MA: National Bureau of Economic Research, 1991).

53. Associated Press, "Pick-6 Odds May Double to Increase Jackpot Sizes," *Asbury Park Press*, November 28, 1983, A12; New Jersey Lottery, *New Jersey Lottery: Milestones*, 3, 15.

54. Zachary M. Berman, "Consider Lotto 48 a Shot at the American Dream," Letter to *New York Times*, March 31, 1987, A34.

55. Peter Applebome, "Lotto Players Make $30 Million Plans," *New York Times,* January 18, 1986, 1.

56. The Center for Community and Regional Studies, Sangamon State University, "Illinois State Lottery: Market Survey Study," June 5, 1987, Folder "Sangamon State University Market Survey Study," Box 35, Lottery Records, Office of the Director, ISA.

57. Jeffrey Zaslow, "Big Jackpots Are Odds-on Choice of Lottery Players," *Chicago Sun-Times*, July 25, 1990, 47; Elspeth Reeve, "A History of Donald Trump's Net Worth Publicity (1988–2011)," *The Atlantic*, April 11, 2011.

58. Associated Press, "26 States Now Running Lotteries to Ease Budgetary Burdens," *New York Times,* February 16, 1988, B5; Terri LaFleur, *The Lottery Book* (Boyds, MD: TLF Publications, 1991), 6.

59. National Association of State and Provincial Lotteries, "History of North American Lotteries," https://www.naspl.org/historyofthelottery; David Tirrell-Wysocki, "Officials: Tri-State Lottery a Winner," *Burlington Free Press*, October 22, 1985, 3B; Associated Press, "Tri-State Megabucks Lottery to Change Odds of Winning," *Burlington Free Press*, November 21, 1985, 5B; *Burlington Free Press,* "Somebody Won Tri-State Lottery," June 16, 1986, 1; Ray Richard, "'I Haven't Come Down to Earth Yet,' Says Mass. Woman After Lottery Win," *Boston Globe*, June 21, 1986, 18.

60. Steve Johnson, "A Lotta Lotto: More and More States Are Joining the Drive Toward the Biggest Game Ever," *Chicago Tribune*, June 13, 1989, C1; Associated Press, "Change in Works for Lotto America," *Statesman Journal* (Salem, OR), February 22, 1992, 4A; Lawrence Hardy, "Lotto America Giving Way to 'Powerball,'" *News Journal* (Wilmington, DE), April 7, 1992, B3.

61. Antonio Carloni to Mario Cuomo, May 11, 1984, Reel 78, Subject Files 1983–1984, Mario Cuomo Gubernatorial Papers, NYSA; Zachary Berman, "New York State's Lottery Has Reached the Point of Lunacy," Letter to *New York Times*, September 18, 1988, E22.

62. Joseph Carbonell to Hugh L. Carey, June 28, 1978, Reel 71, Subject Files, Hugh L. Carey Gubernatorial Papers, NYSA; Joseph Carbonell to Mario Cuomo, December 3, 1983, Reel 77, Subject Files, Mario Cuomo Gubernatorial Papers, NYSA.

63. Larry DeBoer, "Jackpot Size and Lotto Sales: Evidence from Ohio, 1986–1987," *Journal of Gambling Studies* 6, no. 4 (1990): 345–354; Johnson, "A Lotta Lotto."

64. Douglas M. Walker and John D. Jackson, "Do U.S. Gambling Industries Cannibalize Each Other?," *Public Finance Review* 36, no. 3 (2008): 308–333; Will Cummings, Douglas M. Walker, and Chad D. Cotti, "The Effect of Casino

Proximity on Lottery Sales: Evidence from Maryland," *Contemporary Economic Policy* 35, no. 4 (2017): 684–699; Virve Marionneau and Janne Nikkinen, "Market Cannibalization Within and Between Gambling Industries: A Systematic Review," *Journal of Gambling Issues* 37 (2018).

65. In most states, overall lottery sales remained steady even as lotto sales dropped thanks to increased instant ticket sales. *Chicago Tribune*, "Rolling the Dice on Lotto Sales," November 30, 1997, D18.

66. Based on calculations provided in Keith Devlin, "Lottery Mania," Blog post for Mathematical Association of American (June 2000), https://www.maa.org/external_archive/devlin/devlin_6_00.html; National Association of State and Provincial Lotteries Resource Index, https://www.nasplmatrix.org/nri.

67. Alsop, "State Lottery Craze Is Spreading."

CHAPTER 5

1. Maureen O'Donnell, "Chicago Activist Josephine McCord, Worked with MLK, Dead at 85," *Chicago Sun-Times*, December 5, 2016; Barbara Mahany, "West Siders Welcome Nuns' 'Ministry of Love,'" *Chicago Tribune*, March 18, 1983, 2.1.

2. Author interview with Leo McCord, March 13, 2021.

3. Bonita Brodt, "Lottery's Down Side: Road to Easy Street Littered with the Poor," *Chicago Tribune*, May 25, 1986, A1.

4. John Bausch to James Thompson, March 28, 1986; H. J. Ligon to James Thompson, May 29, 1986; and Rebecca Paul to Elsa Littman, February 26, 1986, Folder 54, Box 65, Citizens Assistance Records, James Thompson Papers, Office of the Governor, Illinois State Archives, Springfield, Illinois (hereafter ISA).

5. This estimate of average lottery spending is likely too low, as many of the parishioners would have also bought some winning tickets; Illinois Economic and Fiscal Commission, *The Illinois State Lottery: A Special Report* (State of Illinois, December 1986), 21; Barry Cronin, "'Insulting' Lottery Sign on W. Side Sets Off Boycott," *Chicago Sun-Times*, February 6, 1986, 37.

6. Associated Press, "Priest Organizing Lottery Boycott," *Southern Illinoisan* (Carbondale, IL), March 10, 1986, 2; Eric Zorn, "Lottery Jackpot Not in His Dreams," *Chicago Tribune*, March 19, 1991, S1; Author interview with Thomas O'Gorman, February 19, 2021.

7. Thomas O'Gorman to James Thompson, March 14, 1986, Folder 54, Box 65, Citizens Assistance Records, James Thompson Papers, Office of the Governor, ISA; Stephanie Saul, "Strategic Lottery Advertising Pushes Sales Through the Roof," *Paducah Sun* (Paducah, KY), December 17, 1995, 6E.

8. *Chicago Tribune*, "Not a Lotta Lottery Lovers," March 14, 1984, 2.1; O'Gorman interview; McCord interview.

9. Illinois Economic and Fiscal Commission, *The Illinois State Lottery*, 79; Sharon Sharp to Valerie Cernicky, October 15, 1987, untitled Folder, Box 84, Lottery

Records, Office of the Director, ISA; Mike Tate speaking on Amendment #3 to Senate Bill 1740, June 18, 1986, State of Illinois, 84th General Assembly, House of Representatives, 129th Legislative Day, Transcription Debates, 140.

10. McCord interview; Elizabeth-Anne Vanek, "A Parish in the Projects," *Chicago Reader*, March 26, 1987.

11. Job Roberts Tyson, *Brief Survey of the Great Extent and Evil Tendencies of the Lottery System as Existing in the United States* (Philadelphia: William Brown, 1833), 71, 71 n. 5; on lotteries and lottery advertising in the nineteenth century, see Ann Fabian, *Card Sharps and Bucket Shops: Gambling in Nineteenth-Century America* (Routledge: New York, 1999 [1990]).

12. G. Robert Blakey, "The Development of the Federal Law of Gambling," *Cornell Law Review* 63, no. 6 (1978): 946–949; Robert E. Dallos, "News Media Divided on How to Handle Lottery," *New York Times*, May 24, 1967, 58.

13. Leo Motiuk to Brendan Byrne, "State Lottery Commission Minutes for July 9, 1974 Meeting," Folder "Lottery," Box 6, Records of Dorothy A. Seltzer, Brendan Byrne Gubernatorial Papers, New Jersey State Archives, Trenton, New Jersey.

14. Statement of Ralph F. Batch Before the Subcommittee on Criminal Law and Procedures of the Senate Judiciary Committee, November 21, 1974, Folder "Speeches by RFB," Box 44, Lottery Records, Office of the Director, ISA.

15. *United States v. New Jersey Lottery Commission*, 420 U.S. 371 (1975); Wilfred H. Rommel to Gerald Ford, "Enrolled Bill S. 544-State Lotteries," Folder "1975/01/02 S.544 State Lotteries," Box 18; and James T. Lynn to Gerald Ford, "Enrolled Bill H.R. 1607-Newspaper advertisements of State-operated lotteries," Folder "10/17/76 HR1607 Newspaper Advertisements of State-operated Lotteries," Box 65, White House Records Office: Legislation Case Files, Gerald R. Ford Presidential Library, Ann Arbor, MI.

16. Jon Van, "State Pays $1.5 Million to Push Lottery Dreams," *Chicago Tribune*, July 20, 1974, 3; Illinois State Lottery, "Attitude Study" (July 1974), untitled folder, Box 70, Lottery Records, Office of the Director, ISA; Lee King and Partners, Inc., "Illinois State Lottery: Attitude and Awareness Study," October 1975, Folder "Promotional Materials," Box 73, Lottery Records, Office of the Director, ISA.

17. Illinois State Lottery, "Media Advertising Expenditures by Metro Area, July thru Oct., 1974," Folder "Problems and Opportunities," Lottery Records, Office of the Director, Box 70, ISA; United States Department of Commerce, Bureau of the Census, *1970 Census of Population: Advance Report* (United States Department of Commerce, February 1971), PC(V2)-15: Illinois, 4–19.

18. Don E. Fossedal to Richard W. Carlson and James Sokolowski, "Review of the Daily Game Marketing Plan," March 13, 1980, Folder "Daily Game—on-line, February 19, 1980," Box 4, General Information Files, Department of Revenue: Lottery, ISA; Lee King and Partners, Inc., "Illinois State Lottery Daily Game Marketing Plan, March 1, 1980–February 28, 1981," December 14, 1979, Folder "Lottery Board Control Memos," Box 47, Lottery Records, Office of the Director, ISA.

19. Illinois State Lottery, *1986 Annual Report*, Box 40, Lottery Records: Office of the Director, ISA; Illinois Economic and Fiscal Commission, *The Illinois State Lottery*, Appendix 1; MCA Games, "Advertising and Promotion Plan for Tic-Tac-Dough Christmas Bonus Season Ticket Plan and Tickets as Gifts Promotion" in *Volume 2: Technical Proposal* (September 27, 1979), Box 56, Lottery Records, Office of the Director, ISA.

20. Illinois State Lottery, *1986 Annual Report*; Illinois Economic and Fiscal Commission, *The Illinois State Lottery*, Appendix 2; The Museum of Classic Chicago Television, "Illinois Lottery—'The Daily Game' (Commercial, 1980)," https://www.youtube.com/watch?v=zhjfJ5N_YMg.

21. Kim Kinter, "Illinois Lottery: More Sweat Needed to Sell the Dream," *Adweek*, August 12, 1991.

22. Charles Clotfelter and Philip J. Cook, *Selling Hope: State Lotteries in America* (Cambridge, MA: Harvard University Press, 1989), 205; Illinois Economic and Fiscal Commission, *The Illinois State Lottery*, 79.

23. Raymond Williams, "Advertising: The Magic System," in *The Cultural Studies Reader*, ed. Simon During (London: Routledge 1999 [1993]), 422; Jackson Lears, *Fables of Abundance: A Cultural History of Advertising in America* (New York: Basic Books, 1994), 139.

24. Bozell & Jacobs, Inc., "Wild Game Hunter," August 15, 1985, Folder "Bozell," Box 54, Lottery Records, Office of the Director, ISA.

25. Creamer Inc., "State of Illinois: Illinois State Lottery," May 23, 1980, Folder "Creamer/Lottery," Box 44, Lottery Records, Office of the Director, ISA.

26. T. J. Jackson Lears, "From Salvation to Self-Realization: Advertising and the Therapeutic Roots of the Consumer Culture, 1880–1930," in *The Culture of Consumption: Critical Essays in American History, 1880–1980*, ed. Richard Wightman Fox and T. J. Jackson Lears (New York: Pantheon Books, 1983), 1–38.

27. Lisa Petrison, "That's Rich," *Adweek*, August 24, 1987; on advertising as a funhouse mirror, see Roland Marchand, *Advertising the American Dream: Making Way for Modernity, 1920–1940* (Berkeley: University of California Press, 1985).

28. Nancy Millman, "A Little Lotto Means a Lot in Hard-sell Ad Campaign," *Chicago Tribune*, August 2, 1992, G1.

29. Clotfelter and Cook, *Selling Hope*, 209.

30. Video Monitoring Services of America, Inc. "August Radio and TV Reports," Box 62, Administrative Correspondence and Related Documents, Department of Revenue: Lottery, ISA.

31. *Herald Review* (Decatur, IL), "It Could Be You Next," January 26, 1988, 8.

32. Charles T. Clotfelter, Philip J. Cook, Julie A. Edell, and Marian Moore, "State Lotteries at the Turn of the Century: Report to the National Gambling Impact Study Commission" (April 23, 1999), Table 13, https://govinfo.library.unt.edu/ngisc/reports/lotfinal.pdf.

33. The Center for Community and Regional Studies, Sangamon State University, "Illinois State Lottery: Market Survey Study," June 5, 1987, Folder "Sangamon State University Market Survey Study," Box 35, Lottery Records, Office of the Director, ISA.

34. Mary O. Borg and Paul M. Mason, "The Budgetary Incidence of a Lottery to Support Education," *National Tax Journal* 41, no. 1 (1988): 75–85; Aaron Freeman, *Confessions of a Lottery Ball* (Chicago: Bonus Books, 1987), 33.

35. Nora Zaring to James Thompson, August 5, 1985, Folder 54, Box 106, Citizens Assistance Records, James Thompson Papers, Office of the Governor, ISA.

36. Illinois State Lottery, "Governor Names New Superintendent," *Lottery News* 3, no. 4 (Fall 1981), Illinois State Library, Springfield, Illinois; John Hurst, "Lottery Ads: Soft Sell on a Big Budget," *Los Angeles Times*, April 17, 1985, A11; Dale R. Arvidson to John Bausch, Folder 54, Box 65, Citizens Assistance Records, James Thompson Papers, Office of the Governor, ISA.

37. Mary O. Borg and Harriet A. Stranahan, "Does Lottery Advertising Exploit Disadvantaged and Vulnerable Markets?" *Business Ethics Quarterly* 15, no. 1 (2005): 23–35.

38. Hearing Before the Committee on Governmental Affairs, United States Senate on S. 704 to Establish the Gambling Impact Study Commission, 104th Congress, First Session, November 2, 1995, 28; the ad was originally misquoted by Neal Peirce as "this could be your ticket out" in a nationally syndicated column in 1989; the "this is your way out" version appears to have originated in a 1993 George Will syndicated *Washington Post* column; in his column, Will cites an article in *Notre Dame Magazine* as his source of the billboard text; Neal R. Peirce, "If We Really Want to Come Up As Winners, We'd Begin to Curb Our Lottery Fever," *Los Angeles Times*, May 9, 1989, II.7; George Will, "Gambling with Our Character," *Washington Post*, February 7, 1993, C7.

39. Marilyn Kalfus, "Lottery Foes Say It Preys on the Poor," *Tampa Tribune* (Tampa, FL), July 26, 1987, 42.

40. Beginning in 1975, the National Association of Broadcasters (NAB)'s Television Code—a set of standards and guidelines for acceptable advertising—stipulated that lottery advertising could not "unduly exhort the public to bet." Facing legal scrutiny, the NAB abandoned the Code in 1983; National Association of Broadcasters, "Excerpts from the Television Code," *Antitrust Law Journal* 49, no. 2 (1980): 814; Clotfelter and Cook, *Selling Hope*, 46, 209; Borg and Stranahan, "Does Lottery Advertising Exploit Disadvantaged and Vulnerable Markets?," 24;

41. Alan J. Karcher, *Lotteries* (New Brunswick, NJ: Transaction Books, 1989), 81; National Association of State Lotteries Advertising Code of Ethics, included in *State Lotteries: An Overview*, Hearing before the Subcommittee on Intergovernmental Relations of the Committee on Government Affairs, United States Senate, 98th Congress, 2nd Session, October 3, 1984 (Washington, DC: US Government Printing Office, 1985), 46–48; National Association of State and

Provincial Lotteries, "NASPL Guidelines for Responsible Gaming," updated March 2018, http://www.nasplmatrix.org/rg/files/NASPL_Guidlines_Responsible_Gambling_Final.pdf; Jody L. Furman to Martin M. Puncke, October 30, 1984, included in *State Lotteries: An Overview*, 45.

42. Chris Jay Hoofnagle, *Federal Trade Commission Privacy Law and Policy* (New York: Cambridge University Press, 2016).

43. Sarah Milov, *The Cigarette: A Political History* (Cambridge, MA: Harvard University Press, 2019), 125–134; Pamela E. Pennock, *Advertising Sin and Sickness: The Politics of Alcohol and Tobacco Marketing 1950–1990* (DeKalb: Northern Illinois University Press, 2007), 4, 178, 180, 207, 218–220.

44. Pete Geren, "Truth in Advertising for State-Run Lotteries," speaking on H.R. 3010, March 5, 1996, 104th Congress, 2nd Session, *Congressional Record* 142, no. 28, H1700.

45. State of Missouri, Senate Bill No. 44, Regular Session, 1985 New Laws, 297, Folder "State Lottery Statutes," Box 56689, Zell Miller Papers, Governor's Subject Files, Georgia State Archives, Morrow, Georgia.

46. Sam Vinson speaking on Amendment #2 to House Bill 3083, May 18, 1984, State of Illinois, 83rd General Assembly, House of Representatives, 121st Legislative Day, Transcription Debates, 145; *Chicago Defender*, "Dems Seeks Change in Lotto Advertising," February 12, 1987; *The Pantagraph* (Bloomington, IL), "Social Costs of Gambling Questioned by Think Tank," September 29, 1991, A2.

47. Charles N. Wheeler III, "Thompson's Tax Hike: The Reasons and the Politics," *Illinois Issues* 14 (April 1983); Thomas Walstrum, "The Illinois Budget Crisis in Context: A History of Poor Fiscal Performance," *Chicago Fed Letter*, No. 365 (2016), https://www.chicagofed.org/publications/chicago-fed-letter/2016/365.

48. Neil Milbert, "Illinois OTB Parlors Get Handle on Things," *Chicago Tribune*, March 18, 1990, 8; Don Thompson, "Gambling Available All over Illinois," *The Pantagraph*, September 29, 1991, A2.

49. State of Illinois, 86th General Assembly, House of Representatives, Transcription Debate, January 11, 1990; David G. Schwartz, *Roll the Bones: The History of Gambling* (New York: Gotham, 2006), 440–446.

50. The Illinois Lottery accounted for roughly 41 percent of the total amount gambled but almost 77 percent of profits for the state; State of Illinois, Commission on Government Forecasting and Accountability, "Wagering in Illinois 2005 Update" (August 2005), https://gaming.unlv.edu/abstract/il_1994.html; Illinois Economic and Fiscal Commission, *The Illinois State Lottery*, 8; Illinois State Lottery, *1983 Annual Report*, Box 40, Office of the Director, Lottery Records, ISA; Dale R. Arvidson to Carol Bastian, February 20, 1985, folder "Lottery," Box 106, Citizens Assistance Records, James Thompson Papers, Office of the Governor, ISA.

51. John Matijevich and William Black speaking on House Bill 2889, May 22, 1992, State of Illinois, 87th General Assembly, House of Representatives, 146th

Legislative Day, Transcription Debates, 32–34; Rob Karwath, "Ad Agencies Go All Out for Lottery Pact," *Chicago Tribune*, March 29, 1991, 1.

52. Illinois Economic and Fiscal Commission, *The Illinois State Lottery*, 6, 61.

53. Cynthia L. Tanner to Dennis Wright, March 30, 1992, Folder "Bozell, Inc." Box 28, Administrative Correspondence and Related Documents, Department of Revenue: Lottery, ISA.

54. Roger Chesley and Duane Noriyuki, "Billboard Aims Drinks, Smokes at City Blacks," *Detroit Free Press*, February 5, 1989, 1; Douglas Luke, Emily Esmundo, and Yael Bloom, "Smoke Signs: Patterns of Tobacco Billboard Advertising in a Metropolitan Region," *Tobacco Control* 9 (2000):16–23; Elizabeth M. Barbeau et al., "Tobacco Advertising in Communities: Associations with Race and Class," *Preventive Medicine* 40, no. 1 (2005): 16–22; Brian A. Primack et al., "Volume of Tobacco Advertising in African American Markets: Systematic Review and Meta-Analysis," *Public Health Reports*, 122, no. 5 (2007): 607–615; Ellen Feighery et al., "An Examination of Trends in Amount and Type of Cigarette Advertising and Sales Promotions in California Stores, 2002–2005," *Tobacco Control* 17, no. 2 (2008): 93–98; Andrew B. Seidenberg et al., "Storefront Cigarette Advertising Differs by Community Demographic Profile," *American Journal of Health Promotion* 24, no. 6 (2010): 26–31.

55. Illinois Economic and Fiscal Commission, *The Illinois State Lottery*, 68, Appendix 3; Scientific Games Inc., "Preliminary Analysis of Sales Data of Illinois State Lottery," version I, June 19, 1981, untitled folder, Box 71, Lottery Records, Office of the Director, ISA.

56. Horace G. Livingston to Rebecca Paul, January 12, 1987, Folder "Advertising/Marketing Agencies," Box 41, Lottery Records, Office of the Director, ISA.

57. Bozell, "Illinois Lottery, FY'91 Minority Spending Report," Folder "Bozell," Box 28, Administrative Correspondence and Related Documents, Department of Revenue: Lottery, ISA; "BBV Spending for Illinois State Lottery Newspaper Media, Period: July 1993–December 1993," Folder "Appropriations FY 95," Box 54, Administrative Correspondence and Related Documents, Department of Revenue: Lottery, ISA.

58. Keith Wailoo, *Pushing Cool: Big Tobacco, Racial Marketing, and the Untold Story of the Menthol Cigarette* (Chicago: University of Chicago Press, 2021), 163–166.

59. Robert Stolzberg, "Convenience Stores Thrive Despite Price Competition," *Washington Post*, July 9, 1967, E1; Leonard Wiener, "Convenience Stores Flourish Despite Late Grocery Hours," *Chicago Tribune*, July 4, 1977, C8; *National Petroleum News* "C-Store Industry Hits the Wall," *National Petroleum News* 84, no. 11 (October 1992): 51.

60. Bryant Simon, *The Hamlet Fire: A Tragic Story of Cheap Food, Cheap Government, and Cheap Lives* (New York: New Press, 2017); Marcia Chatelain, *Franchise: The Golden Arches in Black America* (New York: W.W. Norton, 2020).

61. Paul Gilmore, "Grocery Stores and Supermarkets," *Encyclopedia of Chicago,* http://www.encyclopedia.chicagohistory.org/pages/554.html; Ashanté M. Reese, *Black Food Geographies: Race, Self-Reliance, and Food Access in Washington, D.C.* (Chapel Hill: University of North Carolina Press, 2019).

62. Studies show that wealthier neighborhoods have fewer small grocery stores and convenience stores without gas stations, while nonwhite areas have more small grocery stores and convenience stores (with or without a gas station); Kimberly Morland, Steve Wing, Ana Diez Roux, and Charles Poole, "Neighborhood Characteristics Associated with the Location of Food Stores and Food Service Places," *American Journal of Preventative Medicine* 22, no. 1 (2002): 27; Thomas LaVeist John M. Wallace Jr., "Health Risk and Inequitable Distribution of Liquor Stores in African American Neighborhoods," *Social Science & Medicine* 51, no. 4 (2000): 613–617.

63. Steve Dwyer, "C-stores Finally Start Wooing Women," *National Petroleum News* 85, no. 9 (1993): SS5; Karen Blumenthal, "Convenience Stores Try Cutting Prices and Adding Products to Attract Women," *Wall Street Journal*, July 3, 1987, 15; Wiener, "Convenience Stores Flourish."

64. Clotfelter and Cook, *Selling Hope*, 102; Clotfelter, Cook, Edell, and Moore, "State Lotteries at the Turn of the Century," 12–13; Maureen Pirog-Good and John L. Mikesell, "Longitudinal Evidence of the Changing Socio-Economic Profile of a State Lottery Market," *Policy Studies Journal* 23, no. 3 (1995): 451–465; National Association of Convenience Stores, *NACS Lottery Study: Executive Summary* (National Association of Convenience Stores, 1997), Special Collections & Archives, University Libraries, University of Nevada, Las Vegas, Las Vegas, Nevada (hereafter UNLV); National Association of State and Provincial Lotteries, "Sales by Trade Type," NASPL Resource Index, accessed May 2021.

65. National Association of Convenience Stores, *NACS Lottery Study.*

66. Illinois Economic and Fiscal Commission, *The Illinois State Lottery*, 27.

67. Kevin B. Blackistone and Ronni Scheier, "State Lottery Wins Bet on Minority Gamblers," *Chicago Reporter* 10, no. 8 (1981); Lyna Wiggins, Lia Nower, Raymond Sanchez Mayers, and N. Andrew Peterson, "A Geospatial Statistical Analysis of the Density of Lottery Outlets Within Ethnically Concentrated Neighborhoods," *Journal of Community Psychology* 38, no. 4 (2010): 486–496; Brodt, "Lottery's Down Side.

68. Lynn C. Planinac, Joanna E. Cohen, Jennifer Reynolds, Daniel J. Robinson, Anne Lavack, and David Korn, "Lottery Promotions at the Point-of-Sale in Ontario, Canada," *Journal of Gambling Studies* 27 (2011): 345–354; Clotfelter and Cook, *Selling Hope*, 197.

69. Dorothy Collin, "Mayor Isn't Often at a Loss for Words," *Chicago Tribune*, June 20, 1979, 1.

70. Herbert H. Rozoff Associates, Inc., "Meeting with *Tribune* Editors" (n.d. probably 1974 or 1975), Folder "Public Relations," Box 22, Lottery Records, Office of the Director, ISA.

71. David Nibert, *Hitting the Lottery Jackpot: Government and the Taxing of Dreams* (New York: Monthly Review Press, 2000); Kasey Henricks and David G. Embrick, *State Looteries: Historical Continuity, Rearticulations of Racism, and American Taxation* (New York: Routledge, 2017).

72. Michigan and Ohio also used lottery revenue for their general funds initially but re-appropriated this money for education in 1981 and 1983, respectively.

73. Jack McCallum, "The Everywhere Man Alone on the Mountaintop," *Sports Illustrated*, December 23, 1991; Bozell, "School Is Cool," July 22, 1991, Folder "Jordan, Michael," Box 15, Lottery Records, Office of the Director, ISA.

74. Desiree Rogers to Michael Jordan, July 31, 1991, Folder "Jordan, Michael," Box 15, Lottery Records, Office of the Director, ISA.

75. Bozell, "School," Folder "Jordan, Michael," Box 15, Lottery Records, Office of the Director, ISA.

76. W. Perrine, "What Happened to Lottery?," letter to *Journal Star* (Peoria, IL), n.d., clipping in Folder "Korshak—Press Clippsings [*sic*]," Box 49, Department of Revenue: Lottery Records, Administrative Correspondence and Related Documents, ISA.

77. Rob Karwath, "Lottery Contribution to Schools Sets Record," *Chicago Tribune*, July 15, 1992, S4; Laura Yarc to James Thompson, February 10, 1986, Folder 54, Box 65, Citizens Assistance Records, James Thompson Papers, Office of the Governor, ISA; Clotfelter, Cook, Edell, and Moore, "State Lotteries at the Turn of the Century," Table 13.

78. Louis Freedberg, "California Educators Assert Lottery Has Failed to Pay Off for the Schools," *New York Times*, October 4, 1988, A18.

79. Mara Einstein, *Advertising: What Everyone Needs to Know* (Oxford: Oxford University Press, 2017), 119–120.

80. Robin A. Johnson and Norman Walzer, "Privatization of Municipal Services in Illinois," *Illinois Municipal Review* (November 1996), 19–21; Tony Dutzik, Brian Imus, and Phineas Baxandall, *Privatization and the Public Interest: The Need for Transparency and Accountability in Chicago's Public Asset Lease Deals* (Illinois PIRG Education Fund, 2009); *Airport Business*, "Chicago Petitions to Privatize Midway Airport," 22 (March 2008), 4.

81. "Confidential Information Memorandum," likely prepared by Goldman, Sachs & Co., n.d. (probably 2006), folder "Illinois Lottery Memorandum," Eugene Martin Christiansen Papers, UNLV; Matthew Sweeney, *The Lottery Wars: Long Odds, Fast Money, and the Battle over an American Institution* (New York: Bloomsbury, 2009), 241–251; Steven G. Bradbury, "Scope of Exemption Under Federal Lottery Statutes for Lotteries Conducted by a State Acting Under the Authority of State Law," October 16, 2008, https://www.justice.gov/olc/opinion/scope-exempt ion-under-federal-lottery-statutes-lotteries-conducted-state-acting-under (last updated June 23, 2015).

82. Monique Garcia, "State Names Private Company to Run Lottery," *Chicago Tribune*, September 16, 2010, 11; Scott Reeder, "Illinois Lottery Contracts Marred by Conflicts of Interest," *Southern Illinoisan*, April 23, 2012; Northstar Lottery Group, *Proposal for Illinois Lottery Private Manager* (Northstar Lottery Group, 2010).

83. Matthew Walberg, "State Fires Lottery Firm," *Chicago Tribune*, August 16, 2014, 1.

84. Aaron Smith, "Illinois Lottery Winners Are in Limbo," CNN, September 10, 2015; Joe Mahr, "Lottery to Again Delay Large Payouts due to Illinois Budget Woes," *Chicago Tribune*, June 28, 2017.

CHAPTER 6

1. Zell Miller, "Remarks by Governor Zell Miller, National Lottery Convention," October 4, 1998, Folder 100, Box 73, Subseries B, Series IV, Zell Miller Papers, Richard B. Russell Library for Political Research and Studies, University of Georgia, Athens, Georgia (hereafter UGA).

2. Matthew D. Lassiter, "Big Government and Family Values: Political Culture in the Metropolitan Sunbelt," in *Sunbelt Rising: The Politics of Space, Place, and Region*, ed. Michelle Nickerson and Darren Dochuk (Philadelphia: University of Pennsylvania Press, 2013), 82–109.

3. Scholars who have emphasized the harmony between Christianity and free-market values include Bethany Moreton, *To Serve God and Wal-Mart: The Making of Christian Free Enterprise* (Cambridge, MA: Harvard University Press, 2009); Kim Phillips-Fein, *Invisible Hands: The Businessmen's Crusade Against the New Deal* (New York: W. W. Norton, 2010); Darren Dochuk, *From Bible Belt to Sunbelt: Plain-Folk Religion, Grassroots Politics, and the Rise of Evangelical Conservatism* (New York: W. W. Norton, 2011); Matthew Avery Sutton, *American Apocalypse: A History of Modern Evangelicalism* (Cambridge, MA: Harvard University Press, 2014).

4. For example, Thomas S. Dee and Linda A. Jackson, "Who Loses HOPE?: Attrition from Georgia's College Scholarship Program," *Southern Economic Journal* 66, no. 2 (1999): 379–390; Bridget Terry Long, "How Do Financial Aid Policies Affect Colleges? The Institutional Impact of the Georgia HOPE Scholarship," *Journal of Human Resources* 39, no. 4 (2004): 1045–1066; Noel Campbell and R. Zachary Finney, "Mitigating the Combined Distributional Consequences of the Georgia Lottery for Education and the HOPE Scholarship," *Social Science Quarterly* 86, no. 3 (2005): 746–758; Larry D. Singell Jr., Glen R. Waddell, and Bradley R. Curs, "HOPE for the Pell? Institutional Effects in the Intersection of Merit-Based and Need-Based Aid," *Southern Economic Journal* 73, no. 1 (2006): 79–99.

5. Georgians for a Lottery Referendum, "Coalition Formed to Support People's Right to Vote on State Lottery," August 29, 1989, Folder "26th District (1991)," Box 11, Series IV, James F. Martin Papers, UGA; David Beasley, "Racing Backers Push for Lottery Vote," *Atlanta Journal-Constitution*, September 7, 1989, B8.

6. Michele K. Russo to Zell Miller, January 31, 1989, Folder 1, Box 149, Subseries C, Series IV, Zell Miller Papers, UGA; Georgians for a Lottery Referendum, "University of Georgia Poll Indicates Wide Support for Lottery," January 11, 1990, Box 11, Series IV, James F. Martin Papers, UGA; Deborah Scroggins and Betsy White, "Miller Attacks Lottery Foes," *Atlanta Journal-Constitution,* June 30, 1990, B3.

7. David Massey, "Officials Oppose Using Lottery for School Funds," *Marietta Daily Journal*, July 2, 1990, 1B.

8. Maris A. Vinovskis, *From A Nation at Risk* to *No Child Left Behind*: *National Education Goals and the Creation of Federal Education Policy* (New York: Teachers College Press, 2009), 16–17; Martin Gilens, *Why Americans Hate Welfare: Race, Media, and the Politics of Antipoverty Policy* (Chicago: University of Chicago Press, 1999), 28; Gareth Davies, *See Government Grow: Education Politics from Johnson to Reagan* (Lawrence: University Press of Kansas, 2007); Jesse H. Rhodes, *An Education in Politics: The Origins and Evolution of No Child Left Behind* (Ithaca, NY: Cornell University Press, 2012).

9. Vinovskis, *From A Nation at Risk to No Child Left Behind*, 18. The chart considered only the most commonly taken test in each state, meaning ACT scores from Georgia were not considered; William J. Bennett, *Statement by William J. Bennett, United States Secretary of Education, on Fourth Annual Wall Chart Statistics,* February 10, 1987 (Washington, DC: US Department of Education, 1987), 12.

10. US Department of Education, National Center for Education Statistics, *State Comparisons of Education Statistics: 1969–70 to 1996–97*, Report 98-018 (Washington, DC: US Department of Education 1998), 91; W. Daniel Ebersole to Zell Miller, "Local School Tax Increase," January 23, 1989, Folder 18, Box 148, Subseries C, Series IV, Zell Miller Papers, UGA.

11. Cooper and Secrest Associates, Inc., "A Survey of Democratic Primary Voter Attitudes in the State of Georgia (Confidential)," July 10, 1990, Folder 5, Box 193, Subseries C, Series IV, Zell Miller Papers, UGA; John R. Thelin, *A History of American Higher Education* (Baltimore: Johns Hopkins University Press, 2011), 341; Marvin M. Cole to Zell Miller, April 11, 1990, Folder 14, Box 148, Subseries C, Series IV, Zell Miller Papers, UGA.

12. Zell Miller for Governor, "Lt. Governor Zell Miller's The Georgia that Can Be: A Blueprint for the 1990s" (n.d., 1989 or 1990), Folder 1, Box 154, Subseries C, Series IV, Zell Miller Papers, UGA; No Author, "Lt. Governor Zell Miller's Education for the 1990s (First Draft)" (n.d.), Folder 12, Box 148, Subseries C, Series IV, Zell Miller Papers, UGA.

13. Steve Wrigley interviewed by Bob Short, May 20, 2009, Athens, Georgia, ROGP-081, UGA, 29–30; Zell Miller, "Remarks Prepared for Delivery to the Media," October 31, 1990, Folder 3, Box 149, Subseries C, Series IV, Zell Miller Papers, UGA.

14. Jack Schneider, *Excellence for All: How a New Breed of Reformers Is Transforming America's Public Schools* (Nashville, TN: Vanderbilt University Press, 2011), 30;

Premilla Nadasen, *Welfare Warriors: The Welfare Rights Movement in the United States* (New York: Routledge, 2005), 238.

15. Alexander P. Lamis, "The Two-Party South: From the 1960s to the 1990s," in *Southern Politics in the 1990s*, ed. Alexander P. Lamis (Baton Rouge: Louisiana State University Press, 1999), 2.

16. Gil Troy, *The Age of Clinton: America in the 1990s* (New York: Thomas Dunne Books, 2015), 3, 45; Bill Clinton, *My Life* (New York: Alfred A. Knopf, 2004), 361.

17. Zell Miller, *A National Party No More: The Conscience of a Conservative Democrat* (Atlanta: Stroud & Hall, 2003), 44; Richard Hyatt, *Zell: The Governor Who Gave Georgia HOPE* (Macon, GA: Mercer University Press, 1997), 241.

18. Zell Miller, draft of untitled speech (probably for Georgia legislators), n.d. (probably 1989 or 1990), Folder 18, Box 148, Subseries C, Series IV, Zell Miller Papers, UGA.

19. Scott G. Campbell, "Florida Lottery Rings Up $1.6 Billion in 1st Year," *Palm Beach Post*, January 29, 1989, 14; Theron Ussery to "City Councilors, County Commissioners, Editors," January 18, 1989, Folder "Lottery Issues, 1989," Box 9422, Max Cleland Papers, Secretary of State Records, Georgia Archives, Morrow, Georgia.

20. United Methodist Church, *The Book of Discipline of the United Methodist Church, 1980* (Nashville, TN: United Methodist Publishing House, 1980), 98; Zell Miller to James D. Cool, February 7, 1977, Folder "Lottery '93," Box 12083, Zell Miller Papers, Governor's Subject Files, GAA; J. Emmet Henderson, "Which Lottery Statements by Gov. Miller Will Georgians Believe?," The *Christian Index*, September 10, 1992, 6.

21. H. Gary Folds to Zell Miller, October 19, 1992, Folder "Lottery," Box 45043, Zell Miller Papers, Governor's Subject Files, GAA.

22. Zell Miller, "Facts and Figures on a Lottery for Georgia Education," Folder 16, and Steve Wrigley to Zell Miller, "Florida Lottery," January 20, 1989, Folder 18, Box 148, Subseries C, Series IV, Zell Miller Papers, UGA; US Department of Commerce, Bureau of the Census, Decennial Census, Minority Economic Profiles, unpublished data; and Current Population Reports, Series P-60, "Poverty in the United States," "Money Income of Households, Families, and Persons in the United States," and "Income, Poverty, and Valuation of Noncash Benefits," various years, and "Money Income in the U.S.: 1996," P60–193, https://nces.ed.gov/programs/digest/d98/d98t020.asp; US Census Bureau, "1990 Census: Poverty Statistics by County for Persons by Age" (November 24, 1992), CPH-L-106, https://www.census.gov/data/tables/time-series/dec/cph-series/cph-l/cph-l-106.html.

23. Don Melvin, "Georgian Discusses Florida Lotto," *South Florida Sun Sentinel* (Fort Lauderdale, FL), July 22, 1990, 3.

24. Roy E. Barnes interviewed by Thomas A. Scott, October 5 and 26, 1990, P1990-13, Series B, Public Figures, Georgia Government Documentation Project, Special Collections and Archives, Georgia State University Library, Atlanta, Georgia.

25. A. L. May, "Miller Says He'll Make '90 Race for Governor Referendum on Lottery," *Atlanta Journal-Constitution*, January 30, 1990, D3; Ronald Smothers, "Andrew Young Going Afield to Run for Governor," *New York Times*, November 26, 1989, 34; Deborah Scroggins, "Georgia's Case of Lottery Fever," *Atlanta Journal-Constitution,* July 22, 1990, D1.

26. A. L. May, "Miller Still Winner with Lottery Issue," *Atlanta Journal-Constitution*, September 30, 1990, A1; Cooper and Secrest Associates, Inc., "A Survey of Voter Attitudes in the State of Georgia (Confidential)," October 27, 1990, Q10, Folder 8, Box 193, Subseries C, Series IV, Zell Miller Papers, UGA.

27. Tom Baxter, "Miller Hit Jackpot with Lottery Issue," *Atlanta Journal-Constitution*, November 12, 1990, F2; Hyatt, *Zell*, 240.

28. Charles Walston, "Lottery Support Comes from Businesses due to Make a Profit," *Atlanta Journal-Constitution,* October 22, 1992, A1; Mark Sherman and Charles Walston, "Lottery Cost Paid by Miller, Friends," *Atlanta Journal-Constitution*, January 6, 1993, D2.

29. Georgians for Better Education, "Background Information on the Education Amendments: Amendments 1 and 2," n.d. (probably September 1992) and "Governor Forms Group to Urge Passage of Education Amendments," September 3, 1992, Folder 7, Box 262, Subseries E, Series IV, Zell Miller Papers, UGA.

30. Sidney Blumenthal, *The Clinton Wars* (New York: Farrar, Straus and Giroux, 2003), 32; Sarah Eby-Ebersole, *Signed, Sealed, Delivered: Highlights of the Miller Record* (Macon, GA: Mercer University Press, 1999), 75; Chuck Reece, "Press Advisory (For Immediate Release)," July 23, 1992, Folder 10, Box 29, Subseries A, Series IV, Zell Miller Papers, UGA; David L. Carlton and Peter A. Coclanis, "The Roots of Southern Deindustrialization," *Challenge* 61, no. 5/6 (2018): 418–426; Georgians for Better Education, "Background Information on the Education Amendments."

31. Georgians for a Better Education, "The Ticket to a Better Education" (n.d.), Folder 14, Box 156, Subseries C, and No author (perhaps Steve Thompkins), "Georgia's HOPE Scholarship Program: A History," Folder 13, Box 261, Subseries E, Series IV, Zell Miller Papers, UGA.

32. No author (probably Jon Macks and another aide), "Lottery Q&A," n.d. (1992), Folder 10, Box 29, Subseries A, Series IV, Zell Miller Papers, UGA.

33. Miller, *A National Party No More*, 44.

34. See works cited above, as well as Bruce Schulman, *The Seventies: The Great Shift in American Culture, Society, and Politics* (Boston: Da Capo Press, 2002); Daniel K. Williams, *God's Own Party: The Making of the Christian Right* (New York: Oxford University Press, 2010); Robert O. Self, *All in the Family: The Realignment of American Democracy Since the 1960s* (New York: Hill and Wang, 2012); Michael Sean Winters, *God's Right Hand: How Jerry Falwell Made God a Republican and Baptized the American Right* (New York: HarperOne, 2012).

35. Charles Walston, "Lottery Foes Have Tough Job," *Atlanta Journal-Constitution*, September 27, 1992, A1; *United Methodist Women,* "UMW Host 'Vigils Against

the Lottery' During School of Mission Events," (n.d., probably 1992), clipping in Folder "Against Lottery," Box 12083, Zell Miller Papers, Governor's Subject Files, GAA.

36. Barry Horton to Zell Miller, October 26, 1992, Folder "Lottery," Box 45043, Zell Miller Papers, Governor's Subject Files, GAA; Michael Nelson and John Lyman Mason, *How the South Joined the Gambling Nation: The Politics of State Policy Innovation* (Baton Rouge: Louisiana State University Press, 2007), 54.

37. The Body of Christ at Little River United Methodist Church to Zell Miller, February 10, 1992, Folder "Against Lottery," Box 12083, Zell Miller Papers, Governor's Subject Files, GAA.

38. J. Emmett Henderson, "Lottery Turns State Government into Con Artist," *Moral Concern* (Atlanta, GA), (n.d., probably October 1992), 1.

39. Margaret Kelley to Zell Miller, November 6, 1992, Folder "Lottery," Box 45043, Zell Miller Papers, Governor's Subject Files, GAA.

40. Joe Parham, "Support for Lottery Still Widespread," *Gwinnett Daily News*, July 9, 1992.

41. Roy Smith to Zell Miller, n.d. (probably September 10, 1992), Folder "Against Lottery," Box 12083, Zell Miller Papers, Governor's Subject Files, GAA; David Corvette, "Churches' Rally Against Ga. Lottery Draws 800," *Atlanta Journal-Constitution*, July 27, 1992, D2.

42. Margaret Scandrett to Zell Miller, "Gambling," February 7, 1992, Folder "Against Lottery," Box 12083, Zell Miller Papers, Governor's Subject Files, GAA.

43. Joe M. Whittemore to Jim Martin, September 15, 1989, Folder "26th District (1991)," Series IV, Jim Martin Papers, UGA.

44. Benjamin B. Dille to Zell Miller, July 25, 1992, Folder "Against Lottery," Box 12083, Zell Miller Papers, Governor's Subject Files, GAA.

45. EXCEL Excellence Campaign, "Don't Fail Our Kids, Pass Amendment 5," Folder 1, Box 149, Subseries C, Series IV, Zell Miller Papers, UGA; on the Florida lottery referendum, see Patrick A. Pierce and Donald E. Miller, *Gambling Politics: State Government and the Business of Betting* (Boulder, CO: Lynne Rienner, 2004), 75–84.

46. Florida Chamber of Commerce, "The Case of the Disappearance of Enhanced Education Funding," March 7, 1990 (n.p.), Florida Legislative Library, Tallahassee, Florida; Elise St. John, Jason E. Hill, and Frank Johnson, *An Historical Overview of Revenues and Expenditures for Public Elementary and Secondary Education, by State: Fiscal Years 1990–2002* (Washington, DC: National Center for Education Statistics, 2007), 82; Mike Williams, "Lottery No Jackpot for Florida Schools," *Atlanta Journal-Constitution*, September 22, 1990, A1.

47. Georgians for Better Education, "Differences Between Georgia and Florida Lottery Funds for Education," Folder 7, Box 262, Subseries E, Series IV, Zell Miller Papers, UGA; Katherine Chandler to Zell Miller, March 2, 1993, Folder "Lottery '93," Box 12083, Zell Miller Papers, Governor's Subject Files, GAA.

48. Charles Walston, "Governor, Lottery Allies Begin Final TV Ad Blitz," *Atlanta Journal-Constitution*, October 14, 1992, F1.

49. Steve Wrigley to Zell Miller, "'Pops' for the Lottery Fund," March 27, 1989, Folder 2, Box 149, and Steve Wrigley to Zell Miller, "Higher Ed Program," March 14, 1990, Folder 12, Box 148, Subseries C, Series IV, Zell Miller Papers, UGA.

50. Steve Wrigley interviewed by Bob Short.

51. US Bureau of the Census, *Money Income of Households, Families, and Persons in the United States: 1991*, Current Population Reports, Series P-60, No. 180 (Washington, DC: US Government Printing Office, 1992), xxi; No Author, "Georgia's HOPE Scholarship Program: A History."

52. Zell Miller, "Remarks of Governor Zell Miller," HOPE Program Press Events, September 21, 1992, Folder 14, Box 156, Subseries C, Series IV, Zell Miller Papers, UGA; No author, "America's HOPE Scholarships: A Tax Cut to Make 14 Years of Education the Standard for All," June 4, 1996, Folder 32, Box 261, Subseries E, Series IV, Zell Miller Papers, UGA; US Department of Education, *The Condition of Education, 1992* (Washington, DC: US Government Printing Office, 1992), 185; Georgians for Better Education, Press Advisory, September 22, 1992, Folder 7, Box 262, Subseries E, Series IV, Zell Miller Papers, UGA.

53. Eby-Ebersole, *Signed, Sealed, Delivered*, 118–121.

54. Zell Miller, "Remarks by Governor Zell Miller," Governor's Conference on Education, September 19, 1993, Folder 4, Box 156, Subseries C, Series IV, Zell Miller Papers, UGA; Al From Oral History, 2006, Miller Center at the University of Virginia, Presidential Oral History Project; Al From, *The New Democrats and the Return to Power* (New York: St. Martin's Press, 2013), 132.

55. Zell Miller, "Remarks by Governor Zell Miller," State of the State Address, January 15, 1998, Folder 16, Box 157, Subseries C, Series IV, Zell Miller Papers, UGA.

56. *Lotto World*, "Chancellor Gives Governor 'High Marks' for HOPE," August 1996, 22–23.

57. Ira Katznelson, *When Affirmative Action Was White: An Untold History* (New York: W. W. Norton, 2005), 113–141.

58. Charles Walston, "Miller: Preschool Needs Lottery," *Atlanta Journal-Constitution*, September 9, 1992, C1.

59. Margie Eden, "The Georgia Lottery," Letter to *Atlanta Journal-Constitution*, October 31, 1992, A18.

60. *Tifton Gazette* (Tifton, GA), "Promoting a Lottery," September 9, 1992; Earlene Hicks, "Lottery Another Addiction We Don't Need," Letter to *Macon Telegraph*, October 4, 1992.

61. Miller, "Remarks Prepared for Delivery to the Media."

62. Randy Martin, *Financialization of Daily Life* (Philadelphia: Temple University Press, 2002); see also David Harvey, *A Brief History of Neoliberalism* (New York: Oxford University Press, 2005), 33, 161–162.

63. *Atlanta Journal-Constitution*, "'No' on the Lottery," October 22, 1992, A18.

64. J. Emmet Henderson to Jim Martin, "Legalized Gambling," January 26, 1993, and attachment "Georgia Lottery Vote by Counties, 1992 General Elections," Folder "93 Lottery," Box 35, Series IV, Jim Martin Papers, UGA; *Atlanta-Journal Constitution*, "How Georgians Voted on the Lottery," November 5, 1992, C9.

65. David Beasley, "'92 The People Decide: Lottery Faces Strong Opposition," *Atlanta Journal-Constitution*, November 4, 1992, B11; US Bureau of the Census, "1990 Census of Population: General Population Characteristics: Georgia," 1990 CP-1-12 (Washington, DC: US Government Printing Office, 15.

66. Georgia Lottery Corporation, "More than 52 Million Tickets Sold as Players won $25 Million in Prizes During First Week, Lottery Officials Say," July 6, 1993, Folder "94 Lottery," Box 45 and Georgia Lottery Corporation, "First Year Weekly Sales," attached to Georgia Lottery Corporation Background Information packet, Folder "95 Lottery," Box 52, Series IV, Jim Martin Papers, UGA.

67. Gary T. Henry to Louise McBee (n.d., approximately September 1993), Folder 14, Box 3, Series IV, Louise McBee Papers, UGA; Joseph McCray and Thomas J. Pavlak, "Who Plays the Georgia Lottery? Results of a Statewide Survey" (Athens, GA: Carl Vinson Institute of Government, University of Georgia, 2002), 12–17.

68. No Author, "HOPE Awards: Fall 1993 thru Spring 1994 Quarters," June 24, 1994, Folder 1, Box 35, Subseries A, Series IV, Zell Miller Papers, UGA; Carolyn S. Carlson, "Tech Institutes' Enrollment Up," *Macon Telegraph*, October 31, 1993, 1A.

69. Michelle L. Music to Zell Miller, n.d. (probably October 2000), Folder 15, Box 26, Series V, Zell Miller Papers, UGA.

70. Ken Edelstein, "Lottery Money Divvied Up," *Columbus Ledger-Enquirer* (Columbus, GA), January 5, 1994, A1.

71. Nancy Badertscher, "Miller Seeks Millions More for Education," *Macon Telegraph*, January 5, 1994; Rick Dent, "Governor Miller Proposes Expansion of HOPE," September 23, 1993, Folder 1, Box 28, Subseries A, Series IV, Zell Miller Papers, UGA.

72. The HOPE Program, "With the HOPE Program, the Cost of Higher Education in Georgia is Getting a Lot Lower," 1994–1995 academic year brochure (n.d., n.p.), Folder 8, Box 232, Subseries C, Series IV, Zell Miller Papers, UGA.

73. No author, "'Brain Drain' Disappearing in Georgia," n.d. (approximately 1999), Folder 2, Box 6, Series I, Paul Brown Sr. Papers, UGA.

74. Susan Dynarski, "HOPE for Whom? Financial Aid for the Middle Class and Its Impact on College Attendance," Working Paper 7756, National Bureau of Economic Research (2000); Christopher Cornwell, David B. Mustard, and Deepa J. Sridhar, "The Enrollment Effects of Merit-Based Financial Aid: Evidence from Georgia's HOPE Program," *Journal of Labor Economics* 24, no. 4 (2006): 761–786.

75. Christopher Cornwell and David B. Mustard, "Race and the Effects of Georgia's HOPE Scholarship," in *Who Should We Help? The Negative Social Consequences of Merit Scholarships*, ed. Donald E. Heller and Patricia Marin (Cambridge. MA: The Civil Rights Project at Harvard University, 2002), 66–68; Daniel T. Bugler, Gary

T. Henry, and Ross Rubenstein, "An Evaluation of Georgia's HOPE Scholarship Program: Effects of HOPE on Grade Inflation, Academic Performance and College Enrollment," Georgia Council for School Performance Working Paper (1999); *Journal of Blacks in Higher Education*, "Student Aid in Georgia: Less HOPE for College-Bound Blacks," No. 37 (Autumn, 2002), 74–76.

76. Georgia Student Finance Commission, "HOPE Program Information," September 1993, Folder "94 Lottery," Box 45, Series IV, Jim Martin Papers, UGA.

77. *The Journal of Blacks in Higher Education,* "Less 'HOPE' for Black Higher Education in Georgia," No. 57 (2007): 32–33; Jerry S. Davis to Glen Weiner, May 31, 1994, Folder 1, Box 35, Subseries A, Series IV, Zell Miller Papers, UGA; HOPE Scholarship Joint Study Commission Meeting Notes, July 30, 2003, Folder "Chair McBee, 2003–2004," Box 13, Series 1, Louise McBee Papers, UGA.

78. Mike McLeod, "Lottery to Cover More College Costs," *Augusta Chronicle*, March 21, 1994.

79. Christopher Cornwell and David B. Mustard, "Merit-Based College Scholarships and Car Sales," *Education Finance and Policy* 2, no. 2 (2007): 133–151.

80. Carolyn C. Adams to Roy Barnes, October 23, 2001, Folder "HOPE Scholarship," RCB 56394, Roy E. Barnes Gubernatorial Papers, GAA.

81. Maria Donovan Fitzpatrick, "Preschoolers Enrolled and Mothers at Work? The Effects of Universal Prekindergarten," *Journal of Labor Economics* 28, no. 1 (2010): 54, 79; Ross Rubenstein and Benjamin Scafidi, "Who Pays and Who Benefits? Examining the Distributional Consequences of the Georgia Lottery for Education," *National Tax Journal* 55, no. 2 (2002): 223–238; Jisu Han and Stacey Neuharth-Pritchett, "Predicting Students' Mathematics Achievement Through Elementary and Middle School: The Contribution of State-Funded Prekindergarten Program Participation," *Child & Youth Care Forum* 50 (2021): 587–610.

82. Chuck Reece, "Governor Miller Announces Schools to Receive Grants from the Lottery for Education" (Press Release), August 11, 1993, Folder 3, Box 28, Subseries A, Series IV, Zell Miller Papers, UGA.

83. Zell Miller, "Campaign Announcement Speech," April 24, 1994 in Zell Miller, *"Listen to This Voice": Selected Speeches of Governor Zell Miller* (Macon, GA: Mercer University Press, 1998), 159; Harriet Hiland, "Cobb Students to Be Under Surveillance," *Marietta Daily Journal*, July 19, 1994; Gail Hagans, "'Safe Schools, Safe Streets' Campaign Under Way," *Atlanta-Journal Constitution* April 26, 1994, C8; Associated Press, "70 Ga Schools to Meet Students at Front Door with Metal Detectors," *Athens Daily News*, February 22, 1994, B1.

84. *White County Telegraph* (Cleveland, GA), "HOPE a Success," February 9, 1994, 1.

85. Emphasis in the original. Zell Miller for Governor '94, Draft of newspaper advertisement (n.d., probably 1994), Folder 16, Box 154, Subseries C, Series IV, Zell Miller Papers, UGA.

86. Ken Foskett, "Lottery Money Intensifies Battles over Ga. Budget," *Atlanta Journal-Constitution*, February 21, 1994, B1; Ken Foskett, "'94 Georgia Legislature: Miller Proposes $9.8 Billion Budget," *Atlanta Journal-Constitution*, January 13, 1994, E1.

87. Frank Lomonte, "Miller Hoping HOPE Scholarship Will Woo Ga. Voters," *Athens Daily News*, June 26, 1994; *Rome News-Tribune* (Rome, GA), "Miller for Governor," October 9, 1994, 11A.

88. Cooper and Secrest Associates, Inc., "Qualitative Investigation Conducted for the Democratic Party of Georgia (Confidential)," May 1993, Folder 21, Box 157, Subseries C, Series IV, Zell Miller Papers, UGA.

89. Zell Miller, "Remarks by Zell Miller," Georgia Southwestern College, September 21, 1994, Folder 1, Box 28, Subseries A, Series IV, Zell Miller Papers, UGA.

90. John C. Adam, letter to *Atlanta Journal-Constitution*, October 27, 1994, 117.

91. *Atlanta-Journal Constitution*, "Town Meeting Question: 'How Are You Going to Finance Education?'," October 19, 1994, C4.

92. State of Georgia, General Election Results, November 8, 1994, Folder 8, Box 154, Subseries C, Series IV, Zell Miller Papers, UGA.

93. The White House, "Press Briefing by Mike McCurry, Gene Sperling, Bruce Reed, and Governor Zell Miller," June 4, 1996, Folder 31, Box 261, Subseries E, Series IV, Zell Miller Papers, UGA.

94. Nelson and Mason, *How the South Joined the Gambling Nation*, 75; Harold W. Stanley and Christian Grose, "Alabama 1998: Luck Runs Out for the GOP and Christian Right as Democrats Gamble on the Lottery," in *Prayers in the Precincts: The Christian Right in the 1998 Elections*, ed. John C. Green, Mark J. Rozell, and Clyde Wilcox (Washington, DC: Georgetown University Press, 2000), 153–154; C-SPAN, "South Carolina Gubernatorial Campaign Ads," October 1, 1998, https://www.c-span.org/video/?112722-1/south-carolina-gubernatorial-campaign-ads.

95. Mike Carson, "Lottery Sets Siegelman, James Apart," *Montgomery Advertiser*, September 22, 1998, 1A; Analog Indulgence, "Alabama State Lottery Political Ad 1999," https://www.youtube.com/watch?v=Ozvo4ELhGm4.

96. Washington, DC, rejected a legalized gambling bill that included a lottery in 1979 (but approved a lottery the following year), and North Dakotans rejected a lottery referendum in 1988. On the failure of the lottery in Alabama, see Randy Bobbitt, *Lottery Wars: Case Studies in Bible Belt Politics, 1986–2005* (Lanham, MD: Lexington Books, 2007), 79–118.

97. Christopher Cornwell, Maciej Misztal, and David Mustard, "The Effect of Large-Scale Merit Scholarships on State Sponsored Need-Based Aid" (2009), unpublished manuscript, https://citeseerx.ist.psu.edu/viewdoc/download?doi=10.1.1.1077.4852&rep=rep1&type=pdf; Donald E. Heller, "State Merit Scholarship Programs: An Overview," in *State Merit Scholarships and Racial Inequality*, ed. Donald E. Heller and Patricia Marin (Cambridge, MA: Civil Rights Project at Harvard University, 2004), 16; Patricia Marin, "Merit Scholarships and the

Outlook for Equal Opportunity in Higher Education," in *Who Should We Help?*, ed. Heller and Marin, 114.

98. Christian Boone, "Lottery Winner Ignored Wife's Advice Not to Play," *Atlanta Journal-Constitution*, January 7, 2006, B4.

99. This conclusion is contrary to that of education scholar Michael Lanford, who argues that Miller's changes "crippled the HOPE scholarship's effectiveness, damaged its ability to serve equity goals, and potentially endangered its future"; Michael Lanford, "The Political History of the Georgia HOPE Scholarship Program: A Critical Analysis," *Policy Reviews in Higher Education* 1, no. 2 (2017): 187–208.

CONCLUSION: JACKPOT

1. Author telephone interviews with Ashani Acquaviva, July 13 and August 31, 2021.

2. Jerome Christenson, "Gambling Is Really 'The Stupid Tax,'" *Winona Daily News*, July 10, 2019, A7.

3. David Kirkpatrick to Victor Atiyeh, October 11, 1982, Folder 18, Box 88, Administrative Correspondence, Governor Victor Atiyeh Papers, Oregon State Archives, Salem, Oregon.

4. Leah Muncy, "It's Time to Get Rid of the Lottery," *The Outline*, July 31, 2019; George Orwell, *1984* (New York: Houghton Mifflin Harcourt, 1983 [1949]).

5. Eric Dexheimer, "Texas Lottery Sales Surge as COVID Stimulus Money Arrives," *Houston Chronicle*, April 23, 2020.

6. Kurt Anderson, *Fantasyland: How America Went Haywire, a 500-Year History* (New York: Penguin Random House, 2017), 230. For example, Marilyn Gardner, "Getting Rich Too Quick," *Christian Science Monitor*, June 8, 1990; George Will, "Gambling with Our Character," *Washington Post*, February 7, 1993, C7; Tim Stafford, "None Dare Call It Sin," *Christianity Today* 40, no. 4 (April 8, 1996): 42, 34–38; L. A. Williams, "Bill Would Undermine Work Ethic and Degrade State's Rich Sports Heritage," *Christian Action League*, August 6, 2021.

7. Federation of Tax Administrators, "2020 State Tax Revenue," https://www.taxadmin.org/2020-state-tax-revenue; National Association of State and Provincial Lotteries, "NASPL Resource Index."

8. Sarah Ovaska-Few, "N.C.'s Lottery Still a Big Draw in Poor Areas," *NC Policy Watch*, June 17, 2014; Associated Press, "House Budget Doubles Down on Lottery Ads," *Winston-Salem Journal*, June 10, 2014.

9. American Gaming Association, "State of Play," https://www.americangaming.org/state-of-play/. For examples of casinos as tools of economic development, see the cases of Atlantic City, New Jersey, and Bethlehem, Pennsylvania: Bryant Simon, *Boardwalk of Dreams: Atlantic City and the Fate of Urban America* (Oxford: Oxford University Press, 2006); Chloe E. Taft, *From Steel to Slots: Casino Capitalism in the Postindustrial City* (Cambridge, MA: Harvard University Press, 2016).

10. American Gaming Association, "State of the States 2021," May 20, 2021; Ryan Butler, "Where Is Sports Betting Legal? Projections for All 50 States," *Action Network*, December 17, 2021.

11. Commission on the Review of the National Policy Toward Gambling, *Gambling in America* (Washington, DC: US Government Printing Office, 1976); National Gambling Impact Study Commission, *Final Report* (National Gambling Impact Study Commission, 1999), https://govinfo.library.unt.edu/ngisc//.

12. Dan Lewerenz, "Border Stores Do Brisk Business," *Casper Star-Tribune* (Casper, WY), October 12, 2005.

13. Alex Dobuzinskis, "U.S. Lottery Operators Worry as Fewer Millennials Line Up to Play," *Reuters*, February 10, 2017; Zachary Crockett, "Millennials Aren't Buying Lottery Tickets," *The Hustle*, December 17, 2019; Harris Poll, "After Record U.S. Lottery Revenues in 2019, What's Next?," https://theharrispoll.com/after-record-us-lottery/.

14. National Association of State and Provincial Lotteries, "Frequently Asked Questions," https://www.naspl.org/faq.

Index

For the benefit of digital users, indexed terms that span two pages (e.g., 52–53) may, on occasion, appear on only one of those pages.

Page numbers followed by *t* or *f* indicate tables or figures, respectively. Page numbers followed by n indicate notes.